MALRAUX
The Absolute Agnostic

Claude Tannery

The Absolute Agnostic

or

*Metamorphosis as
Universal Law*

TRANSLATED BY TERESA LAVENDER FAGAN

The University of Chicago Press

Chicago & London

Claude Tannery is director of the Institut Français de Porto in Portugal. He is the author of several works of fiction, including *Le cavalier, la rivière et la berge* (1989).

The University of Chicago Press, Chicago 60637
The University of Chicago Press, Ltd., London
© 1991 by The University of Chicago
All rights reserved. Published 1991
Printed in the United States of America
00 99 98 97 96 95 94 93 92 91   5 4 3 2 1

ISBN (cloth): 0-226-78962-4

Originally published as *Malraux, l'agnostique absolu; ou la Métamorphose comme loi du monde,* © Éditions Gallimard, 1985.

Library of Congress Cataloging-in-Publication Data

Tannery, Claude.
   [Malraux, l'agnostique absolu. English]
   Malraux, the absolute agnostic, or, Metamorphosis as universal law / Claude Tannery ; translated by Teresa Lavender Fagan.
    p. cm.
   Translation of: Malraux, l'agnostique absolu; ou la métamorphose comme loi du monde.
   Includes bibliographical references and index.
   1. Malraux, André, 1901–1976—Religion. 2. Metamorphosis in literature. 3. Agnosticism in literature. I. Title. II. Title: Malraux, the absolute agnostic. III. Title: Metamorphosis as universal law.
PQ2625.A716Z943313   1991
843'.912—dc20   91-15554
                                                                     CIP

∞ The paper used in this publication meets the minimum requirements of the American National Standard for Information Sciences—Permanence of Paper for Printed Library Materials, ANSI Z39.48-1984.

To my children,
Éric, Cécile, Christophe, Véronique
To their children
To their children's children
In the hope that, for them, Metamorphosis will truly be the Universal Law

> For me, no more metaphors—
> only metamorphoses.
> —Georges Braque

Contents

Translator's Note / xi
Prologue / 1
Introduction / 5

PART ONE • QUESTIONING MAN

1. The Tragic Existence of Man	13
2. The Tyranny of the Individual	21

PART TWO • ACTION OR THE ABSURD

3. Action, or Rejection of the Absurd	41
4. Rejection of Individual Intoxications	48
5. The Revolution	60

PART THREE • LYRICAL ILLUSION

6. Fraternity Scorned	69
7. History as Fatality	74
8. Man Consumed by the Masses	77
9. Lyrical Illusion	89

PART FOUR • THE METAMORPHOSIS OF CULTURE

10. A Metamorphosis of Man	109
11. Culture: An Agreement of Sensibilities	121
12. Discontinuous History	128

13. A Fraternal Consciousness   154
14. A Fellowship of Difference   177
15. Reconciled Man   197

PART FIVE • Metamorphosis as Universal Law

16. Art Is Not an Antidestiny   215
17. Religions Are Also Mortal   243
18. Metamorphosis as Universal Law   252
19. The Absolute Agnostic   288

Abbreviations / 313
Works by André Malraux / 315
Index / 319

Translator's Note

It has been an honor—and a challenge—to translate Claude Tannery's work into English. As the reader will discover, the breadth of Mr. Tannery's knowledge of and insight into the thought and writings of André Malraux is truly formidable. And I beg the reader's indulgence for my sometimes less-than-comparable rendering of Mr. Tannery's elegant French prose; in an attempt to convey the author's text as accurately as possible, I fear I have sacrificed some of his elegance.

Throughout the text Mr. Tannery cites from a large number of titles by Malraux, both fiction and nonfiction. Parenthetical references are given in abbreviated form with the appropriate page numbers. A complete list of abbreviations and a chronological list of Malraux's works with bibliographical information on French and English-language editions appear at the end of this book (pp. 313–17). Where possible I have cited standard English-language translations of Malraux's works, and the abbreviations used correspond to those editions (in a few cases it was necessary to alter the translation slightly to fit the context in which it is cited). When a published translation could not be obtained, I translated the extract as well as the work's title, but the abbreviation corresponds to the original French edition.

Although a translator essentially works alone, it is the rare translation that is published without the invaluable input of advisers. I wish to thank James R. Lawler for his very helpful critique of my work; Anthony G. Bing for his comments and especially for the use of his library of books by and about André Malraux (of which the most useful was Jean Lacouture, *André Malraux*, translated by Alan Sheridan [New York: Pantheon, 1975]); and Madame Micheline Braun for painstakingly reviewing the final draft of the translation and for providing reassurance to the author.

TERESA LAVENDER FAGAN

Prologue

Death was dead. Sitting on the crenels of the highest tower on the castle, the Sins watched the evening caress the calm city. No change was yet observed.

"And now, to work!" said Pride.

"To work!" repeated the Sins.

"What do we start with?" added Hifili.

There was a long silence, which, after some hesitation, the musician broke by saying:

"Excuse me, dear friends, . . . when I was a man, I was subject to mental anemia . . . So don't be surprised by my question: Why did we kill Death?"

The Sins had hung pieces of its skeleton from their belts as memory joggers. They touched them and repeated, . . . 'Yes—why did we kill Death?'

Then they looked at each other. Their faces were gloomy. And they dropped their heads into their hands and wept. Why had they killed Death? They had all forgotten why. (*LP* 45)

Thus ends *Paper Moons,* Malraux's first book, "a little book in which some of man's lesser-known struggles are related . . . ALL TOLD IN A TRUTHFUL MANNER" (*LP* 13).

The Sins in *Paper Moons* are former intellectuals who wrote propaganda plays, or former artists. They have been metamorphosed into multicolored balloons. They had lived in a world without meaning. They sensed that "great tragic, yet uncertain, things were in the making" (*LP* 35).

Critics seldom grant much importance to Malraux's first books. Some even find it difficult to excuse Malraux for writing them; and others say these youthful works are unnecessary for an understanding of Malraux's work as a whole. I believe, on the contrary, that they are essential.

During the second half of his life, Malraux was unwilling to draw attention to his *For an Idol with a Trunk, Paper Moons, Farfelu Kingdom*, etc., and he often omitted them when listing his works. While not disowning them entirely, since he authorized the reprinting of *Paper Moons* and *Farfelu Kingdom*, he seems to have thought few readers could still grasp them. For the benefit of those readers he offers two clear hints, which cannot be ignored since he placed them at the opening of the two books with the same subject: his life. The first hint appears in the Introduction to *Anti-Memoirs:* "I have called this book *Antimémoires* . . . because it is haunted, often in the midst of tragedy, by a presence as elusive and unmistakable as a cat slipping by in the dark: that of the *farfelu* whose name I unwittingly resurrected" (*A-M* 8). The second, just as clear, is provided by the *farfelu* tale that Malraux places at the beginning of *The Cord and the Mice*, giving the work its title.

When *Farfelu Kingdom* was published, Malraux was twenty-seven years old. He had already published *The Temptation of the West* and *The Conquerors*. The greatest names in contemporary French literature had already rallied to get the appellate court in Saigon to reverse the ruling that had just sentenced Malraux to five years in prison, with no possibility of remission, for taking Khmer statues out of the jungle—statues that he alone had discovered and had hoped to sell. He was working on, and reworking, a book he never finished, *For an Idol with a Trunk*—though he did publish excerpts from it: *The Tame Hedgehogs, Journal of an Aunt Sally Artist, For a Teddy Bear,* and others. These early works prove, if proof is needed, the importance of the *farfelu* in Malraux's thought and writings. While recognizing its importance, however, we must beware of misinterpreting its meaning. In common French usage *farfelu* designates that which is bizarre, fantastic, extravagant. In French literary tradition, and notably in Rabelais, *farfelu* is used to express the Incomprehensible, the Other, everything that is irrevocably beyond the comprehension of mankind. And precisely because this Other is beyond man's comprehension, it must advance masked by mischievousness, fantasy, and poetry.

Farfelu Kingdom is a story intended to create an autonomous universe, as Malraux has carefully pointed out. It is an "exploration of the possible" (*Nouvelle Revue Française* December 1929), supposed to lead the reader toward a world more profound and more real than that of the imagination—a world of visions, which Malraux reveals with humor and detachment because he is quite discreet; visions so intense that they become more real than reality for whoever truly sees them; the vision of a world that could be otherwise; the vision of different relationships among men, different relationships between men and objects, "those strange and familiar objects" (*LP* 13).

Malraux's spiritual quest, starting with the visions of *Paper Moons,* his first book, and ending with the publication of *Precarious Man,* his last, was a long and painful one. As an adolescent he was repelled by a world that was beginning to flirt with the Absurd; he was tortured by thirst for the Absolute, crushed by the relativity of all cultures. But at the same time he was inhabited by expectations of almost incommunicable beauty and almost irresistible power. As a young man he tried to force reality to resemble his expectations, and he took part in the only activity, revolution, which—as he thought at the time—could bring about a change in man's relationship with man, and consequently a change in man's relationship with the cosmos. But the revolution, every revolution, would turn out to be a "lyrical illusion" with the reappearance of organized human degradation. As an adult, Malraux pursued a long inquiry into the "metamorphosis of the gods," looking for the secret of the metamorphosis of man. In his later years he long hesitated to fully accept the only law of the world he acknowledged: the law of metamorphosis.

Having embraced this law, Malraux was then able to rediscover his adolescent intuition: there is no point in trying to kill Death. He rediscovered it full, alive, and enriched by all the experience and knowledge he had accumulated. He realized that giving meaning to Death does not give meaning to Life. He knew that *only* by giving meaning to Life can a meaning be given to Death. And when he discovered what the meaning of life truly is, he could die a simple, banal death, the death of an ordinary man, he whose death had so often bordered on that of the hero or of the *farfelu.*

Introduction

BEFORE SETTING OUT on the path that Malraux took, we must confront a few problems that often hinder the understanding of his work. We need then speak of them no more.

The generations unborn when the first revolutionary battles erupted in China, or when the fascists unleashed civil war in Spain, are astonished by the way their elders used to read Malraux's novels and often still read them. With rare exceptions, they would read them either as Trotsky did or as Jean Lacouture does, that is, as a partisan or as a journalist/biographer. Trotsky saw *The Conquerors* as a fictional account, yet "a source of the most valuable political lessons." Lacouture reproaches Malraux for "the lies" which make up *Man's Hope:* he regrets that Malraux changes "everything he touches into fiction," and speaks ironically of Malraux's tendency to see the world only through "touching embellishments." But who today would venture to reproach Stendhal for transfiguring the Battle of Waterloo or Victor Hugo for embellishing the "Three Glorious Days" of the revolution of 1830.

Gaëtan Picon rightly notes that Malraux's novels treat revolutions and wars with a "nightmarish unreality, as if the poet drew them from his deepest and most private dreams." In a marginal note Malraux responded to this observation by observing: "Artistically speaking, the whole question is summed up there." Those readers who subordinate the artistic question for partisan reasons, that is, for party reasons, should not participate in the debate. Everyone else will be able to follow Malraux when he cites Goya: "Details I have observed supply their accents to *ensembles* I conjure up in my imagination," and when he adds: "This is the novelist's procedure, too" (*VOS* 295).

Today everyone can look at the landscape in Titian's *Shepherd* as a "supreme unreality" (*Ir* 250); everyone knows that Cézanne's painting of Mount Sainte Victoire is an unreality and not a landscape; and everyone admits that the Florentine painters aimed not to imitate an appearance ever more faithfully but "to place that appearance increasingly in the service of creation" (*Ir* 38). And everyone should perceive unreservedly as "supreme unrealities" the streets of Shanghai laid out behind Kyo in *Man's Fate* or the Sierra de Teruel mountains rising behind Magnin in *Man's Hope*. Everyone should acknowledge that historical appearances are used by Malraux in the service of creation. In history, too, there is appearance.

In creating his novels, Malraux made use of observed historical details to give their particular accents to the ensembles he conjured up in his imagination. His novels create "a rival world" (*Ir* 250), just as painting creates a world of its own. *The Conquerors, Man's Fate,* and *Man's Hope* must be fully acknowledged as novels, as artistic creations; it then becomes as futile to reproach them for their "lies" as it would be to reproach Leonardo da Vinci for the unreality of the landscape in the *Mona Lisa*. If we won't acknowledge Malraux's novels as artistic creations, we must explain why they are denied any creative or artistic value. No one has seriously attempted this, for those who challenge the artistic element are really doing so with reference to their political opinions. Prior to 1940, most of those critics were from the right, because Malraux wrote about Communists and revolutionaries. After 1945 they were joined by those who claimed to be of the left, and who accused Malraux of betraying "their" revolution.

Malraux's reply in the public debate over *The Conquerors*—"I am not arguing with my adversaries; I will speak to their children"—might appear somewhat arrogant; yet it expresses a tranquil lucidity. Those "children" read Malraux's novels as they look at an Egyptian fresco, a Romanesque virgin, or a Renaissance Venus. For those "children" the events evoked in Malraux's novels already belong to history books; they have left the realm of politics and entered the investigative field of historians, whose interpretations are as numerous as they are contradictory. Those "children" read Malraux's novels while seeing historical events as simple backdrops. That others might continue to ask whether Malraux's novels serve the ephemeral political causes they have espoused is of little importance. With the passing of time, *The Conquerors* can be read as Emmanuel Berl read it from the beginning: "I consider the publication of *The Conquerors* to be an event of the greatest importance in contemporary moral history. The bourgeois readers who are seduced by Malraux's art will understand tomorrow the danger that Malraux forces them to run, and they will stop looking in the book for information about China, exotic tableaux, a chronicle, or a psychological analysis." With the passing of time everyone will be able to read *Man's Fate* as Ilya Ehrenburg did when the book first appeared, as a metaphysical novel anchored in historical appearance. With the passing of time, everyone, like Montherlant, will see that there is nothing local in *Man's Hope,* and that Spain's presence in it is only incidental.

A second approach to Malraux's novels, as to those of any writer, must be rejected—that of explaining a work through the author's biography, and his art by its conditioning. At the beginning of *Precarious Man,* Malraux recalls that in 1939 he had conceived of his *Tableau of French Literature,* which "defined a new relationship with literature" and "gave more importance to La Fontaine's art than to his biography." Unfortunately, even today, this "tableau" is ignored by most biographers.

The present age delights in unearthing a great man's secrets; for one thing because we like to temper our admiration and also perhaps because we have a vague hope of finding a clue to genius in such revelations . . . The idea is, they say, to get down to the man beneath the artist. So we scrape away ruthlessly at the fresco till finally we reach the plaster, and what is the result? The fresco is ruined and in hunting for the secret of the man we have lost the genius. (*VOS* 418–20)

Malraux often stressed the questionable nature of seeking a posteriori the influence of a life on a work of art. Luckily, "the time is coming when people will say: In the days of biography . . ." (*AC* 231). The day we say this it will become clear that today's biographies were "one of the major literary forms of individualism." Biography is a form that will have lost much of its interest, for "the relations between art and history are changing radically. The search for freedom dominates the search for determinisms. The king is naked. The issues of art are no longer the issues of art history" (*Int* 350).

Like all history, art history has attempted to be deterministic. The future ages that will call our time "the age of biographers" will be ages liberated from that deterministic illusion and capable of being interested in the true life of the artist: they will attempt to account for his "ability to transform." To study Flaubert's life will be to outline his ability to transform a local news item into a universal Madame Bovary. To truly study Malraux's life will be to search for that which enabled him to modify the forms of the Spanish War in order to carve out *Man's Hope*. To study the life of a creator will also, if not primarily, be to look for the ways in which the events of his life have been subject to his creative will—and not the other way around.

It will then be possible to put the "game of keys" back in its rightful place. Except in a novel intended to be a *roman à clef,* that is, a thinly disguised portrait or caricature, there is little sense in trying to establish a correspondence between a fictional character and a person in real life. To attempt to recognize a real person in a novel prevents us from getting to know the character created. To hope to reveal the philosopher Bernard Groethuysen in Malraux's character Gisors, or Philippe Berthelot's brother in Ferral, brings some satisfaction—though rather pointless—but the mind, amused or channeled by this identification, is no longer open to grasping the deep meaning with which the novelist endowed his characters. Every character in a novel is really imagined, created, even if the novelist has used observations made in his daily life. The only fruitful approach consists not of identifying a real-life person behind a character in a novel but of bringing to light the differences that the novelist has created, consciously or not, between what he has observed and what he has imagined. To understand Malraux it would be more useful to know how Gisors in *Man's Fate* and old Alvear in *Man's Hope* differ from Bernard Groethuysen than to know how they resemble him.

In *Picasso's Mask,* Malraux is eager to be precise in this regard: "I had never known Pablo the private person, or his feelings; I had known only Picasso" (*PM* 5). Malraux spoke very rarely about his own private life. His hospitality, his simplicity, his consideration for others surprised all those who knew him. He respected their privacy and expected them to respect his. Although he became a living legend, Malraux nearly always managed to erect a barrier against the immodesty of an age that exposed private lives and made a business of them. Those who knew "André" say little about him and don't write about him. They testify only to Malraux and his thought. Along with the narrator of *The Walnut Trees of Altenburg,* they contend: "I am too firmly convinced that a man's significance depends more on his achievements than on his secret qualities to care much about the secret qualities of those I love" (*WTA* 38).

Malraux often repeated that schools and universities don't teach "literature, but its history" (*HP* 7). Unfortunately, criticism has too often taken the same path. All three have more or less deformed the reader

Introduction

who seeks "an organized thought" in a work of literature and forgets that "literature, as a form of art, escapes without a doubt logical thought to the same extent as music or as poetry when it becomes music" (*AC* 239). Looking for organized thought in *Mirror of Limbo* or in *The Metamorphosis of the Gods,* the disappointed reader closes the book, saying: I don't understand a thing. He is forgetting that "'to understand a work of art' is a no less complex statement than 'to understand a man'" (*HP* 14). Ever since lecture hall psychology spread the illusion that one can *understand* a man (though in fact, like all sciences, it raises more questions than it answers), our age has also harbored the illusion that we can *understand* a work of art.

A pianist knows he is interpreting a sonata, just as a conductor knows he is interpreting a symphony; they are not trying to understand them. A musicologist analyzes and often kills music. We must turn our backs "on the methods which claim to grasp a creative artist in the name of an intelligibility which by his very nature he eludes (*AC* 227). And Malraux himself, more than any other creator today, eludes this type of intelligibility. His style, his form of thought, his sensibility, and even his life are immune to it. His thought proceeds by variations, by modulations; it is never linear. It vibrates and propagates itself like a wave. It takes hold of an idea or a theme, and works it before interweaving it with others. To get inside *The Voices of Silence* or *Precarious Man,* into *The Metamorphosis of the Gods* or *Man's Fate,* one must approach these works as one would a sonata or a symphony—with one's sensibility, and not with one's intellect. A comment of Malraux's illustrates this necessity: "Out of this imaginary world comes the penetrating song of a blindman in the rain of time." The initial reading, like the initial hearing, jolts us, awakens our sensibilities, but doesn't enable us to grasp the whole message. We reread. And quite naturally, since words are concerned, we reread with our reason, we try to understand. "The blindman's song" then becomes inaudible, muffled by a tumult of thoughts. Claudel's prose and plays also demand the same kind of approach as poetry and music. We agree to do this for the Claudel of the *Odes;* let us do the same for Malraux, even though he was an essayist.

In order to find the harmony of sensibility and "the allusive complicity" (*HP* 13) that make *The Voices of Silence* sing and bring *The Timeless* to light, two difficulties must still be overcome. The first results from Malraux's prose style, which progresses by visions, flashes, and not deduction: Malraux's lightning formulas synthesize every complexity, as Angelo Rinaldi has said. Confronted with this prose, the Western mind

Introduction

is baffled, so used is it to formulas that dissect the complex, then attempt to reconstruct it piece by piece. Our passion for puzzles is disarmed by the immediate syntheses Malraux proposes. The second, even greater, difficulty results from Malraux's knowledge of past centuries.[1] Malraux's knowledge of their history and culture was not that of a scholar who has studied them; he sensed them as if he had experienced them. And we are disoriented, since what we know about them comes mostly from reading. Malraux was conceivably the first thinker with this kind of immediate experience of all cultures. His sensibility had prepared him for it, but he was also lucky enough to have been born in an age that invented printing techniques for painting, sculpture, and music that could push back limits formerly imposed by space and time. When Malraux, in *Anti-Memoirs,* tells us that he felt "his youth disappearing in the depths of the time," which exerted "a singular, sometimes physical action" on him, he reveals one of the most profound characteristics of his personality. And when he exclaimed in 1958: "May I make it possible, for all the scattered youth that will hear us tonight, for history to be confounded with memory," he was expressing what for him was already acquired knowledge, but for us still remains a possibility: to sense and know the cultures of the past as we sense and know our own memories.

* * *

From *Paper Moons* to *Precarious Man,* Malraux pursued a true spiritual quest. If we take the attitudes toward his writings that he calls for, it actually becomes possible for us in turn to set out on that quest and on the paths Malraux has opened to us. If we cannot assume those attitudes, what he offers will remain foreign to us.

1. [In the original text Tannery makes use of Claudel's neological word-play, *co-naissance* ("co-birth"; "co-experience") as the more appropriate term for the "knowledge"—*connaissance*—Malraux possessed.—Trans.]

PART ONE

Questioning Man

I

The Tragic Existence of Man

IN THE PALACE of Isfahan, "the princess, surrounded by white kittens, had all the gods of the conquered peoples brought to her in a cellar full of millipedes, and chained them up one by one" (*RF* 322). One night the palace was destroyed by fire. Soldiers emerged from it "carrying magnificent objects on which silk and pearls were seen: manikins; huge, richly dressed dolls; antique toys . . ." (*RF* 327). A rumbling could be heard, at first indistinct, then becoming an uproar: "The gods! The gods! THE GODS! That was undoubtedly one of the great nights of the world, one of those nights when the gods, exhausted, yield the earth to the wild genius of poetry."

Nietzsche's statement "God is dead" has become all-too-familiar. It sometimes obscures the slow, awesome march that begins with Thundering Zeus and ends with the statue of Zeus or Christ in Majesty before reaching the life of the man Jesus. Our era likes to believe it has dethroned the gods, whereas it has only dethroned those that tried to usurp their place in the nineteenth and twentieth centuries. For the other gods, and notably for the Christian God, this era has merely inherited a long process that began in the Renaissance, when it was discovered that the subjects of *Plutarch's Lives* had been great men while owing nothing to the Christian notion of man; when the idea of heathens had to be abandoned and that of antiquity accepted; when people were compelled to admit that the world before Christ had not been chaotic and that there had existed "an eternal Rome compared to which pontifical Rome appeared as a village" (*HP* 58). In order truly to grasp the upheaval of the mind and emotions that resulted from this awareness, we should try to imagine our shock if an archaeologist of our own period had just discovered "in a lost civilization the means of curing cancer or of neutralizing the atomic bomb" (*HP* 59).

With the Renaissance, Western art broke the ties that had until then existed between man and the cosmos. It was in Florence, under Lorenzo the Magnificent, that "questioning man" was born (*Ir* 104), when artists proclaimed that man and the world were yet to be discovered. And only a few years later, in Mantua, mannerism no longer sought to express the secret order of the world. Shakespeare, who considered "the soul of the universe to be a mystery, not a revelation" (*Ir* 241), gave "the heath, the forest, the ocean, madness, death, their great mysterious voice." After Copernicus and Galileo, the sun no longer turned around man's earth. The secret order of the world was shattered. And man himself was to become the subject of research, not of revelation.

Despite the Renaissance, seventeenth-century French culture still managed to impose "its pattern on Europe because it stood for one of the mightiest hierarchies the world had known" (*VOS* 481). It had brought order to "the teeming chaos of the Renaissance" and had maintained God as the keystone—but He was already the God of Molinism. The eighteenth century, despite the legend that surrounds it, failed to substitute an order of its own for the Christian order it was attacking: it substituted the fervor generated by that attack. Its fervor turned to ideas—the people, the nation, reason—which allowed it to forget the Absolute, not to replace it. In the nineteenth century a political deity "stepped into the place of the God of the Jesuits. And soon it, too, rang hollow" (*VOS* 482), while science, daughter of the Enlightenment, maintained the illusion that man could be founded on science and that all discoveries would be in the interests of justice and dignity. Eternity thus withdrew from the world and the human mind attempted to replace it with the only enemy it could find: history. History, too, was unable to reign for long, but from it was born a man who learned that all gods are mortal, the gods of Greece as well as those of Egypt; the gods of Rome as well as the god of Mount Sinai; the gods of Elephanta as well as those of the Alban Hills of ancient Rome.

Truly to accept that all gods are mortal is to assume that we are capable of abandoning the patterns of thought and action that have been instilled in man through thousands of years of belief in immortal gods. The mortality of the gods implies that we are capable of enduring "the vertiginous stress of the void created by the absence of God in the place

The Tragic Existence of Man

where he should be" (*HP* 200). Man was not prepared for that "vertiginous stress of the void," and could "found a perspective only on the tragic" (UNESCO lecture of 1946). For the young Malraux, this tragic reality was not a simple idea or concept; it was a fundamental given of daily life, the unwavering perception of his sensibility. And this is why the subject of his novels would always be "the tragic existence of man" and never "the elucidation of the individual."

No longer knowing with certainty where he comes from, nor where he is going, man finds his relationship with the universe transformed. For thousands of years man and the cosmos were, to a greater or lesser degree, in accord. Since the eighteenth century they have been at variance. Western man has conquered the planet Earth and begun an exploration of space while sacrificing a millenary relationship with the cosmos (cf. *Les Nouvelles littéraires*, 3 April 1952). Can man exist while bound to the universe only by the domination he attempts to exercise over it? All of Malraux's novels reply in the negative, and they can all be understood as quests for a new pact between man and the world.

The discord between man and the world is the principal theme of *The Royal Way*, which concludes with Perken's failure. In *Man's Fate*, Kyo's realization of his political subjugation brings about a far greater and deeper awareness: he becomes aware of his metaphysical subjugation, he experiences "the anguish of being nothing more than a man, than himself" (*MF* 156), and wonders whether he isn't "a moth who secretes his own light, the one in which he will destroy himself" (cf. *MF* 166). In *Man's Hope*, the tragic nature of man's relationship with the cosmos is investigated more than in any other of Malraux's novels, and if we see the Spanish War as a backdrop, we realize that the two main characters in the book are the Universe and Humanity. In *Days of Wrath*, Kassner doesn't only struggle against torture, he also struggles against the indifference and the immense silence of the stars. In *The Walnut Trees of Altenburg*, Berger can only comment: "Nothing remains of the old fellow-feeling between man and earth" (*WTA* 205). In all of Malraux's novels, characters at one time or another run up against the cry of the nineteenth century: "I have nothing in common with the earth." They all try to stifle that cry.

At one time, between the two World Wars, the hope—or the illusion—arose that the Soviet revolution and communism would reconcile man with the world. That hope was quickly shattered, and the resulting disappointment aggravated the discord. Malraux refers to this untiringly, almost like a nagging pain. Living in a "formless world," the West is no longer tied to the cosmos, hence it is no longer tied to a universal notion of man and the human adventure.

In 1926, when Malraux was twenty-five, most artists, at least the most vocal among them, were thrilled with the possibility offered, so they believed, by the death of God: man could be put in His place. But others continued to believe that God was alive. Almost alone at the time, Malraux was contending: "Man is dead" (*TW* 97). That statement remained his great obsession, and he adopted three attitudes with regard to it. In his "*Farfelu* Writings" and *The Temptation of the West,* he asserted that man is indeed dead, and that to believe the contrary would be to deceive oneself. In his novels and in the revolutionary conflicts with which he associated himself, Malraux sought to build a new man. In his monographs he used art and man's creative power as a focal point for his search to unlock the mystery of man.

As an adolescent, Malraux had heard two great voices proclaiming that man might derive everything from himself: Nietzsche and Gide. Their influence on Malraux may have been overstated, for there was also the influence of Dostoyevski, whose "presence is crushing;" Vigny and his "fallen angel;" Nerval and his "man of shadows" and black sun; Baudelaire and Mallarmé; Lautréamont and the *Songs of Maldoror;* Van Gogh and his self-portraits. All had foreseen that the death of the gods would not necessarily bring about the birth of man. Malraux rode in their wake, and after 1920 he went even farther by declaring that "man is dead," well before man would methodically organize crimes against man, and technology and bureaucracy would suffocate the human race. Malraux's premonitory statement forces us to acknowledge that these crimes and suffocation have not caused the death of man, but are the consequences of it.

Like the surrealists, to whom he was close without really ever becoming one of them, in the 1920s Malraux had felt, then analyzed, the terrible conflict between man and what he had created. There were no longer any absolute values to guide man, to give meaning to what he was undertaking. Since the Rights of Man had been replaced by the "rights of the bourgeoisie," civilization was governed by "a ruling class, competent enough but without values of its own" (*VOS* 484). By imposing its standards, its goals, its way of thinking, the bourgeoisie had bred "a structureless world in which the one remaining power was of a practical order" (*VOS* 488). What the bourgeoisie had made people think of as values were merely "objects of desire." What it had progressively imposed through an educational system that initially was remarkably efficient was but a world of realities that kept it from being subject to anything but itself.

While the bourgeoisie was endowing man with an economic and military power that no one would have dared to imagine, a dream was crumbling: the dream that Reason, which was at the origin of that power, would also cure man of the congenital disease of metaphysical reflection. Beyond the ambivalence of science—which is a moral problem—a radical impossibility was developing: the impossibility that science could one day constitute the order of the world. Above and beyond science, Reason itself was attacked. It remained a vehicle for knowledge but had to admit that it wasn't the only one, and that it would never adequately explain man and the cosmos. For those who in the previous 150 years had staked everything on Reason, the shock was great.

An even greater shock awaited them: Reason, of which they had expected so much, now presented them with a universe in which man was "superfluous." Pascal had tragically felt "the insignificance of man" but his faith and his "wager" had allowed him to consider man a privileged creature. His Creator had told him to "have dominion over the fish of the sea, and over the fowl of the air, and over the cattle, and over all the earth" (Genesis 1:26). To Pascal man was of meager proportions, but his Creator had commanded him to be fertile, to fill the earth and to have dominion over it. But twentieth-century man has learned that he belongs to a species like any other; worse, a species that the cosmos can do without. For two and a half millennia, Western man, nourished on Greek and on Judeo-Christian traditions, believed himself to be the center of the world, master of the earth. Today he knows he is superfluous in a world in which his best hope is to be at the forefront of progress. And he has been forced to admit that even that hope may one day be given the lie by cosmic space.

This vertiginous fall leaves man at a loss. In *The Tame Hedgehogs,* the fireman really does think that events in the inn where he is staying with friends are becoming "specious and unjustifiable." While horned ducks waltz faster and faster to the sounds of frenzied gypsy music, other ducks kill one another outside in the hope of being able to enter. Having been made insensitive through habit, the fireman and his friends watch this spectacle without feeling a thing. The next day, hidden in the bushes, the fireman watches as the kitchen boys, armed with skewers, larding needles, and beaters, savagely kill his friends. A fire breaks out. A fireman should extinguish it. The fireman in *The Tame Hedgehogs* leaves without looking back.

Like Perken in *The Royal Way* and Garine in *The Conquerors,* Scali in *Man's Hope* expresses the extent to which man is at a loss because he no longer knows what he is and no longer is able to consider himself the center of the universe. For twenty years, Scali has been hearing about "'the notion of man' and has been puzzling over it. The notion of man is all very fancy when you're faced with men engaged in a life-and-death struggle. Scali was completely unable to sort out his ideas. There was courage, generosity—and there was the physiological side. There were the revolutionaries—and there were the masses. There was politics—and ethics" (cf. *MH* 429). Once "oriented towards Being," today's man is drawn and quartered; he has become a "man capable of being swayed by ideas and acts" (*VOS* 481). "Gone are the days when we thought we should understand later, according to the best traditions! Our petition in bankruptcy has been filed. It's worrying . . . It's very worrying." And the question that then arises: "Does the notion of man have any meaning?" (*WTA* 98).

One reason for Malraux's greatness, and certainly one of the reasons he became a living legend, is that he dared to say, "Man—I don't know what he is," at a time when many of his contemporaries were trying to calm themselves by affirming: "Man! Man!" With a clarity that rejected all comforting illusions and for which skeptics are grateful to him, Malraux repeated that man was no longer free of the human condition. "What weighs on me is—how shall I put it?—my human lot" (*RW* 166), cries Perken in *The Royal Way,* while the artists and intellectuals at the colloquium in *The Walnut Trees of Altenburg* cannot assume the burden of their own condition, for they no longer know upon what values the idea of man may be based.

Man finds himself up against a destiny no longer to be unexplained—a destiny that is "man's consciousness of what is foreign to him and of what drags him along, of the cosmos in its indifference and its deadliness: the universe and time—the earth and death." A creature who knows he is superfluous, not useless, but not indispensable either, a creature crushed by his condition—such a man can only be a tragic figure. But for Malraux, unlike so many of his contemporaries, this tragic reality will never be hopeless, even though certain critics have suggested the contrary. For Malraux, "the tireless inventory of the world [art] on which our century has embarked" (*VOS* 131) is never a hopeless inventory. For

Malraux, the tragedy and the suffering that man experiences at no longer being tied to the universe are the tragedy and the suffering of everything that is born. And this is why he constantly seeks to penetrate the meaning of the long gestation that has led men to put their gods to rest and to reject their well-ordered universes. Malraux constantly confronts "that human mystery" (cf. *WTA* 24) which obsessed him, yet insists that "man is not born of his own affirmation"; "The ground is cleared. Fine! Let's see what we will build upon it" (UNESCO lecture).

There is an essential difference between the human tragedy according to Sartre and the human tragedy according to Malraux. For Sartre, man is tragic because he has affirmed his freedom but knows neither how to explain it nor how to use it; Sartre's tragic vision approaches that of certain Christians: it is the tragic reality of a man who cannot explain his freedom and who doesn't know what to do with it other than move in the direction of his Creator or of history. According to Malraux, man is tragic because he feels dependent on an indifferent cosmos and refuses to lie to himself by affirming that he knows what he is when in fact he does not. To claim that such a man is great is not paradoxical. This is not a pessimist; rather, he is uplifting because he is to be constructed in all lucidity.

Garine in *The Conquerors,* Kyo in *Man's Fate,* Magnin in *Man's Hope,* and Vincent Berger in *The Walnut Trees of Altenburg* have gone definitively beyond Valéry's observation: "Now, on a vast terrace in Elsinore . . . , the European Hamlet watches thousands of ghosts . . . He reflects on the life and death of truths . . . He ponders the folly of beginning the past again, of always wanting to change things" (*Variété* 1). The characters Malraux created between 1920 and 1942 had already gone beyond the man Sartre would introduce after 1945, the man who "lets responsibility for his existence be placed upon himself," who is "in possession of himself" but who basically doesn't know to what end. The fact that man is free and responsible for himself becomes obvious when the gods are put to rest, and it is surprising that some writers and thinkers take such pains to prove it. Perhaps the only reason they have gone to such trouble is finally to put to rest the gods that are still erect in them.

Malraux was obsessed by the question that is central to the colloquium in *The Walnut Trees of Altenburg:* "From beliefs, myths, and above all the multiplicity of mental structures, can one isolate a single permanent factor which is valid throughout the world, valid throughout history, on which to build one's conception of man?" (*WTA* 98). But in wondering whether there is "a single" permanent factor, Malraux poses the question in the purest tradition of unitary thought and brings to light one of the essential, fundamental contradictions with which he was long to grapple. On the one hand, he was looking for a single permanent factor, and on the other he celebrated in all his works the plurality whose richness we are just beginning to rediscover, and the metamorphosis whose Law we still hesitate to accept. How to reconcile in himself metamorphosis, plurality, and unity—this was Malraux's quest. It is also the uneasy quest of man in the waning twentieth century.

In *The Temptation of the West,* Ling says to the Europeans: "You believe that there is in what you call Man, something permanent, which does not exist" (*TW* 87). A few pages later Ling still insists: "For you, absolute reality was first God, then Man; but *Man is dead,* following God, and you search with anguish for something to which you can entrust his strange heritage" (*TW* 97–98). The West, to calm its distress as quickly as possible, yielded to the temptation of bequeathing god and mankind to the individual and the ego. Malraux never yielded to that temptation.

2

The Tyranny of the Individual

FOR MILLENNIA, the divine, or the sacred, had ignored the individual, and when it did acknowledge him it de-individualized him (cf. *Int* 102). In the Christian world, beginning in the Gothic period, this current was reversed, and an individualization of man's relationship with his god was progressively brought about. Under the Gothic impulse, "Christ no longer spoke to all, but to each person individually . . . The reign of the Son replaced that of the Father" (*Int* 285, 294). The communion and prayer of the individual supplanted the community of the faithful and liturgical piety. A new religious sensibility was forged of private prayer and isolation in side-chapels, where the faithful turned their backs to the nave.

Until the Gothic and the Renaissance, "the individual could only admire himself in secret or in sin" (*Ir* 262). After the Renaissance, one acquired the right to admire oneself. With Luther was born the individual responsibility of the Protestant. With Raphael was born the artist who "admired his acts, his mind, his ability to discover the world; abilities he no longer ascribed to God, even if he believed he obtained them from Him." Without negating Christianity, the Renaissance brought the first affirmation of man alone against the cosmos, and it paved the way for that individualistic thought, soon to elevate itself to a philosophy, which would then call itself liberal thought and would henceforth be opposed to all communal thinking.

It is hardly surprising that in an England which had broken with the papacy and had been nourished on Calvinist theology, a true theory of individualism should be developed in the seventeenth century. A product of reason rather than of faith, this theory would invade the eighteenth century and give birth to the French Revolution, "the most vehement affirmation of the individual" (*TN* 10). Having become king, the individual would inherit "the brilliance and imprecision of supreme values" (*Int* 351). Although his royalty was contested from the end of the eighteenth century onward by the state, the nation, and the people, the reign of the individual would "pervade the nineteenth century and part of the twentieth" (*AC* 223).

Ancient and medieval societies had considered ownership to be a social reality that gave rise to obligations and privileges. In seventeenth-century England and in the eighteenth century of the Encyclopedists, ownership was asserted as a right. The primal property, the one from which all others proceeded, the one that served to establish the social order, was ownership of self. Man would conceive of himself no longer as merely a part of a whole, religious or social, but as the affirmation of ownership, and would attempt to negotiate the best possible place for himself in a society whose sole raison d'être was to organize the enjoyment of self-ownership and all other kinds of ownership that flowed from it.

To assert that man is owned by no one but himself, that the individual is the owner of himself, was not enough to establish social obligation. Individualistic thought also had to postulate that the social contract was drawn up between equal individuals. The assimilation of equality with freedom, by which ownership of self was meant, was then the only means that had been thought of to abolish slavery and break the ties of suzerainty. Liberal individualistic thought, later imitated by collectivist thought, would henceforth rest on the idea of an egalitarian society of individuals entrusting a state with the task of organizing and delimiting the enjoyment of ownership. And just as one uses a fence or a hedge to define the limits of a garden one wishes to enjoy alone, so the individual attempted to delimit himself, to delimit his self. A possessive individual, he became an isolated individual without a deep and true bond with the owner next door. Malraux's character Attignies experiences this cruelly in *Man's Hope*. Perching on the wreckage of his plane that has just crashed into the water only a few meters from the beach, he waves desperately to the peasants standing along the shore. In vain, for "each member of a crowd believes that an appeal for help is meant for his neighbor" (*MH* 433). After trudging through the water and sand, Attignies reaches the beach and approaches a peasant. He asks him to help free the wounded men who are trapped in the plane. "Can't swim," replies the peasant." Attignies insists, pointing out that the water is barely knee-high. "I have kids," replies the peasant, walking away.

Ownership serves as such an important foundation for the individual and society that our culture has been instilled with this concept and our vocabulary deformed by it, practically without our knowledge. In French the word *propriété* designates both a characteristic and a possession, and this ambivalence shows the extent to which you are characterized by what you own. The German *Eigentum* can be used as a synonym of *Besitzung*, "possession," or *Kennzeichnen*, "a characteristic." In English, *property* can be used in the sense of *ownership* as well as *quality*. Even more significant is the fact that the same word can mean "to do good" and "to have goods."

By thinking of himself as property and by establishing owner-manager relations with society, man has sentenced himself to basing his life on contractual obligations and thus to transform moral obligations into commercial contracts. By thinking of human relationships as contractual obligations between owners, individualism has allowed money—that instrument for possession—to become the principal agent of the social structure. Malraux emphatically shows this in all his novels.

In *Man's Fate*, Ferral, a character who has received too little attention, incarnates to perfection man bred of possessive individualism. He is the only capitalist in all of Malraux's works, and it is remarkable that as early as the 1920s, having foreseen the evolution of industrial societies, Malraux chose to portray a financial rather than an industrial capitalist. Ferral is the head of the Franco-Asiatic Consortium, which we would today call a holding company. This consortium is the midwife of numerous sister companies "engaged in living by profitable incest" (*MF* 92). Playing the game of finance, Ferral runs a vast group that involves the production of tropical cultures, mineral extractions, industrial processing, as well as public works and trade. All these activities boast of their "civilizing mission" and their "civilizing program." In the thick of the revolutionary struggles between the communists and Chiang-Kai-shek's troops, Ferral is at the heart of political and economic intrigues. Trade union leaders, bankers, presidents of insurance companies, directors of river transport companies, foreign consuls file through his office, and Ferral notes with a certain joy that all of them are directly or indirectly dependent on him. Only Gisors, the old professor, doesn't need Ferral and can tell him what he really stands for: "the will to compel" (*MF* 245), the will to possess people and things in order to compel them.

The postulates that served as foundations for liberal individualistic thought—and were also to serve collectivist thought—created human relationships that led to "a 'reification' of the individual." In the 1920s, Malraux could see that reification was not the lot only of the proletariat; merchants, the lower middle class, white-collar workers are also caught in the fine net of possession that individualistic society has woven. And this subtle net of possession serves as a web not only in social relations but in the relations between men and women. This is shown with extraordinary depth in all Malraux's novels; indeed, male-female relationships may be said to symbolize social relations in his works. And it is perfectly normal that this should be so.

A significant evolution of women characters can be discerned in Malraux's works. In *The Royal Way,* there are only women/objects; in them the adventurer, thanks to quick erotic satisfaction, seeks to forget for a moment his battle with destiny. We find the woman/object again in *The Conquerors,* but here a loving, long-suffering woman also appears. In *Man's Fate,* Malraux introduces almost every type of woman: the woman crushed by her condition as woman and reified both by society and by her husband (Klein's worker or Hemmelrich's invalid wife); the woman as an instrument of erotic evasion; the woman who is willing to give man the illusion of having successfully possessed her (Valérie); and, finally, the woman who fights at man's side to build other relations between men and women and, in so doing, to build other social relations (May). In *Days of Wrath* we find the united couple. In *Man's Hope,* male-female relations are almost completely absent; yet here we do find the woman/pietà, "the millenary people of widows and mothers." And in the last volume of *The Metamorphosis of the Gods,* Malraux evokes the Goddess/Mothers of the highest and most ancient mythology.

In all of Malraux's novels, only two true couples are to be found: Anna and Kassner in *Days of Wrath,* and May and Kyo in *Man's Fate.* Anna's and Kassner's profound and tranquil love, their calm motherhood and fatherhood, correspond only to a fleeting moment in Malraux's own thought and life. Kyo and May, for their part, are charged with significance, and, indeed, *Man's Fate* ends with a dialogue between May and Gisors, Kyo's father. Kyo and May are not just representative of revolutionary fighters hoping to change social relations; primarily they represent all men and women who attempt, at the cost of sometimes terrible difficulties, to build new relationships free of possessive individualism. Kyo has to engage in a formidable battle with himself to root out the reflexes and conditioning instilled in him by his culture. One evening, May informs him that she has taken advantage of the mutual freedom they have given each other and has slept with a doctor from the hospital where she works. The ensuing dialogue between Kyo and May is first set in possessive terms, those the West has used for three centuries to talk about love. We now know that Clara Malraux, on the return voyage from Indochina, gave André Malraux the opportunity to experience the thoughts Kyo first had upon hearing May's confession. Although the strong ties that bind Kyo and May no longer bound Clara and André, Malraux nonetheless seems to have drawn Kyo's reactions from those he himself had experienced.

"Kyo was suffering from the most humiliating pain: that which one despises oneself for feeling" (*MF* 53–54). Confronted with May's confession, he was suffering because of "his feeling that the man who had just had intercourse with her . . . must despise her . . . If he went to bed with her, that was that, but he must not imagine that he possessed her" (*MF* 55). Kyo knows what men think of a woman with whom they've just easily gone to bed, and he believes he knows the thoughts of a woman who, without giving of or committing herself, has agreed to be the object of possession. He suffers because he knows how he and May, "using all their strength to hold each other in a tight embrace," attained true communion, fusion, and thus translated "the common meaning of their lives and deaths." The struggle of the "two" Kyos—the one who has inherited relations of possession and the one who wants to rid himself of that inheritance—is a dramatic struggle. It ends when Kyo decides to leave in an attempt to rejoin the Central Committee despite the risk of almost certain arrest. May prepares to leave with him. For her there is no other choice. Kyo refuses, and at May's insistence he harshly reminds her that she was able to take advantage of her freedom when she wanted to. He insists that she now respect his own freedom to go alone to his death. May is cruelly wounded when in their last moments together Kyo brings up that sexual liaison, which had meant so little to her. In these final minutes she undoubtedly realizes that what is important is not what her act meant to her, but what it couldn't help but mean to Kyo. She makes him realize that this freedom should not have been granted if now, on the threshold of death, it must separate them. She adds bitterly: "There are rights that one gives only so that they shall not be used" (*MF* 212). Kyo is unmoved, even when May asks him: "Have I lived like a woman who needs protection?" (*MF* 214). He leaves alone. On the sidewalk, walking toward his destiny, he begins to become aware of the attitude he has just adopted. "By what right did he exercise his pitiful protection on the woman who had even consented to his going?

Questioning Man

In the name of what was he leaving her? Was he sure that there was in his attitude no element of revenge?... He understood now that the willingness to lead the being one loves to death itself is perhaps the complete expression of love, that which cannot be surpassed" (*MF* 216). With this new understanding, Kyo rushes back. He opens the door. May hurriedly throws her coat over her shoulders and they leave together without a word.

A few pages after this scene, and through a true reverse camera shot, Malraux has us witness a dialogue between Katov and Hemmelrich, both of whom represent all men who feel disoriented and disarmed by qualities of tenderness and devotion they have discovered in their wives. Katov "had sadly proved to himself that he still possessed a remnant of life by treating a little working-girl who loved him with deliberate brutality" (*MF* 221); he had continued his revolutionary activity, but he was doing it now from habit and with "the obsession of the limitless tenderness hidden in the heart" of his wife. Hemmelrich is also disarmed by love; he is the epitome of the "reified" man who "feels like a lamp-post that everything free in the world comes and pisses on;" he can't admit to existing only for "cardiac virtues" and to being consumed by them. He, too, seeks to prove to himself that he still possesses a remnant of life, and he inflicts his sadism on his wife—not with pins, which is rare, but with words, which is far from rare. Neither Katov nor Hemmelrich can establish a person-to-person relationship with a woman.

The most common man-woman relationship in a society of possessive individuals, the one that has become the norm and, of itself, expresses and perpetuates social relations, is the relationship that is progressively established between Valérie and Ferral. For Ferral, apart from the courtesans that can be enjoyed and can entertain one for a moment, the only woman that exists is the woman one struggles with, seeks to possess, and negates. Ferral abhors having to court a woman in exchange for the pleasure he expects from her, for to court a woman is to grant her importance. "The woman who would have admired him in the giving of herself, whom he would not have had to fight, would not have existed in his eyes" (*MF* 244). The possession Ferral seeks is a true negation and it inflicts the deepest and most total humiliation on the woman. By playing with a light switch, Ferral forces Valérie to show "the submissive confession of that possessed face" (*MF* 126). Watching her after she has fallen asleep, he deludes himself: he actually believes that "sleep and her lips gave her over to a perfect sensuality, as though she had agreed to be no longer a free and living being, but only the expression of gratitude for a physical conquest" (*MF* 127). He believes this and shuts himself up in the masculine illusion of the man forged by possessive individualism. The illusion is total. It is tragic. And it is all the more tragic and tenacious since the woman, likewise deformed by the same cultural schemes, agrees to be the object of a conquest and subtly plays on her status as property, destined to be possessed. (Unless she were to adopt the opposite attitude: to make it a point of honor or revenge to possess her partner. That type of woman, once rare and notorious, seems to be multiplying and becoming commonplace.)

Agreeing that the light should remain on, Valérie chooses the warmth that is rising up in her, presses Ferral against her, and "plunges with long pulsations far from a shore upon which she knew she would presently be thrown back, but bringing with her the resolve not to forgive him" (*MF* 126–27). The relentless process of possession has thus begun. Denied, humiliated, momentarily possessed, consenting to such possession, Valérie will seek revenge. A few days later she arranges an encounter in the lobby of the biggest hotel in Shanghai, which humiliates Ferral in front of all the "boys," all the employees, and all the important people of the city. Ferral in turn feels "had," possessed, denied. He cannot but seek revenge. He succeeds in doing so, and the cycle continues. It could have been interrupted if Ferral had understood the letter Valérie had sent to him: "You will probably die without its ever having occurred to you that a woman is *also* a human being . . . I refuse to be regarded as a body, just as you refuse to be regarded as a check-book . . . I am *also* that body which you want me to be *wholly*" (*MF* 229–30). The cycle is not to be broken, for Valérie closes her letter with the revealing confession of a woman deformed by possessive individualism: "Your presence brings me close to my body with disgust, as springtime brings me close to it with joy." Individualists themselves, the Valéries of the world seek not to get closer to their partner's body but to their own; they cannot always live in the springtime, and would rather be brought close to their own bodies with disgust than not at all. The Ferrals take advantage of this preference.

They take advantage but with a bitter aftertaste, for deep down they are not unaware of the true nature of their behavior. After being publicly humiliated by Valérie's revenge, Ferral goes to see Gisors. They speak first of male/female relationships, then of the human condition. Leaving Gisors, Ferral goes in search of a prostitute as if looking for a sleeping pill. Observing the ease and indifference with which courtesans undress, he realizes that by compelling, humiliating, and negating women, "he never went to bed with anyone but himself" (*MF* 245). He suddenly understands that "his will to power never achieved its object." It matters little to him in the end, for by possessing this Chinese woman he possesses "the only thing he was eager for: himself." Kyo, having reached this degree of awareness, would have sent the courtesan away. Ferral approaches her and suppresses the awareness arising in him. Like him, most men forged by possessive individualism submerge awareness when it surfaces.

Possession, negation, humiliation, vengeance—each element carefully cloaked in urbanities and civilities—are the male-female relations of a society made up of possessive individuals. It would be too easy to deny this under the pretext that Valérie and Ferral are only lover and mistress. But husband-wife relations are also made up of rarely interrupted series of little possessions, negations, humiliations, vengeances, suppressed or satisfied, all carefully hidden behind convention and habit. Perceived thus, male-female relations in *Man's Fate* assume the role of symbols for social relations, relations that spin the web of society, relations between bosses and coolies, between Ferral and the employees of the consortium, between employers and employees. All are relations of thinly disguised, subtle possession. All eventually bring about humiliation and consequently the desire for revenge; a desire that often becomes explosive for having been suppressed rather than satisfied.

The humiliation brought about by possession and negation is the opposite of dignity, as Malraux often says; and he makes König, the chief of Chiang Kai-shek's police in Shanghai, the representative of all men who, once having lost their dignity, are tortured by an endless humiliation they can only endure by humiliating others (*MF* 306). Like König but at a lower level, the level of everyday life, all men and women who have ever felt possessed and humiliated, who in their own eyes have lost dignity in their professional, family, or sexual life, will attempt to make others, too, lose their dignity. A cruel destiny for an individual who has affirmed his ownership of self and finds himself caught up in the endless workings of the loss of his dignity. All the mechanisms with which the self-owned individual has thought to enjoy his tranquillity are turned against him. He exhausts himself in his attempt to reconcile the theory—a self-possessed individual—with the reality brought on by this theory—a possessed individual. The individual no longer belongs to himself: he is dispossessed.

The Tyranny of the Individual

Neither society nor the state recognizes the individual; both use him—they consider him to be an instrument of the general interest, which has progressively become the convenient disguise of personal interests that have managed to organize their convergence. Ferral himself learns this to his own loss, however much of a boss he may be. Following Kyo's death, after the failure of the revolutionaries in Shanghai, he goes to Paris to ask the government and banks for help to save the overextended Franco-Asiatic Consortium. In Shanghai, Ferral used coolies, merchants, local bankers, and even the Consul General as mere instruments. In Paris he is discarded like a worn-out object, a thing. Even presidents and chief executive officers experience the "reification of the individual." And the fact that Malraux tells of Ferral's "reification" after Kyo's death and after the great scene of the revolutionaries being thrown alive, one after the other, into the boiler of a locomotive proves, if there were still need to do so, that the meaning of *Man's Fate* is not to be sought only in the events in Shanghai.

In Paris, in the office of the minister of finance, where the presidents of the largest banks and financial institutions are meeting, Ferral observes those present with a certain disdain: "When you're through prostituting yourselves to the state," he thinks to himself, "you take your cowardice for wisdom, and believe that to be a Venus de Milo you need only to be armless . . . Your principal benefits come from your relations with the state. You live on commissions, a function of the importance of your establishment, and not on independent activities" (*MF* 342–45). (Here we marvel at Malraux's ability, as early as 1930, to uncover the dramatic evolution of industrial and liberal economies.) And the minister of finance, too, is only a pawn in a game that goes beyond him and takes away his self-possession. He finds refuge behind the coded language of bankers. He knows very well that the entire discussion about dismantling the Consortium or leaving it intact is nothing but a facade, since other enterprises, this time strictly controlled by the banks, will take up the profitable "civilizing mission" that they are all talking about, while thinking only of benefits and dividends. The minister thinks only of taking care of himself and keeping up appearances. He leaves the bankers to divide among themselves the promising spoils of the Consortium—he cannot do otherwise. He seeks compensation for his lack of real power and finds it in a childish ruse: he offers soft caramels to the bankers, so that they have to struggle to continue speaking with their usual unctuousness.

Having replaced human relations with the relations of contractual obligation, and moral values with commercial ones, liberal individualist society has given money and its modern form—finance—the power to structure society, that is, the power to organize relations between the various parts of the whole. With this development is has become inevitable that one day or another, when the system has sufficiently evolved its own internal logic, the dispossessed individual will come to consider the social order as absurd. To all appearances the liberal social order is coherent, but the appearance covers the cadaver of individualistic thought. To maintain itself, the social order must make ever greater use of coercion, repression, psychological techniques, but must also use hypocrisy and empty conventions. The functioning of justice, emblem of the profound reality of a society, comes to reveal a society that lives contrary to the ideas upon which it claims to be based. In *The Conquerors*, Garine is brought to trial because he helps women obtain abortions. He sees the proceedings as an unreal spectacle in which he has a minor role. "Outside the theatre, stage conventions are only to be found in law courts" (*Con* 55). Malraux too had had such an experience when he went before the court in Saigon. And Camus would also use a trial to show the absurdity of the social order and the way in which justice makes it respectable. But the trial of Meursault in *The Stranger* is above all a personal trial, even though its meaning must be broadened and transposed. Garine's trial in *The Conquerors* is a trial that involves the very roots of family and social organization.

After he has been sentenced, Garine writes to one of his friends: "I do not consider society bad, as it is capable of improvement; I consider it futile ... 'Absurd!' No, I should say unreasonable. The prospect of changing society does not interest me. It is not the absence of social justice that strikes me, but something deeper; my incapacity to adhere to any social order whatever. I am a-social, just as I am a-theist. All this would not matter if I were merely a student; but I know I shall be up against society all my life, and that I shall never be able to enter it without being false to my inner self" (*Con* 56). In Garine, social and metaphysical absurdity are joined together.

Dispossessed of himself and confronted with a fundamentally absurd social order, the twentieth-century individual questions the self with rage and fury and attempts to find in it, if not greatness, at least justification. He exacerbates his individualism. Christian life affirmed the unique character of each individual, but it strictly limited the realm of psychology, for it made man a battleground for a conflict in which the devil was the protagonist (cf. *TN* 27). It introduced an exterior element, the devil, and in so doing masked the fact that in reality that devilish element is found in the depths of one's being. Renaissance individualism was an "ethical individualism" that affirmed "an absolute right to act claimed by the individual" (Preface to *Lady Chatterley's Lover*). The nineteenth century basked in an "unformulated individualism which took root as much in artists concerned with safeguarding their interior world as in the followers of Napoleon, Rastignac, or Julien Sorel, all of them seized by ambition, that social passion of individualism." The twentieth century gave formulation to this unformulated individualism and turned it into a psychological individualism "born much less of the desire to create the complete man than of the fanatical desire to be different."

All of Malraux's works stigmatize this fanatical desire, the true "anguish of virile fraternity." The narrator of *The Conquerors* experiences a base joy in not being like the masses who fill the cathedral. In *Man's Hope*, we constantly encounter individuals who cannot establish themselves in a community and who glorify their difference or their indifference, which amounts to the same thing. The intellectuals at the colloquim in *The Walnut Trees of Altenburg* take spiteful pleasure in dissecting the slightest nuances that differentiate them; their discussions are not enriched by any fraternal breath of air or any true sensitivity, which always leads to communion with something other than oneself. In *The Voices of Silence*, Malraux says of the Impressionists that "this tyrannical impression of the individual does not lead to a tyranny of the impression but to one of the artist himself" (*VOS* 299). Of course, this remark is applied to painting, but we shouldn't hesitate to extend it to psychology and to life. His impressions, which the individual cultivates and scrutinizes like rare plants, do not create a "tyranny of impressions," which would have been conceivable and perhaps momentarily beneficial; they create a "tyranny of the individual."

Under the influence of psychological individualism, the notion of man changed and henceforth rested "on the awareness each person has of himself" (*JE* 138). The cry "Man is the only object of our fascination" is followed by "I am the only object worthy of my fascination" (*JE* 139). The hope of one day being able to know oneself as one would an object inhabits man and becomes a tragic and tyrannical error, which Malraux denounced at the outset of depth psychology. It is an illusion to believe that each individual can base his own Self on his own actions and dreams. "The great Western doctrines have always implicitly allowed that a man can judge himself, can establish constant relations between the principles he has accepted and his own actions" (*JE* 140). But self-judgment is possible only if guided by a superior or supreme value. Without a supreme value, judging oneself becomes an illusion, for one must "attribute to the self-considering conscience traits that belong to it only when it considers others" (ibid.).

A scene at the beginning of *Man's Fate,* to which Malraux would often refer, illustrates the illusion of those who hope to know themselves objectively, to perceive themselves as one perceives others. Kyo hears his voice for the first time on a recording and fails to recognize it (*MF* 21). He tells Gisors, his father, how surprised he is, and Gisors, with a faraway look, replies: "I've had the experience of finding myself unexpectedly before a mirror and not recognizing myself..." and then adds: "We hear the voices of others with our ears." And our own? Kyo then asks. "With our throats: for you can hear your own voice with your ears stopped," replies Gisors (*MF* 48). In *The Voices of Silence,* Malraux gave this scene its full meaning and breadth: "We know, too, that a man's consciousness of himself functions through channels other than those of his awareness of the outside world ... I have written elsewhere of the man who fails to recognize his own voice on the gramophone, because he is hearing it for the first time through his ears and not through his throat; and because our throat alone transmits to us our inner voice, I called this book *La Condition humaine*"[1] (*VOS* 630).

This precision of Malraux's is essential: he entitled his novel *La Condition humaine* because "our throat alone transmits to us our inner voice." And it is also essential that Malraux should have pointed to it more than twenty years after he wrote his novel and more than fifty years after the advent of psychoanalysis. Psychological and psychoanalytical techniques can allow man to hear his inner voice with his ears, just as the techniques of sound allow him to hear his exterior voice. But to go from there to thinking that man will discover the source of his inner self by analyzing his actions or by having them analyzed is a construction of the mind. He will find the external self in them. "With calm distress we are becoming conscious of the profound opposition between our acts and our inner lives. The intensity of the latter cannot belong to the mind; sensing this, the mind revolves emptily, beautiful machine soiled by blood stains ... This inner life is also the most primitive, and its power, which exhibits the arbitrariness of the intellect, cannot save us from

---

1. [Literally "The Human Condition," though translated under the title *Man's Fate.*—Trans.]

The Tyranny of the Individual

mind, to which it says, 'You are a lie, the very means of lying, creator of realities...?' And the mind answers: 'True. But always, when the day ended, men thought they saw rich prizes in the darkness, and the riches you offer are only the last reflections of the dying daylight'" (*TW* 120). Malraux was twenty years old when he wrote those words. Heir of the West, he carried within him the divorce of the West: the divorce of the mind from deep life. All his life he would seek to reconcile them.

When we attempt to know other people we refer, consciously or not, to a coherent world order we have constructed, which we use to make sense of the actions of others. But this referential world is only a code, a screen; it is a system of references in which we believe others move around; it is in no way the real world of the inner self of other men and women. The actions of others don't account for their selves, and yet we use those actions as a way to know them. Likewise, our actions don't account for our own inner self, and yet others use them to know us. Thus, to the divorce between the mind and deep life is added a divorce between the self and other people; a divorce that only love and fraternity can overcome, for they alone open up other roads of access to deep life and the inner self.

Without love and fraternity everyone can lament, like Valérie in *Man's Fate*, "It is not always easy for me to protect myself from the idea people have of me" (*MF* 230); every individual resembles those innumerable characters in *Man's Hope* who agonizingly repeat; "Do you understand me?" for the precise reason that they are consumed with the feeling of being unable to be understood. And since the feeling of being misunderstood is a hell, one may well say that "hell is other people" when no common code, no common referential value, permits either me or others to understand one's inner self beyond actions and words. In the absence of a common supreme value, one's inner self is not only misunderstood by others but misunderstands itself too, even though it has claimed to be the only object worthy of its fascination and is constantly refining the analysis of the elementary particles that make it up. Psychological individualism is locked in a total impasse.

The inner self to which Malraux refers is that of Claude in *The Royal Way*, who falls prey to his own memories and imagination; that of Ch'en in *Man's Fate*, who, possessed by fantastic and threatening images, is afraid to fall asleep; that of the obscure forces that invade Kassner in the solitude of his prison cell in *Days of Wrath*. Above all, it is the self Malraux describes in his monograph *Of a European Youth:* "The self, that palace of silence into which each one of us enters alone, reveals all the precious stones of our provisional dementia mixed with the precious stones of lucidity" (*JE* 141). In 1926, Malraux's writings often referred to dementia and demons which he would later define as "those monsters of the abyss which psychoanalysis catches with nets, and politics with dynamite" (*VOS* 575). In May 1955, in an interview published in *L'Express,* Malraux specified that "the balance sheet of psychoanalysis shows that psychology in the past fifty years has put back the monsters and demons into man." For many, this reintegration renews the hope of rebuilding man anew. This may come about, but first the psychoanalysts must beware of the excesses and the excitement accompanying all beginnings; they must above all rediscover the deep meaning which has been attributed to monsters by all mythologies of all times and on all continents: they are the signal and the guardian of the sacred, the shapeless and monstrous force that the profane man must conquer if he wishes to enter the temple and commune with light.

Malraux always doubted that simply putting the demons back inside man, taming the monsters that everyone carries deep within, could one day build man anew. In 1942, as part of the colloquium at the heart of *The Walnut Trees of Altenburg,* he introduced an essential discussion about psychology and demons. Vincent Berger having exclaimed, "It's our old struggle against the Devil which makes us confuse our knowledge of man with our knowledge of his secrets" (*WTA* 95), Thirard, another participant, responds in terms that are hard to contest: "Secrets reveal man to us in much the same way as science has disclosed to us the meaning of the Universe" (ibid.). This whole discussion begins with a statement: "In psychoanalysis the unconscious, still suspect and *a priori* evil, is the Devil once again!" Did Malraux himself believe the unconscious was "*a priori* always evil"? Perhaps not enough to assert as much himself, but sufficiently so as not to contradict the notion clearly. At the time, Malraux had not yet totally freed himself of the Judeo-Christian heritage of a humanity so guilty that God had to have himself crucified to redeem man, a humanity so sinful that the unconscious could not be *a priori* anything but evil. Malraux progressively freed himself of the Catholic notion of man's radical culpability, and the idea that the unconscious is *a priori* evil is never again found in his writings. Nor is the idea that it is *a priori* good. On the other hand, Malraux's works always express the certainty that the unconscious will not allow man to be built anew. And that certainty is important for the future.

The Tyranny of the Individual

The individual hunting within himself for justification finds dreams, imagination, but also "a chaotic series of sensations" (*TW* 53) over which he has no hold. "By accepting the notion of the subconscious, and by having become fascinated with it, Europe has deprived herself of her best weapons" (*TW* 49), Malraux said in 1927. We should not forget the context of this statement: the most vocal artists of that time gave themselves over to the unconscious and sought to base their creations on it. Malraux always maintained that this was a mistake. He repeated this again in *The Timeless:* "What artist doesn't know that a well-defined unconscious, that of Freud of Jung, never takes into account the *quality* of a painting? And that the undefined unconscious takes nothing into account?" (*Int* 329). Upon publication of the first translations of Freud's work, Malraux foresaw that the individualism of sensibilities that invaded the nineteenth century would be succeeded by an individualism of the unconscious, a psychological individualism. The critic André Vandegans, in his study of Malraux's early years as a writer, is right to underline that Malraux left Europe in 1923 out of disgust with the individualism into which he saw it disintegrating.

The man who recognizes value only in the individual hunted down in the depths is a man who forbids himself any possibility of inner unity and even any possibility of true self-knowledge. The two essays Malraux published in 1926 and 1927, *The Temptation of the West* and *Of a European Youth,* show that *"at the core of European man, ruling the important movements of his life, is a basic absurdity"* (*TW* 40; cf. also *JE* 138). Malraux emphasizes this assertion by italicizing it. In the 1920s, most of Malraux's contemporaries found reassurance either in continued adherence to Christian values, which they hoped to adapt, or in putting all their hopes in the unconscious. Malraux asserted in 1925 that the individualization that had invaded religious life in the Gothic period and had established itself in philosophy in the seventeenth century, in political theory in the eighteenth, in sensibility in the nineteenth, and in psychology in the twentieth century was leading man to a radical absurdity: to his being torn apart by the cosmos, by others, by himself; to a painful division between man's demand for inner unity and the dissolution of his inner self.

In July 1926 (a date that should be noted), Malraux published an essential text in the *Nouvelles littéraires:* "The main contribution our generation has made, I'm convinced, is to proclaim the breakdown of individualism, of all the values, all the doctrines, all the attitudes that are justified by the exaltation of the Self... All the passion of the twentieth century attached to man blossoms into the vehement affirmation of the Self. Well, that man and this self, built upon so many ruins and dominating us whether we want them to or not, don't interest us." This passage is crucial. And none of Malraux's biographers who have tried, more or less sincerely, to show that Malraux became a living legend through his ability to remain on center stage and to get imaginary facts believed, have given this passage enough thought. Malraux's century followed him, even if it did not always truly understand him, because, after declaring that "this man and this self" don't interest us, Malraux plunged into an avid quest to propose another man and another self. He was thus pointing a way to a true epic; and epic always encounters legend. Instead of "endlessly scratching away at the individual" (*WTA* 24), Malraux invited European youth courageously to sustain lucid consciousness and not to find assurance by giving in to the appeal of doctrines or faiths that were all tainted by individualism. He invited it to look truth in the eye: "Europeans are weary of themselves, of their crumbling individualism, of their exaltation. What sustains them is less a thought than a delicate framework of negation. Capable of action to the point of self-sacrifice, but disgusted by the will to act which today contorts their race, they would seek to discover a more profound meaning in their actions"(*TW* 76).

Finally, individualism has only brought about "a conqueror, triumphant but blind" (*JE* 146). Malraux's novels are teeming with men twisted by alienation or humiliation, which corresponds to a shared experience expressed either by an idea, if we are referring to alienation, or by feelings, if we are referring to humiliation. Alienated, humiliated, the individual is devalued. Kyo, in prison, feels "total humiliation." For twenty years Hemmelrich has said "stinking youth!" before saying "stinking old age!" and before "passing on to his unfortunate kid these two perfect expressions of life." Clappique is an individual who lies to others and to himself in an attempt to create some manner of substance for himself. Ferral, too, is a devalued individual: a blind triumphant conqueror in Shanghai; a humiliated instrument in Paris.

A culture and a civilization that turn the individual into their supreme value cannot—either on a social or on a personal level—propose a notion of man that has any substance. Nor can a religious practice that has excessively exalted the individual. And that is why the Christian world has declined since the Gothic period. The man who believes he has found his freedom by affirming that he is self-possessed has really done nothing but give up his freedom. In his social life he has given it up to money, then to the state. In his inner life he has given it up to feelings, then to the unconscious. In his spiritual life he has given it up to the sale of indulgences, then to disputes over Grace. "Still too strong to be a slave, and not strong enough to remain the lord of creation" (*VOS* 603), the individual in no way renounces his own conquest, but ceases to see it as his raison d'être.

The interrogation that has brought about the conquest of the world has not permitted the conquest of man. "An art of Great Navigators" is conceivable, Malraux said, but can we conceive of a culture of "Great Navigators?" (*VOS* 604). Malraux pondered this question for a long time before reaching the point where it posed itself for him in completely different terms. At the beginning of his life, in the 1920s, rejecting the individualism of the unconscious and the essential Absurdity that was beginning to put Europeans on the rack, Malraux sought to escape "the abject surrender to the power of death; the [surrender] of the childless, godless modern man" (*RW* 54). This escape was a sometimes terrifying quest, but he faced up to it and eventually came upon "the mysterious revelation of life" that fills the final pages of his last novel.

PART TWO

Action or the Absurd

3

Action, or Rejection of the Absurd

❦

UNTIL 1930, the absurd is present in all Malraux's works. It makes up their very essence, as if right from the start he were seeking to exorcise the Absurd whose "first apparition" was in the making. In *Paper Moons,* the world is bizarre, comical, vain. In *The Temptation of the West* and *Of a European Youth,* Malraux seeks the roots of the Absurdity that has settled in the very heart of Europeans. He raises the problem that he was to pursue all his life: how to reaffirm man in the face of destiny. In *The Conquerors,* Garine, having become Commissioner at the Revolutionary Propaganda Office in Canton, was momentarily able to forget the feeling of absurdity that had possessed him during his trial and had "come to include everything human" (*Con* 125). At the end of the novel, however, separated from any action and preparing to return to Europe, he once again becomes obsessed with the memory of his trial and with the Absurd, which "is reasserting its rights" (*Con* 125). In *Farfelu Kingdom,* which Malraux published after *The Conquerors,* the world has become strange, impenetrable, except for the mysterious narrator, who in the end sets off for the Islands of the Blessed. Finally, *The Royal Way,* which came out in 1930, is essentially a confrontation between Perken and the Absurd.

In *The Royal Way,* Absurdity, through a stifling progression, becomes universal, radical. In the beginning it resides in consciousness and in the obsession with death, in the obligation to live with "the sweat of death [lying] clammy on [one's] palm" (*RW* 56). It is then nourished by the discovery of what life in the tropical forest truly is, "the ceaseless fermentation in which forms grew bloated, lengthened out, decayed as in a world where mankind has no place" (*RW* 100). In a village of huts, Perken encounters another adventurer, Grabot. The Mois have gouged out his eyes, and have reduced him to slavery: night and day he is yoked to a circular treadmill. He has become a blind beast of burden. The prestigious Grabot is degraded beyond what even death could have accomplished. In an attempt to rescue Grabot from his fate, Perken steps on a poisoned dart, and the end of the novel depicts the slow and inexorable process of his death. Confronted with the failure of the adventure that was his life, Perken then extends the absurdity of it all not only to the universe but also fundamentally to mankind itself, and he exclaims: "To be a living man was even more absurd than dying!" (*RW* 283). But in the final seconds of his confrontation with death, Perken, by a formidable effort at self-analysis, understands that it isn't his death that is absurd, but rather his life. And in a final burst he utters his last words: "There . . . is no death. There's only . . . I . . . I . . . who am dying" (*RW* 290). All of Malraux's subsequent works have their seed in the awareness that surfaces in Perken with his last breath. At the end of *The Royal Way*, but this time without *farfelu* and with tragic depth, intensity, and seriousness, Malraux reaches the same conclusion he reached at the end of *Paper Moons:* killing death resolves nothing; the world and mankind will remain no less absurd.

Between 1920 and 1930, Malraux's awareness of the absurdity of the world and of mankind was not the result of logical reasoning, nor was it the product of thought. The absurdity of the world in which he lived was a given, which he perceived with his sensibility. He didn't think of absurdity; he felt it. He didn't posit the absurd as a theory, he didn't seek to construct a philosophy or an ethics of the Absurd; he suffered the absurdity of the world in which he was born. Although we find portrayed in his work the social Absurd (of which Garine becomes aware after his trial), the individual Absurd (which results from the exaltation of the self), and even the absurdity of the Absurd (when the Sins no longer know why they were so anxious to kill Death), we never find the Absurd portrayed as an answer to the question, But what is the meaning of all this?

In *L'Homme en procès,* P. H. Simon shows the extent to which the desperate young writers of the thirties tried to find assurance in fighting absurdity by exalting a sensual, sexual, and animal way of life. They could be sure that at least such an existence belonged to them. Too bad if it became dull, for it was incontestable. Too bad if nothing could justify it, for it provided a sense of existing. And it was the moment in literature,

Action, or Rejection of the Absurd

concludes Simon, when an existentialist tendency was substituted for a humanist one. But as early as the 1920s, Malraux by way of sensibility had dealt with the philosophical themes Sartre propagated in the forties, and he had already rejected them by the thirties.

After *The Royal Way*, when Malraux was approaching *Man's Fate*, he found himself in an extremely difficult position: he refused to seek support in a humanism that was dead, or to be satisfied with a mankind based on the Absurd. His greatness lies in his search for a way to establish Man upon something other than God, nihilism, or the Absurd. It was also the cause of his suffering, which his detractors all too often forget, for he was forced to live with unanswerable questions, whereas he had within him an almost imperious need to live with affirmations.

If the Absurd represented a reality perceived by his sensibility, it never constituted a temptation of the mind. All the letters written by Ling in *The Temptation of the West* suggest this. Malraux—and young people are beginning to be grateful to him for this as they watch with growing astonishment the efforts made by so many of their elders to raise the Absurd to the level of an Absolute—always believed that the Absurd belonged to a different realm from that of evil or disorder, with which it is often associated. Evil and disorder belong to the realm of the mind: they can be thought. The Absurd, on the contrary, is fundamentally unthinkable. It *is* not. It is merely an absence. It arises only from the fact that the cosmos resists all our efforts to imagine it. "We have turned the Absurd into an answer; it used to be a question," Malraux often repeated. In *The Voice of the West* Malraux's 1974 dialogue with Guy Suarès, he again recalled what he had always thought: "The Absurd is the feeling of Difference negatively felt, like anguish ... [Difference] might be felt as multiplicity, as plurality ... and it might be felt as tragedy. There is no doubt that our civilization has felt it as tragedy and has found the myth of the Absurd in it." Isolated within himself, the individual has cultivated the fanaticism of difference to such an extent that he has eventually been overwhelmed by it. He could experience difference as a manifestation of plurality; he has experienced it as tragedy, neither providing an answer nor having an end.

Although it has not often been pointed out, Camus's position vis-à-vis the Absurd was in the end rather similar to Malraux's. In *The Myth of Sisyphus*, Camus, with the honesty that characterized him, had acknowledged: "I said that the world is absurd, but I was too hasty. This world in itself is not reasonable—that's all that can be said about it. But what is absurd is the confrontation of this irrational and the wild desire for clarity whose call echoes in the deepest reaches of man." Ten years later Camus concluded *The Rebel* with this strong proclamation: "Beyond the ruins of nihilism we are all preparing a renaissance. But few know this." For Malraux, too—and he expressed this when he was an adolescent, from 1915 to 1920—the Absurd is born of the impossible conciliation between the rational demands the Westerner carries within him and the nonrational perception he has of himself and the world. But it follows that the Absurd cannot be the law of the mind. The Absurd entices the mind, questions it, stimulates it, but does not provide a foundation for it. And this is why, in 1925, Malraux had Ling say to Europeans: "Your minor attempts to construct a moderate nihilism do not seem destined to long life" (*TW* 98).

Camus had accepted the Absurd as a point of departure because he asserted at the time: "I can deny everything of that part of me which lives from uncertain yearnings, except the desire for unity, the appetite for resolution, the demand for clarity, for cohesion." Malraux didn't deny the demand for clarity—who would?—but he always wondered about the legitimacy of the "desire for unity," which may not even be within the scope of the human condition. His adolescent visions and the perceptions of his sensibility had taught him that clarity might not come from unity, certainly not from unity such as it had been imagined for several centuries. Ancient cultures, civilizations, and religions emphasized the plurality of manifestations, which did not exclude unity from origins. Judeo-Christian monotheism, despite the Trinity, fought plurality and hypertrophied man's desire for unity. As an heir of the West, Malraux was burdened with that desire, but his sensibilities and his development led him to doubt the legitimacy of such a yearning. The drama and metaphysical anguish in Malraux's life fed on this doubt. They were profound, sometimes tormenting, though modesty rarely allowed him to speak of them in a personal vein. Malraux was tortured by a spiritual thirst that none of the religions or faiths he knew of could quench. By choosing agnosticism on the one hand, and the rejection of the Absurd on the other, he adopted the most uncomfortable position, and undoubtedly the most demanding metaphysical position in an age such as our own. To carry out the quest that alone seemed to be the meaning of his existence, Malraux did not take refuge among any of the gods that had been laid to rest; he rejected the deceptive seductions of the Absurd and chose action instead.

Malraux has often been said to have had the temperament of a man of action; I disagree. He was not instinctively driven to action. It did not represent an imperative in his character. When at twenty years old someone writes truly surrealistic works like *Paper Moons* and *For an Idol with a Trunk,* there is little chance that he belongs to the race of men of action. Indeed, the opposite is true. Malraux had analyzed and stigmatized the tendency that incites Europeans to "desert themselves" and makes them "capable of action to the point of self-sacrifice, but disgusted by the will to act which today contorts their race" (*TW* 76). He took up the same idea again forty years later and developed it in his interview with Nehru: in our civilization everyone is obsessed with action, and today people use action to legitimize their lives. Within our civilization there has been a progressive development of "the intoxication which enables action to brush aside all legitimation from life." (*A-M* 233). Europeans have become like Garine, who at first wanted to be intoxicated by a great action but ultimately had to recognize that his action made him "indifferent to everything apart from it, and, to begin with, to its own results" (*Con* 155). Throughout Malraux's life, from *The Temptation of the West* to *Anti-Memoirs,* there was a continuity in his thoughts on action: he was suspicious of it, and yet he chose it.

The world of pure imagination, to which Malraux joyfully abandoned himself in his early writings and never completely deserted, given the place he reserved for it in *Mirror of Limbo,* is an imaginary world that separates man from reality. On the other hand, while involved in action, man is momentarily unaware of any break, any "gap" between himself and his environment, between himself and the world. If he is not lucid, he will become intoxicated by actions. If he is lucid he knows he will eventually return to the questioning that tortures him, but he hopes the questions will then be posed in different terms. Malraux, unlike many of his contemporaries, saw action not as a diversion, the way Pascal considered it, nor as a drug in which embittered man seeks an escape or a soothing illusion. Malraux felt no attachment either to those men who were bored with anything unconnected to their own action, or to intellectuals like those at the colloquium in *The Walnut Trees of Altenberg* for whom an idea was never born of a fact but always of another idea. And if Malraux chose action, it was to use it as a testing ground for thought. For a man who no longer knows what the cosmos is, nor even what man is, action, if he remains lucid, can represent what experimentation represented for Claude Bernard: it can be a thought seeking its confirmation or its invalidation in experience.

If one refuses to accept the Absurd as an explanation of the world, if one is agnostic not out of refusal or indifference but because no faith can quench one's spiritual thirst, then only action and its experimental properties provide any hope of discovering a new law that might govern the world. "An age that no longer finds the meaning of the world in the soul of men finds it in their actions. As it can" (*TN* 17), Malraux concludes in *The Black Triangle* after pointing out that this groping attitude had begun as early as the seventeenth century, though the eighteenth, impassioned by its battle, and the nineteenth, dazzled by science, had not been fully aware of it.

A true man of action throws himself into action to obtain a result. Malraux conceived of action and lived it as an instrument of conscious thought; indeed, he saw action as the only possible laboratory of conscious thought. The search for efficiency was foreign to Malraux's approach; he tended to participate in acts that led to no immediate success. He had no desire to copy Lawrence; rather, he had more in common with the *poètes maudits,* as Gaëtan Picon correctly pointed out. Malraux accumulated experiences because he lived in an age in which what one could best do with one's life was to convert "as wide a range of experience as possible into conscious thought" (*MH* 396).

When man feels orientated, when he knows what he thinks of the cosmos and of mankind, then, granted, his conscious thought can guide his actions. But if he is not so oriented, he must agree to reverse the terms of his actions and plunge into the painful darkness of tentative and uncertain experiences while maintaining the hope that, once transformed into consciousness, those experiences will lead him to the discovery of a new Law. Of course, we might argue that another approach could be taken: positing a Law and seeking its experimental verification, asserting a consciousness and verifying it through experiences. This is the approach taken by ideologues and, often, by false prophets. But Malraux rejected that course for yet another reason: he knew that, in times such as his, presenting an *a priori* consciousness to an age that no longer had one would be to remain more or less in line with previous consciousnesses that have in fact declined. In other words—the words Malraux used at the end of his life—he challenged that approach because he believed that if an heir has failed to metamorphose his heritage, he can only administer the values that have been handed down to him, even the ones that have been devalued. From his adolescence on, Malraux was inhabited by the deep conviction that our consciousness of tomorrow would be radically different from that of yesterday, as radically different as the Greek consciousness was from the Egyptian, or the Christian consciousness from the Roman. To participate in the birth of tomorrow's

Action, or Rejection of the Absurd

consciousness, to help in the metamorphosis of consciousness, we must free ourselves from the consciousness of the past, we must accumulate experiences, and, with them and them alone, develop a new consciousness. For Malraux, then, action was a metaphysical requirement.

Thus conceived, action enables us to reach "the immense realm of what man draws out of himself to confess, to deny, to magnify himself, or to attempt to live forever" (UNESCO lecture). Ideas can no longer contribute, since we know they are all lies. Action remains the only way to attain "voracious lucidity" (*TW* 122), to truly discover the man in whom is united "the aptitude for action, culture, and lucidity" (*Con* 175), to attain the lucidity that is the opposite of intoxication. In the cultural heritage of the twentieth century, true lucidity does not belong to men of action who, to succeed, must be intoxicated by their actions. Likewise, in an age such as ours, with rare exceptions, lucidity is no longer an aptitude of intellectuals, who rarely confront life with their ideas and often prefer to prove their ideas right despite their being disproved by facts. For Malraux, the demand for lucidity is an agonizing thirst. Without lucidity, man will never be able to stand up to his destiny, which is why, in 1925, he concluded *The Temptation of the West* with this magnificent petition: "Voracious lucidity, I still burn before your tall and solitary flame in this heavy night, while the yellow wind cries, as in all those foreign nights when the wide wind echoed around me the proud outcry of the sterile sea" (*TW* 122).

4

Rejection of Individual Intoxications

WHEN AN AGE is marked by individualism and self-interest—as the twentieth century certainly is—the attitudes toward life and the forms of action available to man are almost always individual intoxications. Some of them tempted Malraux—adventure, terrorism, lies, wisdom—but he rejected those intoxications, however seductive they may have been, for to expect to find lucidity through them, much less a new relationship with the cosmos, would have been futile.

At the beginning of *The Royal Way* a long conversation between Claude and Perken enables them discreetly to reveal what they expect from life and, especially, what they don't expect from it. Claude, a generation younger than Perken, is no adventurer, but he is going to experience an adventure, which is quite different. He understands profoundly that Perken is an adventurer because there are "not so many avenues to freedom" (*RW* 54). He understands "the slave's brief spell of freedom from his master, that men who do not understand it call adventure" (*RW* 56). Gradually he senses the formation of a true camaraderie with Perken, for he has measured just how little that adventurer has in common with those who seek to escape, with adventurers for whom "adventure is but food for dreams" (*Candide,* 1930). He understands how adventure, for Perken, is not "an evasion, but a quest" (*RW* 55).

The great adventurers of the nineteenth century were explorers. Their successors are astronauts and deep-sea divers. Malraux's adventurers—Perken in *The Royal Way* and David de Mayrena in *Anti-Memoirs*—are not out to explore or discover the world, since they consider it absurd; they seek to create a different world. In a world that has become absurd, relations between people and objects have also become absurd, and for a man like Perken, adventure represents the only hope for creating new relations between himself and objects, between himself and others—the only hope for creating different laws of life. He is a demiurgic adventurer. Through adventure Perken expects to find that complete freedom of creation which the *farfelu* brings to the imagination. And he expects this without being tied to any doctrine or ideology. His hope is vain, for it represents a terrible individual intoxication, as evidenced in *The Royal Way*.

Malraux wrote *The Royal Way* six years after his own adventure in the tropical forest, and more than eighteen months after publishing *The Conquerors*. Reflecting on these lapses of time, I have become convinced that Malraux wrote *The Royal Way* in order to exorcize from himself, as from us, the temptation of adventure. Garine, in *The Conquerors,* has been criticized for being an individualist and an adventurer who refuses to humble himself before the revolution in which he is involved. This criticism, which is not, strictly speaking, a misinterpretation of the character Garine but which exhibits a shallow and often biased reading of the novel, was painful for Malraux. He responded by participating in the debate over *The Conquerors;* he responded in particular by showing in *The Royal Way* how greatly Garine differed from Perken, how adventure is an individual intoxication that doesn't free one from the human condition.

When Perken approached the chief of the savage Mois tribe, he thought his life would depend on that chief, whereas it ultimately depended on a poisoned bamboo shoot over which he had already fallen. While walking on, Perken experienced the exaltation of "risking more than death" (*RW* 206), of taking his revenge on the universe, of freeing himself from the human condition. This exaltation was so strong that he "was conscious of an inward struggle, an effort to fight down an overpowering hallucination, a kind of ecstasy" (ibid.). In the end he was not playing with more than his death; he was playing with nothing but death, and he soon fell back into the attitude that "to be a living man was even more absurd than dying!" For Perken, the failure of adventure will be consummated in all lucidity. It will be complete, and Claude manages to learn something from that failure.

Given the meaning of his adventure and his death, there is a contradiction that Perken cannot overcome, one that gives his death a poignancy, especially for Westerners, who have often repressed their secret desire for adventure. The life and death of an adventurer cannot both be significant. If the one acquires a meaning, the other cannot. The adventurer's life is his adventure, but at the very moment of his death that life/adventure ceases to have meaning. At the time of his death, especially when it approaches slowly and inexorably, the adventurer loses possession of his life. The meaning of his life escapes Perken, just as the women with whom he knew only eroticism escaped him: once the sexual act was accomplished, nothing connected him to those women any longer. His possession of women, because it was meant to be possession, was only temporary and fleeting. Likewise, nothing connected him to his life any longer at the moment when that life was leaving him. Perken possessed his life the way he possessed his women: fleetingly and above all futilely, for in the end he had given no meaning to his life, nor had he found meaning in his death, nor had he changed the world or accomplished his great plan.

Having reached the end of his adventure, and looking at his hand, which he no longer recognizes, which seems detached from him, Perken is forced to admit that "nothing would ever give a meaning to his life" (*RW* 286). Anyone who, behind a more or less ordered life, conceals with greater or lesser success a repressed desire for adventure, must make a similar admission. To overcome the senselessness of their life, Sartre suggested they kill the adventurer in themselves and allow the militant to be born. To be a militant, however, one must follow a religion or a doctrine. At the time Sartre was proposing his own doctrine, fifteen years had passed since Malraux had rejected it, for in essence that doctrine was only a resurgence in another guise of the old, failed individualism; it did not establish Man on a permanent, exaltant given.

Confronted with Perken's meaningless death, with that death which took all meaning from life, Claude feels a "desperate fraternity that was wrenching him outside of himself" (*RW* 290). He feels powerless to translate that fraternity into words, and can only put his arms around Perken's shoulders. But the adventurer cannot know fraternity, and Perken looks at Claude as if he were a stranger. The adventurer dies as he has lived, cut off from the community of men. And this is why Malraux boldly says in the chapter in *Anti-Memoirs* that is actually titled "The Royal Way:" "Perken was the incarnation ... of the negative hero ... We have no time for heroes without a cause" (*A-M* 258, 321).

Another individual intoxication—terrorism—occupies an important place in Malraux's novels. For Hong, one of the terrorists in *The Conquer-*

ors, "only action in the service of hatred is neither lying, cowardice nor weakness: it alone is the opposite of empty words" (*Con* 115). The revolutionary leaders are exasperated by the terrorist acts committed by Hong and his friends. They try to convince him to renounce such acts, but Hong, enraged, is defiant: "Politics don't appeal to me ... No social order is anything to me. Life, our one and only life! Not to lose it! There!" (*Con* 117). In *Man's Fate,* Malraux gives an added dimension to the terrorist Ch'en, which Hong still lacked in *The Conquerors.* Ch'en's life is an adventure of violence, an adventure in the same sense as Perken's adventure, a vain metaphysical quest. Thirsting for an absolute, Ch'en "felt, like every mystic, that his absolute could be seized only in the moment" (*MF* 158). His first terrorist act truly represents a rebirth that changes the world as he saw it, and changes Ch'en as well. Previously he had always considered himself to be in revolt; afterwards for a few moments he is closer to the stars. He believes he has found "the meaning of his life," "the total possession of himself" (*MF* 196). To intensify that meaning and possession as much as possible, he decides it is not enough simply to plant bombs, and resolves to throw himself under Chiang Kai-shek's car, for he wants to assassinate the Chinese leader, against the advice of the International.

Although in Malraux's novels the psychology of his characters is never investigated for the interest it holds in itself—which is understandable, since none of his novels, not even *The Conquerors* or *Days of Wrath,* has a major character as its hero—Ch'en's psychological makeup is analyzed in detail in *Man's Fate.* I believe this is not accidental. Malraux wanted—and perhaps needed—to look closely at the psychology of a terrorist, just as he had looked closely at the psychology of an adventurer. The fact that he did this as early as 1930 shows that he had foreseen how terrorism would become one of the most difficult problems at the end of the twentieth century, as it had been for Russia at the end of the nineteenth. The tragedy of Ch'en can be found in part in Camus's *The Just,* and in the thirst of the members of Baader's "Munich Circle."

Ch'en carries a deep anguish within him, which he seeks to control with a certainty. He is obsessed by his nightmares and admits to Kyo that the only things he truly fears are falling asleep and becoming crazy. Yet every night he must fall asleep and encounter the same pestulant creatures (*MF* 157). Ch'en, like Hong, was initially influenced by a rigorous Christian education. He then had Gisors as a teacher, but Gisors was unable to deliver him either from the anguish of the human Fall, which had been instilled in him, or from the permanent and sterile introspection, which is another form of the conflict between the Fall caused by original sin and salvation through grace.

Everything in *The Conquerors* and *Man's Fate* suggests to the reader that terrorists like Hong and Ch'en are only, and remain only, pure individualists. Perken didn't deceive himself; he acted as an individualist, he pursued individual goals, and he admitted as much. Hong and Ch'en, on the contrary, persuade themselves and want to persuade others that they are acting on behalf of the community and in the name of the revolution. Their way of invoking transindividual values, however, remains marked by the purest of individualisms: in the name of their principles they refuse to take concrete situations into consideration; they assume the attitude of moralists—moralists of violence, certainly, but moralists all the same. And their individualism is clearly expressed by Ch'en when he is waiting, a bomb under his arm, for Chiang Kai-shek's car, which he plans to throw himself under: "It was necessary that terrorism become a mystic cult," it was necessary to "give an immediate meaning to the individual without hope" (*MF* 246–47).

An idealist, an individualist, an adventurer in violence—does the terrorist succeed in giving meaning to his life? As early as in *Man's Fate*, Malraux clearly responds in the negative. Before demonstrating this, I must admit my regret that Malraux, although he deals with the objection raised against terrorists for provoking repression and favoring reaction, deals nowhere, either in his writings or his interviews, with the debate over the usefulness or the harm of terrorism in advancing the consciousness of the masses. It would have been perfectly natural for Ch'en to open this debate when defending his plan to assassinate Chiang Kai-shek in front of the delegate of the International; it would even have been perfectly plausible, since Kyo was present at the meeting and had just accused the International of having lost control over the masses through its political tactics. Ch'en might have argued that his act could be used to make the masses aware of the true role played by Chiang Kai-shek. Malraux did not open this debate, perhaps because it might have appeared purely political and even cynical, whereas only Ch'en's metaphysical quest interested him; perhaps also because his position on the issue was not fully established, and he felt no need to present one at that time.

After his first act of terrorism, Ch'en needs to understand the rebirth he feels he has undergone. He goes to see his old teacher, Gisors, and says to him: "I'm terribly alone" (*MF* 62). To experience solitude, to feel separated from others, is a fundamental given of the psychology of the terrorist, so fundamental in fact that it persists in fraternal combat. When two hundred revolutionary groups mobilize for action, Ch'en experiences an uneasy exaltation, but he nevertheless has the sensation of carrying out a solitary action: his own. This solitude, from which he cannot escape, is made vivid through Malraux's description of the attack on the police station. Ch'en and three other men climb up on the roof of the station. They decide to hang on to each other to form a human chain, hanging in the air, which will enable the last link to reach the windows and throw grenades into the station. Ch'en hangs onto the ridge of the roof; he is the one supporting the chain. He feels the weight of the three men pass through his body and through his chest. The first grenades begin to explode inside the station. In spite of "the intimacy of death," in spite of this "fraternal weight," Ch'en feels he is "not one of them" (*MF* 109). The terrorist has no brothers in combat. He remains forever cut off from the community of men.

Ch'en attempts to sublimate the solitude that gnaws at the terrorist, that is impervious to brotherhood: he wants to transform terrorism into a religion. After deciding to blow up the car by throwing himself underneath it, Ch'en first asks two of his companions, Suan and Pei, to join him by also throwing themselves under the car. He is exalted by the decision he has just reached. Like Perken before the Moi chief, he believes "much more to possess his exaltation than to be possessed by it" (*MF* 196). In an attempt to convince Suan and Pei to join him, he contends that "throwing bombs even in the most dangerous way was adventure; the resolution to die was something else—the opposite, perhaps" (*MF* 194). Suan refuses to follow Ch'en because he is fighting for others, not for Ch'en. Pei remains silent for a long time, then agrees to follow Ch'en. Ch'en, however, abruptly changes his mind and tells Pei: "No, today you must bear witness" (*MF* 197). he then asks him to withdraw his agreement in order to be able to write "the gospel of terrorism" (ibid.).

Ch'en's failure is complete, radical. He throws himself under the car. The bomb explodes. A few seconds later he regains consciousness. His legs have been torn off and the lower half of his body is in shreds. He wants to "ask if Chiang Kai-shek was dead, but he wanted to know this in another world; in this world, that death itself was unimportant to him" (*MF* 249). Malraux is working a fantastic turn-around here. Ch'en will not be indifferent to the fate of Chiang Kai-Shek in "another world"; he will still be interested in it in that other world. On the other hand, in the world of the living, in this world, in the world where the general's fate was once so important to him, Ch'en has become indifferent to that fate. And to bring this fully home to us, Malraux makes us wait ten pages before mentioning incidentally, through a minor conversation between dancers in a cabaret, that Chiang Kai-shek was not even in the car.

Ch'en is robbed of Chiang Kai-shek's death not because the attempt failed but because that death is not fundamental: it is not essential, and yet Ch'en wanted to base his gospel upon it. Ch'en's failure, the failure of his life, the failure of the mystical religion he had hoped to establish, is even more complete: Ch'en is robbed of his own death. A policeman approaches his mutilated body. Ch'en manages to grab the little pistol he has always carried in his shirt pocket. He shoots at random, then puts the barrel of the revolver into his mouth. But it isn't he himself who shoots; it isn't he who, with this ultimate gesture, gives meaning to his life and his death. The policeman kicks him violently with his heel. All of Ch'en's muscles contract, and he shoots unconsciously. Like Grabot and Perken, Ch'en's death is taken away from him and he dies a victim of his individual intoxication: he has not changed the world and has not even contributed to it. His action remains meaningless. He has given meaning neither to his life nor to his death.

Like adventure and terrorism, which are ultimate forms of action, lying and wisdom, which are ways of dealing with life, also amount to individual intoxications. Of all the characters Malraux created, the Baron de Clappique in *Man's Fate* is the most surprising. He is a mythomaniac—comic and even ludicrous—who constantly invents biographies for himself, and consciously alienates himself in lies. He doesn't seek banal compensation in lies; rather he discovers the possibility of creating a world in which he has total freedom. The fact that this freedom is illusory matters little to him, for he doesn't want to believe his own lies; it is enough that others, or even just one other person, believe them. He thus enters a world that no longer weighs upon him (*MF* 264), and he experiences true voluptuousness in living "in another person's eyes an altogether different life from his own" (*MF* 279). At the end of *Man's Fate*, Clappique attempts to escape from the police by disguising himself as a sailor, equipped with a pail and a broom, and prepares to board a boat leaving for Europe. He then discovers how changing his clothes has changed the way people look at him, and realizes he has found "the most dazzling success of his life. No, men do not exist, since a costume is enough to enable one to escape from oneself, to find another life in the eyes of others" (*MF* 313).

Rejection of Individual Intoxications

When I first began studying Malraux, the amount of time he devotes to Clappique in *Man's Fate* struck me as excessive. I tended to view this as a resurgence of the *farfelu,* but a degraded *farfelu* that was no longer rooted in the surreal and the fantastic but, rather, in the commonplace and the banal. Today, on the contrary, I believe Clappique deserves a full analysis. Is not the Baron de Clappique involved in almost every important event in *Man's Fate?* Doesn't he serve as an intermediary in the purchasing of weapons? Doesn't he know all the main characters, revolutionaries, capitalists, and police? Doesn't he appear to serve as a slightly unreal link between them? Doesn't Kyo's fate depend on him on two occasions? And doesn't Malraux, as if he wanted to stress the Baron de Clappique's importance in *Man's Fate,* discuss in more than a hundred pages in *Anti-Memoirs* that other Baron de Clappique, the one who in Singapore in 1965 talked about *The Reign of the Devil,* the significant title of the film he was producing about the legend of Mayrena, king of the Sedangs? All these facts have led me to believe that Malraux meant to endow Clappique with enormous significance.

Clappique's attitude toward life thus appears as an artistic transposition of the attitude adopted by the anonymous crowd of those who are neither adventurers, terrorists, revolutionaries, nor anything else. It is the attitude of anyone who can only cope with the human condition by taking a certain dose of lies; lies that they do not truly believe but that enable them to ignore the questions they ask about mankind and about themselves. Lying, elevated to an art by all the Barons de Clappique in the world, or amateurishly practiced, not always consciously, by many human beings, thus becomes the most banal of the attitudes man has adopted since the gods have been put to rest and since man has been dead. Profound life has become comedy, lies; but in living with lies, in accepting his destiny through lies, man has acquired no depth. It is what Gisors is saying when he specifies that Clappique "could not grow old. Age did not bring him human experience, but an intoxication" (*MF* 280).

This interpretation of the Baron de Clappique helps explain why in his interviews Malraux so often cited the advice Vincent Berger gave his son in *The Walnut Trees of Altenburg:* "Bear in mind that a man's most effective weapon lies in reducing the deceitful side of his character to a minimum" (*WTA* 38). It also helps explain the meaning of Malraux's response to Roger Stéphane in 1945: "Intelligence? It is the destruction of comedy, plus judgment, plus the spirit of hypothesis . . ." And it explains why Malraux always reserved a special place for lucidity: lucidity is the only weapon that enables man to reduce the deceitful side of his character; it alone can enable man to come out of the fog of lies in which humanity has taken refuge.

The pattern of lies that enables humanity, for better or for worse, to endure the human condition is the most insidious enemy of fraternity. After encountering "the most dazzling success of his life," Clappique "was stupefied to discover how indifferent his fate was to others—it existed only for him" (*MF* 312). He himself had always been indifferent to the destiny of others, particularly that of Kyo, with whom he had arranged a meeting to warn him of the danger of his imminent arrest. Kyo went to this meeting—his fate depended on it—but he waited in vain for Clappique, who had stayed at a gaming table and had then invented a new biography, incomplete like all the others, for a sympathetic prostitute. The illusory freedom that Clappique had created for himself with a new lie resulted in the arrest of Kyo and all his comrades of the Central Committee. The illusory freedom lying provides causes the suffocation and death of revolutionary fraternity. Believing the lies of the human comedy does not free man from the truth of the human condition.

In many respects the wise man appears to be the opposite of the lying self-deceiver, and Malraux always granted the sage an important place in his novels. There remains, moreover, an in-depth study to be done on the presence of the sage in Malraux's work. Such a study would be quite instructive and would provide profound insight into the differences between Chen-Dai in *The Conquerors* and Gisors in *Man's Fate*, between Alvear in *Man's Hope* and Berger's grandfather in *The Walnut Trees of Altenburg*, and it would certainly illuminate Nehru's presence in *Anti-Memoirs*. Each of these wise men has a unique significance and a personal ethics, which would be useful to compare if we wished to follow in detail the evolution of Malraux's thoughts on wisdom. Here, it is wisdom in itself that concerns us. Malraux was tempted by wisdom, and he often wondered if it could provide a response or represent a valid attitude toward life. To judge from *The Conquerors* and Malraux's description of the sage Chen-Dai, it is obvious that Malraux rejected wisdom as an attitude toward life. But in his last two novels, with the characters of old Alvear and Berger's grandfather his response is more difficult to determine.

In *The Temptation of the West*, the exchange of letters between the Chinese Ling and the young European A. D. appears to be a dialogue on wisdom or, more precisely, a dialogue on the self-denial and submission of Orientals as opposed to the will to act in which Europeans writhe. Ling reminds A. D. that the dreams of Europeans are filled with movements and images, whereas the dreams of Chinese are filled with calm: "The Chinese who dreams becomes wise" (*TW* 57), he writes. The young European resists the temptation to give in to Oriental wisdom, a temptation that has come over the West in successive waves ever since all Western values collapsed, and he replies to Ling: "These dreams, having once possessed us, call up still other dreams" (*TW* 77).

The wise man, as Malraux conceived him when he wrote *The Conquerors*, is above all a moralist of intent in the same way the terrorist is a moralist of violence. Chen-Dai can be associated with a statue of the Commander. He believes in a moral code and wants his life to be a lofty representation of it. But to believe in a moral code in the twentieth century, one must accept values that have failed, or—the nuance here is essential—one must accept values whose form and modalities have failed. A wise man like Chen-Dai can only be a conservator of those forms and modalities. "A noble figure of a victim preparing his own biography" (*Con* 77), he is concerned above all with his moral protest. He teaches men not how to live, but how to detach themselves. He himself is in fact unattached either to men or to the world: he is attached to principles, and foremost to justice. But his conception of justice makes it very distant, very external to real life. It is the justice of those who can preach scorn for material goods and for everyday life, the justice of those who have no problem simply existing. When Chen-Dai writes his will before committing suicide in an ultimate protest against the revolutionaries, he attempts to convince his compatriots that "PEACE, our greatest treasure, must not be destroyed in that confusion into which evil counselors are about to lead the people of China" (*Con* 130). To endure injustice in the name of peace has always been the language of those who are on the right side and who, in addition, are the men who decide on wars. For others, for those who want to exist, who are alienated and humiliated in their work, this language is an insult, even if it is true that the revolution in China had to be conceived and carried out by Chinese and not by foreigners.

In order to adopt wisdom as a guiding rule in one's life, one must be more or less capable of believing either in a god, or in the cosmos, or in man. And if this is impossible, one must at least believe in an ethics or a moral code and be anchored in a system of values. For Malraux, in the 1920s, the Westerner was no longer anchored in any system of values and therefore could not validly espouse wisdom. There is nonetheless a facet of the life of the wise man which interested and even fascinated Malraux: it is the wise man's authority in the face of power. The authority of the wise man is an essential given in *The Conquerors,* and is found in varying degrees in *Man's Fate, Man's Hope,* and *The Walnut Trees of Altenburg.* And it would seem that Malraux thought about this often throughout his life. The noble figure of Chen-Dai, his nobility developed from an exemplary and irreprochable life, makes him a legend and a symbol which are endlessly challenged by the power of Garine and Borodine. These men, who must act, command, and be obeyed, constantly come up against instructions apparently given by Chen-Dai. One day Garine complains about them, but Chen-Dai assures him with obvious contentment that he has given no instructions, not even a signal; he simply uttered an opinion, and that was enough. The exercise of power comes up against something that goes far beyond it and over which it has no control: moral authority.

In *The Walnut Trees of Altenburg* Berger's grandfather protested furiously after the Church cashed in on certain relaxations in the rules for Lent. He went on foot to Rome and succeeded in obtaining an audience with the pope. With about twenty other pilgrims he knelt down when the pope entered. "The Holy Father had walked by, they had kissed his slipper, and they had been dismissed" (*WTA* 30). Berger's grandfather felt a "holy indignation." Ever since that day he was "cut off from the Church but not from Christ," and he attended Mass outside, next to the church. Since he was losing his hearing and was afraid of not hearing the bell that announced the Consecration and the Elevation, he ended up spending twenty minutes on his knees in the nettles of summer and the mud of winter. "This figure with his short white beard and frock-coat, kneeling in the mud underneath his umbrella, in the same spot, at the same time and for the same reason for so many years, presented less the spectacle of a crackpot than of a man of good sense" (*WTA* 31). His enemies tried to disqualify him—he was the mayor of the commune and ran a factory—but they failed. His moral authority was so great that no one dared to oppose him when, despite his intransigent Catholicism, he offered a wing of his house to the Jewish community, to whom the Municipal Council had just refused to rent a building where a synagogue could be established. His son, at first carried away by the attitude of the times, allowed himself to believe for a moment: "Authority is all right, but power is better" (*WTA* 43), then he understood his mistake; he understood that the wise and the just believe and live the opposite.

Rejection of Individual Intoxications

Gisors in *Man's Fate* and old Alvear in *Man's Hope* are not, strictly speaking, wise or just men; rather they appear as reflective men who, in the name of knowledge or art, remain marginally involved in action without being indifferent to it. With an almost certain envy—he was thirty-five at the time—Malraux adroitly describes their moral authority and the power over people that it gives them. Gisors, however, undergoes two trials, which bring to light the limits of his wisdom. When he listens to the questions Ch'en asks himself after his first murder, Gisors measures the great distance separating the universe of blood—his son Kyo's universe—from the universe of ideas—his own. He too becomes aware of his solitude, one which becomes all-encompassing following the death of Kyo, who in the end was Gisors's only link between ideas and reality. With this link broken, Gisors first refuses the consolation of the opium that had so often brought him serenity, and then goes off to Kobe, where he finds definitive refuge away from men and their concerns. Granted, it is he who attempts to teach his daughter-in-law May that one must love life, not death. But the end of his life proves the extent to which even the wise man, in an age like ours, cannot be validly connected either to the community of men or to the cosmos.

5

The Revolution

❧

IF MAN NO LONGER KNOWS what to base his destiny on, if he accepts the Absurd as a way to question the cosmos but rejects it as an answer, if he wants to "exist against all of that" and against the silence of the starry millennia, and if it is lucidity that he aspires to, then man must seek experiences in action which, he hopes, will enable him to discover the foundations of a new consciousness. But as all individual actions, even the noblest, are marked by the failure of individualism and lead to intoxications, the only possible course remaining is participation in a collective action, that is, in an action that embraces the collectivity and therefore can only be religious or political.

After his expedition to search for the statues of the Banteai Srey temple, after the trial that resulted from that expedition, after his prison sentence, and after the founding of the journals *L'Indochine* and *L'Indochine enchaînée*, Malraux knew of no religious faith he could believe in, none to which he wished to entrust his weakness, and above all none that seemed capable of establishing man in the twentieth century and in the centuries to come (*TW* 121). The collective action in which man must seek experiences in order to establish a new consciousness cannot be a religious one; it can therefore only be political. And, as such, it can only be in the service of a new order of things, a new relationship between men. It can only be revolutionary.

Since Malraux's adherence to a collective and revolutionary action was not that of a man who thinks and acts guided by a doctrine, he never found the peace of mind achieved by men of doctrine in action. His adherence was a problematical one. He expected collective action to raise

The Revolution

the question rather than to answer it. He became involved in revolution for metaphysical reasons before he ever did so for political ones. In his novels, revolution appears as the quest of individual man rather than of the citizen or worker. The aspirations revolution must fulfill go far beyond the hope for a better distribution of riches or for a better government run by one class as opposed to another. When Garine evokes the old rancor that led him to join the revolution, and when objections are raised that he has rarely been poor, he vehemently responds: "Oh, that is not the question. My deep-rooted hostility is not so much against the property owners as against the stupid principles on which they defend their possessions" (*Con* 92).

This deep-rooted hostility towards "stupid principles" in the name of which owners of money and power defend their possessions is shared by all the revolutionaries in *Man's Fate* and by all the Republicans in *Man's Hope*. All might have responded as Barca does when Manuel asks him the reasons for his revolutionary involvement: "There are no end of reasons . . . ; the long and the short of it is this: I won't have people looking down on me. Listen, lad . . . , that's how it is. All the rest's beside the point. You're right about the money, I could have fixed it up with them maybe. But those people want to be looked up to, and I'm damned if I'll look up to them. They're not worth it. There's some I can respect, but not them" (*MH* 93–95).

In *The Voices of Silence,* Malraux traces the slow genesis of this deep-rooted hostility toward the principles defended by property owners. Under the feudal system and the monarchy, the king, crowned at Rheims, was "placed at the apex of a hierarchy that claimed man's allegiance emotionally as well as legally, and in which Reason played a negligible part" (*VOS* 483). The bourgeoisie, which appropriated the French Revolution, battled both the king and the Christian religion, unlike the Dutch bourgeoisie, which saw its power as "associated with a return to God" (ibid.). Although the Dantons, the Carnots, and the Saint-Justs were bearers of a triumphant universalism, they were quickly forgotten, and in their wake the rights of the bourgeoisie were substituted for the Rights of Man. The bourgeois, "owing allegiance to no supreme value of their own, discarded those which until now had been shared by all—or endorsed them only insofar as they served their turn" (*VOS* 484). They succeeded in passing off as values what were merely objects of desire. There was no real value system at the base of the bourgeois order, which used the leftovers of Christian values only insofar as they suited it and could be turned to a profit. And that is why, as the nineteenth-century artist and the people of the early twentieth century saw it, the power of the bourgeoisie was being usurped: "It was unjustified" (*VOS* 484).

In a decaying world, a world that can engage neither man's soul nor his mind, a world built by the bourgeoisie upon values of efficiency, revolution presents itself as the only authentic reality, the only geometrical location for actions through which one can seek a new foundation for mankind. By its very nature, revolution goes beyond the individual and appeals to transindividual values. For Perken, adventure is but *one* reality serving to mediate between man and his destiny. For Kyo, for Katov, for May, revolution is *the* reality. None of the revolutionaries in *Man's Fate,* except the terrorists, try to exist as individuals. The hero of *Man's Fate* is a collective hero: it is the revolutionary community and its growth.

Trotsky saw *The Conquerors* as a novel with the revolution as its hero. He was anticipating another novel. Malraux answered him: "The primary emphasis is on the relationship between individuals and a collective action, not on the collective action alone." After *The Conquerors,* Malraux published *The Royal Way,* in which the primary emphasis is on the relations between individuals and individual actions. After *The Royal Way* he wrote *Man's Fate,* with its primary emphasis on collective action, its collective hero—the revolutionary community. With these three novels Malraux presented the triad of attitudes man can have in his struggle against destiny.

At the beginning of *The Conquerors,* the narrator, who is having the situation in Canton explained to him, learns that Borodine's propaganda has not been effective because it did not go beyond telling workers and peasants that they were great guys simply because they were workers or peasants. It was replaced by Garine's propaganda, which was extremely effective because it made the coolies realize that they existed. It made it possible for them to believe in their own dignity and importance. The revolution was "giving everyone his life" (*Con* 17). Malraux's revolutionaries don't hate the happiness of the rich; they hate the respect the rich have for themselves and their lack of respect for the less fortunate.

To avoid any ambiguity about the significance of the revolution, at the very beginning of *Man's Fate* Malraux has several characters reiterate that they are involved in the revolution to seek dignity rather than to win their bread. "To give everyone his life," to enable everyone to have self-esteem, "to teach men the art of living" (*MH* 394), presupposes a transformation of human relations that is possible only by way of a transformation of social relations. A scene from *Man's Hope*—many others could be cited—shows the extent to which human relations can truly be transformed. Ever since the poorly officered *milicianos* fled from Toledo, a certain disorder has been established, and disobedience takes over the ranks. The soldiers elect a committee, which is received by the commander, and it proposes measures to halt the disorder. The elected delegation, made up of four soldiers, stands before the commander just as delegations of workers used to stand: one in front and the three others behind. "It was as if the revolution itself, in its simplest, most significant form, stood there personified by them. For the speaker the revolution meant the right to talk like that" (*MH* 272). This scene is crucial. The respect of the one in command is total. The committee of soldiers is not a committee of palavers; it, too, has authority and efficiency in mind. But leaders and soldiers, commanders and commanded, boss and workers, are no longer face to face in the presence of a blind and degrading submission to authority; they are face to face in respect for the dignity of everyone and in respect for everyone's functions. The commander realizes it and experiences it profoundly. He embraces the chief of the delegation in the Spanish way: "For the first time he was in the presence of a fraternity that expressed itself in action" (*MH* 272).

For centuries, Christianity's strength was in making it possible for each individual to believe that he possessed "some distinct individual life in the eyes of God" (*Con* 91). But in this world the social relationships instituted by Christian individualism have denied each person the right to that distinct individual life. Henceforth, only revolution could offer men the hope of "attaining that individual, independent life, which is in some way regarded as the greatest treasure of the rich" (ibid.). And since there is no dignity possible for a man who works without knowing why he is working, it is essential that work take on meaning, it is essential that man's relationship with his work change: this is one of the fundamental requirements of the human condition. Despite the downfall of the revolutionaries, Hemmelrich can say for the first time in his life why he is working rather than waiting patiently to die, and Pei can write:

'A civilization becomes transformed, you see, when its most oppressed element—the humiliation of the slave, the work of the modern worker—suddenly becomes a *value,* when the oppressed ceases to attempt to escape this humiliation, and seeks his salvation in it, when the worker ceases to attempt to escape this work, and seeks in it his reason for being. The factory, which is still only a kind of church of the catacombs, must become what the cathedral was, and men must see in it, instead of gods, human power struggling against the Earth.' (*MF* 352–53)

"The revolution plays a part that an 'eternal life' used formerly to play" (*MH* 323). Many Christians criticize Malraux for this statement. They criticize him for expecting more from the revolutionary struggle than it can give, and for crowning it an Absolute, when in fact it is impure and provokes not love but hatred. Malraux did not deny that, but he also knew that religions can provoke hatred, and that their temporal battles have not lived up to their spiritual aspirations. And that is why "a man who has been unjustly sentenced, or has run up against more than his share of ingratitude, or baseness, or stupidity—well, he's bound to stake his hope on some new order" (*MH* 323). As long as we ignore the fact that "staking one's hope" has been an essential need of the masses in the twentieth century, we shall be unable to understand in any depth why so many millions, on all continents, have adhered with varying degrees of strictness to revolutionary ideologies.

Before he dies, Kyo takes stock of his life. He is lying in the courtyard of a school next to all his companions, who have also been arrested. In this courtyard the emprisoned revolutionaries are thrown alive, one after the other, into the boiler of a locomotive, whose lugubrious whistle blows as each body is cremated. In order to escape this fate, Kyo prepares his cyanide and folds his arms over his chest, assuming the position of a corpse. His face is made peaceful through serenity. "He had always thought that it is fine to die by one's own hand, a death that resembles one's life" (*MF* 321). His life will have been a struggle for that which, in his time, was filled with the deepest meaning and with the greatest hope. For Kyo, dying could be "the supreme expression of a life" (*MF* 323). Katov, for his part, approaches the locomotive after giving a gift greater than his life: he has given his cyanide tablet to two young comrades who were terrified by every blast of the whistle. The death of the revolutionary hero is a fecund death. Moreno, one of the characters in *Man's Hope*, must recognize this despite his philosophical convictions. "And there's something else which even I, the first Marxist officer in the army, never dreamt of. There's a fraternity which is only to be found—beyond the grave . . . For a month now, I've known dead men can sing" (*MH* 370). Through revolutionary struggles man gives meaning to his death because he has given meaning to his life. Revolution is a "personal apocalypse" in the etymological sense, that is, a revelation.

The Revolution

By entering the "mendicant order of the revolution" (*MH* 319) Malraux's heros attempt to reconcile those two domains in themselves.

If we view revolution the way the West continues to do despite the failures of 1789 and 1917, then Malraux's revolutionary heros have indeed wandered into politics. But Malraux had another view of revolution. In 1948 he asked Nehru how Hinduism had managed to expel a well-organized Buddhism from India, and how it had been able to do so without serious conflict. At the time, Nehru could come up with no satisfactory response, but seven years later he delivered a speech that Malraux thought indirectly provided the answer he had been waiting for. In this speech, Nehru began by recalling that he *busied himself* in the field of politics; then he declared that the best politics should fight the destruction which science brings in its wake, and the violence which humanity carries within it. "We have been failing," Nehru stated, "for so many years, so many generations! There must be some other way than the one adopted by men of my kind and my profession" (*A-M* 227). And Malraux added that this hope for some other way was noteworthy coming from the most effective spokesman for political idealism the world has ever known.

If there is some other way than the one adopted by men whose profession is politics, is it not the one the revolutionary heros in *The Conquerors* and *Man's Fate* are looking for? Like Saint-Just, they are not fighting for a political regime which they consider good, and against a regime they consider bad; they have "the vocation of revolution" (*TN* 115). To be a conscious force in action, to discover the honor of being a man, to conquer one's dignity, to give meaning to one's work—it is a new man Malraux's heroes are trying to bring to life through revolution, a new vision of man that they are trying to transform into a reality.

In 1967 in *Le Magazine littéraire,* Malraux pointed out that for him revolution represented an historical phenomenon, not a social one. That same year in *Anti-Memoirs,* evoking the disagreement between de Gaulle and the communists concerning the arming of militiamen and the union of all the organizations of the Resistance, Malraux concluded: "And we all felt that what was at stake went deeper than [the realm of] politics" (*A-M* 77). Malraux doesn't specify what realm he is referring to, but we can discern it in Napoleon's statement so often cited by Malraux: "Tragedy, now, is politics." Of course, he is speaking here of Greek tragedy, the tragedy that is the result of man's intrusion among forces for which he was only a pawn, the intrusion of the world of consciousness into that of destiny. Malraux's heroes have the vocation of revolution because in

Action or the Absurd

revolution they raise themselves to the level of protagonists. With revolution they cease to be the pawns of obscure, unknown forces: they confront destiny and challenge its blind strength with their awareness.

This ennoblement of revolution is at the root of the first major misunderstanding about Malraux. When Malraux attended the meetings and congresses of revolutionary writers which took place between 1930 and 1939, his contemporaries forgot that *The Conquerors* does not simply seek to conquer a political power, and they forgot that *Man's Fate* is not only about the condition of workers. They forgot that the only struggle that mobilized Malraux was the fantastic struggle man engages in to stand up to destiny. It has sometimes been suggested that Malraux's colleagues hadn't forgotten those things but that they had decided, after an objective analysis of the situation, to make use of his prestige. This may not be entirely false, but then those fair-weather colleagues had no right—except that of bad faith—to claim that Malraux betrayed an idea of revolution to which he had never adhered. If Malraux's *farfelu* writings had been less neglected and if his novels could have been read and understood beyond their local contexts, it would immediately have become clear that Malraux was indeed a revolutionary, but in another sphere and on another level than were his colleagues at that time. Anyone who still doubts this should reread *Man's Hope:* there they will find the themes of "To Be and to Act," "The Quality of Life," etc., which burst onto the streets in 1968 and for a moment almost overwhelmed those who still called themselves revolutionaries of the left.

Goya's enemy, Malraux said, was creation. Goya fought it with an ironic Fantastic, and he knew that his own universe would only become reality through the establishment of a new system of relations between people and objects. The Fantastic, the *Farfelu,* and Fiction enabled Malraux to defy the world in which he lived with total freedom, and to create another universe (cf. *TN* and *Saturn*). For a true creator the world he creates is more real than the reality which surrounds him. Malraux was never more a creator than he was between 1930 and 1939, and when he participated in revolutionary acts it was with the hope of transforming the system of relations between human beings and objects, of incarnating in reality that which he anticipated and imagined. He didn't yet know that he was heading toward a "lyrical illusion"; he didn't yet know that in order truly to establish another system of relations it would first be necessary to set out on another quest and prepare the metamorphosis of politics without which all revolution remains an illusion.

PART THREE

Lyrical Illusion

6

Fraternity Scorned

❦

AFTER HIS TRIAL, it is unthinkable for Garine to be a mere spectator of the first World War. He joins the Foreign Legion. He hopes to take part in the fighting, but finds only "millions of men passive and motionless in the tumult," (*Con* 57) who, for the purpose of clearing out the enemy trenches, are given new, "broad-bladed knives, with chestnut-wood handles, horribly, contemptibly like ordinary kitchen knives" (ibid.). He succeeds in having himself listed as missing and manages to reach Zurich, where he runs a pacifist publishing house. He associates with the Bolshevist group that is preparing the Russian Revolution and quickly understands "that he had now to do with experts rather than with preachers" (ibid.). Unfortunately, these experts of the revolution were soon to become the technocrats of the postrevolution. In the face of ever more powerful and refined technology, used by conservatives and reactionaries alike, the revolutionaries have locked themselves up with this alternative: they can either refuse to use the same technology and be crushed, or they can use it and betray their revolution.

This dilemma, fundamentally a cultural one, is at the very heart of *Man's Hope* and constitutes the tragedy of the work. With uncommon intuition Malraux instantly understood the deep significance of the civil war in Spain. The *pronunciamiento* of the generals explodes on July 17, 1936. Four days later Malraux lands in Madrid! The characters in *Man's Hope* are not revolutionaries like those in *The Conquerors* or *Man's Fate;* they are part of the legally elected government and are defending themselves against a reactionary, fascist insurrection. They fight to keep the power their electors have conferred upon them, and their struggle is rooted in the crisis that was already taking hold of the West at the time: the overwhelming rise of a technology that subjugates rather than serves humanity. Subtly, Malraux gradually reveals how the passion for technology is akin to a more or less conscious adherence to the spirit of fascism. Today we are in danger of forgetting this kinship, for technology now knows how to clothe itself more seductively. A character in *Man's Hope,* the young Maringaud, had been secretary of the worker's union in one of the largest munitions factories. He tells of how the boss, a fanatic for technology, secretly worked alone each night on bolts in order to perfect the machine guns manufactured by the workers during the day, to make those "machine guns 'top-notch, I'm telling you!'" (*MH* 414). The militant workers watched the boss leave around four in the morning, then secretly sabotaged the machinery that the boss had just lovingly perfected. This solemn struggle between technological passion and the workers' solidarity went on every night in the factory. The old boss wasn't a fascist, but his sons were. The passion for technology engenders fascism.

Emphasizing his words with his pipe, Garcia, a member of the Communist party, firmly asserts: "From now on no social change, still less a revolution, can make good without war; and no war without organization on the technical side" (*MH* 115). Magnin, who represents the opposite mentality since he has been able to free himself of the Western cultural heritage, points out to Garcia: "Organization, discipline—I don't see men giving their lives for that!" (ibid.). Garcia hardens his position: "In times like the present, I'm less interested in the reasons men may have for giving up their lives than in the means they have for killing off their enemies" (ibid.). To give lower priority in the name of efficiency to the reasons why men give up their lives is already a betrayal, but the betrayal becomes even more profound, even more radical. Indeed, Garcia suggests that discipline is "an organization of the factors which give an army in the field its maximum efficiency . . . It's a method like any other" (ibid.). Then Garcia expresses the basis for his thought and asserts a principle which, unfortunately, becomes that of all postrevolutionary technocrats: "A popular movement, or a revolution, or even a rebellion, can hold on to its victory only by methods directly opposed to those which gave it victory. Sometimes opposed even to the sentiments from which it started out" (*MH* 117–18). This assertion could not be clearer. Or more terrible. Technology in response to technology is the negation of revolution.

Some revolutionaries have believed that they are only committing a momentary lapse dictated by circumstances by agreeing to employ the same techniques as their enemies. We now know how wrong they are. And at such a price! All techniques—economic, fiscal, judicial, and, perhaps especially, psychological—when they are left to themselves can engender both fascist and reactionary mind-sets as well as totalitarian ones, which mean to be revolutionary but no longer are.

When not subordinated to any true value system, technology can only serve efficiency and thus totally dehumanizes. Only a few minutes after expressing emotion over family photographs, the professor in *The Walnut Trees of Altenburg* who is responsible for supervising the first experimental gas attacks can observe, with complete technological coldness, color variations in the corneas of gassed subjects. Carrying out a command or exercising one's responsibility is seen increasingly as implementing a technique and less and less as exercising personal authority. In *Man's Fate,* for the chief of one of the stations attacked by the revolutionaries, "commanding was a sport, and he gave himself over to it with a joyous enthusiasm" (*MF* 109). His connection with the men he commands is the same as that of a chess player with his pawns. In *Man's Hope,* Manuel knows the tragedy of the leader who, in the current state of culture, must distance himself ever further from his men and thus relinquish fraternity. He is summoned to staff headquarters, where he is given the command of a newly established brigade. He tries to refuse: "But what about my regiment! My own regiment! . . . I know each man in it! Who could . . ." (*MH* 410). There is nothing to be done. On another occasion Manuel tells Ximenes, the career officer who taught him the art of commanding, how overcome he was the day he had to have several of his men executed despite their heart-rending pleas. Manuel concludes his description of that scene by saying that he regrets nothing, he was doing his duty, but he now knows that efficiency and humanity are two irreconcilable principles: "Every step I've taken towards greater efficiency, towards becoming a better officer, has estranged me more and more from my fellow-men. Every day I'm getting a little less human" (*MH* 407–8). Ximenes, so accustomed to commanding that he can no longer ask himself questions of this sort, simply responds: "All I could tell you, my boy, would be things you wouldn't understand. You'd like to lead men and yet remain their comrade; well, in my opinion, no man's big enough for that" (ibid.). For Ximenes, fraternity "was only to be found in fellowship in Christ." Even though it is true that a person-to-person relationship with a god enables one to find the path to fraternity, it is no less true that, for centuries, Christians, business leaders, military or party leaders have taken refuge, like Ximenes, in that very paternalistic and very unpaternal "my boy," and have satisfied themselves with the useful image of a man too small for fraternity and of a fraternity too large for this world. For them, fraternity has become only a promise of the hereafter. When their "boys" were young and untrained, those "boys" very much wanted to believe them; as adults, the "boys" no longer accept that promise, just as they won't accept the promise of a fraternity that can only blossom in the "singing tomorrows" prepared by a totalitarian present.

All powers—the economic, commercial and financial power of Ferral, the police power of König, the political power of Borodine, the military power of Ximenes—become dehumanizing as soon as they begin to seek the greatest efficiency, as soon as they choose efficiency over principles, and in order to achieve those ends employ a technology whose proliferation is carcinogenic. In the 1930s, Malraux was one of very few writers to illustrate the extent to which this dehumanization could be complete, all-encompassing, for it affects leaders as well as followers, governers as well as the governed, commanders as well as soldiers. He was, above all, one of very few writers to illustrate that this dehumanization was not inescapable and was the result of cultural imprinting which for centuries had been influencing the human spirit. For Malraux, being a revolutionary meant trying to rid oneself of that imprinting. Like Magnin. But that revolution was not yet an issue when Malraux became involved in revolutionary struggles. It was somewhat of an issue in May 1968; it has scarcely been an issue since.

The Russian revolutionaries, shaped by the cultural heritage of the Christian West and attacked on all sides by the counterrevolution, the leaders and Western advisers of the first Chinese revolution, the Spanish revolutionaries, abandoned by the democracies—all were revolutionaries only on a social and political level. In a cultural context they were cousins of their enemies. As are the new leaders of China, where, following the perilous quest for a true cultural revolution, we are witnessing the forceful return of the managers, servants of the Golden Calf of "efficiency" that has been erected as an idol in the name of a realism called "situation and international context." The conclusion seems plain that a true cultural revolution, one that would end the dehumanization of man, can only be triumphant in a country where the level of development is such that seeking a minimum standard of living is no longer the highest priority. The fact that the revolutionaries of the 1920s were revolutionary only on an economic and social level, that nothing in their rhetoric raised hope for the end of dehumanization, and that, on the contrary, those revolutionaries seemed bound to accelerate the progress of dehumanization—Garine understood this when in Canton he confronted Borodine and "the businessmen of the Revolution" who sought to manufacture revolutionaries the way Ford manufactured cars. And if Malraux had Garine say so, it was because he, too, had understood and foreseen it.

The profound demand of the entire revolutionary community: fraternity was already celebrated in the Catacombs. But Fraternity has been betrayed by revolution as it has been by the Church. And that is why, in *Man's Hope,* Magnin, Manuel, Alvear, and Scali fight with all their strength not only against fascists, but also against the businessmen of the Revolution. They fight so that Fraternity may be celebrated not only by the dead. They fight so that the response to humiliation may not be egalitarianism—which is but an idea—but fraternity. *Man's Hope* is the outcry of fraternity scorned. It is also proof that we can, like Magnin and Manuel, rid ourselves of the cultural imprints that have been stamped upon us, dehumanizing all humanity. After writing *Man's Hope,* Malraux finally realized that it would never be in the nature of a simple political and social revolution to freely accept fraternity. In January 1945, at the congress of the National Liberation Movement, Malraux recalled that "in 1792, the word "Fraternity" was not carved in the pediments; it was the last to arrive; it was the first to leave." He knew then that if revolution did not first launch an attack against the cultural imprints that have marked men, fraternity would remain but an idea.

7

History as Fatality

FOR MALRAUX'S REVOLUTIONARY HEROES, revolution represents the privileged location of the battle man wages against destiny. This hope is an illusion, as Malraux never hesitated to boldly assert, at the risk of being wrongly accused of betraying his revolutionary ideal.

During the colloquium in *The Walnut Trees of Altenburg,* an approving murmur arises when a participant disagrees with the speaker, proclaiming that there cannot be "any real psychology except in the West" (*WTA* 92). Although he knows perfectly well that all the intellectuals at the colloquium would feel rejected by a world "in which the value of psychology might actually be questioned" (*WTA* 93), Vincent Berger doesn't hesitate to confront them directly and reminds them that "the need for psychology is only to be found in the West. Because the West is opposed to the cosmos, to fatality, instead of conforming to them. And because all psychology is the quest for an inward fatality. The *coup d'état* of Christianity was its establishment of fatality *inside* man—its foundation of it on our nature ... [The Greek] gave his demons an external existence in myths, and the Christian gives his myths an internal existence in demons" (*WTA* 94).

By the second half of the eighteenth century, history was considered to be the daughter of reason, and thinkers turned to history in an attempt to "render the human adventure intelligible" (*VO* 154). And in the nineteenth century there was the illusion of a history that could explain the universe, thus replacing religious explanations. In the name of this illusion the nineteenth century replaced the Eternal with "the only enemy the human mind could find to cope with it—history." More than anything else, historical materialism turned history into "the final incarnation of destiny," but that alone did not free man from fatality, it did not propose a new agreement with fatality; rather, it burdened man with a new fatality—history. In *Man's Fate,* Kyo rightly asserts that "In Marxism there is the sense of a fatality, and also the exaltation of a will. Every time fatality comes before will I'm suspicious" (*MF* 147). For the Catholic fatality implicit in "Suffer pain on this earth in order to reach eternal Paradise," historical materialism has substituted: "Present generations, you must suffer for future generations." Man lost out in the exchange, for if Christian fatality gave man hope for himself, historical fatality only offers hope for his descendants. But man lost even more: history, which was to render the world intelligible and prepare for enlightened tomorrows, rapidly became a new Leviathan. In its temples and on its smoky altars we have celebrated the bloody sacrifice of present man offered up to future ages as an expiatory victim. In one century, the illusion that history could explain the universe and replace religious explanations fizzled out: following the concentration camps and the goulags, no one who confronts an electronic microscope, a particle accelerator, or a space shuttle can seriously believe that we shall one day find the key to the cosmos in the historical adventure of mankind on the planet Earth.

Many Marxists have taught their doctrine as a catechism and have hoped to turn it into a religion. Marx himself never intended to present it as a revelation but, rather, as a logical, rational construction of the mind. In trying to impose this rationality on irrational individuals, Marxists condemned themselves to sink into totalitarianism the primary characteristic of which is indeed the desire to impose a preconceived totality upon the unpredictable in life. A slide into totalitarianism is the fate of any doctrine which, to perpetuate itself, attempts to impose itself and, in order to impose itself, resorts to force.

For Malraux, before the Spanish civil war and even more so after it, the most urgent struggle to be undertaken was the one against totalitarianism, against *all* totalitarianisms, whether reactionary such as those of the fascists, or revolutionary such as Stalinist totalitarianism. The fight against totalitarianisms represented the most urgent and most essential task at hand because totalitarianism rests upon a fundamental negation of man and upon an "organization of debasement." Malraux carried on this struggle throughout his life, and on all fronts. This fact must be emphasized, for some of Malraux's adversaries were quick to accuse him of being a fascist, which could hardly be taken seriously, or asserted that he had narrowly avoided sinking into fascism. At the root of these assertions is a misunderstanding of the essence of Malraux's thought. Thirsting for transcendence, Malraux never hid his respect for the totalization that religion, any religion, provides man. A religious man is linked to other men and above all to the cosmos. He feels he is a member of a Whole. Unfortunately, nearly all religions at one time or another have secreted forms of proselytism or fanaticism that also betray characteristics of totalitarianism, but in itself a religion cannot be totalitarian. When the Islamic revolution in Iran sinks into fanaticism and totalitarianism, it isn't Islam that becomes totalitarian. Despite the Inquisition and despite the forced evangelization of Latin America, "Christendom was not totalitarian." Malraux rightly underlines this truth, adding: "Totalitarian states are born of the search for a totality without religion" (*VOS* 484). Malraux was, indeed, searching for a new totalization, but to accuse him of being attracted to fascism is to confuse political totalitarianism with metaphysical or spiritual totalization.

Malraux observed with concern, almost with anguish, how seductive and deceitful the ersatz totalization proposed by totalitarian states could be, and how tempting it could become for a man no longer connected to the universe and no longer satisfied by the restricted and sterile world of individualism. With even greater concern, Malraux tirelessly repeated in the wake of the Second World War that police and totalitarian regimes were capable of causing fundamental and irreversible metamorphoses in man. In just a few generations, totalitarianism can endow the mind and the culture with forms that then become perpetuated as acquired characteristics. Hence, the fight against those forms was to receive the highest priority. If we want man to stand up to his destiny, we must fight against all those who seek to burden him with a historical fatality, and who attempt to do so by means of totalitarianism, however well disguised.

8

Man Consumed by the Masses

❧

EVER SINCE the eighteenth century "the great values worth fighting for" (*Arts* 11/30/51) accepted by humanity have been the People or the Nation. For Saint-Just, the Nation possessed a value of "quasi-transcendence" (*TN* 9), and it was the Nation even more than the individual or the Supreme Being that Robespierre opposed to Christ. With the French Revolution, the "primacy of the Nation" asserted itself, engendering a nationalism that initially expressed a sense of uniqueness but was transformed following World War I into an affirmation of or a claim to superiority, hiding behind the mask of ideology (*A-M* 85). In Moscow in 1934, Malraux realized "that what was happening was that at last Russia had found in Communism a way to assert her position and prestige" (ibid.). The same could be said about Nazism and Germany, or about fascism and Italy, or about many other regimes on other continents. Between these two forms of nationalism—uniqueness and superiority—there is an essential difference. Indeed, "a weak Russia wants popular fronts, a strong Russia wants people's democracies" (*A-M* 84). And France, more than any other country, has experienced the extent to which communists, when unable to transform a popular front into a people's democracy, would rather return to opposition than manage the daily contradictions of a society in complete change. The imperialist impulse is not unique to Russia, as Malraux emphasized when he added, after evoking the historic course of action Kennedy wished for: "It was no small thing to conceive a course for the world's most powerful nation without its being an imperialistic operation" (*FO* 79). The nationalism of a strong country, no matter which one, nearly always degenerates into imperialism.

When "the primacy of the Nation" wins out, the collective supplants the communal, and the national collectivity takes over the community of the citizens. In *Man's Fate*, Malraux confronted this issue by placing two of his characters—Suan and Pei—in opposition to each other. For Pei, communism was the true means to make China live again. Suan responded: "I don't want to create China, I want to create my people, with or without her. The poor. It's for them that I'm willing to die, to kill. For them only" (*MF* 193). Every one of Malraux's novels shows that, even today, all the Suans of every country lose the battle; those who seek to "create man" are beaten by those who seek first to create the Nation. For this murderous conflict between "creating man" and "creating the Nation" to end, the concept of Nation must be rethought. This is the task of the next century, as Malraux told Roger Stéphane, adding: "Deep down, everyone knows that an empire is something that is condemned to death, whereas a nation is something that develops with the strength of an organism. A nation is like a tree; an empire is like lightning." If one day mankind is able to conceive of the nation as a biological, organic whole, the struggle for life will not preclude the struggle of nations, but it may be possible, within a national entity, simultaneously to create both man and nation. The twentieth century has established the premises of a League of Nations and of a United Nations Organization. Its gropings have made way for the task of its successor.

Without a doubt, "to create men" is Malraux's most profound aspiration in *Man's Hope*. But all the characters in this novel who attempt to "create men" become overwhelmed by political parties. "Intellectuals always believe to some degree that a party consists of men united around an idea." The reality is quite different, for a political party progressively secretes its own finalities and henceforth has need only of militants. Sartre in 1950, in his preface to Roger Stéphane's *Le Portrait de l'Aventurier*, made this cruel and, for him, definitive statement: "The party has no need of irreplaceable members. The militant remains mid-way between the irreplaceable and the interchangeable: He serves, that's all . . . Militants must inherit the virtues of adventurers . . . Entirely devoted to obedience they reserve nothing of themselves, except for that freedom which unreservedly delivers them up." Even if we take Sartre's own ideas into account, there still remains the notion of a man who "serves, that's all." Twenty years before Sartre's preface, Malraux had shown in *The*

Man Consumed by the Masses

Conquerors how greatly this notion of the militant, and thus of the party, differed from the new type of man, who had to be encouraged and in whom would be blended "the aptitude for action, culture and lucidity" (*Con* 175). There is no lucidity and very little culture possible in a man who "serves, that's all."

In *Man's Fate,* seventeen years before Sartre's preface, Malraux had shown how the ultimate demand made by the party is always the demand for absolute obedience. Kyo has come to see Vologin, the delegate of the International, hoping to be able to reverse the order requiring the revolutionaries to give up their arms. Kyo explains why giving up those weapons amounts to signing a death sentence for the Chinese revolution. Vologin first presents arguments that are hardly relevant, which he voices without much conviction. He then uses his only real argument, the only one that shows "a shadow of passion in his voice": "Obedience to the Party is the only logical attitude—in short—of a militant Communist" (*MF* 154). And to bring home the full meaning of this exchange between Kyo and Vologin, Malraux immediately follows it with the speech of the starving stevedores who have just been arrested for attacking the Red Guard for their rations. In their own words and in their own way the stevedores present arguments identical to those which Kyo defended when pleading with Vologin. The man who carries out the interrogation of the stevedores is a former Swiss worker who had labored for fifteen years making watches; he knows all about gears being dependent on each other, and he is content to see himself as just another gear. He remains as closed to the arguments of the stevedores as Vologin was to Kyo's. After attending the stevedores' interrogation, Kyo wanders alone along the docks of Hankow, and he fears that "in all China, and throughout the West, including half of Europe, men were hesitating as he was, torn by the same torment between their discipline and the massacre of their own kind" (*MF* 167). At that moment Kyo is overcome by a sense of impotence.

The divorce between man and the party looms like a menacing cloud behind the action of *The Conquerors* and *Man's Fate*. This divorce dominates every chapter of *Man's Hope*. It has become one of the essential elements of the novel's action. The Negus points out that he and his friends joined the revolution not to build a state, a church, or an army, but "just men" (*MH* 203). He points out that "parties are made for men, not men for parties" (ibid.). But who cares about "creating men" when the battle for power is being waged! When Ramos is asked why he has become a communist after having been an anarchist, he replies: "Growing old, I think... In my anarchist days I was much fonder of individual people. Anarchism, for me, meant the 'Syndicate'—but above all, human relations, human contacts" (*MH* 85). Manuel, after being ordered to perform a dehumanizing exercise of authority, receives this advice from Ximenes: "All that estranges you from your fellow-man is bound to link you up more closely with your Party" (*MH* 408). Manuel cannot accept this and replies that "to be linked more closely with the Party is worthless, if one's to be estranged from the very men for whom the Party's working" (ibid.). Then Ximenes, still just as paternalistic, adds: "And what did you expect, my boy? That you could sentence men to death without a qualm?... But you'll get used even to that" (ibid.). Heinrich also exhorts Manuel: "Surely you don't believe you can change things without being changed yourself?... Your soul is no longer your own... You've already lost your long hair—and the sound of your voice has changed... And now, you must never again waste pity on a lost man" (*MH* 411).

But it is parties and parties alone that decide when a man is lost, and they do so according to their criteria as parties. For a party acts only for itself; it doesn't act for men or even for the militants who "serve, that's all." The impasse is absolute. It will become tragic. No change at all has occurred in the relations between men that revolution was supposed to have changed. The same cultural frameworks continue to underly human relations, even though these relations are established in different social structures. Magnin sums up this tragic impasse at the end of *Man's Hope*. The falangists who died crying "Long live Spain" at the beginning of the civil war now die crying "Long live the falangists;" the communists who died while crying "Long live the Proletariat" or "Long live communism" now die crying "Long live the party." Magnin, who embodies the hope that one day a new way to be a man will emerge, cannot accept this tragic substitution, and says so to Garcia. But the latter, as befits a good communist, has adapted to it and simply responds: "The age of parties is beginning, my friend" (*MH* 505).

The age of parties which was beginning at that time was the age of powerful and methodicly organized parties. Techniques used by political parties were developed in the same way that all techniques have been developed. In the West we often shut out eyes, pretending to believe that these party techniques are the prerogative of fascist or communist parties, and we refuse to see that in liberal democracies as well the age of parties prevails, even if they rest on more subtle or more

Man Consumed by the Masses

insidious techniques. In January 1972, when I said to Malraux that a democratic regime sincerely dedicated to the service of mankind has not yet been conceived, he answered: "That is not even at issue. What is still at issue is the political regime dedicated to serve political parties." Malraux's response did not refer just to France but to democracy in general. All political parties—fascist, communist, or liberal—have espoused party techniques and have amplified the process already in motion: Man's subservience to the group; man's effacement before the group.

After making the comment just reported, Malraux added: "The party isn't very concerned about man. It is enormously concerned about an idea it has of man, one to which it wishes to have man conform." Until 1935, Malraux, like many others, had hoped that communism would be enormously concerned with man. He said as much in the summer of 1934 in Moscow, when he began his speech to the Writers' Congress with: "It will be said of you 'In spite of every obstacle, through civil war and famine, for the first time in thousands of years they put their trust in men!'" (*Commune*, Sept. 1934). Another statement in his speech even better expresses the hope he had at that time: "To the Bourgeoisie, which spoke of the *individual*, Communism will reply: *man*" (ibid.). A few months later, in Paris in November 1934, Malraux once again developed this idea during the meeting which had been organized at the Mutualité to take stock of the Moscow Congress: "We have greatly stressed the distrust that the fledgling Russian society was forced to have weigh upon man. Let us beware of this. That distrust weighs only upon the individual... Soviet society can create a humanism... What is important will no longer be the individuality of each man, but his density" (ibid.). And in June 1935, during the colloquium for the defense of culture against fascism, Malraux once again expressed the same hope: in the face of democracies, which were sinking into commercialism and parliamentarianism, in the face of fascism, which was organizing the enslavement of men on a massive scale, communism alone at that time seemed capable of providing a new humanism.

When Malraux expressed and reiterated that hope in 1934 and 1935, he was writing *Days of Wrath*, and apparently because of the rise of fascism in Europe at that time he gave lower priority to the fears and concerns that had filled *The Conquerors* in 1928. The unpublished fragments of *The Conquerors* which were printed in December 1929 in the review *Bifur* show a Garine standing up even more strongly than he did in the finished novel to the total depersonalization demanded by the communists, and to their desire to set up standardized anonymity. In "The

Question of *The Conquerors*," an article published by *Variété* in October 1929, Malraux responded to those who had seen Garine merely as an individualist. He pointed out that Garine was actually the hero of a resistance against the depersonalization and dehumanization systematically carried out by the Bolsheviks. In the final, published version of the novel, Garine and Borodine are continually opposed on this issue. One day Garine returns furious from a stormy confrontation he has just had with Borodine: "Once again [Borodine] is dominated by this insufferable Bolshevik mentality, this stupid glorification of discipline" (*Con* 159). That particular Borodine wanted to "manufacture revolutions as Ford manufactures cars! It will all come to a bad end, and that, soon," Garine adds. Unfortunately, we know today that he predicted the truth.

For his part, Borodine easily calms himself with the thought that Garine "is outdated" because there exists "a sort of feudal link" between Garine and his comrades. This phrase has been used against Malraux to impute to him something he never even thought of. Malraux never meant to say that Garine was seeking to restore the social relations that existed under the feudal system. He wanted to make his readers *feel* how Garine managed to create, between himself and his comrades, and even between his adversaries, relations that were not just based on discipline or hierarchy but were also established between equal men, equal persons, each individual occupying his place and fulfilling his function. In this, Garine in *The Conquerors* was already preparing the way for Magnin in *Man's Hope*. In the latter novel, most of the important dialogues deal either directly or indirectly with the opposition between fraternity and hierarchy. "The desire for fraternity on the one hand and, on the other, the cult of hierarchy, are very definitely up against each other in this country—and in some others, too, perhaps" (*MH* 207). Anarchists, like the Negus, are "carried away by a fraternity which they know quite well is bound to take a different form one day. And they're quite willing to die after some crowded hours of ecstasy ... or of revenge, in certain cases; dramatic hours in which their dreams come true" (*MH* 208). With less vehemence and excess than the anarchists, millions of men have thought as they did. Neither fascists nor communists can accept this thirst for fraternity, for they must above all form militants just as standardized objects are manufactured, and to do this they use news, propaganda, and physical coercion.

After completing *Man's Hope,* Malraux constantly returned to the theme of man's stupefication by news, propaganda, and psychological techniques. Malraux's very subtle comment on Choderlos de Laclos's *Les*

Liaisons dangereuses may be extended to life in society: he pointed out that the originality of the novel lay not in its eroticism but in the fact that the means of compelling used by its characters was not force but persuasion. For Choderlos de Laclos, lying became "the finest means of compelling: to act upon a part of a person's mind so that that part will compel the entire person" (*TN* 45). With the systematic use of psychological techniques, relations between the governing and the governed, the state and the citizen, the producer and the consumer, have gradually become dangerous liaisons. In the aftermath of World War II, Malraux devoted his Pleyel speech to a warning against those dangerous liaisons:

The values of Europe are threatened from within by techniques born of means that appeal to collective passions—the press, the cinema, the radio, and advertising—in a word, "means of propaganda." In lofty parlance, these are called "psychological techniques." ... In America they are chiefly devoted to the service of an economic system, and they tend to compel the individual to purchase some commodity. In Russia they are devoted to the service of a political system, and they tend to compel the citizen to adhere unreservedly to the ideology of the rulers, and, to that end, commit a man fully. (*Con* 185)

Malraux added this Pleyel speech as a postscript to *The Conquerors* when the novel was reprinted in 1948. The addition is highly significant, all the more so because Malraux specified at that time that "the issue at hand was how to shed light upon the most immediate and crafty menace, namely that of stupefication by means of psychological techniques (propaganda has made giant strides since Garine)" (*Con* 176).

Malraux could see clearly and declared that propaganda has made giant strides not solely in totalitarian states; it has also made them in liberal democracies: "Whether it is a question of selling a cake of soap or of obtaining a ballot, no known psychological technique but is based upon contempt for the purchaser or the voter. Otherwise it would prove useless" (*Con* 189). And one might add today: if those techniques were not based upon contempt for the purchaser or the voter, why have so many consumer or citizen associations been established?

The propaganda that alienates the citizen the way wage earning alienates the worker returns as a leitmotif in the long conversation between Mao and Malraux related in *Anti-Memoirs*. And if we read this conversation with an open mind despite all that is known about brainwashing in Maoist China, we see that for Mao propaganda was not what the word means to us today. The attempt to have a soldier of the Long March exist in the population the way a fish exists in water meant neither indoctrinating him as Borodine wanted to indoctrinate the striker from Canton, nor indoctrinating the population; it meant, rather, that women, young people, and peasants would feel "involved for the first time." Mao added: "If propaganda means training militiamen and guerrillas, we did a lot for propaganda. But if it means preaching... You know I've proclaimed for a long time: we must teach the masses clearly what we have received from them confusedly" (*A-M* 361–62). Regimes that use psychological techniques to act upon a part of the mind in order to compel the entire person can receive nothing from the masses; indeed, quite the opposite is true. "The Soviet government is henceforth incapable of appealing to the masses because it is afraid of them" (*A-M* 371), Mao thought. And his statement was a strange echo of the one de Gaulle made on October 12, 1952, in Neuilly when he declared that those against him in France at the time were "all who are afraid of the people and who tremble at the thought that the people might become directly involved in their own business instead of remaining apart, misled, dispossessed by the cunning networks of electoral divisions."

Religious practice can transform a religion into the opium of the masses. In the same way, political practice can transform an election into the opium of the citizen, as much in a liberal democracy complete with parades and drum majorettes as in a popular democracy with uniform voting registers. With the systematic and refined use of psychological techniques, politics are no longer simply the art of concealment they had been for such a long time; they have also become the art of lying. The world over, the conflict between the manipulated majority and the manipulating minority has superseded the conflict between the proletarian majority and the possessor minority. The struggle for truth is gradually becoming more important than the struggle for capital. The struggle against propaganda is replacing the class struggle. That this is true in Eastern countries where only the propaganda struggle is in the forefront is obvious. In other countries, a subtle and rather tainted situation combines the propaganda struggle with the class struggle. In all cases, the exploitation of men by their fellow-men remains, as well as their resulting alientation. Man's alienation, indeed, may be growing even worse, for if psychological alienation results in less poverty than does economic alienation, it is more subtle and fundamentally more humiliating and degrading. The struggle against psychological alienation is the one lost by Garine in *The Conquerors* and by the Spanish *milicianos* in *Man's Hope*. It is also the struggle that many others have subsequently lost, and the one that will be at the heart of the great confrontations of tomorrow;

and its preferred weapons will be television antennas connected to cables or aimed at satellites. The struggle against psychological alienation is one of the facets of the great struggle between "to be" and "to act," the prelude to which we heard in May 1968 on many continents, and which Malraux, as early as 1937, placed at the heart of *Man's Hope*. It can never be overemphasized that "Etre et Faire" ("Being and Doing") is in fact the title of the central chapter of this novel.*

Party men, all men of all parties, experts in psychological, advertising, or propaganda manipulation have gradually forged a world in which "man has been as much consumed by mass psychology as by excessive individualism" (UNESCO address). This "man consumed by mass psychology" is the culmination of a long process which began in the eighteenth century when Western civilization abandoned "Man orientated toward Being" and sought to form "man capable of being swayed by ideas and acts" (*VOS* 481).

In *Man's Fate,* Kyo and Katov die victims of the political game played by the International when it decides that the time isn't right and that a deal should be made with Chiang Kai-shek. Yet they manage to remain true to themselves to the very end: there is no break between their revolutionary acts and ideals. Ten years later the Spanish revolutionaries can no longer see any connection between ethics and politics. At every moment they are confronted with a conflict between revolutionary action and ideals. Almost every page of *Man's Hope* presents an outcry over or an echo of this conflict.

The Alcazar, still held by the fascists, is besieged by the *milicianos*. During a short truce, a *miliciano* hands cigarettes out to the fascists, another gives them razor blades, while the captain of the *milicianos* accepts a packet of letters that the fascist colonel wants to have sent to his wife. Golovkin, a correspondent for a soviet newspaper, is astonished at this generosity, which would have been unthinkable in the USSR. A discussion ensues. With heated animation the Negus explains the *milicianos'* generosity: "The men will have given their hearts a few day's run. See what I mean? . . . We've no use for 'dialectics' or red tape; delegates are all right, but bureaucrats never! Or an army to defeat the army, or inequality to stamp out inequality, or playing the bourgeois' game. What we are out for is to live the way men ought to live, right now and here; or else to damn well die. If we fail, there's an end to it. No return ticket

---

*The title of the chapter is translated as "Action and Reaction" by Stuart Gilbert and Alastair Macdonald.—Trans.

for me!" (*MH* 200–201). With the rigidity of a technician of action, Garcia, a member of the Communist party, responds to the Negus: If one wants "to make the revolution a way of living, for the mere fun of it, it usually becomes a way of dying" (*MH* 201). The Negus then replies that the communists have turned into something like priests: "You're soaked in the Party, in discipline, in plotting and scheming. If a man doesn't belong, you don't give him a square deal; you've not a scrap of decency towards him. You've lost even your loyalty" (ibid.). Pradas, a member of the technical committee of the Communist party, then takes up the baton from Garcia and tries to explain to the Negus that it is better to be unfaithful to the ideal and capable of prevailing, for there is no point in being loyal if it leads to defeat.

Man's Hope is the struggle of men who cannot allow revolutionaries to betray their ideal in the name of a concrete rationalization of a situation. One day Hernandez asks Garcia: "What's the point of the revolution if it isn't to make men better?" (*MH* 211). Garcia replies that the revolution will be brought about by the proletariat and not by the Stoics. Hernandez is persistent. Garcia then gives an opinion which alone shows the tragic gap between the communists and other revolutionaries: "Moral uplift and magnanimity are matters for the individual, with which the revolution has no direct concern" (*MH* 214). For Garcia, as for anyone who wishes to create men guidable by ideas or actions, the part played by those who wish *to be* is a part doomed in advance, because they live the part politically, while the part itself is not political (Gandhi and Nehru would never have accepted this opinion).

Eventually, Garcia is compelled to go even further in order to justify a betrayal of the revolutionary ideal. He does so in an important dialogue with Scali concerning the questioning of revolutionary action by revolutionary ethics. Garcia refuses to allow that questioning. He begins by reminding Scali that all forms of action are Manichaean and that every true revolutionary is a born Manichaean. Scali refuses to be locked in by this facile reference to the inevitability of Manichaeism in all action. Goaded by Scali's arguments, Garcia searches within himself and, as if confessing, finally recognizes that "for a thinker, the revolution's a tragedy . . . There aren't fifty ways to fight, there's only one, and that's to fight to win . . . For four months all of us have been thronged with corpses! The path that leads from moral standards to political activity is strewn with our dead selves. Always there is a conflict between the man who acts and the conditions of his action . . . There are just wars . . . there's no such thing as a just army . . . one can have a policy that's just, but there's no such thing as a just party" (*MH* 397–98). All of these justifications, which appear to be based on common sense, are in fact stamped with the seal of cultural imprints from which party men have not been liberated. Malraux freed himself from those imprints, which is why he was able to command first the *España* squadron and then the Alsace-Lorraine Brigade. In a conversation with Roger Stéphane, he showed that one can avoid the "boxing match" between a man who thinks out his action and the conditions of that action; he pointed out that one can go beyond the problem of the Manichaeism of action, for, Malraux said, if action is indeed Manichaean, the thought that commands action need not be. The entire problem is summed up there.

For centuries, indeed for two millennia, "the most effective methods [in the organization of action] have been those of the army and the Church, which were taken up by the totalitarian parties and even, to a lesser extent, by the great capitalist and Communist societies" (*A-M* 104). Nor has revolution been able to escape these methods, for revolutionaries have not attempted to erase from their psyches the cultural imprints of which these methods are the byproducts. At the beginning of *Man's Hope,* Garcia says to Magnin, "We are not the revolution ... though we used to talk of nothing else!" (*MH* 114). Magnin replies, "Well, I say: let's be it!" but Garcia can envision only the methods of the army or the Church: "As to those sounds coming in through the window, Monsieur Magnin—I might define them as an Apocalypse of Fraternity. They work on your emotions, I can well understand it. They stand for one of the most moving things on earth, and one of the rarest. But all of that's got to be transformed—or perish!" (*MH* 116). Garcia and those like him will not transform, they will not metamorphose this Apocalypse of Fraternity into the experience of Fraternity; they will kill it with the methods they choose to employ. Nor was Christianity able to transform the Apocalypse of Fraternity that was already being celebrated by Christians buried in the catacombs or martyred in the Roman amphitheaters. In attempting to do so, the Church used methods and means that were contrary to its ethics and to the message it was to convey on Earth. It killed fraternity by reserving it for a world beyond the earth. "My Father" won out over "my Brothers." Revolution followed in the Church's footsteps by allowing the commissioner to win out over the comrade. It believed it was ensuring its own perpetuity by employing techniques contrary to the feelings that had engendered it. In order to survive, the revolution apostatized.

In *Man's Hope,* the communist Pradas repeats what has been said for centuries: "'Nobility' is a luxury no movement can indulge in—in its early phase ... I'm afraid you'll very soon discover that, concretely speaking, that moral code of yours has no utility for practical politics" (*MH* 203–4). An anonymous voice is then heard: "No more has any other moral code." It is Garcia who responds to this anonymous voice, and he does so with a completely surprising statement for a character who throughout the novel has defended the means, methods, and techniques employed by the Party: "And yet the trouble about the revolution, perhaps its tragedy, is that it can't get on without [a moral code]." Considering the great care Malraux always took in constructing his novels it is unthinkable that he inadvertently has Garcia make this essential statement. I believe, on the contrary, that Malraux wanted to destroy the arguments of those who believe, to ease their minds, that communists set one particular moral code up against another. They do no such thing. In the name of efficiency, communist revolutionaries, in Spain as elsewhere, employ methods, means, and techniques that are essentially the same as those they are opposing. In the name of concrete rationalization, revolutionary action turns its back on revolutionary ethics. Many are happy to accept this turnabout, claiming that revolution is "afterwards," whereas "before" there is insurrection and the struggle for power. It is a convenient excuse, but it is tragic because the means employed "before" condition those that will be used "afterwards."

9

Lyrical Illusion

❦

OF ALL THE CHARACTERS in Malraux's novels, only one, Kassner, the hero of *Days of Wrath,* finds his dignity in revolution and derives from revolution his reconciliation with the universe. In the prison cell where the Nazis have locked him up, Kassner struggles against the madness he feels rising up in him by composing a speech that could be told to the darkness. Released by the Nazis through the total sacrifice made by a comrade who passed himself off as Kassner, he clandestinely returns to Czechoslovakia in a two-seated airplane, which is tossed about furiously in a storm. Malraux gives this battle between the airplane, the pilot and Kassner, and the unleashed elements all the weight of a battle against Fatality. Kassner's battle is triumphant, and he achieves fellowship with men and the universe.

Having arrived safe and sound in Prague, Kassner immediately attends a meeting and feels "drunk with humanity" (*DW* 143). He is then reunited with his wife Anna and their son. It must be pointed out here that Anna's and Kassner's child is the only child in all of Malraux's works, with the exception of Hemmelrich's child, who is an invalid and, like his father, overwhelmed by his existence. Anna's and Kassner's son, on the other hand, carries all the hopes and certainty with which Kassner endowed his revolutionary struggle, as if Malraux felt that alone among all his characters only Anna and Kassner could exercise—in the full meaning of the terms—the responsibilities of motherhood and fatherhood. His freedom restored, reunited with his wife and son, Kassner was living "one of those moments which make men believe a god has just been born." It seemed to him "that the true meaning of existence was emerging and that the earth's obscure destiny was about to be realized" (*DW* 172).

Malraux more or less renounced the character Kassner and *Days of Wrath* itself—a "dud," he called it, which is unfair. He wrote it in 1935, between *Man's Fate* and *Man's Hope,* and if he renounced it, even though the novel was centered on the themes always foremost in Malraux's mind, it was by reason of the fullfillment Kassner found in and through revolutionary action. Vincent Berger in *The Walnut Trees of Altenburg* also found fullfillment and a connection with "the most secret life of things"; the meaning of the world and life was revealed to him too, but that revelation did not take place in or through revolutionary action. As early as 1936 Malraux began to believe that the communist revolution, led by communist parties, would never promote man's attempt to stand up to destiny—in fact, the opposite was true. Malraux began to wonder even more profoundly and painfully whether a collective action, a revolution—indeed, every revolution—would not always be a *lyrical illusion* when one pursued the goal he himself was pursuing. After the Spanish civil war, Malraux no longer asked himself that question; he knew the answer, and that is why he called the first part of *Man's Hope* "L'Illusion lyrique" ("The Lyrical Illusion").[1] Revolution, by employing the same means and using the same techniques as its adversaries, by being organized like the Church or the army, by being interested in what people do and not in what they are, did not and could not bring about a new relationship between people and their world.

In order to seize power or to keep it, a revolution seeks to form the largest possible number of militants and to carry behind it the greatest possible number of individuals. To achieve this quickly a revolution uses cultural imprints that have marked the minds of everyone, beginning with its leaders. Revolution doesn't modify those imprints; on the contrary—it ensures their perpetuity. Revolution seeks to modify social relations, it hopes to change the leaders or the ruling class, but it doesn't change the nature of the power exercised, it doesn't fundamentally change the relations between men, and changes even less the relations between man and the universe. The communists in Spain behave like emulators of Borodine, and court the same failure as he. The disputes between Garine and Borodine in *The Conquerors* show that Borodine simply wants to change the holders of power, whereas Garine, like Mag-

---

1. [Translated as "Careless Rapture" by Stuart Gilbert and Alastair Macdonald.—Trans.]

Lyrical Illusion

nin in *Man's Hope,* wants to change the nature of that power. Confined to a hospital bed and knowing he will have to leave Canton, Garine has become somewhat distanced from the revolutionary struggle. He realizes that it was a struggle which would never change the nature of power because essentially it was not seeking to change it. Thus Garine has discovered the Absurd: "It is strange. But after my trial I was obsessed by the vanity of life and of humanity as a whole. It seemed a prey to blind forces. Now this obsession recurs ... Yet it seems to me that in doing what I am doing here I am struggling against this vanity of life ... And that it is reasserting its rights" (*Con* 125). The revolutionary struggle has failed to deliver Garine, and it is with a bitter aftertaste in his mouth that he says: "One cannot cast the revolution into the fire; all that is not the revolution is even worse; one has to admit it even when one is disgusted" (*Con* 126). Because "the aptitude for action, culture, and lucidity" are blended in Garine, he is capable, unlike many others, of an acute realization: he realizes he has become a prisoner of action, sick from action, and that his action has made him "indifferent to everything apart from it, and to begin with, to its own results" (*Con* 155). He also recognizes that in his life there is "a certain rhythm ... a kind of urge, if you like to put it so, from which [he] cannot escape" (ibid.). This line has been used to accuse Garine of individualism, but to do so is to forget that Garine immediately adds: "For some days I have been under the impression that perhaps I am forgetting the main thing, that something else is at hand" (ibid.). This statement, which could be used to introduce the third part of *Man's Hope*—the part that is also titled "Man's Hope"—is essential for an understanding of Garine and, I think, for an understanding of Malraux himself.

Illness plays an essential role in *The Conquerors*. It becomes almost a "character" in the novel. The two principal revolutionary leaders, Borodine and Garine, are ill, and they are confined to their beds each time an important episode in the revolutionary struggle is about to unfold. Their illnesses proclaim that the revolution, too, could become an intoxication. "The graveyards of revolutions are just the same as other graveyards" (*MH* 228). Disillusion becomes overwhelming for all those who, like Malraux, expect revolution not only to modify social structures but to engender another way of living, another way to be a man with one's fellow-men. Malraux never sought to hide this disillusionment, and he expressed it at the end of *Man's Hope* when Garcia says: "For a thinker, the revolution's a tragedy ... And if he is counting on the revolution to abolish his private tragedy, he's making a mistake, that's all" (*MH* 397).

Lyrical Illusion

The road Malraux traveled between *Paper Moons* and *Man's Hope* was an austere one. He participated in a collective action to escape the intoxication of individual actions, he opted to participate in a revolutionary action in order to be one of the catalysts for the transformation of the relationships between people and things, but through these experiences Malraux became aware that he was participating in an illusion. And, even more painful, he realized through his experiences that revolution has not only failed to make man stand tall again, to establish man anew, but rather it can subjugate him and crush him as terribly as reactionaries do.

After writing *Man's Hope,* Malraux knew that in a world that no longer finds meaning either in religion or in science—or elsewhere—politics, all politics, become an end in themselves, and from that fact alone they tend to become totalitarian, either overtly or insidiously. In a world without explanation, in which the only concern is production, either for business purposes or to augment the power of the nation, the citizen is nothing but an instrument. In Machiavelli's world, the Machiavellians still had to maintain some respect for the notion of man that existed in the society of that time. In the twentieth-century world, nothing, absolutely nothing, limits the rights politicians claim to have over men. Nothing, if not the resistance of man.

In 1938, after writing *Man's Hope,* Malraux made the statement which was at the heart of his April 1969 speech in Strasbourg: "A metaphysical problem does not have a political solution." Today it is easy to look condescendingly, as many people do, at the illusionment of all those who, through political revolution, had hoped to find a solution to the metaphysical problem of a humanity in disharmony with the cosmos. This condescension ignores the fact that the goddess Reason, then scientism, then Marxism, and after it still other ideologies, claimed to provide man with an explanation of the world and enabled him to hope that it would be possible to reform the human condition by means of political transformation. This condescension also forgets that we spell with a capital *R* the great Revolutions of 1789, 1917, and 1949—all three of which were fed as much on philosophical and metaphysical thought as on political and social thought. Above all, this condescension forgets that the millions of abused and humiliated men feel deep down inside what old Alvear expresses: "A man who has been unjustly sentenced, or has run up against more than his share of ingratitude or baseness or stupidity—well, he's bound to stake his hope on some new order . . . ;

the revolution plays a part that an 'eternal life' used formerly to play." And Alvear adds: "That explains many of its characteristics" (*MH* 323).

I don't believe Malraux ever completely and unreservedly held the hope that a revolutionary action might resolve the metaphysical problems which had haunted his adolescence, had attacked the balloons/Sins of *Paper Moons* and had fed the dialogues in *The Temptation of the West*. Indeed, in 1930 Malraux wrote in the journal *Monde:* "If the meaning of human solitude and tragedy exists to such a small degree for the communists, it is because Russia, since 1918, has essentially been a mobilized country defending itself. Of course, one must first conquer, but it remains to be known whether, once victory is obtained, man will not once again find himself face to face with his own death and, even more serious, face to face with the death of those he loves."

Kyo was committed to the "before" of a revolutionary struggle, and his death was filled with meaning. On the other hand, in a country whose political revolution is accomplished, one which is "afterwards," men once again find themselves confronted with a banal death, death again becomes death, and the *Farfelu Kingdom* remains *farfelu*. Trotsky, writing about *The Conquerors*—"the book lacks a natural affinity between the author . . . and his heroine, the Revolution" (*Nouvelle Revue Française*, April 1931)—sensed the distance that existed between Malraux and the revolution. The battle waged by the revolution and the one waged by Malraux were not on the same plane, did not belong to the same realm. We should note, moreover, that the main characters in Malraux's novels are always found at a certain distance from the action to which they are committed. Garine keeps a distance from the revolution, Perken from the Moi kingdom, Manuel and Magnin from the victory of the Spanish *milicianos,* and Vincent Berger's father from Ottomanism. They all seem to view their actions as a fleeting companion. They all—like Malraux, perhaps—seem to want to escape from that action mania which keeps the European race writhing and renders people "indifferent to everything apart from it" (*Con* 155). The only exceptions who are truly involved in their actions are Borodine (but he is "a businessman of the revolution"), Kyo (but he is a martyr to his faith in the revolution), and Kassner (but Malraux renounced this character).

Malraux espoused the proletarian revolution because the humiliation and the alienation of the proletariat were the most advanced and most painful forms of the humiliation and the alienation of mankind. But he participated in revolutionary action without being sure that it would give birth to a new form of man. One suspects that Malraux became involved in revolutionary action in order to exorcise the temptation of revolution in himself, to exorcise the hope of a political solution to metaphysical problems. Following his travels in the USSR, and after the Spanish civil war, Malraux knew that revolution would not even be "a means of realizing his ethical desires." In *The Birth of Tragedy,* Nietzsche shows that "the dithyrambic chorus's task is to excite the dionysiac emotion of the audience until the tragic hero appears on stage; they perceive not a man in a monstrous mask but, rather, a visionary form born of their own ectasy." In Malraux's novels, the revolutionary community plays the role of the chorus in Greek tragedy: the revolution excites the reader's emotions, but only in order to lead him to the point at which he will see Garine, Manuel, and Magnin not as revolutionary leaders but as a visionary form of man (*Esprit* 1948). Gaëtan Picon understood this when he stressed that going beyond revolutionary mythology freed Malraux and enabled him to develop his fundamental themes in other forms.

After observing the mentality and behavior of the "businessmen" of the revolution in different contexts, after listening to the first accounts, among them that of Gide, of the methods that were actually being employed in the USSR, Malraux knew that revolution would not be an "Anti-Destiny." He exorcised from himself the almost Faustian temptation to look for a political and social solution to problems that are neither political nor social, and he became aware that "political and philosophical refusals do not attack the human condition in the fundamental realm as described by Goya" (*Int* 78). We might not agree with Malraux on this point, but we cannot deny that he made it. And if we forget, or pretend to forget, that for Malraux "political and philosophical refusals do not attack the human condition in the fundamental realm," we can understand neither his life nor his work after 1937.

"Cézanne was concerned only with 'realizing his vision' . . . ; he envisioned the shapes the forms he saw could take upon his canvas" (*Int* 119). Malraux, too, when he participated in revolutionary actions, was concerned only with "realizing his vision," and, like many visionary artists going into politics, he committed the error of believing that political action is thought and carried out as artistic action is. He approached revolutionary action the way a painter approaches his canvas or a writer his blank page; he believed that the forms he would be manipulating

Lyrical Illusion

would be governed only by his vision and his work. Like a sculptor who learns that his marble resists and that he must often obey it by following its veins, Malraux learned that political matter was not fully malleable. Above all, he learned that in an attempt to create "new relations between men and things," it would be useless to act upon political and social relations so long as the cultural relations that form men's psychism have not been modified. If one truly wanted to act, one should act upon that psychism which has fallen prey to psychological techniques of propaganda or advertising, and also to techniques of certain psychoanalysts who attach too little importance to Freud's warnings in his *Analysis Terminable and Interminable,* in which sofas began to assume on a social level the role previously assumed by confessionals.

In 1941 and 1942, when Malraux was writing *The Walnut Trees of Altenburg,* which he had conceived as the first part of a trilogy of novels, *The Struggle with the Angel,* he was already far from politics, a fact that the polemics over his subsequent political involvements have often prevented readers from perceiving. "He felt himself gradually possessed by an unknown sensation, as he had once been at night in the highlands of Asia, by the sacred presence... In the same way, he now felt the whole of his life becoming odd; and suddenly he felt delivered from it—strangely unfamiliar with the world (*WTA* 68–69). What progressively emerges from *The Walnut Trees of Altenburg,* the point toward which the novel converges, is *an emergence toward life.* To read the novel as Lucien Goldmann has done, seeing Ottomanism only as a transposition of communism, or Turkey and Enver Pacha simply as transpositions of Russia and Stalin, is an erroneous reading which denatures the significance of the work. Even beyond the ideologies of the time, *The Walnut Trees of Altenburg* expresses the futility of all political ideologies and all political actions when the *Farfelu Kingdom* has been chosen as an adversary. Essentially, Malraux never had any other.

Having read Guénon (as Clara Malraux has told us) and Meister Eckehart (as Robert Payne has told us), after finishing *The Walnut Trees of Altenburg* and with plans to write *The Blood of the Absolute,* Malraux got out of politics; he left the political realm. It may appear paradoxical to say that he abandoned politics immediately before becoming, first, Minister of Information in de Gaulle's provisional government, and then an ardent propagandist for the Rassemblement du peuple français, but we must try to suppress our initial reaction to such a statement and attempt to have an in-depth understanding of the facts.

Lyrical Illusion

After witnessing "the organization of debasement," after transforming his knowing that "a metaphysical problem does not have a political solution" into true consciousness, Malraux met de Gaulle. Their first conversation as recounted in *Anti-Memoirs* shows that their point of convergence was found not in the realm of politics but in that of the defense of man faced with all totalitarianisms—a new totalitarianism of the right of which Hitler and Mussolini might only have been sinister harbingers; a totalitarianism of the left whose foundations Stalin was then in the process of strengthening; and a subtle, insidious totalitarianism of an economy and a democracy which were seeking to control the mind of the consumer and the elector through the indirect means of ever more refined psychological techniques. When Malraux joined forces with de Gaulle, he still didn't know what Man was, but he knew it was essential to begin by defending him if one wished to maintain the hope of one day being able to establish him anew.

One might raise the objection that to defend Man does not require becoming a government minister, and that other paths could be chosen. Granted, but at the time when Malraux chose to join de Gaulle it was political ideologies and political practices that were directly threatening man, and it was those threats which Malraux hoped to combat. What Malraux discovered in de Gaulle was the desire and the will—utopian perhaps but certainly sincere—to give another meaning and to impose another mode of existence upon politics; it was the will to reconcile man and politics, divorced since the eighteenth century. Malraux expresses this unambiguously in *Anti-Memoirs* when he states that "what was at stake went deeper than politics," (*A-M* 77) and when he attributes the response "France will go political again!" (*FO* 84) to a de Gaulle who had just said how Gaullism was the feeling that his motives, "good or bad, were not the motives of the politicians." These responses must not be seen merely as an attack on the games parties play. They must be perceived as an entire concept of the Political—another concept unknown to today's politicians; otherwise they would no longer engage in politics in the way they currently do. Having committed himself to Gaullism, Malraux no longer waged a political battle; he was henceforth mobilized only by the defense and the metamorphosis of man, which he pursued through *The Coin of the Absolute, The Imaginary Museum, The Voices of Silence,* and *The Metamorphosis of the Gods*. The character Magnin in *Man's Hope* announced this new Malraux.

Magnin is a revolutionary because he wants "men to know *why* they're working" (*MH* 79), and when he listens to Sembrano or Vallado

Lyrical Illusion

explain the "whys" behind their political involvement, Magnin admires "the intelligence with which these men supported their passion" (*MH* 80). When Vallado remarks that ideas change, Magnin responds, "the people for whom I'm fighting haven't changed. And that's the only thing that matters" (ibid.). Beyond events, beyond ideologies, even beyond religions, there is man, there is life, and there is their perpetuity. Following *The Walnut Trees of Altenburg*, the birth to life and the co-birth of life filled Malraux. He was haunted at the time by "a secret that was far less the secret of death than of life" (*WTA* 70). Like the men in the tank, who come back to life after climbing out of the ditch into which their tank has fallen and discover eternal life in front of an old farm and an old peasant woman, Malraux knew then what the balloon/Sins of *Paper Moons* didn't know: killing death is useless. It is more important to know what life is. After writing *The Walnut Trees of Altenburg*, Malraux knew that wanting to give meaning to life from the meaning one gives to death is an impasse into which most religions have led man. For millennia, man has first given meaning to death or to the hereafter, which amounts to the same thing; he has then conceived the meaning of life in terms of the meaning he has given to death. For Malraux, it was a matter of carrying out a formidable transformation; one had to know the meaning of life and, in terms of that meaning and that meaning alone, to discover the meaning of death. The problem was, as Malraux told Roger Stéphane one evening in 1945 on the Lorraine front, that of reconciling, as Shakespeare did, "life as seen from death" and "death as seen from life."

It would have been useful here to reproduce the final pages of *The Walnut Trees of Altenburg* in their entirety. All night long Berger and his companions struggle with death; under fire, they pull their tank centimeter by centimeter out of the ditch into which it has fallen. At dawn, exhausted but safe, they arrive in an evacuated village; they see ordinary, everyday utensils in a new way; they see animals; they see them as they had never seen them before. "If anyone had told me," says Prade, a peasant, "that one day I might look at some hens and not find it perfectly natural, I shouldn't have believed it" (*WTA* 219). Looking at everything with "eyes of a stranger," Berger expresses thoughts that are among the most beautiful and stirring of all those found in the writing of André Malraux:

In front of us are some watering-cans with mushroom-shaped spouts, the kind I used to love as a boy; and it suddenly strikes me that man has emerged out of the depths of the past simply to invent a watering-can ... What is it in me that makes me amazed—my only feeling since waking has been one of surprise—

that on this well-planned earth the dogs are still behaving like dogs, the cats like cats?... Like a man confronted for the first time with India, I can hear in this picturesque profusion the hum of the centuries buried almost as deep as last night's darkness... O life, how old you are! And how stubborn! (*WTA* 220–21).

Berger then recalls Pascal's pessimistic *pensée* on the human condition—"Imagine a large number of men in chains, and all condemned to death"—blended with the memory of the line his father uttered so often: "Perhaps pain is always the more powerful." But Berger goes farther, transcending this pessimistic vision of the human condition and attaining a revelation:

This morning I am all birth. I can still feel within me the invasion of the earthly darkness when we came out of the ditch, that germination in shadows deepened by the constellations in the gaps of the drifting clouds; and just as I saw the thundering, teeming night rise up out of the ditch, so now from that night there rises the miraculous revelation of day ... I feel myself in the presence of an unaccountable gift—an apparition...; the universe is as complete and mysterious as a young body...; this life which, this morning for the first time, has shown itself as powerful as the darkness and as powerful as death ... I now know the meaning of the ancient myths about the living snatched from the dead. I can scarcely remember what fear is like; what I carry within me is the discovery of a simple, sacred secret. Thus, perhaps, did God look on the first man." (*WTA* 222–24)

For Berger to reach the point where there could erupt within him "the miraculous revelation of day" and the revelation of life "as powerful as death," he first has to understand and contemplate one of the most cruel experiences his father had when serving under Enver Pacha and Ottomanism. One day Berger's father was showered with blows by a madman who had guessed that his father was not a Turk (*WTA* 54). Because of the deference Moslems have for madness, it was impossible for Berger's father to strike back, and he had to overcome his humiliation. This ordeal shattered *the "charm"*—in the etymological sense of a philter— and Berger's father suddenly understood that Ottomanism did not really exist, whereas for months he had been serving it without ever questioning its reality. Undoubtedly the madman had attacked Berger's father at an "opportune moment when the myth, for want of blood, was on the point of collapse," but when it happened is unimportant, for what matters is that Berger's father was delivered through humiliation.

Lyrical Illusion

Revolution and what it had become undoubtedly played the same role for Malraux as Ottomanism did for Berger's father. We must not forget that, two years after writing *The Walnut Trees of Altenburg,* Malraux took the name Berger to represent the Resistance. But in the meantime Malraux must once again have overcome the temptation of resignation. What were his metaphysical and spiritual thoughts between 1941 and 1943? What were his profound thoughts on the possibility of a new notion upon which man could be established anew? We still have too little information to be able to respond adequately to these questions,[2] but it seems clear that Malraux went through a profound crisis during those years. What he had seen in Spain, what he knew of the situation in the USSR, what he thought about the German-Soviet Pact, had contributed to turn revolution into an "anemic myth." The humiliation of the defeat of the Spanish republicans, the humiliation of the French debacle, the armistice, and the Occupation, had awakened Malraux, and while reading Guénon or Meister Eckehart, he couldn't help asking himself: What remained of the man he had wanted to establish anew? Wasn't the metaphysical vacuum, in which man had been living ever since God had died, the source of "the organization of debasement" that was unfolding among revolutionaries as well as among reactionaries?

No religious faith, no spirituality could guide Malraux on the path he wanted to follow. As early as 1926 in *The Temptation of the West,* he explained how and why the Christian faith could never quench his thirst: "Of course, there is a higher faith; the one offered by all the village crosses, and by the very crosses which watch over our dead. That faith is love, and brings peace. But I shall never accept it; I refuse to lower myself by requesting the peace my weakness cries out for" (*TW* 121). Malraux never departed from this attitude, which arose not only from the Church's betrayal of its Founder's message (a betrayal that nourishes many dialogues in *Man's Hope* and a large part of the dialogue between Mauriac and Malraux upon his return from Spain). Malraux's rejection of the Christian faith was more basic, and he expressed it clearly in 1927 in his work, *Of a European Youth.* Approaching Nietzsche's thought, Malraux shows in this work how "Catholicism has created a *submissive* civilization" (*JE* 135), and how it has ultimately separated man from himself. The peace and serenity offered by the Christian faith is paid for with

---

2. Probably only Albert Beuret and Jean Grosjean have the information and documents that might enable us to propose an initial response. They will make them known in due time, and their reasons for this must be respected.

resignation. In essence, the Christian doesn't have the right to judge himself or to do with himself what he will. With original sin and redemption, such as they are interpreted by the Church, "the Christian's fatality has become nature itself... And that's exactly why psychology exists. What does the Christian seek first of all? His salvation. What separates him from it? The fatality of his nature, original sin, the Devil" (*WTA* 94–95). To earn his salvation the Christian must tie himself to a supernatural entity, which wouldn't have bothered Malraux, but that entity is outside man, it is of a different nature than man. And this was what Malraux could not accept, for he was seeking, as all true mystics have sought, to attain the farthest point at which immanence and transcendence have been sublimated in one and the same inexpressible, secret perception.

Oriental mysticism could no more respond to Malraux's profound aspirations than could the Christian faith. The ambiguity of the title *The Temptation of the West* and of the content of this 1926 work have been too rarely mentioned. In this work, through an epistolary dialogue between a young European, A.D., and a young Chinese, Ling, Malraux expresses not only the temptation that a West in the process of disintegration feels in the presence of Eastern forms of spirituality, but also the temptation felt by the East when it considers adopting certain Western attitudes. The Westerner who has lost all connection with the cosmos, who is weary of a devalued individualism, and who is beginning to perceive the limits of the "I," cannot help being tempted by the fundamental attitude of Orientals as described by Ling: "We, on the other hand, do not wish to be conscious of ourselves as individuals. The work of our mind is to experience lucidly our fragmentary nature and to draw from that feeling a sense of the universe..., for the supreme beauty of a cultured civilization is to be found in the careful avoidance of nurturing the 'I'" (*TW* 59). The Westerner who has reached the limits of reason and violence can only feel temptation by, and envy of, an Oriental who asserts: "Our universe is not subject, as is yours, to the law of cause and effect; or, more exactly, although we admit its reality, it has no power over us" (*TW* 83). The Western mind "desires to construct a plan of the universe and give it an intelligible form; that is, to establish between the unknown and the known a relation capable of bringing to light things which have been obscure... The Eastern mind, on the other hand, gives no value to man himself; it contrives to find, in the flow of the universe, the thoughts which permit it to break its human bonds" (*TW* 85–86).

Lyrical Illusion

In the East, forms are "negligible things, born yesterday and already almost dead, like the succession of waves in ageless seas" (*TW* 88). The Westerner analyzes what he has experienced; the Oriental thinks in order to experience. The Westerner seeks to conceive of a world whose rhythm is consistent; the Oriental lives in a world which "is the result of two opposing rhythms" (*TW* 87) whose absolute equilibrium would be nothingness. For an Oriental, "these two rhythms are real only when their opposition is given human expression, whether it be in terms of masculine and feminine or of permanence and change" (*TW* 87–88). Orientals carry within "the concept of rhythm, which contains a powerful exaltation. When idea and exaltation are united, their rising intensity causes a loss of consciousness, which is the point of communion with their source, the unity of the rhythms being found only there" (*TW* 88).

The young European, A. D., experiences the temptation to blend into an All to commune with the profound rythms of the universe, but he suppresses it. He responds to Ling: "Alas! all that seems highly arbitrary to me . . . At the beginning of your quest I find an act of faith. Not as to the existence of this source, but in the value you assign it" (*TW* 91). A. D. believes even more fundamentally that Oriental wisdom and mysticism define as "absolute" not a true absolute but a representation that man creates for himself: "In his ecstasy, the thinker does not identify himself with the absolute, as is taught by your wise men; he merely defines as absolute the furthest point of his sensibility. The argument of your philosophers that all ecstasies are identical, since all begin where the material world ends, seems invalid to me, and invalid the consequences they draw from it" (*TW* 91–92). For A. D., it isn't "consciousness itself" that Eastern mysticism provides, but *a* consciousness. Space does not permit a discussion of Malraux's perception of Oriental mystical philosophies at that time, but we should recall that he was only twenty-five years old when he wrote *The Temptation of the West*. His perception of Oriental mysticism evolved, notably in 1974 during his final trip to Japan. In 1926 he still saw Eastern mysticism as a meaning given to death, and, for him, "the most beautiful theorem of death is an answer only for weakness" (*TW* 92). It was not a "theorem of death," however beautiful, that Malraux sought, but a theorem of life. The serenity, the fusion, the oblivion that Eastern mysticism brings about do not bolster man in the face of destiny; they enable him to forget or to accept it. But Malraux wanted to forge that destiny.

Another realm of reasoning also led Malraux to reject the temptation the West feels in the presence of the East, namely, the inverse temptation, which is progressively invading the East. In his next to last letter, the young European recounts what he was told by Wang-Loh, a noble old Chinese man, tall, with an air of great distinction. Wang-Loh's words paint a picture of destruction and annihilation

> of one of the greatest human systems, one which succeeds in existing without the support of gods or men. The annihilation! China wavers like an edifice on the point of collapse, and her anguish comes from neither uncertainty nor conflict, but from the weight of that trembling roof . . . ; our spirit is gradually becoming *empty* . . . Europe thinks she has conquered all these young men who now wear her garments. But they hate her. They are awaiting from her what the common people call her 'secrets': ways of defending themselves against her. Her effect on them falls short of seduction, and only succeeds in making them realize the senselessness of all thought. (*TW* 102–4)

For Wang-Loh, Chinese life and thought have also become the theater for a "common absurdity" (*TW* 105). When the young Ling replies to A. D. (this is his last letter, which is important to note), he doesn't argue with the opinions of the noble old Wang-Loh; he agrees with them and takes them even further. The only hope Ling can still express is that China, which is creating itself, will be "shaken by one of those great collective emotions which several times have convulsed her" (*TW* 113). This was 1926! Malraux had then ended *The Temptation of the West* with a final letter from A. D.: "There is no ideal to which we can sacrifice ourselves, for we know the lies of all of them, we who have no idea what truth is. The earthly shadow which falls behind marble gods is enough to keep us from them. How firmly man is bound to himself!" (*TW* 121). Malraux could then conclude merely with an invocation to lucidity; the lucidity which alone can enable man to face up to the dizzying void created by the collapse of the great Western and Oriental spiritualities; the lucidity which alone can enable man to hope that tomorrow, perhaps, a new religious sensibility will provide man with a new harmony with the universe.

In order to continue up the path he had set out upon, in order to continue to confront the *Farfelu Kingdom,* in 1941–42 Malraux was helped neither by the Christian faith nor by Oriental mysticism. Once again he was overwhelmed by the temptation of resignation. Like Gisors at the end of *Man's Fate,* Malraux might have been tempted to find refuge in a universe where "even blood, even flesh, even suffering, even death was being absorbed up there in the light like music in the silent night" (*MF*

358). This temptation to give in was not foreign to Malraux. It had already appeared in *Days of Wrath,* where Kassner, in his cell, fights rising madness and then the temptation to abandon himself to serenity. The power of a creative imagination, even one like Malraux's, does not suffice to explain the intensity and the emotion of those pages. To be able to write them, Malraux had to feed his imagination with feelings he had himself experienced, which he transfigured with all the talent and lyricism he possessed.

In his cell, Kassner is overwhelmed by troubling images that pass before his eyes. He fights a Promethean and obsessive nightmare: "A vulture shut up with him in a cage, which with relentless blows of its pick-shaped beak was tearing off pieces of his flesh, all the while staring greedily at his eyes" (*DW* 44). To fight the madness he felt overcoming him, Kassner appeals to music—Russian songs, Bach, Beethoven—which he sings to himself. Little by little the music and its message delivers Kassner from madness and from the nightmare: "The vulture and the prison-cell were being submerged beneath a flooding death chant that enveloped all in a lasting communion, in which music perpetuated the whole past by liberating it from time, mingling all its manifestations even as life and death merge in the immobility of the starry sky" (*DW* 45–46). Note after note, song after song, Kassner then experiences the calm and communion that music brings when it "takes man's head between its hands and slowly lifts it towards human fellowship" (*DW* 48), when it "rises above everything with its intertwined flames that soothe as they consume."

Even if he has been "an animal of action" (*DW* 36), the man who has once known such fellowship, approached such serenity where all is transcended, can't help experiencing the temptation to reject any idea of acting upon the world, especially when "the darkness [is] draining his willpower" (ibid.). Kassner feels this temptation to yield rising within him. To supress it, he has to make "one of the greatest efforts of his life" (*DW* 54). Bolstered by the fraternal messages that the prisoner in the next cell taps out on the pipes, Kassner leaves behind the world of "spectacles" that music has created in him, and seeks to "bring them into the realm of time" (*DW* 57). He regains his will to act, though at first it takes the form of seeking the means to commit suicide, which he believes will enable him to make his death useful.

After finishing *The Walnut Trees of Altenburg* (conceived, as we noted, as the first part of *The Struggle with the Angel,* after sharing Berger's experience of "the miraculous revelation of day," might not Malraux, who

Lyrical Illusion

was first in Roquebrune near Nice, then in Saint-Chamand in Corrèze, have been tempted to yield to resignation? Might he not have felt the need to have everything finally sink into "a contemplative given?" He was over forty years old. Action had always been a means in his metaphysical quest, and in that capacity it had not provided him with any answers. He was working on three manuscripts at the same time: *The Demon of the Absolute;* the second part of *The Struggle with the Angel;* and *The Psychology of Art,* the first segment of which had been published in December 1937 in the journal *Verve*. If at that time he had been aware of a form of spirituality to which he could have "entrusted his weakness," he would undoubtedly have chosen a meditative and contemplative life in which he would have attempted to "rise above everything with its intertwined flames that soothe as they consume." Instead, he became actively involved in the Resistance, following the arrest of his brother Roland in March 1944. After the Liberation he remained in active combat and espoused Gaullism, but his battle, as we now know, was not a political one. Perhaps essentially it had never been one.

In the years that followed World War II, a man like Malraux could have found many reasons to be beaten down. His former friends accused him of betraying their revolution and becoming "an unemployed Leninist"; the Absurd, which for him was a question and not an answer, seemed to be triumphing in literature and philosophy; the communist or socialist ideal was also being tainted: the totalitarianism of the left was gaining strength and was taking over an expanse that had never been covered by the totalitarianisms of the right; capitalism, reinvigorated by the war economy then by the reconstruction, had been revitalised; nowhere—except in China, perhaps, but for how long?—was a new system of relations between people and things being established. Historical and economic materialism were casting their shadows over the earth and taking hold of people.

Under such conditions there are many who would have given up. But when one has believed in man the way Perken and Claude believed, the way Kyo, Magnin, Manuel, and Vincent Berger believed, the way Malraux himself believed, one does not give up. With rare insight, Ramon Fernandez wrote in 1933:

Seen from the inside, M. Malraux's work may be seen as a renewal of the tragic concept of will . . . Will in all its forms, and above all the willed rejection of the world as it is, makes man a hero. But at a certain stage in our development, in our own time indeed, maturity and lucidity are eroding this will from the inside. We can see the vanity, the illusion of our will. Yet if we continue to act, a new sense of tragedy will be born from the very excess of our energy and from the coexistence of our stubbornness and our lucidity ... The lucid Prometheus loses none of his strength. On the contrary, his strength is increased by a discreet but implacable scepticism that serves, as it were, to purify it. In M. Malraux's work, the will begins where it usually ends: after the liquidation of illusions and beliefs. (*Marianne,* 15 December 1933, quoted in Lacouture, p. 149)

After World War II, the field for applying Malraux's "tragic will" changed. In Spain, in Russia, and in France he had learned that it was impossible to create new relations between people and things so long as the cultural imprints that are stamped on the minds of men have not been transformed. He had learned that it was a new culture and a new sensibility that had to be prepared. And it was upon those elements that his meditation and his tragic will for action were henceforth brought to bear.

After coming out of the darkness, after being reunited with his wife and communing with her through tenderness, Kassner feels he is living "one of those moments which make men believe a god has just been born" (*DW* 172); he has the impression of finally holding in his grasp "the eternity of the living and not the eternity of the dead" (*DW* 173). Kassner and Anna "were now going to speak, remember, exchange experiences ... All this would become a part of everyday life, a stairway which they would descend side by side, into the street, under the sky eternally looking down upon the defeats or victories of men's wills" (*DW* 174). Malraux was unable to talk, remember, or exchange experiences with Josette Clotis; she had been crushed under a train at the Saint Chamand station.

Everyday life, going down the stairs, walking down the street, looking at a tree or up at the sky—all these "nothings" in everyday life are shaped by one's culture. And Malraux finally knew that it was essential to metamorphose that culture if one wanted man to be able *truly* to stand up to his destiny.

PART FOUR

The Metamorphosis of Culture

10

A Metamorphosis of Man

❧

IF "THE ORGANIZATION of debasement" had not spread over the earth Malraux would undoubtedly not have made a metamorphosis of culture his highest priority. After Gide's return from the USSR, after the Spanish civil war and World War II, there was no longer any doubt possible for Malraux: only a metamorphosis of culture would enable man to conquer the forces and powers behind the organization of debasement (*A-M* 398); it alone would enable man to stand up to his destiny; it alone would perhaps enable men to live with a new revelation of life "as strong as the shadows, as strong as death."

When Kassner, after being tortured, returns to his cell, and when he has prepared "what could be told to the darkness" (*DW* 93), he is invaded by a childhood memory: the explosion in the mine where already the boy had been working. After the explosion there were still two hundred miners deep within the mine, one of whom was Kassner's father. After forty hours of fighting fire, the inspectors and the workers' delegates decided that there was no longer any hope. The boy had watched as the mine where his father remained was walled up forever. Was he still alive? Was he already dead? Neither the child nor anyone else would ever know. It was the miner's lot. But at least, thinks Kassner in his cell, those were not yet the days of contempt.

Beginning in the 1930s "the will to humiliate" (*DW* 77) made its appearance on earth, and it was to that demon of demons, that absolute evil, that Malraux devoted the last section of *Anti-Memoirs*, which he entitled "The Human Condition." It begins with his long conversation with Mao concerning the Cultural Revolution and ends with the portrayal of "the organization of debasement" (*A-M* 398) which had spread over Europe. The humiliation of the Shanghai stevedores, the coolies of Canton, the workers and peasants of the Asturias, was the result of an economic, social, and political system which used the worker as an instrument, which wasn't interested in acknowledging his quality of being a man, and which didn't allow him to seek that quality in his personal life. With the organization of debasement a threshold had been crossed, a mutation accomplished: humiliation was no longer a result; it had become a goal, an objective. "The will to humiliate" had appeared on earth.

Throughout all time there have existed wars, massacres, repression, torture, but "what had not existed before was this organized debasement" (*A-M* 398), which, born in the twentieth century, employs ever more refined techniques. In the past the goal of torture was "to extract confessions or to punish a religious or political heresy" (*A-M* 399). No nation, even those whose prisons were the most inhumane, had ever made the statement which was at the very foundation of the Nazi concentration camps: "Treat men like dirt, and they will really become dirt" (*A-M* 400). In the Nazi camps, and after them in many other prison camps, "the supreme objective was that the prisoners, in their own eyes, should lose their identity as human beings" (*A-M* 399). The worker in his factory feels humiliated because deep inside he feels like a man. The objective of the organization of debasement is to reach the point where man can no longer even feel like a man.

There are some who easily and quickly reassure themselves by believing that the organization of debasement as such disappeared with the destruction of Hitler's regime. But all evidence points to the contrary. First, there are on all continents those passing or lasting dictatorships which employ methods comparable to those used by the Nazis. Since they do so on a much smaller scale or in a less systematic way, we are eager to ignore or to forget them. Next, there are all the Soviet gulags and hospitals where, under the pretext of punishing political heresy, men are treated like dirt or, what is even worse, given neuroleptic drugs. Prisoners are then so greatly weakened that they no longer put up any psychological resistance, and it becomes possible to shape and "reeducate" them. Finally, and we must not attempt to ignore this, there is the organization of debasement through the use of modern psychological techniques employed by the advertising world and by election campaigns. This type of organized debasement is rampant in countries where, fortunately, defense groups bringing hope for the future can be born and survive—with difficulty, perhaps, but freely, nonetheless.

To some people it might seem scandalous that a parallel could be drawn between the psychiatric hospitals of the USSR or those of popular democracies and commercial or electoral marketing in liberal democracies. But immediate indignation obscures the need to ask essential questions about the techniques employed to keep an office or to win an election. The organization of electoral campaigns/extravaganzas, the search for "slogans" craftily honed by publicity agents, the subtly tinted glow of campaign television programs, the parades with drum majorettes, the distribution of buttons and T-shirts, presidents playing the accordion—the piano of the poor—all these practices, and many others at the level of opinion polls, are based on psychological techniques which fundamentally despise the elector and subtly organize his debasement. "The bigger the lie the easier it will be believed" said Goebbels. He has many unconscious emulators. For example, the organizers of a demonstration who constantly inflate the number of demonstrators, and their opponents who cite equally misleading underestimated numbers, both expend the same amount of energy to have their willful lies diffused as widely as possible by the press, by radio, and by television, which they thus attempt to control as closely as possible. Similar willful lies are diffused via the figures which have invaded political and social life and today constitute its framework: figures on rising prices, unemployment, production, etc. Granted, the stultification and debasement worked by commercial and electoral marketing are carried out in a context of at least formal freedom, and the marketers respect the physical integrity of a person. But they do not respect a person's psychological integrity and in fact seek to harm it all the more when physical well-being is respected. The days of contempt continue. They may even be reaching unguessed depths.

Another realm has also been invaded by the organization of stultification and debasement, one which is more significant than any other. Malraux spoke of it in Oxford in November 1967: "It has been banally said that the machine would fight against the mind; we know today that to all the factories on earth the dream-factories are responding ... Yet the appeal dreams have for all men might be—dream-merchants not being especially dominated by the mind—the most profound and perhaps most tragic appeal to its ghosts and demons that humanity has ever known." Film, television, and record producers use the power of their

The Metamorphosis of Culture

dream factories to play upon what is most instinctive in man and to manipulate trade and high finance. Whether consciously or unconsciously, dream merchants attempt to take control of the spectator by acting upon a part of his mind, and so they become collaborators in the most powerful of potential totalitarianisms. By aiming below the belt and by seeking above all to earn money, they are the chief agents of a new organization of debasement. And this is why their collusion with politicians is so close and so obvious. This is also why the struggle for the control of dream factories is so ruthless. Today it is already possible, if one looks beneath the surface, to see that dream marketing has become a tragic realm where an awesome subterranean battle is being waged by reactionaries and conservers of culture to prevent, they hope, the metamorphosis of culture.

But we must look far into the future and be able to see in the dead, decomposing leaves the humus that will nourish the spring. The organization of debasement will not be victorious, even if it continues to increase the efficiency and subtlety of its means. Malraux makes us foresee and hope for its ultimate failure when he describes the deep, ultimate meaning of the courage and resistance shown by the deportees of Ravensbruck and Auschwitz: they provided an amazingly simple and enormously important response (whose full measure we do not perhaps yet grasp) to the question at the heart of *The Walnut Trees of Altenburg*: "Is there a single permanent factor . . . on which to build one's conception of man?" In the dour struggle carried on by the deportees, "the first victim was death . . . the furious determination to survive which animated most of the resisters was not primarily concentrated against it. They had grasped that in every man there is something more profound. . . . Don't lap up spilt soup. Death was one element among others" (*A-M* 399–400). The balloon-Sins in *Paper Moons* killed Death, but they employed an artifice, a ruse, and in the end nothing changed. The deportees, through their struggle and their suffering, truly overcame the power of Death: They turned it into "one element among others" whereas for millennia it had been considered the essential element of the human condition. The deportees conquered the power of Death because the battle they waged was not a negative one (to kill Death), but a positive one—to maintain their identity as men. "Yet even among the dying there remained enough humanity to divine that the will to live was not animal, but obscurely sacred. The mystery of the human condition manifested itself there, far more than in the cosmic groundswell which sooner or later would sweep tortured and torturers alike to their deaths"

A Metamorphosis of Man

(*A-M* 400). At first vague and profound, the idea of man for which the deportees resisted "now became clear: man was what "they" were trying to take from them ... The extermination camps, in endeavoring to turn man into a beast, intimated that it is not life alone which makes him man" (*A-M* 400–401).

All of Malraux's works, without any exception, as well as his entire life, represent a battle against the culture that had engendered the humiliation of the worker, the debasement of the prisoner or the deportee, the stultification of the citizen/consumer: he waged a battle against the culture that had engendered the organization of debasement so that ultimately a metamorphosis of culture might occur. If, like Garine, we can lucidly recognize that we have no idea what men would do in the aftermath of a successful revolution and that there is every chance that they would in turn become contemptible; if, like Gisors, we believe that the revolutionary is "capable of winning, but not of living in his victory" (*MF* 65); if, like Manuel, we realize that it is currently impossible to exercise a command and maintain a notion of fraternity; if, like Kassner, escaping from hell and feeling "drunk with humanity" (*DW* 143), we bitterly recognize that men can be so inhuman; if, like Malraux, returning to life after his stay at the Salpêtrière hospital (cf. *Lazarus*), we note that men are mainly concerned with the size of their tombstones rather than with their lives; and if we wish to grasp "the eternity of the living and not the eternity of the dead" (*DW* 173), it then becomes clear that the cultural matrices which form the minds of men, the printed circuits which program their sensibilities and intelligence and structure their behavior must first be transformed. It is man's culture that sculpts his way of thinking, feeling, and acting. It is the cultural heritage we all carry inside that fashions our attitudes toward everyday life. It is culture that must be transformed if we hope for the transformation of relations between people and things.

Malraux's early novels illustrate the distance which always exists between everyday life and revolutionary action, between the masses and the revolutionary minority. In *The Conquerors* the coolies are prepared to go back to work despite the orders they've been given; in *Man's Fate* the population of Shanghai seems to be missing; in *Man's Hope* the inhabitants of Madrid carry on their lives as if they have nothing to do with the fighting there. Isn't this almost always true in the cities and countries in the midst of a revolution? Aren't there always on the one hand those who fight in the name of a certain idea of man, and on the other the majority of "real" people who remain outside the fight? But this gap, this separation between the majority of people and the minority of fighters, becomes less and less distinct in each of Malraux's successive works. In *The Conquerors* and in *Man's Fate* the demands of the revolutionaries are primarily abstract and expressed through concepts: dignity, consideration, etc. In *Man's Hope* the demands remain abstract but are sometimes expressed in a more concrete request: don't take any more vineyards; empty the pawnshops, etc. On the final page of *Days of Wrath* a reconciliation between the world of ideas and that of real life is undertaken. This reconciliation becomes complete in *The Walnut Trees of Altenburg*.

It seems obvious to me that it was in the barracks in Provins and then in the Chartres camp that Malraux began to give shape to his idea of man. Thanks to the heterogeneity that surrounded him, and undoubtedly for the first time, Malraux went from the idea of man to the knowledge of men. He discovered flesh and blood men, the peasant or the worker, and no longer had simply the notion of the villager or the proletariat. The end of the first part of *The Walnut Trees of Altenburg* expresses the transformation which took place in Malraux. Returning from Turkey, where he had fought for an idea, a simple idea which had no basis in reality, Vincent Berger disembarks in Marseilles. From the balcony of his hotel room he looks at the Vieux-Port and the Canebière, and he discovers the simplest of things, he discovers real life, he contemplates "the troubled waters" of everyday life, "on earth, toward the end of the second millennium of the Christian era" (*WTA* 60).

After 1942, Malraux, who had been "rubbing shoulders with a world which he thought he knew" (*WTA* 143), then knew what "real life" was; he knew above all that it was that life which had to be metamorphosed, as a plant metamorphoses a leaf into a petal or a pistil, if one wanted flesh and blood man to be able to live everyday life as a man standing up to his destiny. And as Goethe studied plants in order to find the secret of metamorphosis, Malraux undertook an increasingly profound study of the plastic arts in order to get closer and closer to the mystery at the origin of the metamorphosis of works of art, gods, and men. As many Christians might have done, Ximenes answered Manuel: "You'd like to lead men and yet remain their comrade; well, in my opinion, no man's big enough for that" (*MH* 408). Through his experiences in Indochina, China, Russia, Spain, and France, Malraux also realized that "no man is big enough for that." But rather than entrusting this smallness to a Church that reserves man's ennoblement for the hereafter, as Ximenes

A Metamorphosis of Man

did, Malraux maintained his faith in men and did not attempt to look beyond man for the means to make him greater. And in this Malraux was undoubtedly closer to Christ than the Church is. For Malraux his faith in man in no way precluded a search for a transcendence; on the contrary, in fact. But his faith demanded representation of a transcendence that was radically different from all the others Malraux knew of and, above all, that was a representation of an immanent transcendence, one to which all true mystics have sung a hymn and whose path they have explored. It is up to us to turn that path into a royal way.

In *The Walnut Trees of Altenburg* when Berger interrupts the account of his father's life story in order to tell the story of his own, he cries out: "I am in a hurry to get to the point at which writing, at last, is no longer only a change of hell" (*WTA* 189). Can we assume that Malraux is expressing himself through this cry? I believe so. And if this is a statement Malraux might have truly uttered, what incredible depth of suffering it reveals! For Malraux, writing *The Conquerors, The Royal Way, Man's Fate, Man's Hope,* and *Days of Wrath* would have been only a change of hell! We can then understand his thirst and his haste "to get to the point at which writing is no longer only a change of hell"; and why, having got to that point and having experienced "the miraculous revelation of day" (*WTA* 223), Malraux decided not to complete the novels he had begun and to abandon definitively transfiguration through fiction. From that time onward Malraux did not remain in the world of hells, but moved within a universe, the Universe of Forms, where he was able to deepen his revelation of a life "as powerful as death" (ibid.).

In *Anti-Memoirs* Malraux reveals that the passion "which Asia, vanished civilizations, and ethnography have long inspired in [him] arose from an essential wonderment at the forms which man has been able to assume . . ." (*A-M* 197). Malraux must certainly have chosen with particular care the expression: "the forms which man has been able to assume." In it he expresses the depth and the originality of his perception of vanished civilizations. He sensed and perceived the different forms man had already assumed just as he did the different forms given to statuary throughout the ages and on different continents. The discovery when he was yet very young, with its "essential surprise," that man had already assumed "different forms" sustained Malraux's hope for the emergence of yet another new "form" for man.

Malraux saw this hope for a new "form" for man as a necessity. As he confided to me in January 1972: "I don't believe the world can live with the notion of man it has inherited from the West." The context of our conversation suggested that Malraux believed the world could live neither with the notion of man proposed by Christendom, and by those who hope to instill new life in that notion, nor with the one proposed by Marxist philosophy, which is also an inheritance from the West, however rationalistic and scientific it may be. In 1935 Malraux stated in a speech: "The West invented the civilization of quantity opposing a world which had known only that of quality. And our task now is to give quality back to men" (*Commune*, December 1935). Shortly afterward he wrote the weighty dialogues in *Man's Hope* concerning the conflict between "to be" and "to act." If we reread those pages while continuing to hear the muffled echoes of the song of hope that shook the entire Western world in May 1968, it becomes clear that Malraux, in the 1930s, was far ahead of a revolution, or rather it appears clear that the revolutionary battles he waged at that time were rearguard expressions of an earlier revolution. Weren't those battles of the 1930s the continuation of battles waged in the nineteenth century and in no way a prefiguration of future ones? Malraux left the battles of the past behind and committed himself completely to the battle for a cultural revolution, the one which would truly provide man with a new "form." That battle certainly interests men, as Malraux's legacy clearly shows. It is in fact more realistic and wiser to see that the reason Malraux became a living legend is that he brings hope to life, rather than to think, as Jean Lacouture does in his book, that Malraux became a legend because of his lies and mystifications about real life. The Barons de Clappique will never make us believe that Malraux was one of them.

Have we sufficiently asked ourselves why Malraux gave the title *L'Espoir* (translated as *Man's Hope*) to his novel based on the Spanish civil war, which he published after the defeat of its heroes? In his *Introduction à une étude structurale des romans de Malraux*, Lucien Goldmann responds by saying that the novel ends with the republican victory of Brihuega and that Malraux had not wanted to modify his book to encompass the unhappy end of the civil war. Goldmann also believes that the title is associated with the internal structure of the story, in which everything is subordinate to the necessity of sacrificing values to discipline (!). These arguments hardly seem convincing. Others have tried to explain the novel's title by emphasizing the fact that the victory of Brihuega ended up consecrating "the ordeal that was to make or mar the fortunes of the Republican Army" (*MH* 496) and that, those fortunes having been successful, Magnin could think: "The war is only starting now." None of these explanations exhaust the issue, and we must look deeper for the significance of the title, *L'Espoir,* and of its being maintained despite obvious defeat. Indeed, it is a very strong title, devoid of ambiguity.

After hesitating for a long time I have become convinced that the hope Malraux provides, offers us despite the republicans' defeat, is that men will conceive of themselves as men, as Magnin conceives of human beings. It is the hope that men will be voluntarily metamorphosed, just as Manuel allows himself to be. *Man's Hope* is Magnin and Manuel. It would be quite useful to undertake an in-depth study entirely devoted to a comparison of Garine of *The Conquerors* and Magnin of *Man's Hope.* Such a study would most likely confirm that Magnin is a Garine who succeeded. Magnin, even more than Garine, embodies "the aptitude for action, culture, and lucidity." Too often we have been content to see a portrait of Malraux in Magnin and are thus deprived of seeing the true character Malraux created. Garine, conquered by his illness and by Borodine, has to give up his fight. But Magnin plays an essential role in the victory of Brihuega. Garine is on the verge of being intoxicated by his action and becoming indifferent to all that isn't a part of it, even to its results. Magnin never loses sight of the meaning of his action and the fact that it is only a means; he is able to carry out his military command without sacrificing his fraternal notion of leadership. He places himself outside all ideologies and enters into revolutionary action, because he wants "men to know why they're working" (*MH* 79). In battle Magnin feels closer to his men each day, and above all he helps a man like Manuel fully to accept the metamorphosis announced on the last page of *Man's Hope:* Manuel "felt the seething life around him charged with portents . . . Some day there would be peace. And he, Manuel, would become another man, someone he could not visualize as yet; just as the soldier he had become could no more visualize the Manuel who once had bought a little car to go skiing in the Sierra . . . For the first time Manuel was hearing the voice of that which is more awe-inspiring even than the blood of men, more enigmatic even than their presence on the earth—the infinite possibilities of their destiny" (*MH* 510–11). That everyone will be transformed as Manuel was transformed—this is the hope.

In 1945 the French Communist party with Aragon at the helm responded to Malraux's attacks with a violent campaign against him. Garaudy, who was a Communist deputy at that time, published *Literature of the Cemetery,* in which he attacked Sartre, Mauriac, Koestler, and especially Malraux. He first compared Malraux to a Greek god descending from Mount Olympus, witnessing bloody sacrifices, seeing that the warriors were drunk with blood, and going back up, far from human concerns, to amuse himself with metaphysical questions. Garaudy then wrote: "Malraux is the medium of a dying class and of a dying social order because he provides a psychological transposition and a metaphysical justification for their disorder and their anguish." While rereading these lines today it is important to consider the opposition to Malraux that existed at that time, as he had become the political adversary of the communists and, already in 1945, was motivated by the hope—or the illusion—that he would be able to create a true ministry of culture, give life to a vast network of *maisons de la culture*, and transform education with the use of audiovisual methodology.

A medium of the bourgeoisie—Malraux certainly was not that. "Opium of the bourgeoisie," as Régis Debray would later say—he was that perhaps, but it was more their doing than his. The bourgeoisie senses, even if it doesn't accept the idea, that it is a finite class. It no longer believes in the values it once claimed to uphold, and does not itself respect them. In Malraux's time, when the bourgeoisie didn't read his works only to challenge them, it absorbed them the way some people absorb drugs: in those works it found a momentary release from its fears and encountered visions it didn't understand but which brought a temporary escape from reality. Mauriac, unlike Garaudy, sensed the danger Malraux represented to the bourgeois mind Mauriac knew so well, and he wrote pages in his journal to point out that danger.

Far from being the medium of the bourgeoisie, Malraux was the cantor of Metamorphosis as Universal Law: "I am attempting to create a life, the life of someone at a moment in history when we are becoming aware of Metamorphosis as Universal Law" (*Le Monde*, 15 March 1974). It is comforting to know that it is the voice of Régis Debray—a voice that knows what it is talking about and has earned the right to speak—that, in a very beautiful article published a few days after Malraux's death, best expresses the profound meaning of Malraux's life and work:

"We are not Malraux's heirs, nor his victims . . . we are his conquered . . . The cult of Malraux is the opium of the French bourgeoisie, the soul of a world without soul, the sky of the commonplace . . . Malraux has won and we have lost . . . Here, then, is the man who never cared about truth . . . who decided as early as in his adolescence that the real world didn't exist, or existed only as the framework for images and as myth-holder, promoted fifty years later to the role

A Metamorphosis of Man

of model for all those whose lives rest or have rested on two contrary assumptions: the search for truth and the transformation of the real world . . . He was the first to be established at the heart of what is coming and is already overwhelming us—the mythological—the first to sacrifice the idea and the real to the image. As for the rest of us, we have lost . . . We had to disappear into the dead-end tunnels of politics, those slimy labyrinths . . ." (*Le Monde*, 27 November 1976).

If, before leaving for Latin America, Régis Debray could have read *Man's Hope* and *The Walnut Trees of Altenburg* the way we have begun to read them, and the way politics at the time prevented him from doing, his reading would have convinced him that it is still the businessmen, those of trade and finance as well as those of politics and revolution, who believe that only the concrete world should be changed; he would have undoubtedly also been convinced that the real world, the world of appearances, does indeed serve as a framework for our images, and that in the current phase in history it is more important, if we truly wish to transform the relations between men, to transform the images than to transform the framework. Régis Debray might have been convinced of this by rereading *The Conquerors, Man's Hope,* and *The Walnut Trees of Altenburg,* but he undoubtedly would have had to immerse himself in experience—while he was in Latin America, the way Malraux was in China and Spain—in order then to transform that experience into consciousness. Certainly, in his case as in Malraux's, he needed first to experience the "slimy tunnels of politics" in order then to emerge into the light of a personal awareness of the inner reality of people and things. In the same article Debray says that if he went to Latin America "it was quite simply to be involved in revolution, in politics." I have the impression that he, too, came to realize through his experiences that he was involved in a "lyrical illusion," one of the most beautiful, perhaps, but Régis Debray proves to us today, as Malraux did in the past, that for the moment it unfortunately remains an illusion. And this is why one man became a minister and the other a counselor at the Elysée Palace.

To write that Malraux "was the first to sacrifice the idea and reality to the image" is to recognize that he gave a cultural revolution priority over a political revolution. And Malraux was right. The printing press, engraving, the discovery of new lands upset the images that inhabited the minds of men in those times. To realize this fully one would truly have to understand the kind of imaginary those men who didn't know about books and who believed that the sun turned around the earth might have had. It took many generations for new images to make their way into the minds of all men. When those images had been incorporated they engendered the French Revolution and the revolutions of the nineteenth century. And today once again man's imaginary is being shaken up: painting, sculpture, and music have found their printing presses; audiovisual technology is feeling out the vast domain at its disposal; space shuttles are opening up new worlds for man to investigate and for poets to imagine; quantum mechanics and molecular biology are rendering the images of reality and organic life man has created for himself obsolete. From all sides former images are being attacked and new ones are attempting to take over. As we already know, they will be synthetic images. When they have become incorporated by all they will in turn open up possibilities for political and social transformation. But they have not yet been incorporated and in the twentieth century the most important and useful task consists of preparing men for the metamorphosis of culture which is slowly but powerfully occurring from the pressure of new images which have already begun to take root. This primary task must not lead us to forget the essential task of defending the metamorphosis of culture against all those who, consciously or not, attempt to halt its progress because they prefer to rule over caterpillars rather than allow free and luminous butterflies to live; against all those who prop themselves up on aging images and adroitly make use of the general confusion which always occurs with a change of imaginary.

II

Culture: An Agreement of Sensibilities

❧

WITHIN THE LAST few decades the word "culture" has changed meaning. In 1926–27, in his two works *The Temptation of the West* and *Of a European Youth,* Malraux devoted himself to better understanding the change that was going on. In his 1946 UNESCO speech he summed it up clearly: "Within the last twenty-five years pluralism has been born. And for the earlier notion of civilization—progress in feelings, manners, customs and the Arts—we have substituted the new notion of cultures." This substitution conveys a mutation in the thinking of our time which is as important as the recognition of antiquity was for the minds that prepared the Renaissance. It will have equally fundamental consequences.

In the past one rarely spoke of the culture of a period, and when speaking of a person's culture one was referring to the accumulated knowledge a person had of events and works of the past. And if one spoke of the culture of a people or a society, one was referring to the manifestations of its intellectual and artistic life. This limited concept of culture is still maintained by many people today and too often inspires names such as "minister of cultural affairs," the "office of cultural activity," the "center for cultural activity," etc. But for others, the word "culture" has already changed meaning and has undergone a development comparable to the one that the word "civilization" has undergone.

Nourished by the historical studies of the nineteenth century, the early twentieth century gradually abandoned the idea of "the" civilization, whose corollary was an opposition between the civilized and the barbarous, and substituted the idea of "civilizations." Although today this substitution is an acknowledged given, and outdated expressions such as "we brought civilization to them" are ludicrous, it is likely that our era has not yet become fully aware of all the budding implications contained in this change of perspective. It will undoubtedly take longer and be more difficult to realize all the implications which enrich the new meaning of the word "culture." And it will take even longer, will be even more difficult—given the limited notion of culture whose corollary was the opposition between cultivated and uncultivated man—to accept the much larger notion of "cultures," those which the history of ideas and ethnography are attempting to bring back to life.

As the enlarging of the notion of culture is still in its very early stages, the outlines of what we describe as civilizations and cultures remain somewhat hazy—and will undoubtedly remain so for decades to come. When we look at Malraux's writings, we see that even his terminology remained for a long time loose and imprecise, but I believe there can be no doubt about his fundamental thoughts, at least those at the end of his life. For example, he wrote in *The Timeless:* "When civilization changes, when it has transmitted or destroyed the values that wove the homogeneous and tightly-woven fabric of what man constructs or creates" (*Int* 130). His ideas are clear: the realm of civilization is the realm of what man constructs or creates; the realm of culture is the realm of the values which govern that construction or creation. A civilization is a culture's field of action; it is an acted-out culture.

Culture does custom work. It shapes our way of thinking and feeling; it shapes our way of looking at a landscape and a painting, the meaning we give to "big words" and to words we use every day. Talking with Malraux, Picasso made the distinction between paintings which deal with a subject and those which take hold of a theme such as "birth, pregnancy, suffering, murder, the couple, death, rebellion, and, perhaps, the kiss" (*PM* 39). Every culture gives a different form to each one of these themes. Each is metamorphosed from one culture to another. There they evoke different realms of thoughts and feelings.

The culture of a society sculpts the meaning of "big words" and of all words. It creates the meaning not only of "life," "death," "beauty," "suffering," "birth," "god," "crime," but also of "people," "freedom," "democracy," etc. By giving words their meaning culture enables exchange, communication, relationships; it enables us to be connected, to participate. And it is not by chance that the two primary hopes of our era, which will surely be seen by our descendants as not really having had a culture—the hopes which seem to grasp men's minds most profoundly and encourage the most fertile events—are for cultural revolution and

Culture: An Agreement of Sensibilities

participation. Having covered the earth with a sophisticated network of technical means of communication, our era still has no common meanings for "big words." And since it is not yet ready to accept a plurality of meanings, it is experiencing the tragedy of incommunication.

With the existence of contraception, abortion, the oxygen tent, and ultrasophisticated medical equipment, we no longer know where the word "life" begins and ends. The meanings of the words "birth" and "death" have become quite loose. The realm of ideas and feelings encompassed by the word "woman" is in complete flux. The word "people" has become unclear. One must add the adjectives "liberal" or "popular" to "democracy," or else it might evoke contrary meanings. Without common meanings, without a common culture, men of today cannot be connected, they cannot participate, and they must be content to remain juxtaposed. We will undoubtedly one day have to agree to have plurality and uncertainty take hold of the meanings of words as they have taken hold of physics and mathematics, those exact sciences, and we will surely have to construct on them new modalities of dialogue and communication. The cultures our era has inherited have not prepared man for such an upheaval. On the contrary. For minds used to traditional logic abandoning the principle of noncontradiction amounts to traumatism.

Through the meaning it gives to words, a culture sculpts our imaginary. Every culture has its own "magical yet familiar places" which "capture men's imaginaries" (*HP* 63). These are the pyramids and their mummies, the amphitheater and its tragedies, the Coliseum and its gladiators or its martyrs, the cathedral, the opera, etc. The forms among which a civilization lives, its style, are the embodiment of its imaginary, which is characterized as much by its positive feelings as by its negative ones (cf. *HP* 274). We must carefully avoid applying the wrong meaning that is commonly given to "imaginary." Malraux clearly specified that for him "the imaginary is a realm of forms," whereas "the imagination is a realm of dreams" (*HP* 179). The Imaginary Museum is the realm ruled by forms; it is not a place where dreams are assembled. A person's imaginary, like the imaginary of an era, contains the forms, the images, which inhabit that person or that era. The imaginary is a realm of creations; it is not a realm of phantasms.

While presenting the budget of the ministry of cultural affairs to the Parliament, or while inaugurating a *maison de la culture*, Malraux sometimes said that culture is "the knowledge of the greatest number of works of art by the greatest number of men" or yet that it was "the inheritance of the nobility of the world." At the time he was speaking in the way all those who have responsibility for cultural action speak, and he gave culture its earlier, limited meaning. On the other hand, when he responded to the question "What do you call a culture?"—"Let's call it the embodiment of a system of values; and more modestly an agreement of sensibilities" (*Preuves,* March 1955)—he was calling upon the more global and more recent notion of culture, the vast realm of ideas and feelings enveloped by the word "culture" when one speaks of Egyptian culture, of Mayan culture, of Celtic culture, etc. To avoid ambiguities concerning the word "culture" we must from now on always keep in mind that it can have two different meanings: the first is limited—the culture that must be made available so that everyone can be cultivated; and the other is global—the culture, that of an era or a civilization, which enables men of that era or civilization to have a common "agreement of sensibilities" (*Int* 295). Taken in this global sense culture ceases "to signify a degree of civilization, of refinement, and signifies the coherence unique to every civilization." It is the culture of an era that weaves the fabric from which are created all the aspects of civilization; it is culture—when it is one—that gives them their coherence. Like any other structure a mental structure must be organized by a force which organizes the relations between elements. Culture is the structuring force of mental structures.

At the same time that the history of civilizations begins to be written so has the history of cultures. These histories are already bringing to light what ancient cultures have hidden through their lack of universalism: "Every mental structure considers as absolute and unassailable any particular sign which directs life, and without which man could neither think nor act" (*WTA* 104–5). And Malraux could have added: nor feel. Thanks to the history of cultures it is possible today to realize that "humanity's successive psychic states are invariably different, because they do not affect, they do not exploit, do not involve the same *quality* of man" (*WTA* 112). That part of man which was cultivated by (involved in) Athenian culture and that part of man which was cultivated by (involved in) the Middle Ages when cathedrals were being built are always two radically different parts. The history of cultures brings to light the vast secular rotation of psychism. And in this vast twentieth-century crop rotation, the West, if not the entire world, will perhaps appear as an immense fallow field. A new "agreement of sensibilities" is being sought. And it is being painfully sought, for man would already like to know which part of himself will be involved when the metamorphosis of culture in progress is completed. This wish cannot be granted: one can attempt to foresee the outcome of an evolution, but it is useless to attempt to do so with a metamorphosis.

Malraux knew enough not to try. He knew that a culture, like a civilization, is always described after and never before the fact. Only the spinners of theories believe the opposite. But Malraux belonged to the great race of those who are inhabited by pre-vision (let us recall his surprise when he said: "Reality is beginning to resemble my novels"), by pre-sentiment, and he sensed some of the great realms of feelings which might perhaps direct the new agreement of sensibilities created by the culture of tomorrow. And any writer who attempts to follow his pre-sentiment comes up against one of his limitations which must surely be the most painful one: writing with today's words, he must try to foresee what they will mean tomorrow. In Heliopolis, Athens, Rome, and Chartres the word "death" has conjured up different and fundamental realms of feeling. And the realms of feeling conjured up by the word "death" in a Mayan Indian, an animistic African, a Zen monk, a Dominican, or a Hindi untouchable are just as different and fundamental. What realm of feelings will the word "life" conjure up tomorrow? And the word "love"? and "birth"? and "tree"? Will they conjure up a common realm for men of the same community? Or will it be accepted that the culture of a community can live with a plurality of realms of feelings awakened by each "big word"? Before responding, before talking about the new agreement of sensibilities that will give new meanings to words, we must cry out as Jean Tual does in his *Poèmes Cycliques:*

> Mots, je me laverai de vous,
> Ombres foraines
> Dont les déguisements ne se portent qu'un soir.[1]

If a culture can be characterized by the agreement of sensibilities it makes possible, then one of its roles, and undoubtedly its primary role, is to shape man. Malraux stressed this in Athens on May 28, 1959, at the time of the first illumination of the Acropolis: "One can't overstate this: What is encompassed in the very unclear word 'culture'—the totality of the creations of art and of the mind—we owe to Greece the honor of having made it a primary means of shaping man" (*OF* 38). Standing in

---

1. ["Words, I will be cleansed of you, / Itinerant shadows / Whose disguises are worn for one evening only."] From Jean Tual, "Le Chemin de diamant," in *Poèmes Cycliques,* illustrated by Claude Genisson (Paris: Ed. Saint-Germain-des-Prés, 1975).

front of the Acropolis Malraux rediscovered what he had proclaimed at the Congress for the Freedom of Culture in June 1952: "Culture thus appears to us as the knowledge of what makes man something other than an accident of the universe." He also rediscovered what he had confided to José Bergamin in May 1936: "What men express by the word culture is contained in a single idea: transform destiny into consciousness."

In *Felled Oaks: Conversations with de Gaulle* Malraux has General de Gaulle say: "Yesterday, when I was out walking, the shadow of the clouds was passing at my feet; and it occurred to me that fantasies belong to humanity in the same way that the clouds belong to the sky ... So I watch the fantasies pass by. I come indoors. I pick up these books again. They have survived and have perhaps shaped men, as successive gardeners have shaped my trees" (*FO* 104). We find the two meanings of culture perfectly joined here, one giving value to the other. Culture is the gardener of man, and every man, whether or not he is an educated scholar, is the product of a culture. Culture provides a man with the materials he uses to construct his psychological universe and to give himself shape. On this point, as well, the waning twentieth century might indeed appear as an era which had no culture, which allowed man to drift between fragmented shapes that, moreover, attempted in vain to overwhelm the cymas.

Caught up in a metamorphosis of culture whose very slow progress is measured on the scale of centuries, Western man, traveling from one form to another, "remains half-formed" (*L* 112). But there is something even worse: in the twentieth century, what has "begun to disappear is the shaping of man." Industrial civilization, despite the fantastic means at its disposal, cannot give shape to man, and doesn't attempt to do so. This absence of a "shaping of man" is constantly brought up, almost like an overpowering obsession, in most of Malraux's interviews, articles, and books during the last ten years of his life. And Malraux was one of the rare few who rightly sensed that at the very origin of the revolts of May 1968 were the anguish and the disgust in the presence of a civilization which was manufacturing an increasing number of machines when there was no culture to shape men.

Behind a civilization of the machine we see the more or less well-camouflaged influence of the scientific spirit as it was conceived in the eighteenth and especially the nineteenth century. Malraux was right to state: "Science is becoming an omnipotent god, half clandestine, and the arbiter of civilization throughout the world, whether it likes it or not ...

Culture: An Agreement of Sensibilities

Science can destroy the planet, but it can't fashion a man. The humane sciences illustrate this to perfection. Man is not what they posit, but what they seek" (*L* 112). And in the final pages of his last book, *Precarious Man*, Malraux gives an ultimate warning about how serious an absence of shaping for man truly is. Malraux doesn't question scientific method; he says it is approach, research, but not shaping. Scientific method, and the science it enables to develop, possesses "no ordering value" (*HP* 310). In itself, scientific knowledge has no formative power. "Man is no more readied for self-knowledge by science than he is for love by gynecology" (*HP* 311).

However, Malraux didn't have the time or the inclination to study in depth the meaning of the formidable change which, ever since the mid-twentieth century, had been occurring in science and in the minds of today's scientists, who are distancing themselves a little more each day from the minds of their predecessors. Of course today's engineers, those who design and build our environment, still remain marked by the spirit that reigned yesterday, but the true scientists of today are already approaching the spirit of tomorrow. And we will soon see just how the uncertainty and the probabilities of current physics, mathematics, and biology resolutely turn away from the certainties of yesterday. "The new scientific spirit" (cf. Bachelard) has become the most powerful accelerator of the metamorphosis of culture and the richest purveyor of the new agreement of sensibilities.

12

Discontinuous History

AS EARLY AS 1928 in his first novel, *The Conquerors,* Malraux clearly made the distinction between those who wish simply to destroy an obsolete historical situation—the reign of the bourgeoisie—and those who wish to destroy a human attitude, a way of thinking, a culture. Borodine wanted a political and social revolution; Garine aspired to cultural revolution. And Malraux was right, on June 8, 1929, during the public discussion on *The Conquerors,* to respond to those who criticized Garine: "It is not a matter of being right or wrong, but a matter of knowing whether the example provided by Garine acts effectively as ethical creation. Either it acts on the men who read it, or it doesn't. If it doesn't, *The Conquerors* raises no questions; but if it does, I am not arguing with my opponents; I will argue with their children" (Lacouture, 134).

The discussion over *The Conquerors* should be opened up again. The political friends Malraux had at that time, those who were opposed to Garine, were already his opponents. Like Borodine they felt that all ethics are conditioned by what is economic and social. The example provided by Garine could not act on them. It acts, however, on their children, as can already be seen. Many have said that great revolutionary leaders latch onto a character from a novel and force themselves to resemble him. It was thus, suggests Robert Payne, that Lenin identified more or less with Rakhmetev, the intellectual and uncompromising revolutionary created in 1863 by Chernikhovsky in his novel *What to do?* Perhaps tomorrow there will emerge a revolutionary leader who will think of Garine and Magnin, and who will blend in himself "the aptitude for action, culture, and lucidity."

Discontinuous History

Beginning in the 1930s Malraux opposed the old popularization of Hegelianism and Marxism which claimed that all ethics are reconditioned ("Culture," in *Liberté de l'esprit,* no. 1). Malraux didn't deny that there is "a historical datum of thought" (*Con* 183); he didn't deny that there is a certain conditioning of thoughts. But this historical datum does not resolve the problem, as Marxists would like; rather, it introduces the problem. Granted, after asserting that the means of production conditioned the shaping of consciousness, Marx recognized that consciousness could in turn act upon means of production. But for Marx consciousness could only act within the limits of its own dependency: by itself it could not break down the material conditioning which had brought it to life. For Malraux, on the contrary, when man's creative process "enters history, it is linked to history, and not dominated by it" (cf. *VOS* 416). Malraux says this while discussing artistic creation, but the same idea also applies to spiritual and intellectual creation. "*Insofar as he is a creator* the artist does not belong to a social group already molded by a culture, but to a culture which he is by way of building up. His creative faculty is not dominated by the age in which his lot is cast; rather it is a link between him and man's age-old creative drive . . ." (ibid.). All real, sincere artists know Malraux is right: an artist who doesn't accept his age, who doesn't force himself to be of another age, is forced to accede to the timeless; he forces himself to produce a creation that belongs to all ages.

Malraux did not underestimate the weight of economic and social conditions, nor the weight of facts upon ideas, nor the influence of economic and social structures on our consciousness; but he did not accept their constant power to condition ideas. Marxists could not accept this position, and, speaking for them, Aragon launched a violent attack following Malraux's lecture in November 1946 in the large hall of the Sorbonne for the inauguration of UNESCO. Malraux had declared at the time: "It is extremely unimportant for you students whether you are Communists, anti-Communists, liberal, or whatever else, because what is truly at issue is knowing beyond these structures upon what foundation we can recreate man." Aragon replied: "The shamelessness of the jargon against realities has rarely been carried so far." A few months later, in the journal *Esprit,* Albert Béguin described Malraux as "the only authentic French fascist" whereas Mounier wondered "anxiously whether some obscure alliance of unused fervor and invincible despair is not brewing that will throw the living forces of *Man's Hope* to a Europe in the clutches of the conspirators of fear." Involved in violent partisan struggles, and prisoners of the atmosphere resembling that of a "religious war" which pervaded at the time, no one understood that Malraux was giving absolute priority to the fight against all systems of thought and all political systems that subjected man's spirit to historical fatality.

Malraux's thoughts on the exact nature of the relations between facts and ideas, between infrastructures and superstructures, as Marxists would say, are more subtle than is often admitted. "I don't really believe," he told me in January 1972, "in institutions. Certainly they are of some importance, but they are not of decisive importance. Why? Because there is a rather bizarre relationship between institutions and the men who uphold them. The institutions of Sulla are not all that different from those of Caesar. It is the men who are different. There is a dialectic of institutions with the men of those institutions, and a dialectic of men with institutions." Rather than establishing a causal link in which facts dominate ideas, Malraux believed that there is a reciprocal relationship and permanent interaction between these two realms. Malraux picks up and amplifies the strong intuition Victor Hugo expressed in *Les Misérables:* "The history of morals and ideas interpenetrates the history of events, and vice versa. They are two orders of different facts, which answer to each other, which are always linked with and often produce each other ... Man is not a circle with a single center; he is an ellipse with two foci. Facts are one, ideas are the other" (*Les Misérables,* book 7, 1).

Victor Hugo's intuition impels us to distinguish two levels. On the spiritual level almost all traditions and religions use the circle or the sphere as a symbol of divine perfection or the divine realm. Inhabited either consciously or unconsciously by this symbol, many have continued, on a temporal level, to use the circle to represent social organization. For them, cultures and civilizations come out of a single center. If they are spiritualists, this center belongs to the realm of ideas; if they are materialists, it belongs to the realm of facts. Along with Victor Hugo both groups must agree that facts and ideas are two different orders of reality, and that the figure which best represents a society is a figure formed with two centers: the ellipse. The course followed by stars in sidereal space and that followed by the satellites man is now sending up there should help man to accept this elliptical representation of human societies.

Marx, whose ambition was to construct a global theory of mankind, lived in an age when science and thought were first attracted to the concept of energy and were above all obsessed by entropy or the dissipation of energy. Marx and his age were unaware of the concept of information as it is used in its current scientific, not its usual journalistic, sense. Unlike Victor Hugo, Marx didn't have an intuition of the role played by information, and, in his attempt to construct a global theory of mankind, he was unable to incorporate the organizing power of information. He could not account for the negentropy inherent in the power of information; that is, the power of information to oppose the dissipation of energy. If Marx had had an intuition of this power he would not have underestimated the organizing role of culture.

Another concept, which has become familiar to us even if we have not yet explored all its implications, was also unknown to Marx and his age: the role played by genetic codes in the organization of the structure of a living organism. If Marx had had this tool of knowledge and thought at his disposal he would have perhaps recognized that ideas possess a power of organization; he would have perhaps been able to admit that a cultural code could be to society what a genetic code is to the organism. Marxism and historical materialism deny this role, and this is why Stalin, when he cut short the Michurin/Lysenko controversy, was forced to decree that DNA was heretical.

For centuries Western thought, in seeking to know the world and discover the laws that govern it, has used the logic of univocal causality: the same cause, under the same conditions, produces the same effects. This logic, which seemed to account for relations in the infinitely large and in the infinitely small, was shown to be insufficient, then erroneous, when the infinitely complex began to be studied. We know today that the same conditions are never brought together and that the same apparent cause does not always produce the same effects. When Marx studied the infinitely complex, i.e., the social structure, when he developed the theory of scientific materialism, he didn't yet know that the logic of the structure is not classical logic. And he didn't have an intuition of it. By asserting that infrastructures condition superstructures, that facts govern ideas, Marx was applying to the social structure classical deterministic logic, which excluded retroaction and could not account for movements inside all structures.

As early as the 1920s, and thus well before the recent discoveries in particle physics, biology, and computer science were made, Malraux sensed that in every social structure a cultural code exercises an organizing power. This feeling guided and nourished the ideas in his two works of 1926 and 1927: *The Temptation of the West* and *Of a European Youth*. At the other end of his life, in the last volume of *The Metamorphosis of the*

Gods, Malraux makes a statement essential to the understanding of his profound thinking on history and the relations between culture and civilization: "When civilization changes, when it has transmitted or destroyed the values that wove the homogeneous and tightly knit fabric of what man constructs or manufactures, a special metamorphosis takes hold of the images man has created" (*Int* 130). If we agree that civilizations belong to the realm of facts, to the realm of what man constructs or manufactures, to the realm of infrastructures, and that cultures belong to the realm of ideas, values, superstructures, we then see that Malraux is proposing a dynamic and dialectical vision of the relationship between culture and civilization. Culture weaves the homogeneous and tightly knit fabric of the values out of which a civilization is constructed. A civilization transmits these values from generation to generation and can thus be seen as an inheritance or as capital to exploit. But the transmission of values brings about their progressive decline, and the more values decline, the more creators appear who do not belong to "a social group already molded by a culture, but to a culture which it is by way of building up" (*VOS* 416). These creators give birth to new images—a new culture—which progressively weave a new tightly knit and homogeneous fabric out of which a new civilization will be constructed. When we are in the phase during which civilization is transmitting undeteriorated values, then yes, the connection exposed by Marx does exist and facts do condition ideas. But when values have lost their strength, when like an energy they have become too degraded from being overtransmitted, then new images, forged by those who could no longer endure the old ones, take on an organizing power and give rise to new facts and a new civilization.

In the reality and complexity of a living being, the action of facts upon ideas and the action of ideas upon facts cannot be separated. There is no radical alternation. These two actions exist simultaneously, sometimes acting in the same direction, sometimes working against each other. When the values transmitted by civilization are not degraded, when facts and ideas move in the same direction, the two actions are joined. At such a moment the economic and the social strongly influence the cultural, and if creators forge new images, the latter have little hold over facts. On the other hand, when values are much degraded, old images are increasingly challenged and new images are increasingly accepted. As new images are diffused they acquire a power over facts, which resist at first and then give in. This vision of the influences—

Discontinuous History

sometimes convergent, sometimes opposed—of facts over ideas and of ideas over facts gives color to the slow movement of the centuries as Malraux unfolds it in *The Voices of Silence* and *The Metamorphosis of the Gods*. Malraux was not out to construct a theory based on this vision—that would not have been in his nature. But he did intend—and he accomplished this—to carry us over the threshold to a "dialectical history of cultures and civilizations." This is the history of the influences—sometimes convergent, sometimes opposing—of culture on civilization and of civilization on culture. It undoubtedly enables us to view the old conflict between spiritualism and materialism differently, and to see that, if there is a conflict, it is one not of antinomy, but of complementarity. Logically speaking, the conflict between the weight which causes blood to descend and the heart which causes it to rise is an antinomy; considering the logic which animates the vital flow this conflict is but the appearance assumed by a complementarity.

A careful reading of *Anti-Memoirs* shows that the complicity between Nehru and Malraux was metaphysically formed, whereas the complicity between Mao and Malraux was imbued with almost identical perceptions of the relations between culture and civilization. Let us recall the end of the long official conversation between Mao and Malraux. Malraux wants to take his leave of Mao, but the latter decides to accompany him to the parking lot. This is extraordinary. Preceded by the officials who were present at their dialogue, Mao and Malraux seem to be enjoying their private conversation in the long corridors, for they are finally able to broach in private the subject they both feel most strongly about. "The thought, culture, and customs which brought China to where we found her must disappear, and the thought, customs, and culture of proletarian China, which does not yet exist, must appear" (*A-M* 373–74). A bit earlier Mao had cited a statement made by Kosygin at the Twenty-third Congress: "Communism means the raising of living standards" (*A-M* 373), and had dismissed it in a sudden burst of temper. "Of course! And swimming is a way of putting on a pair of trunks!" (ibid.). Mao had also recalled that "Khrushchev seemed to think that a revolution is done when a communist party has seized power—as if it were merely a question of national liberation" (*A-M* 373) whereas Lenin "was well aware that at this juncture the revolution is only just beginning." Mao might have also cited this little-known statement by Lenin: "The political and social revolution in Russia preceded the cultural revolution which imposes itself on us. Today, all we need is to accomplish this cultural revolution in order to become a completely socialist country." Lenin would have surely shown less optimism than is reflected in his "all we need is" if he could have foreseen that a political and social revolution which had not been preceded by a cultural revolution would ultimately be stranded.

Mao had the time to experience how "thought, culture, customs must be born of struggle" and how "the struggle must continue for as long as there is still a danger of a return to the past" (*A-M* 374). Neither the denial of private ownership of the means of production nor the transformation of economic and social conditions can modify thought, culture, and customs. To modify them there has to be another struggle. And, arriving in front of the cars, Mao rather poignantly adds: "But in this battle we are alone . . . I am alone with the masses. Waiting" (*A-M* 375). Then Mao lucidly evokes his premonition of the dangers of revisionism and the tendencies that already prey on the minds of many young people:

Behind our entire conversation [Malraux comments] the hope of a twilight world stood watch. In the vast corridor, the dignitaries have stopped, without daring to turn around.

"I am alone," [Mao] repeats. And suddenly he laughs: "Well, with a few distant friends: please give General de Gaulle my greetings. As for them" (he means the Russians), "the revolution doesn't really interest them, you know." (*A-M* 376).

A few moments earlier Malraux had noted:

The man walking slowly by my side is haunted by something more than the uninterrupted revolution; by a gigantic conception of which neither of us has spoken: the underdeveloped countries are far more numerous than the countries of the West . . . The underdeveloped nations are at the same stage as the proletariat in 1848 . . . Proletariat will unite with capitalism, as in Russia, as in the United States. But there is one country . . . that will never lay down its arms, will never lay down its spirit, before the global confrontation . . . the Chinese era is dawning. (*A-M* 376)

China's current return to norms of economic efficiency and its tactical rapprochement with the USSR seem to belie this monumental thought. But let us not jump to conclusions! Before the end of the twentieth century we will perhaps have proof to the contrary.

When Mao, instructed by twenty years of power, considered it necessary to set the cultural revolution in motion, he inflicted the rudest awakening on orthodox Marxists, who continued to assert that facts conditioned ideas, above all, he represented the most dangerous challenge to those who were hiding—increasingly ineffectively—behind a once revolutionary Marxism classical imperialism and cultural conservatism. Within the last few decades the monumental struggle, of which we have as yet heard only the first grumblings, between the cultural revolution and cultural reactionaries has been taking shape. On this battleground, as well, liberal and popular democracies are objective allies; this is possibly one of the reasons why there is so much free trade between them and why some are so generous in their financing of the foreign trade of others. In liberal democracies those who uphold the old economic and social order react in an attempt to prevent new images from engendering new economic and social facts. In popular democracies the official culture seeks to stifle any cultural manifestation which threatens to undermine political and economic facts. Everywhere, cultural reactionaries, relying on the myth of economy and efficiency, seek to halt the metamorphosis of culture.

Malraux considered it absolutely necessary to reiterate in the preface to the second volume of *The Metamorphosis of the Gods* part of what he had already written for the preface to the first volume. In doing so he wished to respond to all those who had erroneously read the first volume as a history of art: "I thus refer here to the end of the general introduction: I have attempted to make the world intelligible, a world for the first time victorious over time, over the images that human hands created to defy time ... The object of this book is neither a history of art nor a study of aesthetics, but rather an attempt to discover the significance of the fact that throughout the ages man has always sought an answer to the problem raised by the spark of eternity latent in him. Everyone understood the significance of *Remembrance of Things Past* when *Time Regained* came out after Proust's death. Perhaps the significance of this book will not be fully understood until after the publication of the next and final volume" (*Ir* v; cf. *MG* 35). All those who have criticized Malraux for writing a disorganized history of art by basing his work more or less on that of Elie Faure have misread *The Imaginary Museum, Artistic Creation, The Coin of the Absolute,* and *The Voices of Silence.* They have also misread Malraux's earlier works, including his novels; otherwise they would have seen that Malraux didn't believe in history, or at least not in the history that since the nineteenth century has been invading Western thought.

When one rereads *The Voices of Silence* carefully, and especially in the light of *The Timeless,* one sees how Malraux demonstrates that the history born in the nineteenth century is the result, fortunately temporary, of a long process of thought. In Byzantium the Pantocrator was not a god-turned-man, but a majestic god whose throne was in the world above and who endlessly reminded man that the world below was the kingdom of appearances from which man had to escape if he wished to accede to truth. With Roman and especially Gothic Christianity God went from majesty to helpfulness: the God-turned-man, the mystery of the Incarnation and its corollary—the cult of the Virgin Mother—became the center of the divine mystery; the world was no longer one of appearances, but one of the redeemed creation in which everyone could hope to forge salvation from his own individuality. Man's relationship with the divine became individualized: sin and fatality took root in man, and with them anxiety. Expanded in the Renaissance, the exaltation of the individual led the Christian to turn from the Eternal to Jesus, to turn from the majesty of the Father to the mercy of the Son-turned-man. Carrying on this evolution of the divine toward the human, the eighteenth century sought to resolve the problem of man without referring to the divine. The eighteenth century replaced self-possession obtained through an agreement with God with an accumulation of knowledge as a means to self-realization. The directing value was no longer God or Being; it fragmented into humanist values which restored all things to man and which led him to seek an explanation of the world in history rather than in the divine. "History, which now obsesses Europe, much as Buddha's pyrrhonism disintegrated Asia, was coming into its own. No longer a mere chronicle of events, it was becoming an anxious scrutiny of the past for any light it might cast on the dark vista of the future" (*VOS* 541).

Throughout his entire life Malraux was surprisingly consistent in his feelings about history. In 1932 he remarked that all European thought was reduced to "a secret of fabrication." "Temporarily the two great secrets are Comte and Marx, the secret of the cure for metaphysics and the secret of History" (*Nouvelle Revue Française*, January 1932). In 1939, in his *Outline of a Psychology of Film*, he stressed the extent to which Europe had substituted history for annals. In 1943 he created the discussions among intellectuals at the Altenburg colloquium concerning the meaning of history. In 1951 in *The Voices of Silence*, notably toward the end of the book, he meditated at length on the use of art as a means to understand "the song of history" (*VOS* 624). In the final years of his life and in his last two books he frequently reconsidered the exact nature and meaning of "the attempt to make the human adventure which we call history intelligible" (*HP* 45). But it is unquestionably an article Malraux

Discontinuous History

wrote in 1950 which most succinctly sums up his thoughts on history: "Every history is that of an evolution or an intelligible fatality; every history tends to turn the past into a destiny, filled with hope, as in that of Bossuet, Hegel or Marx, or with death, as in that of Spengler" (*Liberté de l'esprit,* June 1950).

The fact that history has become an attempt to render the human adventure intelligible isn't enough to explain why it has taken possession, so quickly and so profoundly, of the human spirit. In truth, history's strength and its fascination come from the fact that it "pigeonholes each religion within a temporal context, thus depriving it of its value as an absolute, a value which syncretic systems such as theosophy are obviously unable to replace" (*VOS* 609). History no longer teaches only the "We Civilizations, we know we are mortal," it also proclaims: "You others, Religions, recognize that you are mortal!" History seemed to have acquired a longer life than religions had, and it derived its strength from that appearance of endurance, it believed it could also derive an absolute from that appearance: the meaning of history. Malraux had to separate himself from those for whom "history aims merely at transposing destiny onto the plane of consciousness" (*VOS* 623), and he concluded *The Voices of Silence* with a reminder that many still refuse to hear: "Hercules' new adversary and Destiny's most recent incarnation is history; but though created by history, man as revealed in the museum is little more historical than the gods of old . . . The vast realm of art which is emerging from the ocean of the past is neither eternal nor extraneous to history; . . . being at once involved in it and breaking free from it" (*VOS* 635).

In all Malraux's works, in his novels as well as in his works of nonfiction, one senses the presence of another notion of history—a notion he neither defines nor specifies, for he is neither a theoretician nor a philosopher, but a notion he perceives with his sensibility, one that he "presenses." "The word 'History' is rather dangerous," he wrote in June 1971 in *Le Magazine littéraire* before continuing: "I would be more inclined to say that Valéry was the enemy of historians more than the enemy of history because, whether one likes it or not, we must indeed conceive of the world as history. Not necessarily 'History' in the sense the word had in the nineteenth century, but History all the same. We have touched on a crucial problem: Can one have a conception of the world which is absolutely foreign to all meaning? I am prepared rather to say that Valéry was an agnostic of History." Since the decline of Christendom Western man has looked to history for the meaning of mankind. But for Malraux it isn't history that gives man his meaning, but rather man who gives meaning to historical facts. History has no meaning. There is no "meaning of History"; there are only historical facts which man attempts to interpret, to endow with meaning. For Malraux there is no acceleration of history, either. During our conversation of January 1972 Malraux expressed that idea, and I told him why it left me rather skeptical. "You are right," he clarified. "I simply wanted to say that I concede to gainsayers the theory of the acceleration of history, which is not absurd; essentially what you say is true ... Events follow one another more rapidly. I can accept that. It's just that what I believe is that that isn't very important."

To admit that history has meaning, direction, is to admit that one must go in that direction and must submit oneself to it; but in that case fatality triumphs over will. "In Marxism there is the sense of a fatality, and also the exaltation of a will. Every time fatality comes before will, I'm suspicious" (*MF* 147). The word "history" is dangerous because man, when he thinks he possesses the meaning of history, no longer looks at the world in and by itself, he sees it as a moment in a historical process, and he explains everything he sees in it by that process. Rather than keeping itself open to life, man's mind can only be guided; instead of acting creatively, his will is henceforth suppressed. Fatality truly triumphs over will, and one must wonder whether it is not at that moment that the slow work of decadence begins. In the second century B.C. Polybius had already propounded a theory of history which justified Roman imperialism and gave Rome, for a certain time, a preferential mortgage on the future. This was the first time an interpretation of history was invoked to justify a political order. At the beginning of *Precarious Man* Malraux evokes "the provocative imperialism of all history of literature" (*HP* 8), and so he makes us wonder whether all history, the very notion of history, isn't imperialistic. The *Annales* certainly were not.

In an interview with Victor Franco, Malraux revealed his very personal attitude toward history: "I perceive History as an interrogation, or a metamorphosis ... Shakespeare's History is not of the same nature as that of historians ... I feel I look at History in a state of constant wonderment, as Shakespeare looked at what he chose ... This state is much more common than we believe, and this is one of the reasons for my audience" (*Journal du Dimanche*, 28 November 1976). That last remark should make us stop and think. Malraux's constant wonderment in the presence of history and his perception of history as a metamorphosis provide hope for everyone who is weary of a linear and unsurprising view of history, of a history which claims to be an answer and not an interrogation, of a history which presents itself as a logical, rational evolution, and not as an ever-astonishing metamorphosis. Malraux provides hope for everyone who is weary of a history which imposes itself as a fatality. This hope also explains his audience and his legend.

During the Altenburg colloquium Möllberg tells how after spending years and years collecting vast documentation in preparation for his work on historical continuity he had thrown every page of his book into the wind during a trip to Africa, when he had learned that continuity didn't exist. Incensed, Stieglitz, one of the participants in the colloquium, stands up and interrupts Möllberg:

"But just a minute! Just a minute, now! The main line of Hegelianism remains intact. The point at issue is the integration in the *Weltgeist* of the facts acquired through our new knowledge, and I can't for the life of me see why what you call the human adventure should not become a history, just as the history of Germany is a history, although consisting of elements which at first glance seem heterogeneous." (*WTA* 112)

"With the suppressed fury of an incurable to whom one has incautiously mentioned his disease" Möllberg replies that he himself had asserted this continuity for years but that, now, he understands how "humanity's successive psychic states are invariably different, because they do not affect, do not exploit, do not involve the same *quality* of man" (ibid.).

In his speech at the Sorbonne for UNESCO Malraux took up this theme and stressed, once again, that the value systems of civilizations were not continuous or progressive. In the first volume of *The Metamorphosis of the Gods* Malraux clarifies his thoughts on this issue and for the first time uses the expression "discontinuous history" (*MG* 32). He thus encourages us to abandon a continuous view of a history governed by a concept, whatever it might be, and to adopt a discontinuous view of a history subject to metamorphosis. "A 'continuous' history ... premises a constant progress, broken though it may be by tragic setbacks" (*MG* 31–32), but we now know that the statues on cathedrals "do not culminate" in Michelangelo's *Night,* that Villon does not culminate in Rimbaud, nor Van Gogh in Braque, and that Athens is not the childhood of Rome. "'Discontinuous' history, the history of civilizations, as formulated in the present century, answers to a feeling profoundly different from that of the continuous history which preceded it. In the latter Egypt used to be identified with the childhood of humanity; whereas in the eyes of the modern historian Egypt represents a form of humanity that has had its day" (*MG* 32).

A continuous view of history is satisfactory for a rational mind, but it corresponds to nothing in reality. In an interview cited by Walter G. Langlois in *Malraux: Life & Work*, Malraux points out what we all know: "The moments in a man's life do not add up in orderly accumulation. Biographies which run from the age of five to fifty are false confessions."[1] The Imaginary Museum has shown how "the continuity of the individual is but an illusion" (*Int* 136). Psychoanalysis, as well. Man easily accepts that there is no continuity in the individual, and he even derives a certain satisfaction from this. But he persists in refusing to accept this discontinuity in the history of individuals, and he invents a Moloch in order to attribute historical continuity to it, a continuity he believes he still needs. This illogical desire to impose continuity on the discontinuous still conditions and influences many decisions in life: the taste for memoirs, for example, but also the organization of education. Educational programs are inspired by a continuous and chronological view of the human adventure. On the subject of poetry Malraux writes, "The student who is sensitive to poetry does not discover poets from the beginning of time to the present; he discovers them in a discontinuous chronology, one governed by their affinities, one which doesn't start at the beginning of time, but precisely in the present—from Verlaine to Villon and not from Villon to Verlaine" (*HP* 8). This is valid not only for literature and music but also for historical events. The gap between the chronological continuity of educational programs and the discontinuity each one of us carries within will most probably be discovered to be one of the explanations for the profound malaise of young people in elementary and high schools as well as in universities in the second half of the twentieth century. On the one hand their magazines, televisions, and microcomputers offer them the means of acquiring knowledge through a succession of discontinuous affinities; on the other hand educational programs at all levels impose a respect for an artificial and conventional continuity. The gap can only be enormous.

Literary and scientific creation—all creation—"turns things upside down rather than bringing them to perfection" (*AC* 233). Why would we want historical creation alone to perfect? "The essence of creation is a break with the past" (*VOS* 623). The essence of history, too. And Mal-

---

1. [In *Malraux: Life and Work*, edited by Martine Courcel (London: Weidenfeld & Nicolson, 1976), p. 19.]

raux invites us to learn all our lessons from the fact that "we no longer believe that a chronology of events (and which ones?) suffices to establish a History, because a History doesn't go beyond chronology unless it becomes an interpretation of the human adventure; no chronology in itself contains Hegelianism, Marxism, or theories of culture" (*Ir* v). Just as earlier ages built places of worship—temples, churches, mosques—where men went to connect with the cosmos, the nineteenth and twentieth centuries, because they believed they had found an explanation of mankind in History, transformed the palaces of the past—museums, libraries, historical monuments—into sanctuaries. But these palaces have revealed in only a few decades how the continuity of the past is only an illusion, and how history is a succession of "invariably different" psychic states (*WTA* 112).

When the human mind will have disengaged itself from a continuous view of history it will be able to free itself both from the pessimism of the young Valéry and the temptation to rely conveniently and dangerously on "a direction to history." For everyone who has already accepted the transformations of man's sensibility which the histories of civilizations and cultures have brought about, for everyone who has allowed the transformations brought about by reproductions of all works of art from all countries and all time to operate within them, Valéry's "vanished worlds" and "sunken empires" are no more the childhood of a continuous history than they are the ghosts of an inexplicable history. Elam, Nineveh, Babylonia are no longer "beautiful, hazy names," as they were for Valéry, nor are they promising young children, as they were for Marx. They are moments in the history of humanity that do not involve the same *part* of man, moments that are invariably different.

In his last work Malraux seems to have presented a new perspective on the discontinuity of history. He alludes to the "parallel society in which Rastignac becomes more historical than Guizot, and Vautrin more historical than Louis-Philippe" (*HP* 99). Through this incidental remark Malraux invites us to extend the notion of appearance, already familiar in philosophy and theology, to the realm of history. In his preceding book, *The Timeless,* at the end of his meditation on art and creative power, Malraux was led, as Nietzsche had been through other paths, to look once again at the world of appearances. Today everyone is finally admitting that the goal of the Renaissance artist painting a *Madonna and Child,* or of Rembrandt working on *Nightwatch,* or of Goya drawing *Los Caprichos,* was not to imitate, but to express another world using forms that appeared in their own. For many readers already, and perhaps for everyone tomorrow, Rastignac, Vautrin, Julien Sorel, Raskolnikov, Madame Bovary, and Roquentin have become individuals whose presence is more real than that of many individuals encountered in real life. These fictional characters, for a true reader, possess a real presence which is denser and of a different nature from that of the presences perceived within the multiple relations of daily life. For those readers Rastignac is, in fact, more historical than Guizot, and Vautrin more than Louis-Philippe, in the same way that the landscape behind the *Mona Lisa* has become more real for us than the landscapes which existed at the time Leonardo da Vinci painted. One must, therefore, be prepared to extend to the realm of literature that which is admitted for painting: Guizot and Louis-Philippe belong to the historical landscape of their era; Rastignac and Vautrin belong to the world which endures from metamorphosis to metamorphosis and which is no longer the world of appearances. At this point historians will protest, just as art historians have protested against *The Imaginary Museum*. For everyone else the evidence will be accepted: Guizot and Louis-Philippe have entered into the past, as do all appearances, whereas Rastignac and Vautrin have entered into the world of presence. Through his discontinuous perception of history, which joins our corpuscular and discontinuous perception of even the densest matter, and through the demonstration of a world in which Delacroix and Rastignac become more historical than Guizot, Malraux invites us to see that in history there is historical appearance just as in metaphysics there is physical appearance.

For a historian, Rembrandt and Van der Helst are seventeenth-century painters. For an artist, and for anyone who is sensitive to art, "there is nothing in common between the historical survival of Van der Helst, which is a result of his testimony and is related to the survival of a document, and the *presence* of Rembrandt" (*Int* 131). Every artist knows that there is an evolution of humanity and of painting, but "what he admires about Tintoretto escapes this evolution and belongs to a world in which Tintoretto, Poussin, Delacroix, and Manet are simultaneously present. Determinisms legitimize the succession and the plurality of styles, but they in no way account for the existence of *the* style ... *The history of art cannot give an account of the world of art*" (*Int* 132). In historians' history determinisms also attempt to legitimize the succession and the plurality of civilizations and cultures, but the history which results from that cannot give an account of Man.

In *The Myth of Sisyphus*, Camus justified his commitment by proclaiming: "Given History and the Eternal I chose History because I like certainty. At least I am sure of history, and how can I deny that force which crushes me. There is God or time, this cross or that sword." Nor did Malraux have an Eternal. Malraux, too, had a personal involvement in historical events; but for Malraux history was never a force which crushed man, and he always proclaimed in one form or another: "The soul of history, underneath the Roman armor or Gandhi's robes, is human will" (*Rassemblement*, 26 June 1948). However, Malraux's "will" in no way resembles Hegelian will. Throughout his entire life and in all his works Malraux always sought to give man back what many philosophies of history had taken from him, and he always repeated that history depends on man, not man on history. For Malraux what we call history is the incarnation of human will.

That successive forms of the incarnation of human will are discontinuous, that they are invariably different, that they do not involve the same part of man will not surprise those who "have become aware of Metamorphosis as Universal Law" (*Le Monde*, 15 March 1974). It is obvious to them that Malraux's view of history in no way resembles that of Spengler, although such a claim has often been made. In *Precarious Man* Malraux is explicit on this subject: "The Imaginary Museum first seems rather Spenglerian. But not for long, because for Spengler every culture is destined to die, whereas for the Museum every great style is destined for metamorphosis" (*HP* 220).

Once again we are forced to note that Malraux is proposing a rather exciting view of man. But this view is equally rather demanding, because for Malraux no predetermination, no divinity in the usual sense of the term, no Leviathan, no historical materialism, no nothingness is available to make excuses for man. And this is why Malraux was able to say: "There is something more important than History; it is the constancy of genius" (*Arts*, 5 June 1952). We mustn't define genius here as it has been defined in the nineteenth and twentieth centuries; we must define it as Malraux does: "The work of genius is not a mere lucky fluke but an act of autonomous creative power" (*VOS* 614). Man believed history was very important because after he stopped appealing to religions, man asked history to render the human adventure intelligible. Having recourse to a transcendent god made Western man so accustomed to seeking an explanation outside himself and the world that he did the same with history and first conceived of it as being external to man. Malraux rejected the sort of history in which man is the product, and he tried to convince us that what is most important is not the succession of appearances seen as the incarnation of human will, but rather the constancy of man's exercise of autonomous creative power.

"Those obsessed with history are also obsessed with time . . ." (*Le Magazine littéraire*, July 1971). Malraux was seventy years old when he made this statement in an interview with Jean Vilar. He responded at that time with strength and wisdom to the question he had asked himself thirty years earlier, and which Möllberg raises during the Altenburg colloquium: There is undoubtedly something behind history. Is it "perhaps our consciousness of time" (*WTA* 105)? In the first volume of *The Metamorphosis of the Gods* Malraux stresses that the world of history and the world of art are "akin yet adverse" (*MG* 31) even though they were born together. Both of them have been haunting the West "ever since their joint influence caused the world of faith to disappear." They have been haunting the West "ever since a sequence of philosophies, voicing that *sense of time* which seems to be an obsession with our present age . . . has taught us to see in Time man's chief [interlocutor]." Man at the end of the twentieth century, who seems weary of a linear, continuous history, also seems just as weary of having time as his chief interlocutor. And we must remember here Camus' cry in *The Myth of Sisyphus:* "The absurd man is he who does not separate himself from time."

By accepting the historical view that has developed since the nineteenth century, by agreeing to have chronological time as their chief interlocutor, men have conceived of themselves as "men of a special period" (*VOS* 631) and no longer "simply as men" (*HP* 293). In the world of art what causes a painting, a sculpture, a sonata, or a novel created in the near or distant past to become a work of art is its presence. It is presence which separates the work of art from the object and which separates it "thus from history" (ibid.). The object belongs to a particular time; the work of art belongs to all time. Objects belong to "a passing of time related to chronology" (*Int* 126); works of art escape that passing time. By turning man into a "man of a special period" history and chronological time have turned him into an "object" also ruled by chronology. And a revealing similarity in vocabulary here highlights words favored by a whole trend in philosophy: object, objectification. By accepting time as a chief interlocutor man has been turned into an object, and he is rebelling today because he feels and he knows that he is *also* a subject.

"Outside our biographical life there exists a self-consciousness that is indifferent to chronology" (*Int* 134), and this is why man cannot ac-

Discontinuous History

cept being considered as an object ruled by "the passing of time related to chronology." The consciousness we have of ourselves is not chronological, or if it is, it is so only occasionally. It sometimes becomes so because the consciousness others have of us is always chronological, except in love or friendship. "Every man's life is chronological for others" (ibid.). Time is the means others use to get to know us, exactly as it was for a long time the means physicists used to learn about the universe. Time is a means used for investigation and knowledge, but the image it gives is deformed, because that image is built upon chronology and cannot correspond to nonchronological reality. Or, in other terms, chronological time can account for the succession of appearances; it cannot account for inner reality, which is not chronological. As Goethe demonstrated, to say that the fruit comes after the flower is an artifice of thought and language which can be useful provided one remains aware that this artifice corrupts reality because the fruit is contained within the plant even before the flower blooms.

In 1967 Malraux replied to Emmanuel d'Astier: "Man is not constructed chronologically" (*Evénement,* September 1967). In 1976 he clarified his thought by writing: "[F]or all men events converge more than they follow one another. The West has become used to calling chronological time history, which makes rather simple problems insoluble" (*Int* 135; cf. *HP* 282). Although depth psychology has shown how chronology has come apart inside us, history still claims that the past of all men is a historical and chronological past; it attempts to have man live within a unique and linear notion of time, whereas man, as we now know, can live within notions of time that are very different from each other. The expression "in that time" found in the Gospels expressed a notion of time that "gathered together the past of chronicles when necessary" (ibid.), but which turned all those pasts into avatars. "In that time" was in a certain sense an "eternal time." Centuries with faith had man live in this "eternal time." History makes men live in a particular and linear time. The attack on chronological time has begun. It has begun through the contemporary novel, as Malraux shows in *Anti-Critique.* It has also begun in the most recent of films. Curiously enough, biography, which in its current conception still obeys the rules of chronology, is very successful in bookstores when at the same time a great number of novels and films refuse to obey chronology any longer. The paradox is only apparent, because these biographies do not have the same audience that the novels and films have. Today's biographies and autobiographies satisfy an audience which has not yet freed itself of the view of history inherited from the nineteenth century. This audience likes memoirs and does not yet understand *Anti-Memoirs*.

The attack on chronological time has begun because it could not maintain for very long the status-favored interlocutor which science and then history had given it. Sooner or later its usurpation had to burst apart in broad daylight since, as Bergson, whom Malraux cites, wrote: "The intemporal is inside us, and in it we find a less falsified, a more real awareness of ourselves and the world" (*Int* 135). Malraux adds to this fundamental statement: "This is undoubtedly why we have endowed upon images which are today called works of art the life foreign to chronological time which was once the life of the supernatural, of eternity, of immortality." And yet if we truly carry the intemporal within us, why have we had to wait so long for it to emerge? It is because the essence of the intemporal is the "questioning of time" (*Int* 138), and because all cultures and civilizations before ours assigned religions the task of questioning time. Through a formidable collective transfer men conferred to the gods the intemporal they carried within them and which life itself carries within. Men asked the gods to undertake the questioning of time for them. Today, aided by the scientific spirit, which no longer assigns time the favored role science had given it for so long, man takes it upon himself to question time. This is not the least important reason for the angst which takes hold of certain insufficiently prepared souls. One does not easily make contact with the relativity of time and with the intemporal when they have been hidden for so long. The reversal of the situation is complete: historical and chronological time, which had assumed primary roles and dethroned religious absolutes by also inscribing them in time and history, through that fact alone prepared the conditions for its own abdication, for it is that time which has enabled man finally to hear the intemporal he carries within and no longer to go looking for it outside himself.

The intemporal was long in emerging because "the intemporal is a remains" (*Int* 138). We must assign the same meaning to "remains" that alchemists give it. Indeed, Malraux immediately clarified: The intemporal "becomes what it is when it is no longer dissolved in the eternal or in the unreal." When in his internal crucible man has dissolved then burned the ashes of chronology, he then discovers the pure "remains" and can then realize the intemporal he carries within. We are experiencing "the Epiphany of the Intemporal" (ibid.). Malraux employed this powerful expression, which should make anyone who can fully feel it

Discontinuous History

sing with joy and happiness, immediately after he exposed "the shattered chronology" we see on television screens, and, I will add, in many novels and on many movie screens. This is a good opportunity to remark that the great developments in audiovisual technology, made possible through the technological advances of the end of the twentieth century, have brought about rediscoveries rather more than they have created an innovation; if there is innovation it resides in the breadth of the phenomenon and not in its nature. For millennia, humanity lived within an oral tradition which did not exclude libraries but which did limit them. An oral tradition is audiovisual. For several centuries, no more than four or five, the rise of the printing press led to the belief that humanity would henceforth live in a written tradition. This is wrong. Audiovisuals of the past, those of oral tradition, enabled man to enter into a vast time frame, which was sometimes eternal, sometimes motionless. The audiovisual technology of today and tomorrow, by way of its small and large screens, will shatter chronology and gradually open the doors of the intemporal to all men.

Ever since man has been able to inherit all cultures and civilizations, everyone knows, and often intuits, that there isn't just one but several notions of time. Everyone knows the time of the Middle Ages, which was an "everlasting present" (*WTA* 106) when a cyclical flow of time reigned, "in which a Christmas day was closer to all former Christmas days than to the day that preceded it in the calendar and in human life" (*Int* 125). Everyone is familiar with chronological time in which the flow of time is linear. Everyone is familiar with the time in which "it takes twenty-eight kingships of Indras to complete a day and a night of Brahma" (*A-M* 181), that in which the flow of time seems immobile like "a continuity without history" (cf. *VOS* 30). Everyone also senses that a new perception of time will be born of the physics and mathematics of the twentieth century, of space/time in which space and time are measured in the same unit. Many people, if not everyone, have already become aware of the arbitrariness which has ensured that since Aristotle time has been measured by means of movement and movement by means of time. Anyone who has already worked on his perception of time can affirm that on demand he can sometimes feel one of these times, sometimes another, and sometimes even another. It has become possible today to admit and to accept the fact that time, like perspective, is a simple convention of the mind, perspective being relative to space. Time is not a reality but an instrument forged by the mind to enable communication, exchange, the comparison of personal experiences which would otherwise be untransmittable. Time is an instrument forged by the mind to objectify perceptions.

Knowing that man can live with invariably different notions of time, accepting that time is a convention created by the mind, we can then allow the intemporal we carry within to emerge, and completely accept "a-chronism." The world of art, as we understand it today, that is, the world of "the presence in our lives of what should belong to death" (*HP* 293), has prepared us for this acceptance. When we can simultaneously admire the sculptures of Sumer, those of the Parthenon, and those of Chartres, when we feel within ourselves the simultaneous presence of Aeschylus, Villon, Shakespeare, and Goethe, "it is art penetrating into a realm which we don't call eternity but which we truly experience as an 'a-chronism'" (ibid.). For millennia, in an attempt to attain "a-chronism," man has sought to assume the essential attribute he had endowed upon the gods—immortality—the immortality which the labors of Heracles, his pyre, and his marriage to Hebe promised to any man who was worthy of conquering it, the immortality which had become eternity, that which the Resurrection of the flesh and holy communion promised to Christians. Today man can attain "a-chronism" by becoming aware of the intemporal he carries within.

A work of art which spans the centuries doesn't belong just to its own age but to all ages. It doesn't express just the notion of time which was prevalent when the artist who created the work lived; it also contains and expresses all notions of time possessed by everyone who has looked at it and who will look at it as a work of art. An Egyptian sculpture and a contemporary sculpture, a Fra Angelico and a Braque, a tragedy by Aeschylus and a play by Brecht all encompass the times of their creators as well as the times of the people who admire and internalize them. Works of art belong to the intemporal as do the Christian saints who incorporate both the time in which live the devout who pray to them and the "eternal time" of divine eternity in which they participate and of which they are the favored mediators. By enabling us to sense either clearly or indistinctly that it encompasses all times, a work of art reveals the intemporal we all carry within. The work reveals it but does not unveil its nature. It brings it to light but renders it even more mysterious.

To admit that a man shaped by a linear notion of time can enter into fellowship both with a *Nativity* painted by an artist whose notion of time was cyclical and with a Buddha head from which emanates the artist's entire notion of an almost motionless time forces one also to admit that all these different times, although they are invariably different, are times

Discontinuous History

which can also enter into fellowship. We are then seeking *the all-encompassing* that contains them. Since the establishment of the Imaginary Museum the immobility of the Sphinx, the immortality of Zeus, the avatars of Vishnu, the eternity of Jesus, the cycles of the *Popol-Vuh*, can no longer be the "all-encompassing" containing all time within themselves. All have become particular expressions of the intemporal; of that intemporal we feel inside but whose mystery becomes increasingly deeper the more it is revealed to us. It is certainly in this way that the very enigmatic statement with which Malraux concludes the three volumes of *The Metamorphosis of the Gods* must be interpreted: "Born together, the Imaginary Museum, art's enigmatic value, and the intemporal, will undoubtedly all die together. And man will then see that neither is the intemporal eternal."

In the speech he delivered in Mougins after the inauguration of the exhibition "Malraux and the Museum Without Walls" organized by the Fondation Maeght, Malraux declared that each person's own Imaginary Museum was an "All-Encompassing, which has taken the place of nature or of God" (*PM* 220). Few statements have provoked as much thought, sensibility, and imagination. In the Imaginary Museum the power which triumphs is not one of the powers found outside of man in which he has put his trust for so long. Nor is it the power to seduce which for a time—fortunately brief—art was believed to possess. No! In the Imaginary Museum the power evoked is "the creative power," "the power to conquer time through its irresistible intermittence of which metamorphosis has made us aware." The creative power that sings in the Imaginary Museum "establishes the metaphysical power of art." The Imaginary Museum doesn't create the intemporal, it unveils it. In unveils the fact that creative power belongs to the intemporal.

Malraux prudently points out that man has perhaps "sensed a distancing in space and time in a biological way just as he once felt the dawn and the birth of the day" (*Int* 386). With the twentieth century the feeling of distance in space has disappeared. The airplane, the written press, and televised news have brought a sense of spatial proximity, even to those who don't travel. The sense of temporal proximity, on the other hand, has not yet been achieved by everyone, and it remains a privilege, despite the condensing of time made available through museums, libraries of books and records, and video libraries. To sense the closeness of all time, as one feels close to all cities, remains the privilege of those who have been able to liberate themselves from a chronological and continuous view of history. For Malraux the sense of distance in time exists no more than does the sense of distance in space, and in this he most probably prefigures one of the essential characteristics of the sensibility and the culture of tomorrow. While reading *The Voices of Silence*, *The Metamorphosis of the Gods*, or *Precarious Man*, one can't help being troubled at first, then seduced by the overwhelming presence of Malraux, friend to all ages. He is as close to Rembrandt as he is to Picasso. He talks about the time of Chartres or the time of Tutankhamon the way he talks about his own time. He internalizes every age as if he has lived in it, and doesn't simply ponder it as a scholar would. Malraux accumulated vast knowledge of the facts and events of all ages, but this knowledge was only food for his sensibility. He communed with the art of an age as one might commune with the heart and mind of a loved one. Art historians have reproached him for this. It was impossible for there to have been a dialogue between them and Malraux. For art historians art is matter for the accumulation of knowledge which they consider objective. For Malraux the world of art is the realm of communion, and he has no use for an objectivity which is often only the screen of objectification. Communion is first comprehension, that is, a communal way to perceive. It is not nourished by objectivity, which, however, doesn't mean that it isn't fed on lucidity and tolerance. Malraux never presented his perception and his comprehension of all art of all times as the only true ones. But he had the testimony of his senses, nourished by all the knowledge he had gathered. And everyone knows that the testimony of a lucid subject carries more weight than does the report of an observer who claims to be neutral and objective, yet never is.

To all those whose sensibility enables them *truly* to enter into the world of art, the Imaginary Museum offers a communion which is stronger than time and stronger than death. Like the communion of the saints, the Imaginary Museum proposes a fellowship in the undying creative power of man, in the undying creative power of life, in the genesis always at work. The Christian knew very well that St. John lived before St. Francis, but he communed with them in the eternity of Christ. Malraux knew that Rembrandt lived before Cézanne, but he communed with them in the intemporal. Rational minds who always favor knowledge acquired by the mind over consciousness brought about through sensibility cannot accept this fellowship in an "a-chronism" of that which, for them, is only successive. And yet, if they truly looked inside themselves they would see, in a disturbing simultaneous presence, the communion of the immobile smile of the Buddha and the enigmatic smile of the Mona Lisa, the questioning of Hamlet and the challenge of Faust.

Discontinuous History

It was impossible for Malraux to write a chronological autobiography; it would have been foreign to his perception of the world and life. Memoirs, which are based on chronology, are distorting mirrors. Our age accepts them, even studies them carefully, for they provide the illusion of possessing time. Malraux didn't need this illusion since he had liberated himself from time. And when he specifies that he called the book of his life *Anti-Memoirs* "because it answers a question which memoirs do not pose, and does not answer those which they do" (*A-M* 8), he leaves us to understand that the question memoirs attempt to answer is one which doesn't interest him. To seek to repossess time is but the desire to capture an appearance. Malraux understood Proust's satisfaction at the end of *The Past Recaptured*, but he himself didn't need to look for satisfaction in lost time; beginning in his adolescence Malraux lived in transcended time. As for the satisfaction derived by writers of memoirs, whether important or not, who overwhelm bookstores with their deceptively fabricated chronologies, or the satisfaction of biographers who attempt to fabricate a convincing chronology, Malraux was unable to experience such satisfaction, so weak and pale did it appear to him, as it does to everyone who has felt deep inside the warmth and light of a transcended time which has fundamentally no importance, or rather which has only as much as do incarnations and appearances.

To consider chronology as appearance, to sense the fusion of all time within oneself: it is surely here where Malraux's readers have the most difficulty in following him, just as they experience difficulty in understanding the poet Jean Tual, who ends "Le Chemin de Diamant" with this sumptuous stanza:

> En moi, privé de forme et d'ombre,
> Tous les âges s'entredéchirent
> Merle oublié, dont le bec jaune
> Va tâtant les murs d'une nuit
> Seuil de triomphe.[1]

But the consequence of not following Malraux here is that one is also unable to follow him upon the metaphysical shores he reaches in proclaiming that "Metamorphosis is the Universal Law." By transcending time without the help of gods, Malraux invites a new Copernican revo-

---

1. ["Deprived of form and shadow, / All ages tear themselves apart in me / Forgotten blackbird, whose yellow beak / Goes tapping on the walls one night / Threshold of Triumph."]
From Jean Tual, *Poèmes Cycliques*.

lution, the way contemporary scientific thought also invites one. To be convinced of this we need only to look at one example. The way of seeing the galaxies and interstellar spaces, which question contemporary man so intensely when he truly looks at them, rests on the notion of light-years which inhabits that man. The view of the universe and the questions it raises depend on the distance and the speed traveled by light during 365 days. But speed and day are notions that depend on the idea one has of time. If man calls upon the intemporal he carries within, if he modulates the idea he has of time the way a painter escapes from the optical conventions he uses for perspective or the way a musician escapes from the acoustic conventions he uses for tonality, if man thus modifies his perception of time, then his perception of light-years will be modified, and therefore so will his perception of the universe. Today, for "men of a particular (and linear) time" the light-year and its billions of kilometers appear beyond the human scale, but for men living "in this time" or in that time, living within another notion of time and speed, light-years can take on surprising familiarity and proximity. Space shuttles, and the speed which allows them to move around in a time which is not our own, have already changed the questions man asks himself about cosmic spaces and "the icy face of the moon," questions which still haunted Teilhard de Chardin. The questions will not be silenced, but the starry millennia will undoubtedly move from an inhuman and crushing scale to reside on a more welcoming one. And should anyone doubt this he needs only to search his memories and recall an August evening during which, with the wonderment of a child, he raised his eyes toward the Milky Way and was astonished that evening to feel the stars so close.

By condensing or by dilating our perception of time, we can manipulate our perception of the infinitely large or the infinitely small just as we can alter a photo we want to take by opening or by closing the camera's lens. An intense condensation of our perception of time enables us to see the cosmos as no longer being on an inhuman and crushing scale. Likewise, an extreme dilation of our perception of time enables us to view no longer with alarm the frequencies recently discovered in the infinitely small. If one maintains the common perception of the latter, it is indeed alarming to think that the quanta of a hydrogen atom undergo seven million billion (7×10^{15}) beats per second. On the other hand, if we dilate our perception of the infinitely small to the extreme the rhythm of this frenetic pulsation becomes strangely similar to the rhythm of the slow geological flow of time. For those who know how to go beyond "the doors of perception" (Huxley), it is even possible for them to dilate and condense their perception of time in such a way that the dance of the quanta and the march of the stars vibrate to the same tempo. When they then return to a conventional perception of time the difference in rhythms they once again perceive pose no more difficulty for them than do the instruments of an orchestra, some of which play thirty-second notes, and others rounds.

To live in the intemporal where Michelangelo and Braque, Chartres and Angkor, Isis and Jesus commune with surprising simultaneity is to live in a cosmos where the light-year, an essentially temporal notion, has lost its titan quality and where the expansion of space and worlds confronts man in a more amicable way. Throughout his life Malraux sought this intemporal which he had sensed within him when he was just an adolescent. In his early writings, and particularly in *Farfelu Kingdom*, places and times are mixed together without any regard for geography or chronology; space and time in these writings lose all substance and consistency, which enables the narrator—barely sixty years old—to set off for the Islands of the Blessed. In his novels Malraux always uses a narrative technique that explodes linear time and which rests on a strongly emphasized temporal discontinuity. At the end of his life Malraux had not solved the mystery of the intemporal, but he truly lived in it, and this is why his last two books devote so many lines to a meditation on time.

For millennia the struggle against destiny was first a struggle against time, a struggle against the "you'll never know what it all meant" (*A-M* 1). The very formulation of this overwhelming enigma implicates time by opposing the future of "you'll never know" to the past of "what it all meant." This enigma, like that of the Sphinx, is only an enigma in the temporal. In the intemporal it is dissolved, it is no longer present, and therefore does not call for a response. This enigma bears the seal of the religions that have kept the intemporal outside of man instead of revealing the intemporal within him. And yet almost all the founders of religions have been preceded by prophets who transcended time and announced that the "Son of Man" lived "in that time." If the next century, or the following ones, experience a spiritual upsurge, whose advent Malraux so often envisioned, it will be one which will reintegrate the intemporal in man, instead of alienating it outside him.

13

A Fraternal Consciousness

DURING THE SECOND HALF of the twentieth century biology seems to be assuming the role that history once had in the nineteenth century. The biologist of today, like the historian of yesterday, willingly believes that his discipline will forge "the next myth about man" and will render the human adventure intelligible. And if the future brings a biological materialism which will also be seen as a complete philosophy, we may fear that such biological materialism will engender a totalitarianism more terrible and insidious than that which is already based on historical materialism. Genetic manipulations in the name of a philosophy of biology would be much worse than concentration camps and deportations in the name of a philosophy of history.

The beginnings of a great debate occurred between Jacques Monod and André Malraux, which could have become crucial. In the *Revue des Deux Mondes* of February 1955 Malraux published his article "Le mythe de la science et le destin de l'homme." In 1967 in the newspaper *Le Monde* he wrote: "For the first time a civilization doesn't know its *raison d'être*" (29 November 1967). Jacques Monod responded: civilization doesn't know it "because it lives with, affirms, and teaches systems of values whose foundations are in ruin, whereas it owes its emergence to the adoption of an ethics of knowledge whose sources, rules, and nature are unknown to it." Monod also asserted that knowledge is not a means but an end. For Malraux there could be no ethics of knowledge, and knowledge was in no way an end in itself. Monod's and Malraux's positions were much too far apart for there to have been a truly useful dialogue between them.

A Fraternal Consciousness

For Malraux, "experiencing the universe is not the same as systematizing it, no more than experiencing love is the same as analyzing it. Only an intense awareness achieves understanding" (*TW* 87). This statement, which Malraux wrote when he was twenty-five years old, could be a motto for his life and his work. With his astonishing memory Malraux accumulated knowledge in a way few men have been able to do, notably in art and ancient civilizations, but he never used it to devise a system or to analyze things. His works of nonfiction do not form a history of art, which would be a system, and they are even less a theory of art; they uncoil the spiral of a long meditation on the "Why?" of art and on "the honor of being human" which is made manifest through art.

For several centuries Western man has been confusing knowledge with the accumulation of facts. Just as the West has gradually gone from enlightenment to enlightenments, it has gone from knowledge to the knowledge of many things. For the Westerner knowledge is no longer the ability to formulate a just idea, to establish just relationships; it has become the ability to amass a large quantity of information. And it was necessary for Claudel to write "co-naissance" for the true meaning of the word to be remembered. For a Westerner knowledge must be objective. Knowledge turns what it studies into an "object." Knowledge deals with objects, and therefore it only takes into account, or only seeks to take into account, the visible world. For millennia the world of facts and objects was only the world of appearance. The "Enlightenment," then the nineteenth century, gave that world "an invincible promotion" and turned it into "reality" (cf. *Int* 7): a reality that claimed to be the only one in existence, the only one worthy of interest, and the only one capable of establishing a new ethics. In the world of art, as in science or philosophy, the world of appearance sought to impose itself and to exclude all that wasn't part of it (cf. *Int* 76). After centuries of the unreal during which illusion was created through perspective, shadow, and distance, in a few decades the real hoped to come into its own in official painting, photography, "hyper-realism," concrete music, and official realism. All these realisms sought to annex the imaginary and the unreal in order to have them submit to an ultimately victorious appearance (cf. *Int* 88). All were manifestations of the imperialist will of the world of knowledge. Fortunately, the revolt of the surreal soon erupted and proclaimed how unconscionable the claims of "reality" truly were. The revolt of the surreal also proclaimed (through the character Gisors) that there is "a world more true than the other because more constant, more like himself" (*MF* 73–74).

Malraux foresaw the birth of an Imaginary Museum of audiovisuals, which would be as different from our current Imaginary Museum as the latter is from the Louvre. In the final chapter of *The Timeless* Malraux presents a stimulating series of questions concerning the change in sensibility and the culture being prepared by modern audiovisual technology. "Audiovisuals are perhaps alone capable of connecting us with a work of art by separating us from the 'rest' (this 'rest' is called the world).... The time and the place of the Imaginary Museum were almost concepts; those of audiovisuals are almost sensations" (*Int* 385). And let us not forget here that in *Man's Fate* Malraux had written magnificently: "He who seeks the absolute with such uncompromising zeal can find it only in sensation" (*MF* 158). It is already possible to foresee that audiovisuals will make us "see what we couldn't seize from the imperceptible" (*Int* 381). The electronic microscope not only enlarges what we can already see; it shows us what we haven't yet seen. Audiovisuals do not simply show what we have already seen in a different way, they establish new relations and offer them up to our capacity to feel.

Audiovisuals, by diffusing sensations and not concepts, speak directly to the consciousness they form, or deform. For the first time two means of formation—formation through knowledge addressing intelligence, and formation through sensations addressing consciousness—fight for preeminence and thus do not allow any formation of man. For a century education, obligatory for all, has been seeking to form students through the accumulation of knowledge. "We have been taught to know Corneille, not to be moved by him" (*HP* 202). As long as this was the only means of formation it was accepted and studied, all the more so because the formation of consciousness was carried out at home. Today, "those who frequent libraries, record libraries, and Imaginary Museums, are connected through emotion to the masters of the past" (ibid.). We are not connected to them through knowledge, which doesn't mean, of course, that having knowledge about past masters is an obstacle to obtaining a quality and intensity of emotion—indeed, quite the opposite is true. The adolescent who has been moved by Cinna or Phaedra on television can't tolerate the analytical way Corneille and Racine are scrutinized in school or university classrooms. Those who have been inspired by a series on Richelieu or Amazonia can no longer tolerate a traditional course in history or geography. As long as their elders struggle to continue to impose the mode of cognitive formation which they themselves endured and which they consider to be the best, there will be indifference, and possibly even disgust and revolt, among all those who have grown up with access to a mode of formation aimed at the senses. A new mode is being sought in conjunction with the values in the name of which that formation should be undertaken. And the fact that this mode is neither completely thought out nor therefore truly organized is no excuse for remaining blind to it and denying the promises it holds. It is still like a newborn baby who cries and gesticulates in order to get attention.

Humanity has already known great periods in the formation of consciousness. In the past this formation was ensured by religions that reserved knowledge for a very small minority and left matters relatively obscured for the majority of minds, not out of contempt or disdain, but from the profound belief that knowledge was not essential to attain immortality, nirvana, or eternity. Malraux foresaw a new formation of consciousness based on a massive diffusion of knowledge, a formation which would lean on that diffusion and would turn knowledge into a means. We know, along with Malraux, that this is what is at stake in the current struggles.

At the end of *Days of Wrath,* Kassner, free of his prison cell and torture, looks at the lines of his hand immediately after winning the battle against the elements he fought during his return flight to Czechoslovakia on board a small two-seated airplane. He "smiled upon seeing once more the long life-line in the palm of his hand and the line which he had made one day, ironically, with a razor" (*DW* 133). Kassner then muses that all the lines which mark his destiny have been made in that way, by patient and steadfast blows of determination. "What was man's freedom," he adds, "but the knowledge and the manipulation of his fate? . . . [O]n this earth of prison-cells and sacrifices there had been heroism; there had been holiness, and there would perhaps at last be simple consciousness" (*DW* 133–34). By speaking in this way Kassner was formulating a wish whose realization finally seemed possible. Garcia, in *Man's Hope,* goes further and proposes a maxim for life: "converting as wide a range of experience as possible into [consciousness]" (*MH* 396). Jean Grenier, in a letter he wrote to Malraux in January 1938, and which he later used as the conclusion to his *Essai sur l'esprit d'orthodoxie,* declared: "You thus define all of your works in that way. Experience is vast, consciousness worthy . . . you fill your destiny magnificently. And it would have been another destiny to convert as profound a consciousness as possible into experience." It would indeed have been another destiny, but for a man like Malraux it would have required another era. Our era no longer has a consciousness, and it is impossible to convert a nonexistent consciousness into experience, or rather, it is only possible for isolated or solitary people who are also preparing the way and will take on the role of beacons. True to his nature and to his personal destiny, Malraux worked to prepare, through experience, the foundations of a new consciousness; in this way he, too, was preparing the way for those who, later, would be able to convert that new consciousness into experience.

When Malraux stated in front of UNESCO that "the first European value is the will to consciousness. The second is the will to discovery," he gave the impression of expressing a wish rather than stating a fact. It is indeed difficult not to recognize that ever since at least the eighteenth century the will to discovery has triumphed over the will to consciousness. Europe's *crisis of consciousness* will only cease if the will to discoveries, that is, the will to knowledge, becomes subservient to the will to consciousness. This has already occurred among certain isolated people, of whom Jean Grenier assuredly is one; it has not yet occurred on the scale of a modern civilization.

"The quality of man, and not an accumulation of knowledge, is the ultimate objective of any culture" (*Liberté de l'esprit*, July 1950). As early as 1937 Malraux had placed at the heart of *Man's Hope* the demand that civilization and culture be concerned with "the quality of man." This demand, this hope, feeds the most important dialogues in the novel and is found at the center of the chapter which Malraux in fact called "Etre et Faire." Gide, through his works and in his journal, had raised the same question for the individual. In 1937 in *Man's Hope* and in 1968 in his analysis of the events of May, Malraux raised the issue for society, civilization, and culture. Faced with the preeminence of knowledge and the will to discovery which have engendered "acting" and which are concerned above all with quantity, the characters in *Man's Hope* fight so that one day the quality of man, "being," may triumph. And when Jean Lacouture writes that in Malraux's collected works *Man's Hope* represents the triumph of objective truth over the imaginary, and of acting over being, he has read Malraux less attentively than Régis Debray has, and he is seriously in error (cf. Lacouture, 273). Jean Lacouture should have immediately explained, which he didn't do, that for Malraux this victory of acting over being is only superficial and temporary. The final pages of the novel show this: being will one day triumph over acting.

After 1945 Malraux's former friends, who had become his political adversaries as he had become theirs, attempted to hide the true meaning of *Man's Hope*. Georges Mounier, for example, wrote that with *The Wal-*

A Fraternal Consciousness

nut Trees of Altenburg, "one is at the opposite extreme of *Man's Hope,* all the heroes of which, indeed, worked so that history could have meaning and so that starting with us, at least, it might be possible for man to be a continuous fact" (*Les Lettres Françaises,* 7 June 1946). His misinterpretation is total, but it is understandable, for shortly before that he wrote: "My main problem is understanding what has happened since *Man's Hope,* and how the fellow-traveler of that time has become the rather surprising anticommunist of General de Gaulle's cabinet." When it became obvious that Malraux had never been a Communist, or even a fellow-traveler, the men of the left, and especially those who merely professed to be leftist, attempted to claim *Man's Hope* for their own, even if they rejected its author. They succeeded somewhat in temporarily hiding the true meaning of the novel. Above all they didn't want readers to see how *Man's Hope* showed that "the age of fundamentals is returning," that "reason has to be rebuilt on a new basis," (*MH* 325) and that despite the apparent victory of acting it is being that will triumph one day, regardless of what the "businessmen of the Revolution," who do nothing more than oppose certain techniques of know-how to others, think about it. The hope Magnin and Manuel provide is that know-how will one day be used in the service of "knowing-how-to-be;" that knowledge, when it is redefined anew and is no longer sought as an end in itself, will become the servant of consciousness.

The seventeenth century elevated reason to the status of a supreme value. Choderlos de Laclos and Saint-Just, despite their differences, would have been in agreement on this supreme value, as Sade and Bonaparte, and Montesquieu and Voltaire, would have been. But toward the end of the eighteenth century reason began to trifle with men and feed squalls of passion which it attempted in vain to justify. Today, "the knowledge that the thinking mind is incapable of regulating even the most ordinary activities of life has come to play a leading part in our modern civilization—which, moreover, declines to regulate its irrationality" (*VOS* 496). Some still hope that reason will one day once again be able to unveil the mystery of man. Their approach resembles that of musicologists who believe that analysis can unveil the mystery of a Mozart sonata. Musical analysis, like any analysis, can enable us to deepen our knowledge of a work, but only the consciousness of the performer—provided he doesn't belong to the group of technocrats of music who have also surged to the forefront—can give life back to a work and establish it as a work of creation.

In *Man's Hope* the dialogue between Scali and old Alvear is undoubtedly the one which illuminates the whole book and which best helps us to grasp its true meaning. Scali came to Madrid by car expressly so that old Alvear could leave the city before the arrival of the fascists, who would probably arrest and shoot him. Old Alvear refuses to leave. His refusal is explained neither by indifference nor by resignation, but by a serenity and a wisdom which already allow him to live in another realm. For Alvear, beyond the revolution, beyond the avatars of the moment, beyond all that threatens his life, "there is a terrifying and profound hope in man . . . The age of fundamentals is returning . . . Reason has to be rebuilt on a new basis . . . It wasn't the gods who created music, it was music created the gods." (*MH* 324, 325, 326). In a novel entitled *Man's Hope* it is inconceivable that Malraux would have old Alvear say that "there is a terrifying and profound hope in man" without asserting a connection between Alvear's statement and the book's title.

Left to itself reason runs on empty, like a motor which is connected to nothing. Even worse, it races if it is given too much fuel. Not only can reason not account for man; it can't account for itself. It must be "established *anew.*" And not *once again*. The notion of humanism with which the West has been living for several centuries can no longer be accepted. Pierre-Henri Simon summed up this notion in *L'Homme en procès*: "Among the multiple and multivalent meanings of this word [humanism], let us always agree upon its most correct and simplest one: 'humanist' implies a confidence in the rational nature of man . . . Let us therefore call humanists those who . . . attempt to give weapons back to unarmed reason." For Malraux this notion of humanism is a mutilation, indeed even a castration. Man is irrational to the same extent that he is rational. Both contribute to his greatness just as they can contribute to his downfall. But to truly grasp Malraux's thinking we must follow its evolution in the face of the irrational.

During his adolescence and the first years of his adult life, Malraux seems to have been greatly attracted by the irrational. Indeed, it seems he was truly driven toward it. All the same, this attraction and drive were accompanied by a certain uneasiness and even mistrust. Although his early writings almost appear as a hymn to the irrational, his first two works of nonfiction, written at the same time, often appear to contain a warning against the irruption of the irrational. In truth, in 1926–27, Malraux, who was only twenty-five years old, had not yet clearly delineated, within himself and for himself, the boundaries of the realms of the irrational and the instinctual. Freud's appearance in French intellectual life

A Fraternal Consciousness

and the first manifestations of surrealism were at most only a few years old, and they encouraged this imprecision. In 1926 Malraux was already asserting that the "I" is irrational and that one cannot have an awareness of it as one is aware of others. He boldly asserted that "our deep life, intensity, cannot belong to the mind" (cf. *JE*) and that the mind is "a lie, the very means of lying, creator of realities" (*TW* 120). But at the same time he was already thinking that the instincts, the unconscious, and psychological individualism could never establish man, and this is why he ended *The Temptation of the West* with an invocation to lucidity. Malraux might therefore appear either opposed to his age or lagging behind it. In truth he was ahead of it: he had already understood that the movement of ideas which was in the forefront had as its goal the undermining of a worm-eaten edifice rather than the building of a new one. In the second half of his life, after meditating for a long time on the irrational, Malraux made the distinction between instinct and the unconscious, dreams and the imaginary, impulse and imagination, the life of depths and deep life, and he was then able to assert without restriction or reservation the double nature of man: rational and irrational.

Ever since cassette tape-players have become so widespread, it has become difficult to truly imagine what the character in *Man's Fate* might have felt when he first heard his voice on a recording and didn't recognize it. Today everyone can hear his voice at will either through his throat, from the inside, or through the ears, from the outside. The development of psychology and psychoanalysis, when they haven't gone astray, also enables everyone to either listen to his "I" from the inside, or to become aware of it from the outside. In the past the inner consciousness of the "I" was provided by religions, which brought the irrational under control. Today, man is faced with a rational which no longer has a foundation and with an irrational which is also left to itself. He is unsubjugated, or worse, he is under the control of his instincts.

In *Precarious Man,* which is to literary creation what *The Voices of Silence* is to the creation of plastic arts, Malraux retraces the slow rise of the irrational in the novel. The writer, in order to justify his perfect knowledge of his characters' intimate feelings, that is, in order to respond to the "How do you know?," for a long time used either the biographical convention of characters who are observed by an omniscient narrator, or the fiction of an epistolary novel. Thus literature, particularly in theater, associated itself more with personalities than with characters. The author directed "personalities he created more or less rationally" (*HP* 131) and he left aside "the irrational to which the character owed everything" (*HP* 105). This coherent rationality seduced and reassured the reader. In the nineteenth century, when literature was more interested in character than in personalities, the novelist began to "take up residence in the soul of his characters," to live in them. This was equally a convention. It was above all a "surprising metaphysical carom, for never had anyone attempted to take hold of man from the inside as well as from the outside at the same time" (ibid.). It was then believed that psychological analysis would be the privileged weapon of the novelist. In scarcely a few decades one had to admit the obvious: "The most extensive analysis is accompanied by the most unsubjugated irrationality, as Dostoyevski and Proust have shown" (*HP* 196).

The Cid and *The Miser* were coherent. Their behavior was rational. Their natures dictated their behavior. Racine didn't live in Hippolyte, nor did Molière live in Harpagon. They had conceived of a personality type and portrayed the acts engendered by that personality. Balzac lived for a moment in Père Goriot, and Victor Hugo in Valjean, and Flaubert in Madame Bovary, and Zola in Gervaise. But Dostoyevski crossed an altogether new threshold: he continually switches back and forth between Raskolnikov's inner and external lives, between his least obvious rational and his most unsubjugated irrational. The irrational had attained free reign in literature. Which was certainly not foreign to the attempt at a rationalization of the irrational which Freud was undertaking at the time. For a moment the modern novel might give the impression of having abandoned that attainment and of attaching itself to the cold and meticulous description of facts and gestures seen by the most neutral observer possible. In fact, the modern novel expects its reader to recreate the irrational in the characters for himself using the facts and gestures which have simply been described.

Finding himself faced with his most unsubjugated irrational side could only upset a man who had attempted to exist either while denying that irrationality or letting it be controlled by the gods, and almost always while devaluing it. Camus, better than anyone else, expresses this unsettling of modern man. In *The Myth of Sisyphus* he writes: "I said that the world is absurd, but I was too hasty. This world in itself is not reasonable, that's all that can be said. But what is absurd is the confrontation of this irrational and the wild longing for clarity whose call echoes in the human heart." A few pages later Camus writes, even more significantly, "Our appetite for understanding, our yearning for the absolute are explicable only insofar as we can indeed understand and explain

A Fraternal Consciousness

many things. It is useless to absolutely negate reason. It has its domain in which it is efficacious. This is in fact that of human experience. This is why we want to make everything clear. If we cannot do so, if the absurd is born on that occasion, it is born precisely at the very meeting of that efficacious but limited reason and the forever regenerating irrational." Camus later discovered the full and complete universe he portrayed in *A Happy Death,* but when he wrote *The Myth of Sisyphus* he tended to rely above all on reason, for he felt able to write about reason what he had written about history: "At least of that I am certain."

Malraux gives the impression of having always been more certain of the realm which doesn't belong to his reason than of that which does. The metamorphosed Sins in *Paper Moons,* the narrator in *Farfelu Kingdom,* Garine in *The Conquerors,* Claude in *The Royal Way,* Kyo and Katov in *Man's Fate,* Vincent Berger, who has the miraculous revelation of day at the end of *The Walnut Trees of Altenburg,* and Malraux, himself, all have a common characteristic: they attach more importance to what they perceive through the irrational than to what they construct through reason (cf. *TW* 87). For them what is essential is not to analyze what one experiences, but to think in order to experience. It is the irrational that for them paves the way to fellowship and consciousness, whereas the rational only provides for the accumulation of knowledge. But we must be careful here of the ambiguous meaning of irrational. Too often we limit the irrational to what reason cannot explain and immediately add that the progress of knowledge is increasingly pushing back the limits of the irrational. Thus storms, lightning, rain would have at one time belonged to the irrational only to have then entered into the realm of the rational: Zeus' lightning bolt lost its mystery and became a simple electrical discharge. When Malraux speaks of the irrational, and ennobles it, he is speaking about another realm.

He is speaking above all of the realm which will never be explained by relations of cause and effect, those which are the foundation of knowledge forged by reason. Today science, built upon these relations, must acknowledge its limitations. It must accept relations of probabilities, of unpredictabilities and uncertainties. Mathematicians, physicists, and biologists are already paving the way for a mode of thinking for which causality and laws—physical laws—will appear as exceptions. They are paving the way for a mode of thinking which will no longer uphold the search for a single equation summing up a generalized causality as the scientific ideal. Granted, this new mode of thinking might still be called "reason," but we must realize that it no longer has anything in common with the reason we have known up until now. Malraux was approaching this thought process, and that is why so many of his contemporaries found his nonfiction obscure. When reason is established anew it will be upon principles it has been unaware of up to now, and even upon principles it had rejected as being irrational.

When Malraux speaks of the irrational he is also and above all speaking of another, even more extensive realm, that which arises not from man's "thinking abilities," but from his "sentient abilities"; the realm of sensibility and not the realm of thought; the "I feel therefore I am" of Gide, and no longer the "I think therefore I am" of Descartes. For several centuries anything connected to sensibility has been considered an ornament, a luxury, and often a trap. Everything acquired through the senses has been considered suspect, and only what is learned through reason is seen as truly worthwhile. Should anyone doubt this, he need only recall how reason has attempted to govern even the world of art. This was the case, for example, with the often reductive literary analyses encouraged by so many universities, or yet the rationalizing analyses encouraged by so many art historians. But the example Malraux gives is even more all-encompassing and more probing. He underlines how the myth of Racine, which is very different from Racine himself, "for two centuries imposed under the frivolous name of taste: the most complete rationalization of art that had been known since Aristotle" (*HP* 74). Disarmed temporarily by the *poètes maudits,* by cubism, surrealism, abstract art, and depth psychology, reason is raising its head once again and is waging an ultimate battle: it has launched an assault against psychoanalysis into which it is attempting to reintroduce causality, determinism, and conditioning. Indeed, how many analysts are aware that in their daily practices they are reintroducing the reductive principles of "the same effects are produced by the same causes"? (Principles Freud would never have accepted in the second half of his life.)

"Reason has little power when confronted with sensibility," Malraux states in the preface to *Mademoiselle Monk*. And we can already sense that the day is dawning when rationalists will accept this; when they will fully admit that the faculty of reason is subservient to that of feeling. Audiovisual technology will encourage the dawning of that day following which "the thinking reed" will no longer be seen as a metaphor for man, and when we will fully accept man as "an imagining animal" (cf. *TW* 66): an animal making his imagination the forever new servant of his sensibility. We must stop here and pay close attention to a primary and essential point: for Malraux, and for everyone who is grateful to him for having always emphasized this, the imagination, the imaginary, and the sensibility must not be confused with dreams, madness, and the unconscious. Surrealism was a vital and beneficial reaction against the reasoning mental structures which had invaded the Western mind, but in wanting to free man from the stifling guardianship of reason, some surrealists, literary ones in particular, favored dreams, madness, and the unconscious. They thus only freed an aspect, and not necessarily the most interesting one, of the irrational. Their provocative and cleansing role was indispensable. This is why Malraux never attacked them. But the realm they opened up was too limited, and that is why Malraux never joined them. The author of *Paper Moons* should have had a place in *La Révolution surréaliste.* He never wrote for it. André Breton and his closest friends sensed that Malraux was avoiding them. The special issue *Variété* devoted to "*Surréalisme en 1929*" (June 1929) contained spiteful words against Malraux, who merely replied with humor in a simple letter to the director of the journal. This letter was published in the August 15, 1929, issue.

Unlike surrealism in painting, the literary surrealism of André Breton and those he didn't alienate gradually moved away from true surrealism—that, for example, of Hieronymus Bosch or Rabelais, in whose works the real and the surreal, each invigorated by the other, are so interpenetrated that nothing, no boundary, separates them. A "surrealism" where the real and the "sur-real" express the double nature of man. Malraux couldn't assert, as André Breton wrote in *Le Manifeste,* that surrealism was "a psychic automatism through which one attempts to express either verbally or in writing or in any other way, the real functioning of thought. A dictate of thought in the absence of any control exercised by reason, outside any esthetic or moral concerns." Moreover, André Breton, by ultimately behaving like a veritable pope of a veritable Church, by carrying out anathemas and excommunications, proved that for him the "sur-real" did not vivify the real; that the "sur-real" remained on the level of ideas; that it didn't bring about awareness, and therefore remained incapable of modifying human behavior. This remark and any reservations we have must, however, in no way alter the gratitude we owe to André Breton for having forcefully led the battle of surrealism, and for having done so much to upset reason and its imperialistic pretensions.

By attaching itself to the waking dream, the unconscious, and madness rather than to imagination, sensibility, and the imaginary, a certain surrealism involuntarily contributed to the diverting of the irrational. It

The Metamorphosis of Culture

is now up to us to put it back on course. Malraux was correct in writing: "Surrealism, far from proposing to further culture, repudiates it in favor of the dream" (*VOS* 575). Repudiate the mentalities which had invaded the Western mind: Yes. To do so in the name of dreams: No. Dreams are not imagination. Onirism is not the imaginary. Man's greatness is not found in the power of his waking dreams; it is found in his ability to create forms and to govern his creation. Unfortunately, we are forced to note that our age, on the whole, is placed opposite this greatness and delights in "the industrialization of dreams" (*A-M* 236) which makes the imaginary subject to instincts. "The owners of the dream factories are not unaware of this. And they are not here to help people, but to make money" (ibid.). Paradoxically, at least in appearance, this "civilization, which satisfies the instincts of the masses in a way they have never been satisfied before" (ibid.), is at the same time a civilization that resurrects the works of the past. The paradox is only apparent, for only these resuscitated works seem "powerful enough to withstand the powers of sex and death" (ibid.). If our age did not invoke those resuscitated works our civilization "would become more enslaved to instincts and to elementary dreams than almost any civilization the world has ever known. It is there, I [Malraux] think, that the problem of culture forces itself on our attention" (ibid.).

At the opening ceremonies of the *maison de la culture* in Bourges on April 13, 1964, Malraux was already developing this theme: "We have invented the most prodigious dream factories humanity has ever known ... All of humanity is invested with immense powers of fiction, and these powers of fiction are also powers of money or political powers whose natures are the same ... We have discovered that in each one of us there is a vulnerability to dreams, but at the same time those who live off dream factories have discovered how to take advantage of that vulnerability ... What is most powerful over men's dreams are the sinister realms of the past which were considered demoniacal: the realm of sex and the realm of blood." In the past the gods channeled the powers man couldn't control either in the universe or in himself. Mythologies and cosmogonies controlled these powers. Reason has proven that it can't control them, and that it will never be able to do so. It has left these powers to themselves. The dream factories and machines have taken control.

Promoting instincts and dreams in order to free oneself of a reason which had become imperialistic represented a necessary step, but stopping in midstream could not encourage the promotion of the irrational. Only a true culture is capable of doing this. The culture of the Middle Ages was above all a culture of the soul. The culture of the Renaissance and those of the eighteenth and nineteenth centuries were primarily cultures of the mind. The slow and painful metamorphosis of culture which we sense at work seems to be preparing a culture in which the rational and the irrational parts of man will be reconciled and cultivated equally without man's alienating either one or the other in favor of images he might project outside himself.

In *Man's Fate* Kyo realizes that it is not just one's own voice but also one's own life that is heard from the inside, whereas others hear it from the outside. For himself man is "a kind of absolute, the affirmation of an idiot: an intensity greater than that of all the rest" (*MF* 59), but for others man is what he does. Between the perception one has of oneself and one's own life and the perception others have of one there is an abyss, and out of this abyss rises solitude, a complete, all-consuming solitude. This is why Malraux noted in the margin of Gaëtan Picon's essay: "I believe we know no one," which is, moreover, a thought Gisors has almost word for word in *Man's Fate* (cf. *MF* 67). Indeed, Gisors knew that the awareness he had of himself and the awareness he had of others were irreconcilable, for they were acquired through radically different means. And knowing this he lived in "a forbidden solitude where no one would ever join him" (*MF* 73).

The Christian message, which was founded on fraternity and love, might have delivered man from his radical solitude, but the Catholic Church betrayed its message, starting in the seventeenth century certainly, if not earlier. In Barcelona, where the churches had been burned, the Christian Ximenes said to the anarchist Puig: "God should not be dragged into man's family squabbles" (*MH* 31). Puig replied: "It's no use telling people who've been having their cheeks slapped for the last two thousand years to 'turn the other cheek' ... to teach poor people, workers, to accept what happened in the Asturias ... And to do so in the name of love—I ask you! Could anything be more disgusting?" (*MH* 32–33). For certain revolutionaries it would have been better to burn banks rather than churches. Puig didn't agree with that: "Leave that to the bourgeoisie; it's in their line. The priests, that's another matter" (ibid.). Having betrayed the message by making fraternity possible only in the hereafter, the Church did not deliver man from his solitude, and today, "there's more [fraternity] right here in this street than in any old

Cathedral" (*MH* 45). A scene in *Man's Hope* illustrates this perfectly. The journalist Slade is trying to find a subject for an article. Lopez proposes he write one on the necessity of painting the walls of the city white so that they can be offered to painters. Upon those walls, he says, masterpieces won't be turned out, but a style will be created. "It's unthinkable," Lopez resumes, overwhelmed, "that given people who have something to say and people who are willing to listen, we won't create a style. Just give them a free hand, give 'em all the airbrushes and spray guns, all the modern contraptions they can want and, after that, a chink of modeling-clay—and then you will see! . . . One day that new style of ours will catch on in the whole of Spain, just as the cathedral style spread over Europe" (*MH* 46). (While reading these premonitory lines written in 1937, one can't help thinking of the walls almost everywhere in the world that have begun to talk since 1968, and whose messages are so strong that films have been made about them, such as *Les murs mûrs!*) After listening attentively to Lopez, Slade, wondering whether or not he is going to devote his article to Lopez's project, watches men passing in front of him, "exulting in their carnival of liberty" (*MH* 47) and sharing "with their painters in the dark, underground communion that Christianity had once provided, that today the Revolution gave them" (ibid.).

Indeed, for a time there was hope that the fraternity of the Marxist International would deliver man from solitude, but the gulag and the race of sputniks buried the "comrade" just as the Inquisition and the temporal power of the pope buried the "brother." Kassner, "deprived of [fraternity]" by Nazi torture, felt that "solitude was about to return" (*DW* 92), and Malraux felt that, as well, when he wrote the novel of fraternity, *Man's Hope*. Fraternity was once again undermined. It was undermined by the businessmen of the revolution just as it had been by the clergy, but in the end it didn't really matter, for hope remained. Hope was Hernandez agreeing to send Moscardo's letters to his wife; hope was Magnin carrying out his command while keeping the fraternal notion of the leader; hope was the communion of the peasants of Linares and the wounded airmen in the Sierra de Teruel; hope was Manuel regrouping those who had fled from Toledo and experiencing a deep emotion because for the first time he was in the presence of a fraternity that expressed itself in action. In *The Conquerors* the fraternity to which Garine aspired was still an idea, an abstraction. After *Man's Hope* fraternity became a real, experienced fact for Malraux, a fact which was not yet powerful enough to be victorious but which was strong enough to encourage a lucid hope. The opening pages of the novel assert this unambiguously:

A Fraternal Consciousness

"[T]he darkness was all fraternity" (*MH* 11), and then Manuel understands that the car he had so much trouble buying in order to go skiing was no longer important to him. "[The car] had ceased to be: nothing remained but this memorable night, fraught with a vague and boundless hope, this crowded night when every man had his appointed task on earth" (*MH* 13). And to ensure that the reader sees the true meaning of *Man's Hope,* that he can measure the extent of the metamorphosis that takes place in Manuel, Malraux alludes in the very final lines of the novel to the car evoked in the first pages. Manuel then "felt the seething life around him charged with portents"; he knew he "would become another man, someone he could not visualize as yet; just as the soldier he had become could no more visualize the Manuel who once had bought a little car to go skiing in the Sierra" (*MH* 510).

In *The Walnut Trees of Altenburg* fraternity has become powerful enough to momentarily shake the established order. The Germans have just launched a gas attack at Bolgako on the Vistula: trees, leaves, daisies, horses, birds, soldiers—all become viscous and gluey like peat. Lieutenant Berger tries to regain control of his men, who have abandoned the battle and wearily return carrying an enemy soldier on their shoulders, as if they are carrying a drowned man. Their gestures are those of a "pathetic, clumsy comradeship" (*WTA* 169). Soldiers and under-officers refuse to obey: "It's nothing to do with me ... there aren't any orders any more" (*WTA* 167, 172) they reply, when they reply at all. Lieutenant Berger himself gradually becomes incapable of doing his duty as an officer; he, too, carries a gassed enemy soldier on his shoulders; he does it for the same reason all his men did it, not out of a feeling of pity but out of "something a good deal deeper, an urge in which pain and brotherhood were inseparably united, an urge that came from far back in the past—as though the sheet of gas had yielded not those Russians, but only the friendly bodies of men in the same file" (*WTA* 184).

While reading and rereading this scene involving Lieutenant Berger it is once again impossible not to remember that Malraux, two years later, took "Berger" as his Resistance name, and it was with this name that he carried out the command of the Alsace-Lorraine Brigade. In addition, Malraux used that scene once again in *Lazarus,* the hymn to fraternity he wrote after his stay at the Salpêtrière hospital where, in 1972, he truly experienced, and for the third time, a return to life, a return to the world of the living. Malraux explains clearly why he evoked that scene again: the Bolgako attack, he says, is an example "of man and death overwhelmed by the instinctive fraternity embedded in man—

'programmed,' our sneering computers might say" (*L* 6). That scene, he also says, "embraces a confrontation between fraternity and death and that element in man which today is fumbling for an identity, and is certainly not the individual" (*L* 4). The explosion of fraternity that took hold of all the men in Bolgako "exercises on me," continues Malraux, "the same powerful and perturbing effect as the great myths and the defiant 'No' of Antigone and Prometheus" (*L* 5). (In *Mirror of Limbo,* of which *Lazarus* became a chapter, Malraux speaks of "the great myths of revolt since Antigone.")

We must fully understand the meaning and the strength of the expressions Malraux chooses: "an urge that came from far back in the past . . . the fraternity embedded in man—'programmed,' our sneering computers might say." But then if it is embedded in man, if it is programmed in him, why is fraternity always rejected? Is it utopian to think that one day the social and religious orders will no longer be the gravediggers of fraternity? Is it useless to hope that one day, as on the Vistula (but more durably), fraternity will become stronger than the established order? (*MH* 207). Is it idealistic to believe that one day, as before the Alcazar, "the need for fraternity will triumph over the passion for hierarchy"? Is it idealistic to hope that like certain religious or initiatory orders fraternity and hierarchy in civil society will no longer be irreconcilable enemies? All Malraux's works reply that it is not utopian to have those expectations, that we must prepare them, and that such preparation implies a complete metamorphosis of culture.

In his hospital room at the Salpêtrière, after having to crawl on the floor where he had fallen in the middle of a terrible, black night, Malraux undergoes a somnolence "accompanied by an intoxicating flow of images" (*L* 116) in which "fraternity is rarely absent." All the scenes of fraternity Malraux has ever known pass before his eyes. His "brush with death" does not call up in him the film of the events of his life nor the memory of the people he has loved; he calls his memories of fraternity "the only sentiment which, until the fever returns, will dare to contemplate death" (*L* 118).

People think they understand the feeling of fraternity "because they confuse it with human warmth" (*L* 116). It has been turned into a "comical utopia in which no one is nasty to anyone else" (*L* 116–17). But if one can rise above this trivialized fraternity, then what belongs to true fraternity "will reverberate with the same profound resonance as love, sacrifice, the supernatural, and death (*L* 117). Through laziness or seek-

A Fraternal Consciousness

ing an easy way out men willingly believe that "fraternity was added on as a makeweight to more profound sentiments like justice or freedom. But it is not just a superficial appendage. Like the sacred, it eludes us if we strip it of its primitive, irrational element" (*L* 117). After attempting throughout his entire life to discover how man could stand up to destiny, after believing for a time that art could be an "antidestiny," the Malraux of the Salpêtrière—he who had had a brush with death, which before had only come near—that Malraux became possessed by fraternity, by the "fraternity which fate does not obliterate" (*L* 116; cf. *MF* 359). And that Malraux, he who wrote *Lazarus,* might also have said that the passing of time which drew him closer to death didn't separate him from the world, but rather tied him to it in a serene accord. He lived for four more years.

The fraternity that appears as one of the clues to Malraux's works is not the individual feeling one person might have for another; it is a common, communal state of mind, the one Mao evoked when he said: "It was a question of reestablishing fraternity much more than of conquering freedom" (cf. *A-M* 360). A communal fraternity which in the end becomes one of the cornerstones of civil society. A fraternity which tried to make the streets and cities ring out in May 1968, and which those who were unable to understand it, since they were too busy fearing for the established order, will never be able to conceive of. A community of feeling which explains that "if the Feast of the Federation on July 14 convulsed France, it was because it was the Feast of Fraternity" (*L* 117). A communal fraternity which Kassner celebrates in his prison cell when he prepares what can be told to the darkness: "You, my Chinese comrades, buried alive, my Russian friends with your eyes gouged out, my German friends around me with your ropes, you in the next cell who have perhaps been beaten to death, what I call love is the thing that binds us together" (*DW* 98).

"I have spoken of love. 1925, or thereabouts. Like most young idiots at the time, I did not believe in its existence" (*L* 117). Personal confidences from Malraux are so rare that we must see how very important this one is, all the more so since in it one senses a regret, almost an anger, at having momentarily adopted the positions of the "young idiots at the time." When exactly did Malraux begin believing in the existence of love? It is difficult to say with certainty, but it does seem that it was with Josette Clotis, shortly before World War II. Beginning in 1933 in *Man's Fate* Malraux proclaimed that only fraternity and love could free man from his solitude, that they alone attacked the human condition. Ultimately it matters little whether at the time Malraux was writing *Man's Fate* true love was still only a hope and an idea for him, or whether he had already experienced it, for what is important is that in a magnificent scene Malraux celebrates the metaphysical power of human love. The pathos of the scene in which this celebration occurs enables very few to be able to perceive it.

Kyo and all his comrades have been arrested. Lying down in what used to be a school yard, they know that one after another they will be thrown alive into the furnace of a locomotive whose lugubrious whistle blows each time it swallows a revolutionary. Kyo has a cyanide capsule in his possession which will deliver him not from death, but from a death that would have been stolen from him. Stretched out on his back in the position of a corpse, Kyo thinks about his life before taking the saving bite of the capsule. He feels it is fine "to die by one's own hand, a death that resembles one's life" (*MF* 321), a death that is "the supreme expression of a life" (*MF* 323). He feels the calm brought on by the satisfaction of having "fought for what in its time was charged with the deepest meaning and the greatest hope" (ibid.). Kyo, who incarnates the revolutionary community so completely, knows that what has delivered him from solitude, the fate of the human condition, is not his battle, but his love for May. This crucial realization was carefully prepared by Malraux through the scene in which May informs Kyo that she has taken advantage of the freedom they have granted each other, by going to bed—without attaching any importance to the encounter—with one of the doctors from the hospital where she has been working. Faced with this confession Kyo has to overcome all the old reactions instilled in him by the old culture; he has to accept that one cannot possess another person; he rebels against the thought that the doctor might have believed that he possessed May; he has to stifle his jealousy, which is often only possessiveness; he has to stifle the desire for vengeance. And having won all those battles with himself he then realizes that only love destroys solitude (cf. *MF* 59): for everyone else it is what he has done; for May alone it isn't only that. Love enables one to "hear" the life of another as one "hears" one's own, that is, with one's throat and not only with one's ears. Love establishes immediate communication between people without the need for mediation. Love attacks extreme solitude, and that is why Malraux entitled his novel *Man's Fate,* as he specified on numerous occasions (cf. *L* 141). Without love, "men are not my kind, they are those who look at me and judge me; my kind are those who love me and

A Fraternal Consciousness

do not look at me, who love me in spite of everything . . ." (*MF* 59). And at the precise moment Kyo swallows the cyanide capsule, a moment when one certainly does not lie to oneself, when one is invaded by the serenity of making one's death "the supreme expression of a life" (*MF* 323), he rediscovers his certainty: it is May who has delivered him from all solitude; only love can destroy the solitude of the human condition.

To sense the depth of the thought Malraux expresses in this scene, we must sense how the love May and Kyo forged and tempered no longer has much in common with the sometimes too sentimental, sometimes too imperfectly sublimated love which invaded the West beginning with the myth of courtly love. To be convinced of this we need only compare, for example, the love found in Saint-Exupéry's work with that found in Malraux's. In Saint-Exupéry's novels love is almost omnipresent; in Malraux's it only appears discreetly. For Saint-Exupéry's heroes, who are bound to their planes like knights to their mounts, love is a crucial element, but they idealize their lady and seek the strength they need to fight for that idealization. The woman is not their equal. She inspires an idealization which is a transposition of the divine eternal over the feminine eternal; a love which is at the origin of the impossible love in which the West, with a certain masochism, delights. For knights this love could inspire the Quest for the Holy Grail; for ordinary men, who must survive and cannot live with an ideal or with sublimation, this love degenerates when it comes into contact with reality, and their women, who are not their equals, become their possessions. For Lancelot du Lac as for Tristan and Romeo, love is inaccessible on this earth. Far from being as strong as death their love will only blossom out of death. Far from delivering man from his solitude their kind of love makes man feel his smallness and his solitude on the earth below.

Granted, Kyo also dies, but he doesn't die because he loves May; he dies because the community he incarnates cannot yet triumph. Just as the new relationship between men which the revolutionary community wanted to bring about could not yet be established, the love which May and Kyo have forged is not yet able to find a place for itself. And if Malraux continues *Man's Fate* beyond Kyo's death, if he ends his novel with the painful dialogue between Gisors and May, it is to demonstrate clearly the meaning of the book, a meaning which is found well beyond revolutionary events. Following Kyo's death Gisors retires to Kobe. He believes his love for his son is as great as May's, and he tells her so. Gisors was attached to other men only through his son, only through his paternal love, and Kyo's death is "a metamorphosis" for him (*MF*

355). It changes his life. He discovers music. He is delivered from anguish, "from death and from life" (ibid.), he accedes to worlds where "there is no real," the "worlds of contemplation—with or without opium—where all is vain," where everything—blood, flesh, suffering, and even death—is absorbed "in the light like music in the silent night" (*MF* 358).

Gisors has trouble truly understanding the love that united May and Kyo. He has trouble understanding a love made of battles fought together, even those that are won. For him love is "the confident contemplation of a beloved face, the incarnation of the most serene music" and he doesn't understand why May's life hasn't changed after Kyo's death. May answers him by saying that her life hasn't changed "like the body of a living person who becomes a dead one does not change" (*MF* 359). May contemplates the serenity of Gisors' face almost with horror, and would willingly see it as cowardice brought on by opium. With her pain fastened up inside, May will carry on the battle out of loyalty to Kyo, to their love; she will carry on the battle so that some day relations will be established between men and women, relations which she and Kyo knew were possible and not utopian. By ending *Man's Fate* with this dialogue Malraux repeats what he so often said in the body of the novel: Only love and fraternity deliver us from the human condition. But he also repeats that there are two possible roads to love: the road of serene contemplation to which Gisors has acceded, even if he is unattached to the community of men, and the road of a committed and fraternal battle, the battle which has united May and Kyo and which May will carry on. For men who do not retire from the world, the road to the advent of love is open; it passes through the woman, through women like May, even if, unfortunately, still too few women have been able to understand her message and follow her example.

When Malraux asserts that love alone delivers man from solitude, he is not just thinking of affective solitude, he is also, and above all, thinking of metaphysical solitude; otherwise he wouldn't have entitled his book *Man's Fate*. Once again, and this time on a metaphysical level, one notes how for Malraux the man/woman relationship is the symbol of relations among all humans, of their relationship with the cosmos and their relationship or nonrelationship with their gods. An old mandarin man had said to Gisors: "Woman is subjugated to man the way man is subjugated to the State." The state protects its members, the boss protects his subordinates, the man protects the woman, the believer begs the protection of his god, but in all cases the counterpart of such protec-

A Fraternal Consciousness

tion is possession. To be protected man agrees to be possessed, even if he rebels from time to time. May and Kyo fight to erase those psychic imprints which have been stamped on human beings for centuries. Kyo is repulsed by the idea that a man might believe he has possessed May. May asks Kyo: "Have I lived like a woman who needs protection?" Kyo fights with himself to expel the reflex thoughts which make him want to exercise "a pitiful protection." Kyo and May succeed in freeing themselves from relationships built upon the notion of protection and which engender psychological and spiritual alienation. They are the symbol of a mental structure, of a culture which will no longer see love and fraternity as inaccessible utopias; no longer consider man too small for fraternity; no longer consider love to be possible only in divine perfection; and no longer delight in the deaths of Tristan and Yseult or of Romeo and Juliet, and in order no longer to delight in them, will no longer consider love and fraternity to be simply more or less romantic inclinations, but rather to be the embodiments of a will to be. In this May and Kyo join the company of Pamina and Tamino, the couple who undergo all the trials of regeneration and who disengage themselves from the undertakings of the Queen of the Night; the couple for whom Sarastro waits to turn over the government of the world to them and retire, for he is but a single man; the couple who enables humanity to sing:

> When virtue and beneficence inspire the great with counsel wise
> Then Doth the heavenly reign commence
> And mortals emulate the skys.[2]

If Kyo and May become the rule rather than the exception, if fraternity and love are no longer seen as unattainable in the world below, if all Kyos are no longer compelled to take cyanide so as not to be thrown alive into the furnace of a locomotive, if all Mays are no longer forced to carry on the battle as widows without the child they always wanted to have, if the false belief, ultimately useful enough, that man is to man automatically and obligatorily a wolf is rejected, then yes, man will become a brother to man, and man will be delivered from solitude. That it be so starting today is a utopian hope, and this is why Kyo dies. That it will be so tomorrow is a possibility, and this is why May carries on the battle.

In the hymn to fraternity which Malraux sings in *Lazarus*, one rediscovers hopes and visions that had already illuminated *Paper Moons* and

---

2. [Mozart, *The Magic Flute*, act 1, scene 26. Translated by Natalia MacFarren. (London: Novello & Co., 1929).]

Farfelu Kingdom. But in the meantime Malraux encountered Kyo delivered from solitude through his love for May; he encountered Magnin and Manuel transformed by that fraternal night in *Man's Hope* when every man had a task to do; he encountered Vincent Berger, who experienced within himself the meaning of the ancient myths of beings torn from death; he encountered—and oh how much—the royal trembling of the hands of Rembrandt and Van Gogh's governing their creations. These encounters completely freed him from the obsession, inherited from past centuries, of wanting to kill the Queen of the *Farfelu Kingdom*, and revealed to him that for man to live among his own kind, for him to tear himself from the complete solitude he feels deep inside and which attaches him neither to others nor to the cosmos, he must live among the images of the only sentiment which is as strong as death: fraternity (cf. *L* 118).

14

A Fellowship of Difference

❦

ROGER STÉPHANE, in *Le Portrait de l'aventurier,* correctly states that "the exercise of authority constitutes one of the fundamental pleasures of sadism." He thus makes fully obvious a fact which is too often forgotten: the surprising number of loyal readers of Sade in Europe is explained less by an attraction for sexual sadism than by a subtle complicity between the basic spirit of sadism and the mindset of those who hold power. In *Man's Fate* Malraux notes: "Sadism with pins is rare; with words, far from rare" (*MF* 220). The exercise of any sort of power—the power of a man over a woman or a woman over a man, of a commander over soldiers, of a boss over workers, of a secretary-general over militants—is almost always accompanied by a certain enjoyment. And the need to constantly augment or refine that enjoyment, which if it isn't improved risks getting dull, is at the origin of the subtle and ferocious game holders of power play in order to continually enlarge the field of their power.

In the exercise of power the spirit of possession has also wreaked havoc. The man one commands is an individual whom one sees as a possession, and even if the ownership is no longer legal, as in the time of slavery, it is psychological. Even today, for many the exercise of power is the exercise of ownership, of possession. The fact that the sense of ownership may be unconscious does not render it less real or profound. When it is not the beautiful will whose praises Nietzsche sings and which some continue to misunderstand, the will to power becomes the will to compel, the will to experience the pleasure of having compelled or of being able to do so. What fascinates men "is not real power, it's the illusion of being able to do exactly as they please . . . Man has no urge to govern; he has an urge to compel" (*MF* 242). Manuel, in *Man's Hope*, says that what three-quarters of Spanish fascists dream of "is not authority, it is having a good time." Authority is subject to something that goes beyond it. "Having a good time" is an enjoyment one offers oneself and which is sought as an end in itself. When Ferral, the president of the Franco-Sino Consortium, declares that intelligence is "the possession of the means of coercing things or men" (*MF* 239), he is a perfect representative of the great majority of current leaders and directors. Ferral, König, the president of the League of Bankers—they all justify their power by using cultural, civilizing, economic, or financial considerations, which enables them not to look inside themselves and not to become aware of the exact nature of the pleasure they experience in governing or directing. Borodine and all the businessmen of the revolution are also unaware of this, and more than anyone else they avoid anything that might awaken them. None of them can understand when they are told that their way of exercising power denies dignity to their subordinates. Ferral cannot understand Valérie's demand for dignity, nor that of the coolies; König can't understand Kyo's, and Borodine sees Garine's request that the dignity of others be respected, including that of his enemies, as belated individualism.

In *Man's Fate* the portrait of the prison guard is a caricature of all those in power who exercise that power as they would an ownership and who derive subtle enjoyment from it. Like all caricatures it exaggerates the features in order to reveal the true spirit. The guard's vileness doesn't seem fully real to Kyo, but "at the same time, it seemed to him a foul fatality, as if power were enough to change almost every man into a beast" (*MF* 300). The words Malraux chooses here are quite strong: "a foul fatality," turning man into a beast. All varieties of beasts are possible: the prison guard changes into a wild and bloodthirsty beast; König, the police chief, changes into a cynical and revanchist beast; Ferral, the captain of industry, changes into a refined and subtle beast; the director of the budget, the bankers, and the minister of finance change into hypocritical and saccharine beasts. It is nevertheless possible to escape from this foul fatality. Malraux gives an example of how. Roger Stéphane, still in *Le Portrait de l'aventurier*, continues writing: "I have only heard one man discuss any exercise of command without sadism—André Malraux, who said to me one day, 'For me, commanding has never consisted of anything but showing a fraternal superiority.'" The accounts of all those who served under Malraux's command in the Alsace-Lorraine Brigade echo Roger Stéphane.

A Fellowship of Difference

How, then, can one escape the "foul fatality" which seems to change almost all men into beasts as soon as they hold any power? How can one escape this destiny, how can one stand up to it? These questions are present in all Malraux's novels, without any exception. Sometimes they surge to the forefront and take center stage, as in *Man's Fate, Days of Wrath,* and *Man's Hope.* At other times they remain less obvious. At all times they impose themselves as questions which man must answer if he wishes one day to be able to answer other questions and truly stand up to the totality of his destiny.

If in all his novels Malraux illustrates the insidious way in which power is exercised in a society which has inherited possessive individualism, he also sketches a new exercise of power which is no longer a will to compel marked by subtle sadism, but an exercise which has become the manifestation of a "fraternal superiority," one which is no longer paternalistic, but fraternal. Ximenes, the Catholic career officer who out of legalism refused the command which the *pronunciamento* of the fascists offered to him, sums up in a wonderful formulation in *Man's Hope* the problem which confronts all the Magnins and all the Manuels of the earth, that is, all those who seek the modalities of this new exercise of power: instead of using "military discipline," which is a possessive and sadistic form of commanding par excellence, how can one succeed in forging a "republican discipline" which is fraternity in action? (cf. *MH* 171).

In 1936–37, after exercising the command of the España Squadron, and after observing how commands were being carried out around him, Malraux knew it was useless to hope that new relations between men might be established if the same techniques of command continued to be used, and especially if the spirit which had given rise to these techniques was maintained. In 1967, after wielding power at the government level and no longer just at the level of a squadron or a brigade, Malraux returned to this subject at length in *Anti-Memoirs.* "The organization of action is the primary task of the statesman . . . the most effective methods in this field have been those of the army and the Church, which were taken up by the totalitarian parties and even, to a lesser extent, by the great capitalist and communist societies" (*A-M* 104). For millennia great legendary figures with political power—with the exception of great kings—have derived legitimacy for their power and for their having entered into history from their military successes, e.g., Alexander, the Roman consuls, Napoleon, Kemal Ataturk, etc. In the twentieth century more than in any other many political men wear the uniform of a military leader in an attempt to establish their power and increase their authority: Stalin, Hitler, Mussolini, and a great many dictators in South America and perhaps soon in Eastern Europe (Jaruzelski will have emulators!). In the twentieth century the methods of the army and the Church—they are not fundamentally different—seem to have found unparalleled success, but perhaps in reality they have known only the excessive, uncontrollable expressions of their death throes. Indeed, two great figures, Gandhi and Nehru, rose up to challenge not one technique of power with another, but an old mindset with a different one.

A reflection on the mindset which supposedly animates and justifies power is the subject of the two lengthy dialogues between Nehru and Malraux. Behind Nehru's "friendly and clearheaded" observations showing regret that India's organization was in the process of becoming electoral, Malraux senses "the inescapable necessity which Lenin, Mao, and Mussolini had come up against, and which was not only the power of the Party but also that of the State, which alone could ensure India's survival and its destiny, the state, which had perhaps haunted Alexander and had certainly haunted Caesar and Charlemagne and Napoleon . . ." (*A-M* 137). Lenin wrote: "There is no instance of a revolution which did not end up by increasing the power of the state" (cf. *A-M* 136), and Nehru sadly questions the extent to which a state can be founded upon nonviolent action, and the extent to which what he has wanted to establish is indeed a state. When Malraux asks Nehru what has been his greatest difficulty since independence, Nehru replies without hesitation: "Creating a just state by just means" (*A-M* 139). And Malraux concludes from that: "Nehru was attempting one of the most profound metamorphoses in the world" (ibid.).

This metamorphosis of power haunted Malraux as he created the character Garine, just as it haunted him as he was writing *Man's Hope* or carrying out his command of the Alsace-Lorraine Brigade, or later performing his role as minister of cultural affairs. It also haunted him as he was reflecting on his life and writing *Anti-Memoirs*. In all Malraux's works Magnin best incarnates what the exercise of power can become when the metamorphosis of power is completed. Magnin won't accept "any conflict between all that revolutionary discipline stands for and those who still are blind to its necessity" (*MH* 116). Magnin wants "each individual man to have a life that isn't classified in terms of what he can exact from others." With a few words, then with a few brief commands, Magnin knows how to reestablish order and calm the minds of the men

A Fellowship of Difference

of the España Squadron. Scali has assumed its command in the interim. He has to confront a revolt of the mercenary airmen. Being an intellectual, like the majority of those who exercise power in contemporary society, he attempts to explain himself to the rebellious men, to convince and seduce them. He would be extremely surprised if someone told him that in truth he is unconsciously attempting to compensate for the fact that he knows only how to compel. He gradually loses ground. Magnin returns just as the tension is about to take a dramatic and irreversible turn. In only a few seconds he has the situation back in hand, and is able to do so without the use of persuasion, seduction, or a stupid exaltation of discipline: he manifests "the supreme fraternal superiority" which characterizes his command throughout the entire novel.

In the introduction to *Malraux: Life and Work,* Martine de Courcel unfortunately repeats an error made by many commentators: "The first question that springs to mind in reading this book," she writes, "is whether Malraux does not have a sort of ontological repulsion for anything organized or established" (p. 4). She then discusses Malraux's being horrified by all that is institutionalized. Malraux's entire life proves the contrary. If Malraux does show revulsion—and he did, indeed, seem to have shown some—it is not revulsion at what is organized or institutionalized; it is at the principles behind the current organization. Malraux didn't reject organizations and institutions either consciously or unconsciously; he didn't deny their necessity; he simply wished for organizations and institutions which would be based upon different relations between men, different principles. With a few exceptions, our institutions and organizations are the heirs of Imperial and Pontifical Rome. The fact that the columns of Roman law and those of canon law were built in the same city is not by chance! The hierarchizing principle of our institutions is based on subordination and multimanagement. Every party cell receives and executes the orders of a higher-up who is *exterior* to it, and who himself receives and executes the orders of another superior. These principles of organization, which were, at best, acceptable in relatively simple societies, become inoperative and unacceptable in increasingly complex and overwhelming societies. As early as in his adolescence Malraux rejected these principles that had become dehumanizing and dreamt of organizations and institutions which would create new relations among men. His early writings and his first works of nonfiction strongly suggest this.

Like Vincent Berger in *The Walnut Trees of Altenburg,* Malraux felt "completely useful and enthusiastic only in the service of something he had himself conceived or helped to conceive" (*WTA* 50), and he undoubtedly felt that this was true for all men. Being neither a theoretician nor a doctrinarian, Malraux never expounds a theory of power, but through his novels, through his dialogues with Nehru and Mao, through his conversations with de Gaulle, one senses the presence of the idea that in the near future power will be a regulation of complexities, all of which participate in the functioning of the whole, and that it will no longer represent a relationship of subordination resulting in the possession of some men by others. A biological image may be used here, without, however, its being used as an analogy. Only a few decades ago, everyone considered the brain to be "the boss" of the other organs in the body; it was considered to be a president or a commanding general toward whom information converged and from whom orders were issued: the movement of muscles, the rhythm of heartbeats, the secretion of glands, etc. Today we see the brain not as an organ to which the other organs are subordinate, but as the most complex organ participating along with all the others in the regulation of the entire body. And we know that the brain can be affected by the disfunctioning or the lack of participation of another organ. Today the organization of a living being appears as a group of functions interconnected through mechanisms of regulation. The structuring power of the living being is not a power through subordination. Large industrial and commercial enterprises are beginning to learn lessons from this. Of all our institutions they are the closest to the example of a living organism. The more complex they become the more they realize that power through subordination results in asphyxia and the more they seek new structures for organization.

A living being is not organized around relationships of subordination. Organs do not carry out orders. Life is organized around participation. When in *Anti-Memoirs* Malraux tells how Mao summed up the way in which the army of the "Long March" was organized, one is struck by the absence of a reference to the notion of command, at least in the way the word is usually used in the army or the Church. Another mindset underlies Mao's words, another notion of power. A notion whose early roots were still fragile and threatened, as Mao well knew. The French ambassador stated that Chinese youth were oriented toward the future that Mao envisioned for them, but Mao, more of a realist, replied that large segments of Chinese society were still "conditioned in such a way that their activity is necessarily orientated toward revisionism" (*A-M* 369). Mao is right. Like all metamorphoses, the metamorphosis of power will take a long time, and centuries, if not millennia, of conditioning, of power through subordination, will not be erased in one or two generations.

If one always finds the hope for and even the necessity of a power based on other principles in Malraux's works, one also finds the idea that there are always authorities opposed to power. In all of Malraux's novels an authority stands up to the wielders of power and limits their freedom of movement. Sometimes this moral authority is invested in a totem such as the Mois of *The Royal Way* or Queen Sebeth of *Anti-Memoirs*. More often this authority is exercised by men who are portrayed as sages, like Chen-Dai, or as just men, like Grandfather Berger. In *Anti-Memoirs* Malraux conveys that Gandhi was an authority before he became a leader. In Malraux's novels the separation of the functions of the king and the sorcerer, or of the leader and the wise man, is presented as obvious, normal, natural; but this separation is never presented as a consequence of a separation between the temporal and the spiritual; it is presented as a necessary balance, as protection against the abuses of power.

In the crucial scene of *Man's Hope* and in the extraordinary images of the film *Sierra de Teruel* which show Magnin and the peasants of Linares climbing into the mountains to look for the wounded airmen, then carrying them down in a huge procession, we cannot overemphasize how Magnin seems to have transmitted to this group of people all the fraternity he possesses. It is highly significant and revealing that Malraux places Magnin's lengthy meditation in this scene. His meditation begins with Magnin's noticing an apple tree, "the only living thing among the rocks, living with the mute ageless indifference of endlessly reincarnated plant life" (*MH* 473). It then leads him to the realization that, in the fraternal procession descending the mountain, "it was not death which harmonized with the mountains at that moment; it was triumphant human will . . . And all that long line of black-clothed peasants, the women with their hair hidden beneath the scarves which they had worn from time immemorial, seemed to have more of the character of an austere triumphal progress than a relief party bringing home wounded men" (*MH* 484). Anyone who has ever been caught up in a truly fraternal procession knows how fraternity sculpts a triumph which is stronger than death.

Two years after commanding the Alsace-Lorraine Brigade Malraux wrote to Father Pierre Bockel: "You know how this type of command implies not solitude (I have encountered almost constant fraternity) but partial isolation" (letter of 25 February 1947). A year later he specified further: "Several times, with soldiers as well as with my closest companions, I sensed the presence of the fraternity I was looking for" (letter of 10 October 1948). Malraux knew from experience that it is wrong to assert that exercising a power and working for greater efficiency are ineluctably opposed to fraternity. Up until now it has always been believed that the exercise of a power was incompatible with fraternity, except sometimes in religious orders. There has never yet been a social, economic, or political group formed whose primary goal is the attainment of and the respect for fraternity. How can it be otherwise in a culture which believes that no man is "big enough" for fraternity? How can it be otherwise when the only religion that made fraternity one of its pillars is also the one which has incited the most cruel of fratricidal wars, developed one of the least fraternal proselytisms, and tolerated the most dreadful pogroms. For a new culture to welcome fraternity, as the old one has welcomed possession through subordination, it is perhaps first necessary that liberty be given free reign. For a long time it has seemed utopian and unthinkable that a state, a commune, a company could be made up of men who are free from each other. This utopia has become a reality today, even if freedom remains to be gained in two out of three countries, and must be endlessly defended everywhere else. Even today many still believe it utopian to assert that life in society might some day be organized around fraternal men who are each other's equals; many still consider it utopian that power and fraternity might be reconciled the way Magnin and Malraux reconciled them. But all those who thus too easily strip the word "utopia" of one of the most fundamental hopes of our time should at least recognize that the hope that one day the "Garines" of the world will no longer be overcome by the "Borodines," the hope that the "Magnins" will one day people the earth, and the hope that fills *Lazarus* upon Malraux's return from the Salpêtrière, is a hope untainted with naiveté which rests on no illusion.

It is not the man of the old culture who will forge fraternal groups and societies; Malraux knew this and said as much. At one time he had hoped that Soviet society would create a new humanism and enable man to defend "not what separates him from other men, but that which enables him to join them outside of themselves" (*Commune*, November 1934). In 1934 Malraux still thought that Soviet society was not threatening mankind, only the individual. He was wrong and realized it. The following year Malraux published excerpts from *Days of Wrath* in a journal. In response to the criticism these excerpts provoked, Malraux wrote a preface for the book's publication in which he outlined "very briefly," a few ideas he was holding on to for later development (*DW* 3). This "very briefly" forced Malraux to write one of his most concise and densest texts:

> The world of a work like this, the world of tragedy, is the ancient world still . . . individual antagonisms, which make possible the complexity of the full-length novel, do not figure here . . . The history of artistic sensibility in France for the past fifty years might be called the death-agony of the brotherhood of man. Its real enemy is an unformulated individualism which existed sporadically throughout the nineteenth century and which sprang less from the will to create a man whole than from a fanatical desire to be different . . . The individual stands in opposition to society, but he is nourished on it. And it is far less important to know what differentiates him than what nourishes him. (*DW* 3–6)

This 1935 text expresses a position which Malraux always held, and which he developed on several occasions in his writings on art. For example, in 1950 he writes: "Every great style of the past impresses us as being a special interpretation of the world, but this collective conquest is obviously a sum total of the individual conquests that have gone to its making" (*VOS* 334). At the end of his life Malraux would have undoubtedly avoided the reference to collectivity, which had in the meantime taken on another meaning; but that isn't of great importance, for his thinking is clear: The individual, when he is not possessed by the fanaticism of difference, is nourished by the community, and the community is nourished by individuals. How many times has it been said or written that Malraux was an individualist and even that he was a belated romanticist! I don't know of any claim that is further from what André Malraux truly was. And the biographers who have constructed their biographies upon this idea seem to me to have been more carried away by their own temperament than carried along by the life and works of Malraux. André Vandegans was right when he specified in the conclusion of his work on the literary youth of André Malraux that, in Malraux, "the 'I' glorifies itself to escape emptiness, then loses itself in the 'we,' where it assumes its essence of a man." Like certain mystics Malraux *sees* in the strongest sense of the verb *to see;* that is, he can envision the whole in the part, and the part in the whole. Like Vincent Berger in the presence of the venerable walnut trees of Altenburg, Malraux senses "an impression of free will and of endless metamorphosis" (*WTA* 115); he sees the tree in the leaf and the leaf in the tree. For Malraux the "I" without the "We" has no more meaning than does the "We" without the "I." And this is why, in *The Temptation of the West,* the young European A.D. cannot follow his friend, the Chinese Ling, when the latter asserts that "the supreme beauty of a cultured civilization is to be found in the careful avoidance of nurturing the 'I'" (*TW* 59). Here we arrive at the heart of the spiritual battle Malraux waged throughout his life and which he won only at the very end: the one he waged to escape the disfiguring opposition between the individualist consciousness taught by Christendom and Western philosophies on the one hand and, on the other, the careful avoidance of nurturing the "I" taught by Oriental religions and philosophies. For a very, very long time, Malraux sought a way for man to reconcile within himself "the sensation of being a particle of the universe" and "the awareness of being a living organism, complete, discrete" (*TW* 33). For almost all his life, Malraux remained torn between the two sensibilities which inhabited him at the same time and nourished his constant thoughts on internalized givens: the sensibility which led him to sense man as a unique whole and that which led him to perceive man as an ephemeral particle.

For Malraux this sense of being torn apart, such as most mystics have endured, continued until his descent into the realm of the dead, until the Salpêtrière hospital, in November 1972. When he returned to the realm of the living, life presented itself to him in a new light. From that moment Malraux saw metamorphosis no longer as just the law of the world of art; it became the law of the entire universe, and in it he reconciled the whole and the particle he felt himself to be. He was then ready for the revelation he experienced two years later when he found himself for the first time in front of the Nachi waterfall.

To assert that the "I" has meaning only in the "We," to assert that man is simultaneously an ephemeral particle and a unique whole, is obviously to place oneself on a metaphysical plane. But for men like Malraux or like Gandhi and Nehru, metaphysical assertions, profoundly sensed and not simply intellectualized, are meant to be transformed into realities; they inspire the actions which then seek to change the relations between the individual and the group. *Man's Fate* and *Man's Hope* endlessly establish this dialectic concerning the relationship between the individual and the group. Until now all cultures have believed it impossible to truly reconcile the individual and the group, even when they forced themselves to see that the encouragement of the one wasn't too much to the detriment of the other. All cultures, until now, have believed it impossible to build societies in which the individual has meaning only within the group, and in which the group has meaning only vis-à-vis the individual. In *Mémoires d'outre-tombe* Chateaubriand sums up this centuries-old mentality when he asserts that society dwindles when the individual grows in importance, and vice versa.

In the Orient the individual, who has no essential metaphysical reality, also has no reality with regard to society. In the West, following the birth of gothic religious individualism, the notion of society is crystalized around the idea of the protection of individuals and their property. The excesses of these societies born of possessive individualism resulted in the eighteenth and nineteenth centuries in forging the notion of societies responsible for the common good. Actually, the nineteenth century rediscovered and adapted the Roman Imperium and, like it, paved the way for imperialism. The individual, having become an instrument of the group, is subordinate to it, and especially to the greatest of groups, the state, which produces its own finalities and pursues only them. All groups have gradually done the same thing: their members, their elements, are nothing but their servants. It is possible to observe the cruel way in which this occurs even in liberal societies; they, too, in the name of the general interest, have ended up pursuing their own societal ends and considering their citizens as instruments to be used to achieve those ends. Associations have undergone a comparable evolution, and more particularly those associations known as unions and political parties. Confronted with commercial institutions established in order to attain their own objectives, to grow and make a profit, the aim of associations has been to defend their members and see that their needs are taken into account. But as soon as an association succeeds, as soon as it grows to a certain size, it becomes much more interested in its own problems and in the pursuit of its own objectives than in representing and listening to its members. To be convinced of this we need only to observe the increasing frequency of the situations in which leaders of a group are "overwhelmed" by their members, and the frequency of a hypocritical corollary: the declarations of leaders asserting that they listen to their members.

In *Man's Fate* the problem of the relationship between the individual and the group is constantly raised. Ch'en wants to transform terrorism into a religion in order to legitimize the individual as he confronts the group. Clappique invents successive biographies for himself and finds "the most dazzling success of his life" (*MF* 313) in a lie which is designed better than any other lie, because he is a pure individualist and can find no place in any group. Gisors takes refuge in opium or isolates himself in Kobe because he can't conceive of himself as an individual, nor can he adhere to any group around him ... Only Kyo, Katov, and May incarnate the reconciliation of the individual and the group. Granted, Kyo and Katov die, but their action, despite the repression that has beaten down an exhausted China, remains "incrusted like the inscriptions of the early empires in the river gorges" (*MF* 359). May, the woman, who can carry life inside her, carries on the battle. She had been inhabited by an "always passionate desire" to have a child by Kyo (ibid.). She will never have that child, nor any other, for after Kyo's death that desire seems to be a betrayal. The child that Kyo and May might have had assumes the value of a symbol. Malraux would most likely have given them that child, as he had given one to Anna and Kassner, if Kyo's and May's battle had been victorious. For Kyo and May to have procreated, for their offspring to have been able to live, it would have been necessary for the individual and the group to be reconciled not only on a metaphysical level, but also in everyday life, in social life. For Malraux they were not yet reconciled on the metaphysical level and even less so in social life. Kyo's and May's child would not have been able to live the values it would have represented, and this is why May didn't have a child. All the same, one can't help thinking that Magnin and Manuel in *Man's Hope* greatly resemble the offspring that May might have had.

The revolutionaries of *Man's Fate* are beaten by the capitalists, but that happens only because their leaders sacrifice them to the situation of the moment as they see it, and to the "general interest" as they perceive it. Going up the river toward Hankow, Kyo experiences "how difficult it was for him to get a solid basis for his activity if he no longer consented purely and simply to obey the instructions of the International. But the International was wrong" (*MF* 155). Kyo comes to Hankow to meet with Vologin, the delegate of the International (cf. *MF* 144). During the meeting Vologin "was much more ill at ease than he appeared ... he was there to see that the decisions made by more qualified, better informed comrades than he were carried out." The "objective" analysis of the situation as seen from Moscow, the "general interest" as seen from the offices of the Kremlin, called for compromises, even if they should lead to the destruction of the revolutionary community of Shanghai. It is also in the name of the general interest that Ferral has to bow down before the hypocritical demands of the Parisian bankers who expect to divide up among themselves the promising spoils of the Consortium by hiding behind the safe appearance of a minister of finance concerned with the common good. For the financial capitalists as well as for the businessmen of the revolution, the general interest has become a ruse.

At one time the general interest was seen as the interest of the many opposed to that of the one: the monarch who gradually ended up no longer seeing himself as the Lieutenant of God in his kingdom. Today, the general interest serves as a front to hide the interests of the social group, whichever it may be, that truly wields power. The general interest has become the deceptive covering of individual interests that have organized their lasting or momentary convergence. On April 17 1948, in Marseilles, Malraux, at that time the propagandist for the Rassemblement du Peuple Français, cried out: "We then gave for the first time a serious content to the idea of general interest . . . We have brought back to a country that had forgotten it since the death of Hoche and the death of Saint-Just this idea of the general interest on which France will, in the future, be based" (Lacouture, 377). The immediate future—"on which France . . . will be based"—Malraux employed in 1948 was too optimistic, but that fact isn't very important, and will most likely not be important to future generations. What is important is that in this speech Malraux expressed what had already been expressed in so many dialogues of *Man's Hope:* the belief in a general interest that would be something other than the ruse which had been used for the last two centuries. Malraux's reference to Saint-Just is significant. For Saint-Just, institutions were "the rule of an immense convent where the cockade replaces the cross" (*TN* 119). In Saint-Just "the Republic found its principal incarnation, far from politicians and imposture." For Saint-Just and for many of those who listened to him, "the Republic wasn't just a system of government; it was first and foremost an Apocalypse, and the hope for an unknown world" (*TN* 126). The Republic Saint-Just hoped for didn't have time to exist, since most of his contemporaries only wanted "to reestablish the State in order to have power within it" (*TN* 127). No one as much as Saint-Just "hoped so passionately to *change man.*" He wanted to create institutions to shape men. But Saint-Just would not have respected the diversity and plurality of beliefs and opinions. Indeed, he possessed "an apparently intellectual monotheism, which was truly ethical and almost religious" (*TN* 125). The passion for totalization which animates great religious figures made Saint-Just "passionately totalitarian" (*TN* 121), just as it turns most religious leaders who become worldly leaders into totalitarians.

"If only each man would direct upon himself one-third of the efforts he devotes nowadays to politics, Spain would become quite a habitable country" (*MH* 323), thought old Alvear at the height of the civil war (cf. *MH* 322). He prayed for a society which would seek to make men responsible, not to a cause—even to that of the oppressed—but to themselves, which, he added, is the hardest thing of all, whatever people may say. Until the present time societies as such have never considered their goal to be the shaping of man or his quality as a man, or his responsibility to himself. These concerns were passed on to religions, and as a result religions degenerated, for they were forced to grant more importance to morals than to spirituality. Like old Alvear, Malraux hoped for societies whose primary goal would be the shaping of man, and in many respects Malraux's life seems to have been a struggle to prepare the way for such societies. For Malraux a great culture is a shaping of man. He hoped and even predicted that after societies whose objectives are to exercise the imperium of the state, to ensure the protection of the property of individuals, to produce and distribute wealth, there will be societies whose primary aim is the shaping of men in a respect for the plurality of opinions and beliefs. After imperial and police societies, after societies of production and distribution, Malraux was preparing the advent of cultural societies. It is in this sense that we must understand what Malraux optimistically said in the continuation of his April 17, 1948, speech in Marseilles: "We have given this country a certain number of ideas it has needed. We have made France understand that the idea of democracy, the one that was defended by people you are aware of was an imposture pure and simple; France now understands that democracy remains to be created . . ." And we must see the same meaning in the statement Malraux attributed to de Gaulle in 1971: "True democracy is ahead of us, not behind us; it has still to be created" (*FO* 124).

Saint-Just lived "with a truth that called for fellowship, not adherence" (*TN* 126), but Saint-Just's truth excluded all other truths, and in that he announced the totalitarianism of fascisms and communisms with their "unique and all-powerful party" (*TN* 121). Malraux also hoped for a society in which men could live in fellowship and not through adherence, but unlike Saint-Just, the fellowship Malraux sought could not be based on the belief in ONE truth and thus on the exclusion of all others. The fellowship Malraux sought had to be based on the respect for all truths—political, ideological, cultural, and religious.

Always present to a certain degree in Malraux's novels, the themes of fellowship and community take increasingly distinct shape in each successive work. In *The Conquerors* Garine seeks fellowship and not discipline. In *The Royal Way* Perken, who is cut off from the community of

A Fellowship of Difference

men because it requires too many "absurd or calculated compromises" (*RW* 27), gradually comes to feel a fellowship with the Mois. And if in the end he is destroyed by the Mois, it is because he gives them the impression that he is on the side of the French state, which, like all states, excludes fellowship and is concerned only with lengthening its railroad lines (cf. *RW* 255). In *Man's Fate* the main character is the revolutionary community and not such and such a revolutionary hero. In *Days of Wrath* the feeling of fellowship in fraternity saves Kassner from madness. In *Man's Hope* Malraux emphasizes from the very beginning the union achieved for the first time between liberals, anarchists, republicans, union members, socialists, and communists who "joined in an attack on their common foe and his machine-guns" (*MH* 22); for the first time an "underground fellowship" fills the darkness, which "was all fraternity" and where "each man had something to do on earth" (*MH* 11). Finally, in *The Walnut Trees of Altenburg* the theme of fellowship grows to the dimension of a cosmic fellowship, to a fellowship with life.

In June 1936 in his lecture on "cultural heritage," Malraux declared: "For my part I willingly agree to see the rebirth in all men of fellowship in the fundamental realm of human emotions." Thirty years later, in his speech on the occasion of the first illumination of the Acropolis, and after praising the genius of ancient Greece which had given man strength in the face of his gods and despots, Malraux asserted that "among all the values of the spirit the most fertile are those born of fellowship and courage" (*OF* 44). Convinced when he was just an adolescent that man could only be reborn through participation in communal values, Malraux sought throughout his life to discover what that fellowship might be and upon what it could be established. As early as 1935 in front of the International Writers' Congress for the defense of culture against fascism, Malraux developed the theme of fellowship and difference, a theme he subsequently never ceased to elaborate and which formed the essential part of the preface to *Days of Wrath*: "It is difficult to be a man. But it is not more difficult to become one by enriching one's fellowship with other men than by cultivating one's individual peculiarities. The former nourishes with at least as much force as the latter that which makes man human, which enables him to surpass himself, to create, invent, or realize himself" (*DW* 7–8). In 1973, in his conversations with Guy Suarès published under the title *Malraux, the Voice of the West,* Malraux seems to lengthen the preface to *Days of Wrath* and enrich it with reflections from an entire life. These conversations are crucial but unfortunately too little known. From the beginning Malraux, referring to when he was twenty years old, specifies: "I sensed the difference between civilizations, between mental structures, to be a fundamental notion of man. Or, if you wish, I experienced the vague feeling of difference as an essential mystery of the civilization in which I had been born." A bit later he adds: "I told you earlier of the fundamental feeling of Difference. I believe that the Absurd is the feeling of Difference sensed negatively, experienced as anguish and pain. Difference can be experienced with indifference, with exaltation, as multiplicity, plurality . . . and it can be experienced as tragedy. There is no doubt that our civilization has experienced it as tragedy and has found the myth of the absurd in it" (*VO* 20).

This text is crucial because in it one rediscovers, in another form and on another level, the reconciliation between the "I" and the "We" for which Malraux had been looking for so long. In metaphysics as well as in politics (we are finally beginning to realize the connection between these two realms), Malraux attempted to reconcile two apparently contradictory necessities: the need to solidify one's fellowship with others and the need to cultivate one's difference. Malraux sought to reconcile two feelings which have always been antagonistic: the feeling that only sharing communal values can enable man to be reborn and the feeling of difference as a mystery and as the basic foundation of man.

An Oriental is indifferent to the sense of his difference. The Westerner, on the other hand, first finds a momentary exaltation in it, then discovers tragedy and anguish. This first opposition results in a second which is paradoxical only in appearance: being indifferent to the sense of his difference, the Oriental easily admits that differences are irreconcilable. The Westerner, on the other hand, who has ultimately found only anguish in the exaltation of his sense of difference, attempts to reassure himself by basing his scientific and philosophic thoughts on analogies and resemblances which deny or devalue difference.

Malraux agrees that "cultivating one's difference" can represent one of the means which enable man to realize himself, but under the condition that it doesn't end in "an effort at self-development, the only aim of which is to acquire power" (*TW* 118–19). For Malraux, the feeling of difference can be experienced without tragedy or anguish under the condition that it be an affirmation and a recognition of multiplicity and plurality. Plurality, which is the daughter of metamorphosis, constitutes one of the principal themes of *Anti-Critique*, the beautiful postscript Malraux wrote for *Malraux: Life and Work*. Malraux proposed to call this type of

A Fellowship of Difference

collective book *Colloquies,* as opposed to biographies, since its basic characteristic is plurality. "When the awareness of metamorphosis comes to dominate evolution and to create its own history, will another attempt to grasp man, a new kind of biography, take shape over and above the one we already know? Under what name should this ever-increasing type of book be known? The old title *Miscellanea* springs to mind, but they are as inconclusive as the others were affirmative, even when they do not give rise to any questions. Let us therefore call them *Colloques*" (*AC* 224). Through its method alone the Colloquy "regards its pluralistic approach as important" (*AC* 232). In his three last works—*Anti-Critique,* the final chapters of *The Timeless,* and *Precarious Man*—Malraux presents remarkably coherent and calm thoughts. He returns to pluralism all the significance of which it had been stripped by a narrow view of monism, theist or not. He trusts in the colloquia of tomorrow, because the colloquy truly understands metamorphosis; because "the Colloquy conspires with hazard to be on the lookout for the irrational aspects of the world" (*AC* 250).

Under the influence of catholicity the Westerner became used to thinking that there couldn't be fellowship on this earth, and that in order to experience fellowship it was necessary to wait for the fellowship of the saints. A scene in *Days of Wrath*—we could cite many others in Malraux's other novels—illustrates what a fellowship of the living might truly be. Kassner, freed from prison by the ultimate gesture of fraternity of the comrade who passed himself off as Kassner, escapes to a little tourist plane which will secretly take him out of Germany. The weather is very bad. Kassner doesn't know anything about the pilot except the passion which animates him and that together they are going to risk their lives. It stirs Kassner even more deeply "to feel that they were united not in their persons but in their common devotion, as if each step toward the machine was bringing him nearer to an austere and powerful friendship of a sort rare on this earth" (*DW* 120). An individualist can only feel connected to a person he knows; for such an individual only the personal tie, the tie between each person, can create a union. But that alone means his field of possible unions is restricted, it cannot result in true fellowship. Malraux, like Kassner, had no need for personal ties to feel connected. He who was always so discreet about his personal feelings, expressed this clearly to Guy Suarès: "I always feel involved in a human relationship, either personal or impersonal. I have no personal ties with the Glières, where I am to speak on Sunday, but I have a human connection, and I feel strongly involved" (*VO* 169). People's relationships with each other in the West of possessive individualism are relations strongly characterized by appropriation and possessiveness. Paternal and maternal loves are most often possessive loves. The concept of family—first aristocratic, based on the ownership of a title and of land; then bourgeois, based on contracts signed in the presence of a notary—clearly expresses the appropriation which is at the base of familial relationships (it might be suggested to whoever doubts this that he look carefully at how the first phases of many analytical treatments are carried out; he might then see how remembrances serve first to wash away relationships of appropriation which have been all the more traumatic because they have taken the place of love relationships). Relationships between men and women, even when true feelings exist, most often reflect a mute possessive struggle, a mute struggle for the appropriation of the one by the other. Ultimately, social relations are essentially reflections of an ownership of the means of production and of the goods which the individual may or may not possess.

Fellowship is not based on ownership and cannot result in appropriation. It is based on community. The blossoming of communities, or the sometimes clumsy attempts at establishing a community, which has been occurring since the second half of the twentieth century, reflects the agony of possessive individualism and the fundamental need for true fellowship. The very notion of ownership is in the process of changing, and its judicial content is weakening: from co-ownership into multi-ownerships, it is undergoing a transformation through which, in the guise of adapting to current circumstances, it is gradually being emptied of itself and is being prepared to dissolve in the presence of the community. Individualism cultivated appropriation and the fanaticism of difference. Collectivism and totalitarianism have attempted to respond to it by encouraging a leveling of differences and by challenging plurality. In Malraux one always finds the avoidance of these two phases and the hope that once the metamorphosis of culture has been achieved, it will be possible for a fellowship of differences to flourish, and for there to be born a man who will invent, create, and surpass himself by deepening his fellowship *and* by cultivating his difference. Malraux's hope joins that of biologists and other scientists who know today that the genetic code inscribed in the DNA of an individual is not enough to explain the variety of forms each individual can assume. They know they will have to call upon another code, this time belonging to the species, and perhaps even upon a more fundamental or more primordial code which theoret-

A Fellowship of Difference

ical hypotheses are already attempting to imagine and describe. The relationship between the "I" and the "We" is at the heart of contemporary science just as it is at the heart of the philosophy (political or not) and of the metaphysics of today and tomorrow.

A chrysalis crawling on the ground cannot imagine the perceptions and sensations of a butterfly flying from flower to flower. In the same way, it is impossible to imagine what the fellowship of differences and its modalities will be when the metamorphosis of culture in progress is achieved. In order to do so, we would have to wash words like "person," "group," "individual," etc., of their current vague meanings; they would have to have already taken on their new meanings and have awakened the new realms of feelings they will awaken tomorrow. An image, however, might help to imagine how a collectivity might truly be transformed into a community; the image of an orchestra rehearsing. When through his culture and mentality the conductor still adheres to possessive individualism, in this case enlarged to the extreme by stardom, the musicians, under the conductor's baton (the French expression, "chef" ["leader"], is significant), seem drawn in by his talent, by his magnetism, and often by his authoritarianism. The work of rehearsing is then choppy, and if cohesion is created, it is accomplished through the conductor and in the conductor. The more the musicians are individualists attempting either consciously or not to cultivate their differences and those of their own instruments, the more the authority and the magnetism of the conductor are necessary. The conductor then has the crucial role of forcing the musicians to surpass their individuality. The work of an orchestra and its sonority are completely different when the conductor has freed himself from an individualistic mentality and when he assigns himself the task of giving birth through the musicians to a fellowship of differences. Chamber music represents a realm where this fellowship can be experienced to the fullest. When musicians in a quartet or a quintet have been assembled for the first time, their individualities, their differences, and their difficulties in finding a fellowship fill the acoustic space and fill it all the more when each of the musicians is a star. If, on the other hand, they are used to working together, to interpreting together the violin's difference, that of the viola and that of the cello are no longer cultivated in and of themselves, but are affirmed in order to blend into the communal score. True chamber music brings to the listener the beneficent feeling of being admitted into a fellowship of differences more easily than does symphonic music. And we can thus undoubtedly understand one of the reasons for the general public's recent enthusiasm for this music which was once considered too difficult for the average listener.

The fellowship of differences Malraux sought is completely opposed to the view of the group which Teilhard de Chardin proposed in 1945 in *Quelques réflexions sur les droits de l'homme*. Teilhard writes that the society of the future must "combine everything for the completion of the individual through a well-constructed integration of the latter into the unified group in which one day humanity must organically and physically end up." The choice of words—"integration" and not "fellowship," "unified" and not "united," "completion," "culminate," etc.—reveals the profound thinking by which Teilhard de Chardin's reflections were always nourished. It is the vision which, through an excess of monism, presents a cosmos as completed, culminating, being integrated into an omega point toward which everything converges and in which everything is unified. In Malraux's works one never finds the idea of completion, which would, moreover, be irreconcilable with that of "Metamorphosis as Universal Law." In his vision of humanity to come, Malraux was closer to Leopold Senghor, who evoked "communal cooperation which throughout all time has been held in high honor in Africa and which has never taken on the collectivist form of the aggregates of individuals." Malraux was also closer to Nehru, who saw socialism as "cooperation in the service of the community."

In Florence in the fifteenth century painting caused a world governed by the unreal to succeed a world governed by fellowship. The great ebbing of fellowship had already begun. Stage by stage man has thus slowly made his way toward "the jolting of the individual obsessed with rivaling transcendence and community" (cf. *Ir* 47; *Int* 300). Today, the individual knows he will not be the winner in this rivalry, and he can't help asking himself the fundamental question upon which Malraux concludes his preface to *L'Enfant du rire* by Father Pierre Bockel: "It is possible for a believer to first see in transcendence the most powerful means to his fellowship. It is certain that for an agnostic the most important question of our time becomes: Can there exist fellowship without transcendence, and if not, upon what can man establish his supreme values? Upon what unrevealed transcendence can he establish his fellowship?"

15

Reconciled Man

IN MADRID, pounded by pro-Franco artillery, a small-caliber shell explodes in front of a church. The pigeons that have flown away return and, intrigued, look at the new fissures in the frontons. All Malraux's novels contain numerous scenes that, like this one, present vegetal or animal life reigning above or beyond the life of men and their human struggles. Malraux particularly liked to cite what had been told to him by a friend who had begun collecting butterflies when he discovered that his illness was terminal: "Often now I put myself in the position of the butterflies . . . They have existed for two hundred and sixty million years, and the average life of a butterfly lasts two months . . . In Java, in Bali, they were there long before man . . . They surely must exchange butterfly stories: the flowers left the trees to become offerings, to deck the hair . . . Surely they must say, we have been the same butterflies for so long, and the puny stories of men . . . seem so frenzied and irrational." (*FO* 38). When Malraux told this story to de Gaulle he added, "If the universe is not viewed as a dependency of man, mankind is just one event among many. I quoted to my poor friend from the sacred Indian text the passage where, after the battle, large butterflies 'come to settle on the dead warriors and the sleeping conquerors'" (ibid.).

In *The Royal Way* man is tormented by vegetation that invades everything, and by insects that swarm over the rocks of the temples. The vegetal and animal conditions seem stronger, more durable than the human condition. To reach the goal he has set himself, Claude must conquer a hostile nature. There is no profound connection between him and that nature. Nature and he are enemies and they fight each other. As a product of his culture, Claude has distanced himself from nature, not only because he is a Westerner and finds himself in a tropical forest that is foreign to him, but much more fundamentally because nature, for him, is only an element to be conquered; this is true for Perken, as well. Nature, in its wildest form, takes its revenge on them, especially on Perken.

After freeing the adventurer Grabot, whom the Mois had reduced to nothing more than a beast of burden harnessed day and night to a treadmill, Claude and Perken impotently witness the preparations of the Mois who will capture them at dusk. They appear to have no other choice than to submit to the savages or flee into the forest—but the forest would be stronger than they, and they know it. In the end Perken manages to strike a deal which saves them: Grabot will be exchanged for jars, one per warrior in the Moi village. But when Perken approaches the Moi chief to negotiate with him he falls on a poisoned dart. His slow descent into death begins. It lasts for days on end while in the background we witness the struggle between the wild, savage tribes and the military unit whose orders are to "clean up" the region before the arrival of crews coming to construct a railroad line. In his final death throes Perken is reduced to nothing: he has lost his authority over the savages and he realizes that his presence alone is no longer enough to prevent the state from taking over "his" region: "For them, too . . . I'm a dead man" (cf. *RW* 260). The entire game of Perken's adventure is forfeit. He played his game between the savages, whose cultural code is to live like nature, and the state, whose cultural code is to blindly dominate nature. He played his game between the "barbaric menace" (*RW* 272) and "the white man's madness" (*RW* 275), and he lost. And when Perken in a penultimate burst of energy attempts to return to "his" region, Claude realizes "how much the older of the two Perken was" (*RW* 244). Despite the quality and the intensity of the friendship that links them, Claude realizes how much Perken and he are "utterly unlike," how much they seem "men of alien races." In fact, Claude contains the seeds of another attitude toward nature, of another relationship between the mineral, vegetable, and animal kingdoms of which man is a part; another relationship which is gradually crystalized in the novels Malraux wrote after *The Royal Way*.

For many years Malraux seemed almost fascinated by ruins: ruins of Khmer temples, ruins of the Queen of Sheba, future ruins in which "no trace will then be left of the [Florentine] palaces which saw Michelangelo pass by, nursing his grievances against Raphael; and nothing of the little Paris cafés where Renoir once sat beside Cézanne, Van Gogh be-

Reconciled Man

side Gauguin" (*VOS* 641). This fascination was interrogative. Those ruins questioned Malraux, and Malraux questioned them. Even more than dead planets, more than geological indifference and the silence of the starry millennia, ruins placed Malraux in a terribly concrete and sensitive confrontation with a force which belongs to the earth of mankind, that is superior to man, and makes humanity "an event among others." A confrontation with a force which radically undermines any anthropocentrism. "The day may come when, contemplating a world given back to the primeval forest, a human survivor will have no means even of guessing how much intelligence Man once imposed upon the forms of the earth" (*VOS* 641). The three great monotheist religions centered everything around man. What obsessed Malraux, on the contrary, what pushed him along on his spiritual quest, was his feeling that man was no longer the oldest enigma, nor even perhaps the most constant or the most important one. In answer to the anguished imploring of Perken, who in an outburst of revolt and impotence asks, while pointing out "the tremendous menace of the night: To live on in defiance of all that—can you realize what that means?" (*RW* 168), Garine provides an initial response: "You must never let go of the earth . . . those who want to let go of the earth find it sticking to their fingers" (*Con* 162–64). But Garine's response is only a first step. The true response is given by the apple tree in *Man's Hope* and especially by the two walnut trees in *Altenburg*.

The apple tree in *Man's Hope* is the one that Magnin observes intensely when he climbs in search of the airmen who have crashed in the Sierra de Teruel. This apple tree is "the only living thing among the rocks, living with the mute ageless indifference of endlessly reincarnated plant-life" (*MH* 473). Its apples had not been picked. They had fallen and formed "a ring of decaying, [seed-filled] fruit" (*MH* 482) around the tree. While descending the Sierra, Magnin passes once again in front of the apple tree and sees it in a completely new way, for in the meantime he has become aware, thanks to the huge fraternal procession that carried the wounded, of the fact that it isn't death which rules the mountain, but triumphant human will. "The ring of decaying fruit" could then take on its full significance: it "seemed to typify the passage from life to death that was not only the doom of men but was an immutable law of the universe" (ibid.). It is also an attentive look at apple trees that introduces Vincent Berger's meditation, then his contemplation in *The Walnut Trees of Altenburg*. In Malraux's works the apple tree is not the tree of forbidden fruit; it is the tree which leads to the path of a revelation of life. And one can't help thinking here of the verse in Genesis in which Yahweh voices his fear that man, after eating the fruit of the first tree, would proceed to the fruit of the second: "Behold," said Yahweh/God, "the man is become as one of us, to know good and evil: and now, lest he put forth his hand, and take also of the tree of life, and eat, and live forever ..." (Genesis 3:22). Then Yahweh/God chased man from the garden of Eden and placed at its entrance "Cherubims and a flaming sword which turned every way, to keep the way of the tree of life" (Genesis 3:24). Thus through his fears, his words, and his actions Yahweh/God seems to have authenticated what the Serpent said to Eve: "Ye shall not surely die: For God doth know that in the day ye eat thereof, then your eyes shall be opened, and ye shall be as gods, knowing good and evil" (Genesis 3: 4, 5).

Vincent Berger's great meditation and contemplation occur shortly after the end of the Altenburg colloquium. Vincent Berger leaves the room where the colloquium has ended without the participants having answered the question which was the theme of the gathering: "Is there any factor on which we can base the notion of man?" With his ears still ringing with the intelligent, but ultimately vain words that have been spoken, Vincent Berger walks through fields and along roads. "The sun was setting, kindling the red apples on the apple-trees. Idle thoughts, orchards eternally re-born, which the same fears always kindle like this evening's sun" (*WTA* 114). Continuing his walk and easing his mind, Vincent Berger reaches a level of communion with the universe which is not easily communicable, for it doesn't belong to the realm of thought or reflection, but to the realm that is opened up through contemplation when silence is accomplished inside oneself and when one's entire being fuses with the spectacle it beholds.

Vincent Berger stops in front of some big trees: firs, lindens, and above all two magnificent walnut trees. The sight of these trees first reminds Vincent Berger of the wooden statues which decorated the room where the colloquium was held. But those statues are the fruit of human will, and the memory of them has to be erased in the presence of the will of the cosmos. "The magnificence of the venerable trees was due to their great bulk, but the strength with which the twisted branches sprang from their enormous trunks, the bursting into dark leaves of this wood which was so heavy and so old that it seemed to be digging down into the earth and not sprouting from it, created at the same time an impression of free will and of endless metamorphosis" (*WTA* 115). In the distance, between the trunks of the two walnut trees, Vincent Berger could see the steeples of the Strasbourg cathedral and, closer, the vineyards that rolled down to the Rhine and gave proof of human patience and labor. For Vincent Berger, absorbed in his contemplation, cathedral and vines are only "an evening decoration round the venerable thrust of the living wood" (ibid.). Slowly, gradually, contemplation becomes vision, an almost Franciscan vision: "Instead of supporting the weight of the world, the tortured wood of these walnut trees flourished with life everlasting ... Between the statues and the logs there were the trees, and their design, which was as mysterious as that of life itself" (*WTA* 115–16).

If one perceives the true depth and significance of Vincent Berger's meditation and vision, one can then begin to understand the reasons why Malraux entitled his novel *The Walnut Trees of Altenburg* and not the colloquium of Altenburg. If one can join Vincent Berger in his contemplation, if one can share Walter Berger's feeling that thanks to Nietzsche's singing in the St. Gothard tunnel, "the millennia of the starlit sky seemed as completely wiped out by man as our own petty destinies are wiped out by the starlit sky" (*WTA* 73), then one can understand how in the final pages of *The Walnut Trees of Altenburg* the narrator—is he also Malraux?—dares to say: "[T]his morning I am all birth. I can still feel within me the invasion of the earthly darkness ... so now from the night there rises the miraculous revelation of day ... I feel myself in the presence of an unaccountable gift—an apparition ... With its trees branching out like veins, the universe is as complete and mysterious as a young body ... the biblical dawn in which the centuries jostle" (*WTA* 222–24).

Throughout his *farfelu* works and his novels, Malraux attempted and succeeded in freeing himself from all his cultural inheritance that influenced relations between man and nature. He freed himself easily from the mentality that advocates more or less openly a submission or an abandonment to nature and to the cosmos. He freed himself with slightly more difficulty from the Judeo-Christian heritage, which advocates man's domination over nature; a domination which God prescribes to Adam and Eve: "Be fruitful, and multiply, and replenish the earth, and subdue it: and have dominion over the fish of the sea, and over the fowl of the air, and over every living thing that moveth upon the earth" (Genesis 1:28). Malraux freed himself from all that inheritance, and when he completed *The Walnut Trees of Altenburg,* which was to be his final novel, he acceded to a vision of the cosmos in which all forms of life fuse into a single destiny; in which all artificial and deforming distinctions between nature and culture are abolished. We must be careful here of the way we define the word "nature." It is not the nature dear to Jean-Jacques Rousseau, and is even less the nature which so moved Lamartine. In the eighteenth and especially the nineteenth centuries, although man was learning formidable techniques which would enable him to truly dominate and subdue nature, he seemed at the same time to rediscover nature, although his discovery was at that time more sentimental and affective than fundamental. For that man nature was still limited to the flowers of the fields and to nostalgic lakes. All the same, poets were beginning to ask: "Inanimate objects, do you in fact have a soul?" For Malraux, the nature which was present during the battles in *Man's Hope*, the one which provides an answer the Altenburg colloquium couldn't provide, is extended to encompass the entire universe, the entire cosmos, and the endless metamorphosis which governs it, as well.

Beginning in the 1930s Malraux set out on the road toward a reconciliation of nature and culture: a reconciliation which science and philosophy in turn pursued a few decades later. Nothing is more foreign to Malraux's thought than the theory of "natural man." In *The Unreal* Malraux traces the great stages in the movement of thought which ended up in the diffusion and the generalization of that theory, the premises of which one finds in the writings of Saint Thomas Aquinas, but which was asserted above all after the fifteenth century (cf. *Ir* 165). After man's relationship with his God was individualized in the gothic era, after God the Father was overshadowed by the Son made man, theology, and notably that of Nicholas of Cusa, asserted that Christ was the perfection of human nature. But it was then necessary to explain how Christ, the perfect man without sins, could be the perfection of man the sinner. To do so the notion of natural man, the one who lived in the Garden of Eden and who, two centuries later, was at the origin of the myth of the "noble savage" was invoked. "This natural man was the man of philosophy substituted for the man of theology and above all of Revelation" (*Ir* 166). The theology of the fifteenth century having shown the way, philosophy and political thought proceeded to be swallowed up in the notion: England in the seventeenth century and France in the eighteenth century granted particular importance to the ideas of "a state of nature," of "natural right," which today appear to have been primarily weapons forged to fight the theories of divine right and the form of monarchy that took advantage of it and which deviated increasingly from the sacred monarchy.

One of the aftereffects of the theories of "natural man" and of "a state of nature" was the distinction, perhaps even the opposition, that arose between nature and culture. As Edgar Morin sums up admirably *Paradigme perdu,* "we saw homo sapiens detach himself in a majestic leap and out of his wonderful intelligence produce technology, language, society, culture." Malraux never accepted this vision, which thrived in the seventeenth and eighteenth centuries and in part of the twentieth century; indeed on the contrary he rejected it when he was only an adolescent and set out on the road toward an awareness of the total unity of the "nature/culture" duo. As early as 1940 Malraux asserted in his own way what today the human sciences are asserting and what Edgar Morin sums up in writing that at present we see nature, society, intelligence, technology, language, and culture coproduce homo sapiens in the course of a process which has lasted several million years. For Malraux, this process, which is still going on and will go on forever, is a process of continual metamorphosis. After 1942 Malraux's works, all his essays on art but also his *Anti-Memoirs* and *Precarious Man,* contained a constant affirmation and strengthening of his certainty that culture, far from being opposed to nature, is a part of nature; that culture and nature are only categories created by the mind to talk about facets of a single and same reality; and that culture represents what a cyberneticist would call the *information* of nature.

For centuries the human order was presented in opposition to natural disorder and the orderliness of a classical facade to the disarray of an untended forest. Today we know that the human order is not as ordered as we thought, and that natural disorder is not as disordered as we claimed. Step by step we are beginning to rediscover that there are affinities and communication between plants; step by step we are beginning to better understand the order which organizes animal societies; step by step we are seeking to decipher the secret of the information which organizes the course of the stars just as it organizes the circular path of quanta; and thus, step by step, we are beginning to admit that the gnarled wood of the two walnut trees of Altenburg, instead of supporting the weight of the world, can flourish with life everlasting.

Well before space shuttles began to modify our imaginary by making us internalize—and no longer just intellectualize—man's relative smallness on a cosmic scale, well before the excesses of societies of production encouraged a surge of theories on the ecosystem, Malraux had urged man to reconsider his relations with all that is not a part of him, and to realize that contemplating rocks, walnut trees, and stars makes one aware of the presence of continual metamorphosis just as much as contemplating works of art created by man does. In proposing this vision of the world and of man living in the world, Malraux is not reducing man's stature. On the contrary, he is enlarging the field of metaphysical interrogation. For approximately twenty-five centuries the questioning of Western man, heir to Greece, was focused on man, his destiny and his death. Nature and the silent stars played only the role of accessories to this interrogation, as scenery or motifs secondary to the primary anguish. Following the path of Nietzsche contemplating, questioning the flowers in a prairie in the spring, Malraux urges man to discover, just as Magnin discovers during his descent from the Sierra de Teruel, that the will of the mountains exists and that it is part of the same will as that of men; he urges us to accept that there is a destiny of trees just as there is a destiny of men; and that the life and death of man can be given meaning only if all the rings of decaying fruit full of seeds surrounding all the apple trees are also given their full meaning. And Malraux urges us to accept this, not by abandoning our cultural heritage as Westerners and assuming an Oriental heritage, but by allowing our own heritage to be metamorphosed.

The true character of the relations which exist between a civilization and nature can be described by the tools and machines used by that civilization, and by the way in which work is organized within it. Even more fundamentally the meaning a civilization gives, or doesn't give, to work reveals its true relationship, or its absence of relationship, with the cosmos. These themes appear magnificently and with powerful lyricism in *Man's Fate* and *Man's Hope,* but they are rarely noticed because the very subjects of these novels, the context in which they were published, and Malraux's political involvements caused most people to undertake only a political and social reading of all that Malraux wrote about work. Today one can and must undertake a detached reading of the events in the books, attempt to truly understand what Magnin meant when he replied to Vallado that he was a revolutionary because he wanted men to know why they work (cf. *MH* 79). Today we must seek truly to understand what Gisors means when he teaches his students that one must not escape work but rather find one's raison d'être in it. (Unfortunately, many young people in the second half of the twentieth century, weary of not being able to find their raison d'être in work, and deceived by the completely momentary ease to be found in a society of consumption, have not yet learned Gisors' lesson and avoid work instead of carrying on the struggle so that man can find his raison d'être in it.)

In the first pages of *Man's Hope* a factory siren bellows out in the Barcelona dawn. At first it seems to be just one of the many sirens which

Reconciled Man

are heard every morning calling people to a job where they go only in order to survive. But soon ten, twenty sirens join the first, and finally all the sirens of the city are heard. Then, "as in Spanish cities of old all the belfries jangled a summons to the townfolk in the hour of peril, so now the proletariat of Barcelona answered the volleys with the tocsin of their factory whistles ... Shrilling all together, the sirens had no longer the funereal accent of a liner putting out to sea; rather they seemed to voice the jubilation of a revolting fleet" (*MH* 18). In this opening scene of *Man's Hope* Malraux reintroduces a theme that is present in *Man's Fate:* From ancient slavery to the feudal system, and from the feudal system to salaried employment, the worker has gained in freedom, but not in dignity. We must see the full significance of the fact that in the last pages of *Man's Fate* Malraux had May, the woman who can give life and who will carry on the battle, read a letter in which the lecture Gisors gave is repeated: "A civilization becomes transformed, you see, when its most oppressed element—the humiliation of the slave, the work of the modern worker—suddenly becomes a *value,* when the oppressed ceases to attempt to escape this humiliation, and seeks his salvation in it, when the worker ceases to attempt to escape this work, and seeks in it his reason for being. The factory, which is still only a kind of church of the catacombs, must become what the cathedral was, and men must see in it, instead of gods, human power struggling against the Earth ..." (*MF* 353).

To believe that tomorrow work can become a value in which man will find the means to be and no longer simply the means to exist, to believe that the factory can become a cathedral—what a utopia! some, if not everyone, will exclaim! Those people need only remember, however, that Nero would have cried "utopia" before the tortured body of Peter if he had been told that a chorus of thousands of slaves would be celebrating mass in churches risen from the catacombs, and that one of his successors would build the Vatican Basilica on the very tomb of the man he had just martyred. No one yet knows which temple will be built upon the school yard where the revolutionary community of Canton was burned alive in the furnace of a lugubrious locomotive, but there is no doubt that one will be built there.

In an article published in December 1933, shortly after Malraux was awarded the Goncourt Prize, Mauriac wrote: "We are living in a strange society; it is old, it is bored, it excuses whoever knows how to distract it, even if that be by frightening it, by giving it goose flesh. Here is a fellow [André Malraux] who beginning in his adolescence has approached society with a disapproving eye, with a dagger in his hand ... And his works show the strict alliance this furious young man has formed with all the forces summoned up for the ruin of the old world. And yet, he has talent ... !" In the indulgence of this old society, which is bored and placates its enemy, Mauriac saw "the profound instinct of a very old lady who says to her child who is challenging her, 'It is no use; despite the abuse you are heaping upon me, you are mine through your intelligence, your culture, your style; you are mine through all the talent of your mind. My heritage sticks to your skin. You study the mysteries of Asia in vain; you will never disrobe yourself of my spirit with which I have clothed you.'" Mauriac concluded his article by stressing that Malraux was a completely despairing man (which shows that Mauriac was seriously wrong about the meaning of the works that had already been published), and that such despair cannot resist the charms and attractions of success. Mauriac concluded: "Will we see him climbing one by one the rungs which the old, astute world places under the feet of young conquerors; and will we one day see, on that tragic face, the radiant smile of a satisfied man?"

Today it is clear, despite appearances, that Mauriac was wrong. In my opinion Mauriac was trying to reassure himself rather than truly to perceive the movement Malraux's sensibility and thought were engaged in at the time. Mauriac had rightly sensed the dangers Malraux represented to the culture and society to which Mauriac belonged with all the fibers of his being; and for reassurance Mauriac tried to convince himself that that society and culture would retrieve Malraux. Like Mauriac, many people are still reassuring themselves by saying that Mauriac was right since Malraux became a government minister, and a minister of de Gaulle. But those people should not be reassured too quickly, for our successors will undoubtedly grant more importance than we did to de Gaulle's proclaiming that it was necessary "to abolish the humiliating conditions in which an outdated economic organization is keeping most workers" (1 May 1949); to de Gaulle's stating that "capitalism contained the motives for a massive and perpetual dissatisfaction"; finally, to de Gaulle's telling bastilles that they should "be ready to willingly open their doors. For when the battle is waged between the people and the bastille, it is always the bastille that ends up being wrong" (14 July 1943). Granted, de Gaulle and Malraux did not abolish capitalism, nor did they succeed in convincing bastilles to willingly open their doors, but it was still too early! One day it will appear more clearly than it does

Reconciled Man

today how the *maisons de la culture* Malraux established prepared for the fall of the cultural bastilles which attempt to prevent the metamorphosis of culture. If this were truly not the case, then why, after Malraux's departure, was such an attempt made to rein in or to stifle the *maisons de la culture?*

"My heritage sticks to your skin ... you will never disrobe yourself of my spirit with which I have clothed you," said Mauriac. Malraux never denied that he was the heir of the society in which he was born and of the culture in which he had been steeped; he even admitted as much in 1927 when he wrote in *Of a European Youth:* "Our primary weakness comes from the necessity we feel to learn of the world through a European screen, we who are Christians no longer." For Mauriac, to inherit meant to receive goods, to manage them as well as possible, to preserve them, and to prepare oneself to pass them on. For Malraux, "a heritage involves a metamorphosis" (cf. *VOS* 633). For Malraux, the culture he inherited was not a family estate whose charm and habits are maintained even when a few pieces of furniture or a few walls are moved; it is the food that enables the chrysalis to become a butterfly. Malraux didn't inherit the Moissac Portal the way Mauriac did. Mauriac wanted to conserve that inheritance and pass it on through a will. Malraux received that inheritance in order to return it to life by putting it back into the flow of metamorphosis.

As early as in his adolescence Malraux sensed that the cultural inheritance he had received belonged to only *one* culture and to *one* society. In 1917, that is, at a time when it was still neither very common nor very easy, Malraux sought to be the heir to all cultures, and not just the heir to the society which was bored, the one about which Mauriac spoke. If Malraux remained apart—benevolently, of course, but apart all the same—from surrealism and dadaism, it was because he accepted his cultural heritage. In *Anti-Memoirs* he stressed how Gandhi, Mao, and Nehru were also men who accepted their heritage (*A-M* 224, cf. *A-M* 239, 373). What interested Malraux, what had always interested him ever since *Paper Moons* and until *Precarious Man,* was not the destruction of the old culture—he knew it was living its final moments—but the preparation of the final phase of the metamorphosis of that culture. In the culture Malraux had inherited and from which he had freed himself by allowing it to be metamorphosed within him, man is a tragic figure, a man of scorned fraternity, a man who experiences history as a fatality, a man weary of individualism and a man chewed up by the masses. "What

The Metamorphosis of Culture

irony ... in this closed-off man who is permeated only by the discordant elements of the universe!" (*TW* 119). And when Malraux said in his speech during the inauguration of UNESCO that he expected culture to "enable man to reach an agreement with it, and once this agreement is reached, to attempt to make his destiny more profound," he summed up in that single statement the quest which lasted his entire life.

In Malraux's novels the airplane appears as the favored instrument for man's reconciliation with himself and with the cosmos. In the 1930s the airplane still represented a new human conquest, one which gave man new dimension. Only a few years earlier the *Spirit of Saint Louis* had enabled Lindbergh to cross the Atlantic for the first time. The Guynemers, the Mermozs, and the "Night Pilots" incarnated both a myth and an ideal. In Malraux's novels the airplane assumes the role the boat had in certain novels of the past, and the role which the space shuttle will have tomorrow in novels whose authors will know how to use it. In Malraux's works the airplane takes on a symbolic value: it is the catalyst for cosmic reconciliation. Each time Malraux describes such a reconciliation, he is drawing from events he himself experienced intensely, and he then transfigures them.

In *Man's Hope* it is possible to see how for Malraux the airplane brings about the establishment of relations between men different from those which usually exist. Individuals, like Leclerc, who are incapable of sustaining these new relations exclude themselves from the squadron. In a crew of airmen each person has his function: the pilot, the spotter, the gunner, the mechanic ... each person is essential to the success of the mission and the survival of everyone; there is a leader, of course, because one is needed, but this leader exercises authority rather than power; in the airplane the conflict between the individual and the group is overcome; the differences in functions and in hierarchy do not preclude fraternity; on the contrary, in fact: the fraternity established on an airplane goes beyond the simple fraternity of battle to accede to human fraternity, and even to cosmic fraternity, the one whose voice is heard in the Sierra de Teruel. While commanding a squadron Magnin is able, unlike Manuel, who commands a regiment, to command while maintaining "the comradeship that bound him to his leader" (*MH* 473). And if one wishes to perceive the full significance of the fraternity that exists on board the Orion, Magnin's airplane, as it does on board all the planes of the España squadron, one needs only to remember the fraternity which had filled Kassner in the tourist plane carrying him clandestinely

Reconciled Man

to Czechoslovakia and in which he had waged and won a battle with destiny.

While he is approaching the plane, Kassner senses that the ties which bind him to the pilot go beyond themselves and draw him closer "to an austere and powerful friendship of a sort rare on this earth." As soon as he is seated at the controls the pilot takes on the value of a symbol for Kassner: he is "the answer of those whom Kassner had saved by destroying their names" (*DW* 123) and by resisting all tortures. The silent throngs of his comrades who had filled the darkness of the prison seem "to people this region of fog" that then surrounds the plane. They seem to fill "the immense gray universe inhabited by the obstinate motor, more responsive than a living creature." When the hurricane is unleashed Kassner feels that the fraternal struggles of all men are with the pilot and him, "in the fuselage against the hurricane" (*DW* 127). Kassner's and the pilot's battle against the elements takes on the dimension and the significance of the struggle of the human condition: this struggle is "some fatality" (*DW* 124). For directions Kassner has only imperfect instruments and the clouds make any navigation by sight impossible. When the plane is in the eye of the hurricane it begins to spin on its own axis. The compass follows the rhythm of the plane and spins around in its case. Nothing—no visibility, no observation, no magnetic north—can guide the pilot, just as nothing can guide many any longer. "The cosmic fury was refracted with precision on [the] minute sensitive surface" (*DW* 128 and *A-M* 63) of the compass case, as it, too, is shaken by the enormous, fabulous life force which shakes men and bends trees. (In *Anti-Memoirs* Malraux tells of how in 1934 he had lived through a similar battle against a cyclone, one which provided him with the experience of a lifetime by making him encounter the cosmos of the *Iliad* and the *Ramayana*.) Despite the controls which have become useless and despite his awareness of his infinite smallness in the eye of the hurricane, Kassner continues to believe in "human domination" (*DW* 127), owing, notably, to the constancy of the motor. It is obviously not a question of man's domination over the hurricane, nor over the cosmos, but of his domination over fear and his destiny.

Finally, in an attempt to escape from the storm the pilot puts the plane into a nose dive at the risk of crashing into the ground. When he finally arrives under the clouds and regains a little visibility, he has to make the plane nose up as quickly as possible, because the tops of the hills are only fifty meters below. Kassner then notices "a pallid lake which branched into tentacles that reached up the valley and reflected with a strange geological calm the low, colorless sky" (*DW* 132). As the plane gets closer to the lake Kassner realizes that its calm is not as great as it had at first appeared, and that the water's surface is agitated by a scudding wind. The strange calm of the lake was only an error in perspective as was the geological calm or the silence of the starry sky. In the finally peaceful airplane Kassner feels the stubborn world of men rising "toward the last russet gleams in the sky with the sacred voice of infinity—with the very rhythm of life and death" (*DW* 133). Kassner can then remove his hand, which has been holding the windowpane so it wouldn't shatter under the hailstorm, and he "smiled upon seeing once more the long lifeline in the palm of his hand and the line which he had made one day, ironically, with a razor; the lines which marked his destiny had been made, not with the stroke of a razor, but with patient and steadfast determination" (ibid.). Yes! man can create his destiny.

Seen from the plane the lines of roads, rivers, and canals on the earth resemble those of an "immense hand" and "assumed the features of fatality" (*DW* 134). From this earth there rises up a serenity of a life that knows how to organize its fatalities. "An immense peacefulness seemed to bathe the newfound earth, the fields and the vineyards, the houses, the trees and their sleeping birds" (*A-M* 64). With the help of the airplane man wages and wins a cosmic battle with destiny. Triumphant, he is no longer at odds with the cosmos, nor with the earth of men. He knows that man's freedom is "the knowledge and the manipulation of his fate" (*DW* 133) and when he comes back down to earth he can do so with hope, for "upon this earth of prison cells and sacrifices there had been holiness, and there would perhaps at last be simple consciousness."

The "return to earth" Malraux experienced above the Aurès, and which he lyrically transfigured in *Days of Wrath,* opened the doors to a reconciliation with life and the cosmos. This reconciliation developed in him slowly, gradually, and didn't become complete until after another "return to earth," in the opposite direction, one might say: the return to earth which reconciled him with the forces of death, the one he experienced three times, first when his tank turned over into a ditch. He transfigured the story of this first return to the realm of the living and turned it into an initiatory tale, the tale which concludes *The Walnut Trees of Altenburg.*

Each time Malraux tells the story of a return to earth, he describes the mask of childhood and the face of innocence man wears while his return is occurring (cf. *DW* 128; *A-M* 63; *WTA* 222). Childhood and innocence here must be understood in the meaning Dostoyevski attributes to them when he tells of the dialogues that the "Idiot" had with the children of the Swiss village where he was recuperating: "In the presence of children, the soul becomes healthier." Having contemplated the face of innocence and the mask of childhood, Vincent Berger, and undoubtedly Malraux as well, is able to say: "I feel myself in the presence of an unaccountable gift—an apparition . . . this life, which, this morning for the first time, has shown itself as powerful as the darkness and as powerful as death . . . I now know the meaning of the ancient myths about the living snatched from the dead . . . Thus, perhaps, did God look on the first man."

We must never forget that this line—"Thus, perhaps, did God look on the first man"—is the last line of Malraux's last novel. After writing it Malraux worked on yet another novel, *The Struggle with the Angel,* but one day he wrote on the manuscript that the novel would never be completed and he then ceased writing novels *forever.* "I am in a hurry to get to the point at which writing, at last, is no longer only a change of hell" (*WTA* 189), Malraux wrote a few years earlier. He had surely arrived at that point thanks to the apparition he had—fugitive, as are all apparitions—of a man reconciled with the forces of death and life, including the life of the cosmos. Following that apparition, writing novels could no longer satisfy the need Malraux carried inside: to deepen the message that apparition had revealed to him, and, if possible, to rediscover its forms. Questioning *The Voices of Silence,* hunting down the secret of *The Metamorphosis of the Gods,* was no longer "a change of hell" for Malraux, as writing novels had undoubtedly been. It was a long, slow, and often painful meditation on the mystery of life, a life as strong as death, a life which in all its forms is governed by metamorphosis.

PART FIVE

Metamorphosis as Universal Law

16

Art Is Not an Antidestiny

❦

THE MIRACULOUS REVELATION of day does not silence questions posed by the human condition any more than faith silences doubts, and Malraux, after his "return to earth," asked himself these questions just as much as he had done earlier. All the same, he was no longer plagued by them, no longer their prisoner. His interrogation came from higher above and also seemed impregnated by the "immense peacefulness that seemed to bathe the newfound earth" (*DW* 135; *A-M* 64).

In order to find the answers or an answer to the questions he had been asking since his adolescence, Malraux henceforth cultivated one single realm: the plastic arts. The preface to *The Metamorphosis of the Gods* confirms this: "My aim [in this book] is neither to write a history of art (though the very nature of artistic creation sometimes obliges me to keep pace with the process of time) nor a study of esthetics; it is to try to discover the significance of the fact that throughout the ages man has always sought an answer to the problem set him by the spark of eternity latent in his being—a problem which has assumed a new complexity in our modern culture, first of all cultures to realize and recognize its ignorance of man's significance" (*MG* 35). The preface to the second volume underlines this again, because many readers of the first volume had not been aware of the preface: "Like my novels, like *Anti-Memoirs*, like *The Voices of Silence*, *The Metamorphosis of the Gods* deals essentially with man and destiny" (*Ir* VI).

We must go even further and boldly assert that painting and sculpture always represented the primary foundations of Malraux's interrogations, whereas writing novels on the one hand, and, on the other, his participation in the events in Indochina, China, Spain, and France, were only detours in his principal metaphysical advance. His quest was always directed by his reflection and meditation on "art's struggle against destiny" (*Ir* VII). When only twenty-five, he attempted an in-depth search to discern the fundamental differences in sensibility and culture which characterize Eastern and Western art. In 1930, in *The Royal Way,* Claude Vannec already conveyed ideas to the director of the French Institute of Saigon which Malraux would develop twenty years later in *The Voices of Silence.* In 1932, Malraux published *Gothico-Buddhist Works of Pamir.* In June 1935, at the Congress for the Defense of Culture, where Gide spoke mainly in favor of a communism which would respect freedom and democracy, Malraux devoted the essence of his address to the power of art and, at that early date, to the metamorphosis of works of art. *The Voices of Silence,* published in 1951, is dated by Malraux "1935–1951." All these facts, and many others not mentioned here, clearly confirm that "art's struggle against destiny" was always the focal point around which Malraux's deepest reflection and meditation were organized.

After 1945, Malraux the writer devoted himself entirely to that meditation. One may wonder whether it might have been the sole theme of Malraux's writings, after that of the *farfelu,* if he had not been imprisoned in Indochina and placed brutally in the midst of the political and social realities of the colonial administration at that time. Malraux's writings began to be published in 1921. From 1921 to 1928 he published only *farfelu* stories or essays. From 1928 to 1942 he published six novels. In 1946 he gave up writing novels forever, and until his death in 1976 he published only works of nonfiction. Writing fiction thus took only about twenty years of Malraux's life, roughly a third of his life as a writer—but what an impact that activity made!

In his battle with destiny, Malraux successively, and sometimes simultaneously, used three weapons. First, the *farfelu* and the total freedom it gave to the creator; next, the revolutionary struggle and its transfiguration into novel form; finally, the creative power of the artist and of life. After 1945 when Malraux-the-writer devoted himself exclusively to "art's struggle against destiny," he renewed contact with his primary concern, which was always his essential concern. All of these facts provide additional confirmation of the apparent paradox I have already suggested: when Malraux espoused Gaullism and became a guest of official residences, it was no longer political struggles that interested him, nor even politics, but the metamorphosis of culture and the defense of man threatened by the organization of debasement.

Art Is Not an Antidestiny

In 1945, as before the war, Malraux was not the kind of person to remain an intellectual signing manifestos and petitions or haranguing crowds from the platform at intellectual gatherings. His experience had taught him that communist parties and Soviet Russia too were spreading a terrible and massive organization of debasement over the earth, and that by preaching an official culture they were becoming the champions of a reactionary culture. As early as 1945, Malraux proposed measures that would have caused an upheaval in education, and thus in culture, if they had been adopted (they would also have prevented the disasters that have befallen national education since 1962 and especially since 1971). It is not the purpose of this study to discuss whether Malraux was right or wrong in making the political choice he made at the Liberation. In order to debate this fully and seriously we must wait for partisan and ephemeral passions to fade into the historical past, whereas Malraux's works will remain in the present of the world of art. On the other hand, this is the place to assert once again that Malraux's motivations transcended politics and that the only thing that mattered to him, as his writings prove, was the necessity of protecting humanity from debasement; a humanity all the more threatened in that it still had no point of reference, in that the absurd at the time gave the illusion of being triumphantly in control, even though Malraux had shown twenty years earlier that the absurd was a question and not a response.

Very few people have truly understood the nature of the battle Malraux waged in the second half of his life. His new allies were overjoyed by his choices because, they believed, those choices reflected their own; but those choices remained for the most part foreign to Malraux's true concerns. Like Mauriac, his supporters believed that "an old, bored society" had brought Malraux back into the fold. They congratulated themselves that "their" minister of cultural affairs was cleaning up Paris, but they smiled ironically, and often condescendingly, at the hot air that, in their opinion, came out of the *maisons de la culture*. His former allies reproached Malraux for having betrayed "their" revolution after the Liberation, and continued to reproach him for that. Yesterday as today, because of their partisan struggles, they were unable to perceive the plane upon which Malraux was located. To all these we must add the people who are unable to truly *read* Malraux-the-writer because they refuse to forgive Malraux-the-minister for remaining essentially silent about the torture that went on in Algeria or, on the opposite end, the execution of a colonel who had rebelled.

After the Liberation, Malraux chose a primary adversary: communism. For Malraux it was a cultural adversary even before it was a political one. More adamantly than anyone else, the communists could not accept the idea of a metamorphosis of culture which would have made them appear laggards of the official culture, incapable of accepting plurality and battling it ferociously with totalitarianism, that is, with the rejection of all differences. Today, Malraux's political friends and adversaries are slowly withdrawing into the past, just as Dante's and Victor Hugo's political adversaries once did. Today, new generations are reading *Man's Hope* and *The Timeless* the way they once read *The Divine Comedy* and *Les Misérables,* that is, by leaving historians and literary critics the task of endlessly discussing the conflict between the Guelfs and the Ghibellines, or the "Three Glorious Days."

Malraux's long meditation on "art's struggle against destiny" went through several phases, several revolutions. It developed like an ascending spiral. Inattentive, hurried readers have believed that Malraux was turning in circles because, they said, he kept returning to the same themes and citing the same works. The truth is that Malraux, although drawing on the same source for his essays, placed himself each time on a higher plane and each time offered a different perspective. In an initial phase, which corresponded to the preparation and publication of *The Voices of Silence,* Malraux believed it possible to assert that the creative power of the artist provided a valid response to destiny. Art appeared to him at that time as an antidestiny because it provided a victory over time, a constant rectification of creation and a means of acceding to fellowship.

In all Malraux's nonfiction, one idea returns continually and is expressed in multiple forms: a work of art, a work born of an artist's creative power, does not belong to time as do objects or events. "The surviving work of art reaches us in a double time, which belongs only to that work: the time of its author and our own" (*HP* 16). A Rembrandt, painted in 1660, cannot be confined to that date anymore than it can be confined to the date we look at it or to the date our successors will look at it. A sacred or religious work of art, for its part, belongs to three temporalities: the time of the artist who created it, the time of the person who looks at it, and the time or the absence of time of the religion that inspired it. A statue of Isis, a statue of Buddha, and a statue of Christ all belong to the times of the sculptors who created them, to the times of those who look at them, and to the times of the Egyptian cycles or Buddhist immobility or Christian eternity. There is no word to express this idea of belonging to different temporalities, and "we seek an All-

Encompassing, like the atmosphere for man or water for fish" (*Int* 124). The idea of an All-Encompassing containing all time and even the absence of time resurfaces frequently in Malraux's writings.

Since the Renaissance, it has been claimed that a work of art survives because it is "beautiful." Today we say that it survives because it is a work of art, which is the same as saying that "we call art its power of resurrection" (*MI*, I, 54). In *Precarious Man*, Malraux emphasizes the fact that we rarely speak of "the giant resurrection in which we are living because it goes without saying," but that if one is careful to *truly* reflect on it, one can only remain pensive in the presence of that "giant resurrection" (*HP* 276). It is the real presence of works of art within us, works we have chosen as our own, that reveals the resurrection in which we are living and makes us seek the All-Encompassing that contains them all; the All-Encompassing which will enable us to understand how all times can be fused and abolished within it. "The river of chronological time is lost in the time of art; it has no current; it is like a lake with invisible shores" (*HP* 281). Sailing on a lake so vast that one cannot discern its boundaries induces the strange and comforting sensation of being enclosed in a limited space that one takes pleasure in perceiving as an unlimited one. Those who have ever experienced the strange sensation of truly feeling within them the fusion of all the presences of a work of art—the presence it had for its creator as well as the presence it has for the viewer, will have for the viewer's children, and once had for the viewer's ancestors—have also experienced the strange sensation of feeling apparently unlimited time condensed to the point of being contained entirely in those communing presences. The world of art sumptuously ignores the realm of time. It is "the world of the presence in our lives of what should, normally, belong to death" (*MG* 31). We deeply experience the existence of that world, and yet we "do not know its nature" (ibid.).

Man had to learn to escape time without resorting to divinities in order to become capable of seeing "the river of chronological time" turn into "a lake with invisible shores." And that lake is probably the same one that sings in Jean Tual's *Poèmes Cycliques:*

> Plus haut, plus haut que la clameur des blés,
> Rayons laissés à mi-chemin,
> Chante le lac secret qui m'aime.[1]

---

1. ["Higher, higher than the clamor of the wheat, / Rays left in midstream, / Sings the secret lake that loves me."]

In the past, different art worlds were mutually exclusive, just as religions have always been exclusive (ecumenicism, unfortunately, is not acceptance of alterity; it is the search for the smallest common denominator). Today, the world of all arts has become a single world; it is the world "of the images that human hands created to defy [time]" (*MG* 35); it is the world "for the first time victorious over time." The world of art enables us to be connected to a time that is neither the time of men nor that of the gods. The world of art offers "a gleam of that eternity which, it seems, belongs to art alone" (*MG* 33). From the beginning of the twentieth century, the confrontation between Oriental and Western art resembled "a conflict of eternities" (*Int* 224). A conflict between Oriental eternity, which suggests the precarity of the individual, and Western eternity, which exalts the individual and encourages him to win individual and eternal salvation. By accepting all the representations of eternity already imagined by man, by fusing them all inside itself, the world of art, which admits all gods of all time, allows man to enter into intemporality. "The intemporal is born when resurrection has become a mystery" (*Int* 130). The resurrection or the reincarnation of religions was a mystery of faith. The "giant resurrection" within which the world of art enables us to live is an obvious given of the senses, even though its obviousness remains mysterious.

Despite all the facts history provides for a knowledge of a work of art, history "can never account for it completely; for the Time of art is not the same as the Time of history" (*VOS* 623). The Imaginary Museum does not deny that there is an evolution of humanity, or that there is an evolution of painting, but it brings together Tintoretto, Poussin, Delacroix, Manet, Braque, etc., into a world where they "are present simultaneously" (*Int* 132). For a historian, Rembrandt and van der Helst are painters of the seventeenth century, a century which, moreover, preferred van der Helst to Rembrandt. For an artist, Rembrandt is present, van der Helst is not. The shards found in the caves of Lascaux are historical objects; the bisons that are painted there reach us through their presence. Despite "the jubilation with which the nineteenth century, schooled in beauty, discovered 'products of history' in works of art, we now know that there is no determinism in art and that history does not account for art" (*Int* 125). The world of art, such as we conceive of it, was born in the nineteenth century at the same time as history, but it grew up "with history like an enemy/brother" (*Int* 134). Whereas history was seeking to give itself a *meaning*, art had to accept itself as a mystery, and ultimately had to accept the fact that the timeless presence

Art Is Not an Antidestiny

of works of art could be explained by no other value than "the mysterious value of art" (ibid.). To the *meaning of history* and to the tyranny of time imposed by that *meaning,* art contrasts its presence freed from history and proves "invulnerable to the rise and fall of empires" (*MG* 33). Just as the tree, rooted in clay, escapes from the clay and rises toward the sky, so the artist takes root in history and escapes from it at the same time. The work of art, which has entered into the world of art, is seated on "the assembly of presences delivered from the irreversible course of centuries" (*Int* 164). The creative power of the artist is "a power that transcends history and summons forth the centuries" (*Int* 13).

During the Altenburg colloquium, Möllberg asserts: "The everlastingness of man can be conceived, but it's an everlastingness in nothingness" (*WTA* 110). Möllberg at one time believed in history, but in Africa he comes to understand that it doesn't exist, and he throws to the winds—between the Sahara and Zanzibar—the manuscript he has been working on for fifteen years, which was to present "a ruthless and perfectly coherent interpretation of man . . . , a synthesis of Hegelian proportions." Since he no longer believes in history, Möllberg no longer has an answer to the question, Is there any meaning to the idea of man? "In other words: from beliefs, myths, and above all the multiplicity of mental structures, can one isolate a single permanent factor which is valid throughout the world, valid throughout history, on which to build one's conception of man?" (*WTA* 98). Although Möllberg, an orphan of history, no longer has an answer, Vincent Berger could suggest one: art. In *The Walnut Trees of Altenburg* Malraux began to outline the idea he would develop eight years later in *The Voices of Silence:* art is a permanent given, valid throughout time and space, valid throughout history, and upon it there can be established a notion of man. (Between *The Voices of Silence* and *The Metamorphosis of the Gods,* Malraux was led to question this assertion.)

Through his creative power, through "the lure of the evasive," through his "refusal to copy appearances," the artist pulls "forms from the real world to which man is subject and [makes] them enter into a world of which he is the ruler" (*VOS* 320). The world of art is the world in which man's total freedom is manifest. In response to the fatality history imposes when it attempts to make the past intelligible and give a *direction* to the future, art replies by proclaiming freedom. And that is why those who accept the fatality of history cannot tolerate the freedom of artists.

"Though always tied up with history the creative act has never changed its nature from the far-off days of Sumer to those of the School of Paris, but has vouched throughout the ages for a conquest as old as man" (*VOS* 639). The Imaginary Museum is the place where all the *possibles* of the past are assembled and where all the *possibles* of the future are proposed to us. As early as 1933, in his preface to Faulkner's *Sanctuary*, Malraux voiced an idea which he was often to repeat: in writing a tragedy in which destiny is the main character, the Greek poet expressed what fascinated him, and he did so not in order to deliver himself from it but to change its nature. He brought destiny into the realm of what is imagined and dominated. It was long believed that representing a fatality was the same as submitting to it. "But it's not, it's almost possessing it. The mere fact of being able to represent it, conceive it, releases it from real fate, from the merciless divine scale" (*WTA* 97). In Greek tragedy the poet "challenges Destiny on equal terms" (*MG* 62). Works of art also challenge it on equal terms.

Because they connect us with the passing of centuries, because they survive when centuries pass, works of art prove that the artist has been delivered from his dependency. In the presence of a Greek tragedy, as in the presence of a work of art, what fascinates the viewer is "its simultaneous revelation of human servitude and man's indomitable faculty of transcending his estate, making his very subjection testify to his greatness" (*VOS* 590, 630). We must keep that passage in mind if we wish to fully understand the contention that art is an antidestiny, a "revolt against man's fate" (*VOS* 639), which Malraux made in 1951; we must not take this statement out of context, which is, unfortunately, easy to do when it appears in isolation on a page. The consciousness of greatness and that of subjection are not mutually exclusive; they do not alternate, they coexist, they are simultaneous. Destiny remains. But through art, victorious over time, man is introduced as a partner in the game of forces in which he was previously only a pawn. "Every masterpiece... tells of a human victory over ... destiny" (*VOS* 630). The tamer in a cage knows that the wild beast, even tamed, remains a beast; the spectators in their seats know it too; that is why they have come. The artist, delivered from his dependency, erasing through his works the millennia of the starlit sky, yet knowing that he himself will be erased by that sky, proves it is useless to kill the queen of the *Farfelu Kingdom* as the Sins in *Paper Moons* sought to do. Tamed destiny, which growls behind every masterpiece, attests to the fact that the queen of the *Farfelu Kingdom* is powerless over the world of art.

Art Is Not an Antidestiny

Many people continue to believe that an artist creates in order to *express himself.* Malraux knew how wrong that opinion was. Beginning with his first writing on art, he specified that it was the need to *create* that forces an artist to express himself. In *Precarious Man,* Malraux forcefully states that "the artistic vocation is born of an emotion experienced not in the presence of a spectacle but in that of a power" (*HP* 152). The emotions someone wishes to express do not make an artistic vocation; they make a Saturday poet or a Sunday painter. An artistic vocation responds to a necessity, the need to allow a creative power to well up. The artist himself is not always fully aware of that power at the beginning of his life but becomes increasingly conscious of it as his mastery is affirmed. Before the nineteenth century, that power was only suspected, for it was considered at that time to be subordinate to other powers, of which it was seen as the servant. In *The Timeless,* Malraux describes the slowly rising awareness of the autonomy of an artist's creative power. After Manet it became clear to painters that painting in itself had *an existence independent of reality, of the imaginary, or of the sacred it was expressing* (*Int* 110). Thanks to the Imaginary Museum, we have in turn become aware of this *autonomous existence* of painting, and Malraux invites us, notably in *Precarious Man,* to go even further and attribute to all the arts the autonomous existence of the power of creation.

The museums and libraries of all media confront man with "the inexhaustible power of creation, which survives through the centuries" (*Int* 161). Ever since the metamorphosis of his looking, reading, and listening has enabled man to have access in the world of art to the works of all times and all places, he has become aware of the permanence and the universality of the creative power of the artist. For an artist, but also for his viewer, his reader, or his listener, creation appears as the expression of a power which "summons forth the centuries" [qui fait "la sommation des siècles"] (*Int* 13). We must point out here the three meanings that can be attributed to the French word *sommation:* an imperative summoning; the calculation of a whole or of a sum; a result produced by several stimuli, each one of which in isolation would remain ineffective. With "*In summoning forth centuries,*" the power of artistic creation calls upon *all time* to obey its injunctions, it creates a Sum which encompasses all the centuries and which would be of a different nature if any one of them were missing. It is the summoning, or challenge, that a conqueror issues.

Malraux often elaborated on the idea he expressed for the first time in

Moscow in 1934: art is not a submission, it is a conquest. Here Malraux joined Nietzsche, who stated that art is redemption, in the sense not of redemption from sin, but redemption of a right. Art is a conquest because it appears as a "rectification of the world, a means of escaping from man's estate" (*WTA* 98). This idea, which Malraux expressed as early as 1942, is strongly developed in *The Unreal*: by attaching characters and landscapes to the universe of which it is the sole creator, art delivers us from the human condition (cf. *Ir* 251). The world of art is not a subjugated but a sovereign world. In the world of art, contemporary man finds "his obscurely Promethean greatness" (*Int* 11). Through his creative power the artist raises a "protest of mankind" against the human condition, and anyone sensitive to art is a part of that protest, which is stronger than the passing of centuries since it "summons them forth."

When art was subordinate to a supreme value, it expressed that value. Since the time that the world of art has existed in and of itself, since it became an autonomous and sovereign world, "it has connected, by encompassing them, all the values it has ever expressed" (*Int* 156). All supreme values that have at one time been accepted by man are rediscovered in the world of art, which therefore presents artists as "intercessors of the superhuman" (*Int* 11). The world of art is peopled with those who have the will and the power "to wrest forms from the real world to which man is subject and to make them enter into a world of which he is the ruler" (*VOS* 320). The relationship between people and things proposed by a work of art is a relationship "of a different nature than that imposed by the world" (*VS* 275). In his *Outline of a Psychology of film*, written in 1946, Malraux specified that for him a work belonged to the world of art if it was "the expression of unknown and suddenly convincing relations between people or between people and things." Photography and official painting suggest, if there is still need to do so, that art has always created correlations other than those of life, correlations other than those that appear in life (cf. *Int* 75). Today it is finally being admitted that in centuries of sacred art, and, later, in centuries of art of the Unreal, the artist did not choose forms from among forms apparent in life but "created forms that rivaled the world of appearance" (*Int* 146). For centuries, for millennia, in fact, man had lived in two relatively well-connected and concordant worlds: the world above, which was given to him by the sacred or the divine, and the world of everyday facts and gestures, which was the world of appearance and the ephemeral. In the West at the end of the nineteenth century, what until then had been only apparent became real, indeed the only reality. As Buddhism had turned the world into unlimited appearance, as Greece had turned it into the residence of Mortals, and as Christianity had made it the earthly world, so the nineteenth-century Western world believed it could turn the world into the ultimate reality. In protest against this world of reality, which claimed to be the only true one, artists proclaimed the world of art and waged a merciless battle "to attain the sovereign world that delivers them from appearance" (*Int* 164). From their battle was born the awareness that a pictorial fact exists prior to a painting, a poetic fact prior to a poem, and a musical fact prior to a quartet. According to a still rather widespread illusion, Van Gogh would have seen a landscape in Arles and then have decided to transform it. In reality, "he hardly saw an Arlesian landscape; he fore-saw the pictorial fact, which he drew from it" (*Int* 107). The landscape became "an appeal to creation."

Cézanne once said: "The pink and the white of *Olympia* lead us to the pictorial truth of things by a path of which our sensibility was ignorant before those colors" (*Int* 48). For Manet, for Cézanne, for their immediate successors, nature was not the appearance of the *pictorial truth* in which they believed, "it was the secret of it" (*Int* 49). They sought to decipher nature in an attempt to attain the *secret* beyond the appearance, and in this they joined the artist of the Far East and his search for the *sign*. Gauguin, with his aphorism "Art is abstraction," prepared the path magnificently explored by Kandinsky. The world of art, which refers only to itself, will also be able to open up the Imaginary Museum that contains it. For those people—fewer in number than one thinks—who can *truly* learn from their Imaginary Museum, but also from their internal literary and acoustic libraries, that art is neither an imitation of nature nor an illustration of supreme values to which it has successively appealed; for them, the insistent continuity of artistic creation reveals that "genius has always drawn the forms of another world from appearance" (*Int* 147). In Sumer, in Byzantium, in Chartres, artists also drew forms from appearance, but they did so in order to link them to the divine. Twentieth-century art declines to link the forms it derives from appearance to any sacred or to any divine, and it therefore boldly asserts that there *really* exists a realm of nonappearance, a surreal. "What is being called in question once again is the *value* of the world of appearances" (*VOS* 592), but this time it is being done by man alone, by man who has found within himself the world of nonappearance and has not entrusted it to the gods.

For anyone truly sensitive to art, a sonata, a poem, or a painting leads to the discovery that there exists a musical world, a poetic world, and a pictorial world. All these worlds together form the world of art, which rivals appearance and is "a world different in kind from that of reality" (*VOS* 320). For anyone who truly internalizes a work of art, the real is devalued by art just as it was by religion. The real is devalued by the creative power of man, by his power to go beyond appearance and to accede to a higher world, which is the world of art—victorious over time, over the ephemeral, and over appearance. Art rests on the conviction that "the only world which matters is other than the world of appearances" (*VOS* 598).

What we call reality is basically only a system of relations, a system we attribute to the world, one that we use to explain it. In the past it was believed that artistic creation was "the faithful or idealized transcription of these relations" (*HP* 159). We know today that nothing of the kind is true, and that artistic creation is based upon *other* relations. The Imaginary Museum and our inner literary and acoustic libraries reunite all the works through which artists, "whether overtly or covertly, replaced the data of visual experience with a new vision of the universe" (*MG* 33-34). One need only place side by side a Van Gogh and a Sunday painting, a novel by Dostoyevski and a detective novel, an African mask and a Mardi Gras mask to immediately sense that the latter belong to the world of appearance whereas the former belong to a world other than that of appearance, though not the world beyond. Works of art proclaim that there exists here on earth "a Truth beyond and above appearance" (*MG* 13). Artists have always opposed "successive worlds of Truth" to appearance (*MG* 25). Today these successive worlds fuse into a single one, the world of art.

In *Anti-Memoirs,* Malraux tells of a personal experience that profoundly marked him and, he notes, gave direction to all his reflections on art. If we wish to follow Malraux's spiritual quest during the last twenty years of his life, it is essential to be aware of this experience. In 1955, Malraux was in Egypt, in front of the Sphinx, which he hadn't seen since 1934. "It was then," he wrote, "that I distinguished two languages which for thirty years I had been hearing as one. The language of appearance..., the language of the ephemeral. And the language of Truth, of the eternal and the sacred" (*A-M* 32–33). We must pay crucial attention to the words chosen by Malraux. Starting in 1955 he *distinguishes* the two languages which up until then *he had been hearing as one.* Those two languages which had been confused became distinct. Malraux could henceforth hear them at the same time, he could distinguish them from

Art Is Not an Antidestiny

each other, as a musician can distinguish the voices of a fugue. Now able to distinguish the language of the ephemeral and the language of Truth, Malraux *immediately* began to write the first chapter of *The Metamorphosis of the Gods*. He thus began a quest which lasted more than twenty years. That quest is evident in *The Supernatural, The Unreal,* and *The Timeless,* whose profound significance is perceptible only if one constantly keeps in mind the fact that in those works Malraux sought to hone his distinction between the language of appearance and the language of Truth. To avoid misinterpreting the three volumes of *The Metamorphosis of the Gods* and Malraux's fundamental thought, it is essential not to attribute to Truth, which Malraux wrote with a capital *T,* a meaning he *never* gave it. We must always remember that in *Anti-Memoirs,* after describing his experience in front of the Sphinx, Malraux states: "Art is not an end product of the ephemeral in people's lives ... but of the Truth which they have each in their turn created" (*A-M* 33). And we must always remember that at the beginning of *The Metamorphosis of the Gods* Malraux writes: "The artist created images of Truth in the same way as man created his gods and the world they illuminate" (*MG* 25).

In an epigraph to *The Metamorphosis of the Gods,* Malraux cites Van Gogh's cry: "In life and painting I can quite well dispense with God. But, suffering as I am, I cannot dispense with something greater than myself, something that is my whole life: the power of creating." In *Paper Moons,* the joyous claim of the Balloons-Sins remained limited: they believed creation needed touching up, and they thought "its harmony would have gained much if they had been invited to its establishment" (*LP* 31). In *The Metamorphosis of the Gods* there are no longer claims, only affirmation: the affirmation of man's slow awareness of his creative power. The Imaginary Museum does not provide the sight of a simple touching up of creation; it provides "an awareness of art's impassioned quest, its age-old struggle to remould the scheme of things" (*VOS* 15). With the passing of time, each of the great styles of the past appears "as a special interpretation of the world" (*VOS* 334). This interpretation is a collective victory, the victory of a culture and a civilization, but it is made up of individual victories which are "victories over forms, achieved by means of forms" (ibid.). Whether conscious of it or not, an artist conquers the world by reducing it to forms he chooses or invents. Through that alone he becomes "a transformer of the meaning of the world" (ibid.), like the philosopher, who reduces the world to his concepts, or the physicist, who reduces it to his own laws. But the physicist, with the exception of certain quantum physicists, presents laws that merely transform the meaning of the world of reality, of appearance; he transforms the meaning of the world by revealing yesterday that the earth revolves around the sun or that the planets and the stars are attracted to each other, by perhaps revealing tomorrow that the sun and the galaxies themselves revolve around a yet unknown center. The artist, however, through the forms he invents, transforms the meaning of the world that is not the world of appearance; he transforms the meaning of the world whose existence is "independent of the real, the imaginary, or the sacred" (*Int* 110).

Like Michelangelo, many artists know "the royal trembling of the hands that order the secret of the cosmos according to the governed forms" (*Int* 117). "The Creative Process"—the title of the third part of *The Voices of Silence*—is Malraux's slow meditation on the power possessed by great artists when they seek to free themselves from inherited forms and to invent their own and thus respond "to the call for a new significance to the world" (*VOS* 361). When a great style dominates an age, it proposes a certain meaning for the world. The forms it has invented remain convincing until the artists for whom that meaning and those forms are lies speak out. Those artists then invent new forms, which propose a new meaning.

In contemporary art the dislocation of forms, the explosion of colors, the disappearance of shadow and depth represent a groping for new forms which might express a new meaning of the universe. When Picasso said, "I must absolutely find the Mask," he meant, Malraux specifies, I must find "the emphasis that a great style confers upon the human face" (*PM* 68–69). In a surprising battle against himself, Picasso "dared prohibit plumbing the depths solely to control the sequence of his styles" (*PM* 18). Throughout his life he battled not only against earlier forms invented by others, but also against the forms he had himself invented. Whereas the painters he admired, whose canvases made up his personal collection, were almost all artists who had struggled to probe ever more deeply into their style, Picasso himself believed that "the continuity of style is hell" (*PM* 18). I have long been astonished and even intrigued by Malraux's passionate interest in, and even fascination with, Picasso. Today I believe that if Malraux, in quest of Metamorphosis, had such an interest in Picasso, it was because Picasso was "unequaled as an inventor of forms" (*PM* 153). In an age such as ours, ignorant of its values and of what significance it should give to the world, Picasso was one of those artists who denounce a culture rather than propose a new one. He was one of those artists who prepare the transformation of the significance of the world by scouring, sometimes corrosively, what still remains of the earlier one. Picasso had intended that "his rebellion be incurable; and it was" (*PM* 258). His painting is "the most enraged accusation of painting" there is (*PM* 101), but life bubbles in it as it bubbles in the boiling waters of original chaos. A tree branch picked up during a walk, a plastic cap from a bottle, a metal wire from a champagne cork, a simple bread crumb from the table—in Picasso's hands everything took on a surprising form. "He appropriated to himself all the leaven of metamorphosis" (*PM* 32), and with him it is no longer just pictorial power that is in question: "It is demiurgic power" (*PM* 62).

Cézanne, "alone with his truth," had discovered the mistake of all masters, the one Titian had already sensed: they "believed artistic creation to be in the service of Virgins, Doubles, or Nature; Nature, Virgins, and Doubles were meant to serve creation" (*Int* 156). In the centuries of the Unreal, "the autonomy of demiurgic power" (*Ir* 202) slowly emerged. Botticelli, one of the first to realize it, had foreseen "the victory of art over the world of God" (*Ir* 169). And the word "Renaissance" entered the vocabulary of art "to express the gradual discovery of the power by which the artist . . . creates the exalting unreal, in which the dependence of the creature and the transcendence of the creator disappear together" (*Ir* 168). This statement is crucial for whoever wishes to understand Malraux's profound thinking. Judeo-Christian culture, which shaped the West, has always emphasized the transcendence of the Creator and, consequently, the dependence of the Creature; it has always insisted on separating the City of God from the City of Man. In Western culture, man has been excluded from the world of God by the sin of the first day, that of Adam and Eve, and by the sin of the second day, that of Cain. Human existence is thus considered to be a lifelong atonement without which man can never enter the City of God. Atonement is essentially an individual affair, even if it occurs within a religious community. Even nonbelievers have been marked by this culture, which for centuries has impregnated the sensibility of the entire West. Malraux, marked by it like every Westerner, began in his adolescence to feel outside the culture, and to free himself he had to endure the terrible twisting suffered by flowers when they are turned 180 degrees and must slowly rearrange all their fibers to turn once again toward the sunlight. Meditating on the meaning of art, Malraux discovered at ever deeper levels the dazzling manifestation of the demiurgic power of the artist. He discovered a creator who did not transcend his creation, and a creation that travels through the centuries, from metamorphosis to metamorphosis, completely independent of its creator. Meditating on the world of art, Malraux discovered a world in which the transcendence of the creator and the dependence of the creature disappear together.

"Posterity," says Malraux grandly, "means the gratitude of coming generations for victories which seem to promise them their own" (*VOS* 464). That is true, and that is why "the Museum succeeds the Cathedral," as Joseph Hoffmann wrote. And I would quickly add that all the victories won by artists, bearers of a hope of victory for every man, explain why the *maisons de la culture* are already succeeding churches and chapels, despite their initial stammering. The artist of today provides man "the most compelling echoes of his liberation" (*VOS* 464), as did the high priest or the saint in the past.

On several occasions Malraux stressed how irritating it is, when speaking of art, to use a religious vocabulary, but how one can hardly escape from it because a religious vocabulary has always served to express the fact that people consider manifest "the existence of two distinct worlds" (*HP* 150). Art is not a religion, as Malraux often repeated, but it does unite "the intercessors of the superhuman, those possessed by the unknown" (*Int* 11), and above all it unites them in a fellowship of the living, in a fellowship with wine, and sometimes with blood, of the creative power of man, in a fellowship devoted to the passion of the creator.

Until the twentieth century the value of works of art had been legitimated either by the sacred, by the divine, or by beauty. Today, works of art that survive in the Imaginary Museum, exist beyond any of those legitimations. Today the steadiness of Isis, the immobility of Buddha's smile, Christ's crown of thorns, are not legitimated by the religions of the artists who painted them; they are legitimated because they bear witness to the creative power of man and because they are the sounding boards for the most persuasive echo of a possible liberation. Today the world of art is a world that reflects solely the demiurgic power of the artist, that is, the creative power of man. Art has thus acquired all the attributes of a supreme value, even though, as Malraux often states, that value remains secret and imperceptible. But isn't it the nature of all supreme values to be imperceptible? Did Siddhartha or St. John of the Cross express themselves otherwise when they spoke of their supreme values? "The creative power establishes the metaphysical power of art" (*HP* 294). Few statements better characterize the three volumes of *The Metamorphosis of the Gods,* which often resound as a powerful amplification of Nietzsche's outburst: "Art, man's redemption ... Art, suffering

Art Is Not an Antidestiny

man's redemption ... Art has *more value* than truth ... Art is the true task of life, art is life's metaphysical activity." If one can accept and endure this demand for *The Will to Power*, carried on by the song of *The Metamorphosis of the Gods*, then one can understand how from Turin in January 1889, a few days before definitively locking himself up in a perhaps protective silence, Nietzsche could write to Jacob Burckhardt: "Dear Professor: I would have ultimately preferred, and very much so, to be professor in Basel than ... to be God! But I didn't dare push my personal egoism to the point of losing sight, on his account, of the Creation of the World." At about the same time Nietzsche wrote to Peter Gast: "Sing me a new song: the world is transformed and all the heavens rejoice."

I have already pointed out that Malraux often wrote about the feeling of total solitude which invades man when he realizes that his inner voice will never be heard by others the way it is heard by himself; others hear it with their ears, from the outside; a man hears his own voice with his throat, from the inside. Fraternity and Love attack that solitude. So does Art. As of 1929 Malraux wrote: "It is man's destiny not to be able to communicate his intimacy with others, nor to apprehend that of others, but art attacks that destiny" (*Variété*, 15 October 1929). The relationship between a work of art and a person who is sensitive to it is above all one of fellowship. For historians and for many professors of art history, a work of art is above all an object to be studied and an occasion for dissertations. For someone who appreciates art, a work is primarily a source of sensations, which doesn't mean that the quality and depth of those sensations are not nourished by knowledge—quite to the contrary. To be sensitive to a work of art is above all to allow oneself to establish a dialogue of sensibility and a fellowship of perception. Art establishes communication with the most profound part of a person, the part in which words become powerless to express intimacy. Braque correctly pointed out that "what is most important in a painting is always what one cannot say." It is also what is most important in a Mozart symphony, or even in a novel by Dostoyevski, although in literature the illusion of being able to say what is most important in a work rests on the fact that the artist, here, uses words as his materials.

The feeling that a work of art speaks to the most secret and most profound part of our intimate selves is the source of the emotion one experiences at the sight of that work. Like the silence of love or the look of fraternity, the song of a work of art is not monodic: it is the chorus of inner voices in harmony, those that feel they are communing. Lopez rightly wanted to give the walls of the city to the painters so that the song of underground fellowship which opens *Man's Hope* would rise up even more clearly. And what did Malraux hope to do in the *maisons de la culture* if not to multiply the number of places and conditions in which the greatest possible number of men, women, and children could commune through art and attack the destiny that sentences them to solitude?

In the world of art today, El Greco doesn't destroy or exclude Botticelli, Apollinaire excludes neither Villon nor Hafiz, and Dutilleux no more excludes Schubert than Chartres excludes Nara. Unlike the world of philosophers and religious figures who excommunicate each other, the world of art is a world based on the total acceptance of plurality. In itself and through itself the world of art achieves a fellowship of differences. What is more, it preaches the fellowship of differences and does so without looking for any syncretism. In *The Voices of Silence,* Malraux emphasized the extent to which, ever since the influence of ancient Greece, our communions have been oriented toward what is similar, whereas the communion provided through Oriental art and primitive art forms were oriented toward what is dissimilar. And Malraux wondered at the time, nostalgically, it seems, whether a communion based on dissimilarity was possible for a Westerner (cf. *VOS* 567). The answer given to this question points out the separation between two mentalities and thus two sensibilities. For some, who do not always realize it, the world of art remains the world of masterpieces that express the values—whether sacred or profane matters little here—in which they believe or to which they adhere. For those people the road to a communion of differences is not yet open. For others, on the contrary, who have opened up their sensibility, art has truly become "the communion of creations," the community which welcomes all creations equally (*Int* 120). For those people the world of art is the community that brings together brothers who, outside of the community, would be enemies. For those people the world of art "gathers together works which have become fraternal from so many civilizations which once hated or ignored each other" (*OF* 58), and which often continue to hate each other. And because the world of art gathers them together, "our civilization senses a mysterious transcendence in art and one of the yet obscure means to its unity" (ibid.). Each word of this statement seems to have been carefully chosen by Malraux.

Our civilization has not yet found its unity in art, but it senses it is there, though the means to this unity still remain obscure. One day, perhaps sooner than we think, the younger generations will destroy the unacceptable gap between the national rivalries created by backward politicians or the religious rivalries of narrow-minded missionaries, on the one hand, and, on the other, the international community that will be formed with the help of tourist buses unloading waves of tourists into all the museums of the world—tourists who have come to commune more or less consciously and deeply with an inexhaustible artistic creation. The younger generations of today will undoubtedly demand tomorrow that there be extended to everyday life the spiritual communion that enables Argentinian music lovers to go to a Buenos Aires concert hall to hear an English orchestra accompany a Russian pianist who has come to play a rhapsody composed by an American. Art which is victorious over time is also victorious over borders and national rivalries. And, as Malraux often stated, the seventh art, film—when it is an art—will do more than any other art form to render the fanaticism of national differences unacceptable. Already the youngest people today are deaf to the speeches of their elders and are being accused a little hastily of lacking patriotism. On the other side, unfortunately, we hear the reaction of those who want once again to extol religious or national fanaticisms. In the face of this formidable reaction, art—alone today, absolutely alone—holds forth the possibility of a communion of differences and seems to promise the yet obscure means to a union.

Art establishes a fellowship between creators and their faithful "who are their laity" (*Int* 118), but it also provides both with "a fellowship of man with what surpasses him," a cosmic fellowship. In the last few decades, millions of famished people have begun to approach the tables of this communion. They are regarded ironically by "cultivated" men from the old culture who find them too little and too poorly dressed. Who cares! For these famished souls, art is true communion, even if they are not yet fully aware of it. All together they form "people of all lands, hardly aware of what it is they have in common, [who] seem to be asking of the art of all time to fill a void they dimly sense within them" (*MG* 34).

For Malraux, to look for an answer to the question, What is Art? was the same as looking for an answer to the question, What is Man? (*Les Nouvelles littéraires* 3 April 1952). He stated this clearly in April 1962 to Gilles d'Aubarède. It seems to me, however, that Malraux had to live for more than thirty years with the suspicion that his meditation on art would not provide him *the* answer he so hoped for. In response to Roger Stéphane, who cited Gide's words, "There is no problem for which a work of art is not a sufficient answer," Malraux replied: "That's garbage" (*Carrefour* 28 July 1954). This statement dates from 1954, that is, barely three years after Malraux wrote that "art is an antidestiny" in *The Voices of Silence,* a comment that prompted many misinterpretations of his thought. A question confronts us here: If by 1954 Malraux believed and affirmed that "art resolves nothing," why did he nevertheless continue to look to art for the answers to the spiritual and metaphysical questions that had been tormenting him since his adolescence? Two explanations may be attempted. First, Malraux, despite his assertions of 1954, may have continued to hope that art could provide an answer. I find this explanation unconvincing. I have the impression, on the contrary, that Malraux continued to probe the question, What is Art? after 1954 not in the hope of finding an answer to the question, What is Man? but in the hope of finally being able to modify the way in which man was to ask himself that question. In 1954, or even earlier, Malraux might have intuited that only a complete change in the terms of our interrogation could enable our successors to find a new answer. That is why he would have resumed his entire reflection on art and undertaken *The Metamorphosis of the Gods.* One might hope that someday a painstaking and in-depth study will be devoted to the difference in tonality and lighting which can be perceived between the first works on art—*The Imaginary Museum, Artistic Creation, The Coin of the Absolute, The Voices of Silence*—and the final three—*The Supernatural, The Unreal,* and *The Timeless.* Malraux broaches the same themes in all of them; he often studies the same paintings and sculptures, but the mindset with which he does so is no longer the same. Following *The Voices of Silence,* and after 1954, he knew that "art doesn't resolve anything," that his meditation on art would only allow him to better formulate his question. He knew it and, I believe, suffered because of it.

In all his novels, too, Malraux pursued only one goal: to clarify what Man is. In 1942, at the beginning of his final novel, *The Walnut Trees of Altenburg,* he wrote: "As a writer, by what have I been obsessed for the last ten years, if not by mankind?" (*WTA* 23–24). In 1946, in his UNESCO address, Malraux believed he could assert that "with man's questioning his destiny, the destiny of mankind, man begins and destiny ends." This grandiose hope was to collapse, and in the 1950s, while preparing to write *The Metamorphosis of the Gods,* Malraux knew that if man begins—perhaps!—destiny doesn't end. Despite *The Voices of Silence,* despite *The Imaginary Museum,* Malraux rediscovered Vincent Berger's fundamental assertion in *The Walnut Trees of Altenburg:* "Man knows the world is not on the human scale, and he wishes it were" (*WTA* 96). He then took up again from the beginning all his reflections and meditations on the songs that resound "under the infinity of the night sky" (*WTA* 189). And since "art doesn't resolve anything" (*Int* 9, 122), he began untiringly to pose the questions, "What is Art? What is Man?" (*HP* 201), no longer seeking to answer them, but in an attempt to formulate them in a new way.

Religions, like destiny, even if they didn't protect man from death, did protect him "by connecting him to God or to the universe." After hoping for a time that art would connect man fully to the universe, after telling Roger Stéphane in July 1954 that the same was true of art as of religion, Malraux repeated loudly and clearly in his final books that "art is not a religion." He went even further and issued a *formal warning* to everyone who had not followed the evolution of his meditation: "To try to discover whether art has become a religion makes no sense, for it legitimates neither destiny nor death" (*Int* 122). Malraux does not deny that art fills our lives and transcends death—on the contrary, he reaffirms it—but even the victory over time, which he had celebrated in *The Voices of Silence*, becomes relative and loses part of the attributes with which Malraux had at first endowed it. Malraux does not question the basic notion of the survival of works of art any more than he questions that of a world of art formed by the presence among us of what should belong to the past and to death. But that survival and that presence, instead of being affirmative, instead of providing an answer, themselves become questions. This essential evolution in Malraux's thought is expressed for the first time in *Anti-Memoirs,* when Malraux, describing his visit to the Cairo Museum in 1965, writes: "What now strikes me, in this doomed museum, is the precariousness of artistic survival, its complexity" (*A-M* 43). A few lines later he concludes this reflection by asserting: "And already this museum is no longer an assurance of survival . . . the world of art is not a world of immortality, it is a world of metamorphosis."

When in Egypt in 1965, Malraux went through a personal crisis akin to those great nights of doubt which, once over, leave you quite different. His break with Madeleine Rioux was complete. His self-questioning was total. Standing in front of the pyramid of Cheops he decided to write his *Anti-Memoirs,* which is profoundly significant when we remember that he had just become aware "of the precariousness of artistic survival." The awareness of this precariousness, which Malraux had at first underestimated, must have been a tragedy, for it demanded a complete questioning of his thoughts on art. He found himself pondering an idea he had expressed several years earlier: "Destiny is not death" (*VOS* 630).

Metamorphosis as Universal Law

He had known this ever since writing *Farfelu Kingdom;* he had not entirely forgotten it, especially in his novels, but he had not yet truly incorporated it into his meditation on art, so preoccupied had he been with bringing fully to light the demiurgic power of man, the power that "can erase the starry millennia."

Aware of "the precariousness of artistic survival" (*Int* 134), compelled to accept that "already the museum no longer assures survival," and remembering that "destiny is not death," Malraux was faced with the mystery that had long been the most painful for him: "No perceptible value legitimates the victory over the centuries" (*Int* 134).

This statement more than any other shows how difficult it was for Malraux truly to free himself from the heritage and culture of the Christian world. Indeed, one might reply to Malraux that the desperate will and urgent need to find *one* perceptible value to legitimate the victory of art over the centuries are, typically, a will and a need shaped by Judeo-Christian tradition. An Oriental would respond simply and tranquilly that the victory of art over the centuries is legitimated by life, of which art is one of the manifestations. Malraux, as we shall see, finally opened the door that led in this direction, but he did so because he could no longer endure the tragedy of all the great painters from Manet to Picasso: "To hold painting as their supreme value—without knowing why" (*Int* 156). Our world of art, Malraux often said, refers "first to that which exists only through art" (*Int* 56), our art is "the first whose supra-world is the world of art" (*Int* 166). But since he could not resign himself to be immersed in immanence, he continued to search for *one* transcendence, which would legitimate the world of art as being its own supra-world. For the benefit of what, or of whom, did our art extract from appearance that which it represented? And since the answer eluded him—no doubt because, formulated in that way, the question has no answer—Malraux, in *The Timeless,* his final essay on art, painfully gives expression to "the solemn mystery of art." He had already spoken of it in 1960 in his speech to save the monuments of Upper Egypt. But in 1960 this enigma, full of the mysteries of the Sphinx, seemed only solemn. In 1976, in *The Timeless,* it became painful: "When the human adventure succeeds that of the species, there appears the enigma of the consciousness of death, which today joins that of art" (*Int* 405).

In *The Timeless,* Malraux no longer allows himself any escape and sees himself as naked as Job before the enigma of art. Religions had hidden that enigma because they offered a supreme value to which art referred. Later, people believed in "art for art's sake," but that belief also masked

Art Is Not an Antidestiny

the fact that art is enigma. The mask fell off, and the enigma became glaring. In *The Voices of Silence*, a few lines before the well-known *art is an antidestiny*, Malraux had already said that "art does not deliver man from being a mere by-product of the universe" (*VOS* 639), but he had then added that art "is the soul of the past in the same sense that each ancient religion was a soul of the world"; he had also added that art provided "that deep communion which would else have passed away with the passing of the gods." A quarter of a century later, after again taking up his meditation on art, Malraux asserted that, on the contrary, "art annexes the human adventure less and less" (*Int* 391), and he asked the question: "In the pursuit of the adventure of the species, on the tiny peninsula where man has been tossing about for his forty millennia, what becomes of the confrontation between his adventure and his art?" (ibid.).

At the conclusion of his meditation on art and man, Malraux honestly announces the point at which he has arrived: the world of art is not an answer, it "is a constant interrogation" (*Int* 400). When Albert Béguin wrote in the October 1948 issue of *Esprit* that Malraux was "a martyr of his time," he was surely unaware of the premonitory nature of his statement. It seems obvious that in any other age than our own Malraux would have been a strict believer in the supreme value which then ordered the world and linked man to the cosmos. But at the time in which he lived, none of the supreme values Malraux knew of was an ordering value, and all were problematic. He must constantly have suffered in being unable to adhere to any supreme value. Recall the conclusion of *The Temptation of the West*, written when Malraux was twenty-four years old: "There is no ideal to which we can sacrifice ourselves, for we are familiar with everyone's lies, we who have no idea what truth is ... Of course, there is a higher faith ... That faith is love, and brings peace. But I shall never accept it; I refuse to lower myself by requesting the peace my weakness cries out for." He surely suffered in knowing that he would join the starry millennia before the spiritual event would occur whose coming he had so often proclaimed. He surely also suffered—and it seems no exaggeration to say that he suffered as a martyr—knowing that he would not participate in that spiritual advent, but only in its preparation. And it is surely because millions have recognized their own suffering in that martyr that Malraux's writings, although little read, have found their audience.

To consider art as enigma upsets perspective and forces the Imaginary Museum "to question some of the ideas upon which it believed it was based" (*Int* 281). Few statements must have been so costly to Malraux. And it is because we have considered art to be a supreme value without knowing which one that we have been so quick to question Dogon masks and Voodoo fetishes. They too express a mystery; but we are dealing here with a mystery internal to man. This questioning of the inner world, which had become vital, as Freud well understood, also explains the fascination of twentieth-century artists for the paintings of the insane. Malraux proposes a startling explanation for that fascination: every artist, he said, "more or less refracts the culture of his society ... even if he is opposed to it." The madman, on the other hand, refracts none of that culture, "for what he has lost is the element that links a man to his community" (*Int* 295). Thus, the fascinated artist hopes to find in the insane the manifestation of fundamental man, man freed from cultures, the manifestation of the inner world unmarked by any cultural imprint. But that world won't be found there, Malraux concludes formally, for "faced with the ingenuous, demented or prisonlike exercise of painting, the adventure of art imposes itself upon us like a coded secret whose unknown code is no less evident than is the secret" (*Int* 300).

Faced with this coded secret whose code is unknown to us—a secret and a code that constitute the enigma of art—Malraux was again forced to ask the fundamental question: "Does the artist create the way he thinks he does, or does he grab a power on the wing, which would awaken if it were not paralyzed by the 'pictorial culture,' that is, the Imaginary Museum?" In the first half of the twentieth century it was thought that the conflict between "the will to expression," that belonging to the artist, and "the will to accession" which had been unique to the sacred arts, could be decided in favor of "the will to expression." Malraux was no longer so sure of this, and he predicted that audiovisuals, by showing everyone "the contrast of four millennia of attainment and of a few centuries of expression" (*Int* 355) would also show that "creation often combines the will to express and the will to attain." We are already forced to question once again the idea that the will to expression is "the principal and constant agent of creation." We are also already forced to see in Van Gogh as in Picasso a will to accession; accession to an *unknown* perhaps, but accession, all the same. Malraux's perspective is now reversed, and Malraux, after revealing the demiurgic power of the artist as well as its metaphysical significance, wondered whether that power was not also a means of accession to an even greater power.

In 1942, in *The Walnut Trees of Altenburg,* Malraux wrote "the greatest mystery is not that we have been flung at random between the profusion

Art Is Not an Antidestiny

of the earth and the galaxy of the stars, but that in this prison we can fashion images of ourselves sufficiently powerful to deny our nothingness" (*WTA* 74). After tirelessly questioning those fashioned images for more than thirty years, Malraux happened upon an even greater mystery: the mystery of the language emitted by all the forms of all those images, the mystery of a "metalanguage" of all the forms created by art. Just as interstellar space emits waves, which we can catch but cannot yet decode, works of art emit "scrambled ultrasounds, which we perceive but cannot decipher" (*Int* 336). Art is enigma; the language of forms remains mysterious to us; we hear it but we have not decoded its ciphered secret. Faced with the power to create that is within us, we can only say: "We still don't understand its language; we only hear its voice" (*PM* 233). Malraux said this in 1973 before the Imaginary Museum that had assembled at the Maeght Foundation, and until the end of his life in 1976 he avidly questioned "that voice" in an attempt to understand its language.

Ever since art ceased to express the sacred or the supernatural, ever since the Imaginary Museum resuscitated all the forms of the past and gathered all the forms of the present, we have believed that our view of works of art was a liberated one. What we are really doing is looking at them with an experimental eye. We look at them the way we look at a crowd of people in which we are searching for a friend. We project the image of our friend on many people, thinking we recognize him in them. Every age, including our own, has projected its experimental eye on works of art (*Int* 245). The canons of Autun, who had the portal of their cathedral walled up, saw it with an eye different from ours, and neither of these views corresponds to that of the Roman sculptors who fashioned the portal. The language we hear in front of works of art is the language we impose on them, it is not their own; it is not the *metalanguage* that all the forms drawn from ourselves can speak to deny our nothingness. Arriving at this stage in his reflection, Malraux enlarged the field of his interrogation as he had never done before, and he asked himself a fundamental question that gave new color and new tonality to his thought in the final two years of his life. Confronted with the multiplicity of the forms gathered in the Imaginary Museum, with the voice they make us hear, with the metamorphosis of those forms depending on the specific way of viewing imposed on them by man, Malraux wondered: "Can we assume that human beings carry within them a language of forms that transcends civilizations?" (*Int* 311).

In answer to this question, which is literally upsetting, that is, which dramatically changes the way we listen to the voices of works of art, Malraux replies in the affirmative. He goes even further and invites us to discover and agree that if we are capable of simultaneously hearing the voice of an Ellora sculpture and a sculpture from Chartres, that of a Rembrandt and of Takanobu, that of Picasso and of a Voodoo fetish, it is because *primordial forms* do exist: "The irrational creates forms that we would call archetypes if that word didn't have so many meanings. Let us call them primordial. They are born, as is horror of the octopus, in a quasi-biological realm much deeper than collective forces: they are on the order of destiny" (*Int* 311). Art is an antidestiny, not because it is opposed to destiny, but because it allows a blending into it. Art is the unceasing quest for "primordial forms," which are on the order of destiny, and therefore art is the highest form of fellowship with destiny. And if there is "a language of forms that transcends civilizations" (*Int* 297), if there are "primordial forms," then the question whether the artist creates or whether he grabs a power on the wing, the question whether the artist invents or whether he discovers his creation, is raised in different terms.

At the end of *The Timeless* and on the threshold of *Precarious Man,* Malraux was in the presence of the "phosphorescent eyes of forms ... Never has their enigma struck man more with its confused and startling presence" (*Int* 405). Malraux completed his patient inventory of the forms created by all irrationals, he scrutinized the various ways of viewing that man had already imposed on all these forms, and—like Goethe, who made an inventory of plants and their forms and, while looking for the *Ur-Pflanz*, discovered the metamorphosis of plants—then sought "primordial forms" and the law of their metamorphosis. Rembrandt, Picasso, and the Little Man from the Cyclades "who still has something to say" (*PM* 267), remain and will continue to remain together in Malraux's Imaginary Museum because they incarnate one of the forms that primordial forms can take, and because they speak "the language of forms that transcends civilizations," a language that is within man, even though he has not yet deciphered it.

It seems almost certain that it was in Japan, in May and June 1974, that the belief in the existence of primordial forms must have arisen in Malraux. He tells us that as he was walking down the stairs leading to the Nachi waterfall he experienced—for the first time in front of a waterfall—"the transmission of the sacred" (*Int* 208). Describing the anonymous fourteenth-century cylinder depicting the Nachi waterfall, in the Nezu Museum in Tokyo, Malraux says that, like all masterpieces of the

Far East, it is not a representation but "a sign," not "the sign of a spectacle" but "the symbol of a mystery" (ibid.). Following his trip to Japan, Malraux worked on *The Timeless,* of which chapters 7 and 8 are a long meditation on the arts, which pursue inner reality beyond appearances, and attain it. Since writing *The Temptation of the West,* published in 1926, and even since his adolescence, Malraux had been thirsting for inner reality, but at that time nothing enabled a Westerner to find the inner reality of beings and things within himself. "The West is unfamiliar with the concept of inner reality because our individualism considers all inner reality to be subjective" (*Int* 218). For centuries, all Western thought has rested on the ideal of objectification and on the danger of the subjective. Inner reality, it was believed, could only be subjective. Western religious thought, too, steered away from inner reality. Based on transcendence more than on immanence, it asked its faithful to turn toward an exterior transcendence. That is why the Church tried to stifle the blinding light of its mystics, who had found within themselves the burning fire of the inner presence of their transcending God, and why, when the church failed to dim that light, it recuperated those mystics by turning them into saints like any others.

From the time of his first trips to China and Japan, Malraux constantly sought to understand what inner reality might be for a Far Easterner. He had taken those trips, however, either between the ages of twenty and thirty, or during periods in his life when art had not yet become an enigma for him. He was *studying* inner reality at that time; he had not yet *experienced* it. In May and June 1974, in front of the Nachi waterfall and in the temples of Ise, Kyoto, and Nara, Malraux no longer thought about inner reality; he experienced it. He then *sensed* the true meaning of the statement: a Japanese artist, while painting a sign, "hopes to have received the confidence of the world" (*Int* 222). He experienced it deep within him; he sensed that "the world of inner reality is more subtle than the cosmos" (*Int* 236).

The revelation of inner reality is too intimate a revelation to be easily transmitted. An image may help portray what it represents. An orchestral conductor, a violinist, a pianist work for years on the score of a symphony or a sonata, they perform increasingly more profound interpretations of it, they know the score note by note, and yet they live with the feeling that the essence of the work still escapes them. And then one day, suddenly, they feel they are entering into the score and finally reaching its inner reality, its music. In front of the Nachi waterfall, whose sign he had known of before he saw a manifestation of it, Malraux had a comparable revelation: out of the manifestation and with the help of the sign, he attained its inner reality. Having been able to attain it, he discovered "the language of inner reality, which exists before art and is revealed by art" (*Int* 224), and he discovered above all that "inner realities converge" (*Int* 284). In light of this *convergence* and in an ultimate attempt, Malraux then went on to rethink the entire significance of the Imaginary Museum: "Our Imaginary Museum closes at five o'clock; it is four thirty, and for us it has lost its share of the unknowable."

In *The Voices of Silence,* Malraux asked himself what purpose modern art served when it took what it represented from the world of appearances (*VOS* 592). After his 1974 trip to Japan, Malraux could unify into one huge vision the *sign* of the Shigemori of Takanobu, the *unreal* that serves as a landscape for Titian's Shepherd, the *abstraction* of contemporary paintings, and the *stylization* of Braque's Birds: he united them in the world of inner reality, and having acceded to that world he discovered the existence of "a language of forms that transcends civilizations"; he discovered the existence of "primordial forms." Malraux could then integrate into his meditation what he had until then neglected. He went on to question *all* forms, not just those created by the artist. He questioned the driftwood, the septaria agates, and all "the crafty bountifulness of nature" (*Int* 302). He finally knew that museums and libraries do not just assemble, as was believed, "successive answers to the question raised by death; today, taken as a whole, they incarnate the question more than the answers" (*HP* 291). An All-Encompassing that is vaster than the Imaginary Museum must be questioned. And to question it, which Malraux was quick to do in *Precarious Man and Literature,* he rediscovered the Word—In the beginning was the Word, he seemed to affirm, and the Word took form. Thus uncertainty was born.

17

Religions Are Also Mortal

❦

AT THE CONCLUSION of his spiritual meditation, which had chosen art as a support, Malraux had to accept the obvious: all the temples of art—museums, book and audio libraries—built by the first civilization that was heir to the entire earth propose changing incarnations of the question, "What is Man?" but they provide no answer to it. Malraux then rediscovered what he had first written in 1950 at the end of *The Coin of the Absolute,* and what he would have preferred to invalidate: art provides "a string of ephemeral answers to an invincible question" (*Psy. Art.,* III, 147). Religions proposed an answer and told man what he was. The world of art doesn't tell him. The survival it proposes is precarious, which also renders its victory over death precarious. The immensity of the time it provides is not infinite. It, too, is a world which seeks its world above. Faced with these limitations, which he had hoped to overcome, Malraux, with all the honesty he possessed, concluded his writings on art with the statement: "And man will realize that even the Timeless is not eternal" (*Int* 415). To write that statement must have been painful for Malraux. Thirty-five years earlier he had proclaimed, "As a writer, by what have I been obsessed if not by mankind" (*WTA* 23–24). Did he encounter a spiritual impasse, then? Did he meet with ultimate failure? Some have affirmed this a bit too quickly. I believe on the contrary that Malraux explored the means of access to a new spirituality, which he felt was in the making.

In *Paper Moons,* written when Malraux was nineteen, the Deadly Sins, setting out to attack Death, stated as an aside, and thus as a fact without much consequence, that God had already "changed His name and His clothes many times" (*LP* 27). In *Farfelu Kingdom* the dead gods had become mere toys. Through all of Malraux's works on art, one idea weaves like a leitmotif: the survival and resurrection of works of art metamorphose the absolutes that those works celebrated. The artists who expressed their belief in Isis, Buddha, Vishnu, Zeus, or Jesus Christ saw these figures as absolutes; the faithful who prayed to them prayed to an absolute. For us, heirs to religions of all time and all places, those absolutes have become "metamorphosed absolutes" (*VOS* 636), "relativized absolutes" (*MI*, I, 48; *Psy. Art.*, III, 139). There may be an eternal part of man, but "civilizations that claimed to possess it, possessed it only on their own terms" (*VOS* 407). Religions, as well. The strength and significance that was once attributed to history rested on the fact that history pigeonholed "each religion within a temporal context, thus depriving it of its value as an absolute, a value which syncretic systems such as theosophy are obviously unable to replace" (*VOS* 609). Even though history has lost the place it once usurped, one of its major teachings nevertheless remains: every religion is relative to an age and often to a geographical area. In the twentieth century the enduring movement of thought that began in the Renaissance, when the Christian world had become "a world among others and when, for Dante, Virgil was no longer damned" (*HP* 34), has finally ended. In just a few centuries, all religions have become relative. "It is one of the major metamorphoses of humanity" (*HP* 33).

We must be aware of the different meanings the adjective "relative" can have. Too often we only think of the meaning "partial, incomplete, imperfect," which it has in a phrase like "someone of relative integrity." This meaning is a derived, deduced, weakened one. The primary meaning of "relative" is that which exists only in relation to something else; that which forms or implies a relationship. When each man has truly integrated relativity into his culture, as many scientists have already done, he will then more readily accept the proclamation that arises out of the Imaginary Museum: religions only exist relative to "something else," they establish relationships, they are relative. Laymen will probably accept this more readily than will clerics.

The absolute that religions claimed as their own, most particularly the revealed monotheist religions, "had ruled out the possibility of any mutual understanding on a deeper, universal level" (*VOS* 609). Claiming to be the only true expression of the absolute, each religion also claimed to be as absolute as the absolute to which it prayed; it could not conceive of itself as the expression of *one* relationship and it became threatening

Religions Are Also Mortal

to all those who did not relate in the same way that it did. Today, we should note the full significance of the title *The Coin of the Absolute* (*Monnaie de l'absolu*), which Malraux chose for his third essay on art. The word *monnaie*, prior to its meaning as change given for what you have paid, means currency, or coin, the very means of exchange, and it measures the terms of that exchange. And in this sense all religions should be considered as a Coin of the Absolute. The verbal forms and the edifying images a religion proposes are not the absolute; they are an expression of it; they are a means of exchange, of communication, of relationship with the absolute.

We must take this even further: history, and then the Imaginary Museum, have not only made it fully clear that religions are relative, they have also shown that religions are mortal. After the "We Civilizations, we know we are mortal" that so many minds have had trouble accepting for their own civilization, there must merge today the "We Religions, we accept ourselves as mere mortals." Religions are also relative to an age, that is, to time. Our inheritance of the entire earth is made of "the succession of values changing with each civilization" (*VOS* 633). The ethic of Taoism, Hindu submission, the Greek spirit of inquiry, the medieval communion of men, the cult of Reason and then that of history—all these values, even supreme values, "decline once they lose their power of rescuing man from his human bondage" (ibid.).

Under the pretext that Malraux, when writing *The Voices of Silence*, was speaking of the decline of supreme values, some critics believed his thinking was approaching that of Spengler. It was not, as Malraux said and repeated, for he emphasized the metamorphosis of values and not their death. A supreme value, because it is supreme, possesses the power to metamorphose itself, to be incarnated in variable, multiple, and successive forms. A religion is always based upon *one* of these forms, and it belongs to the realm of what must be metamorphosed. It doesn't belong to the realm of what endures beyond form. It is a formation and disappears with the form. It is mortal. In every religion's founding myth there are historical, even subtle facts. Nietzsche, in *The Birth of Tragedy*, showed how the interpretation of myths tends to become narrower throughout the centuries and how religions close themselves up in an orthodox dogmatism when their founding myth becomes more restricted. When the culture which has given birth to a religion, or the one upon which a religion has leaned to establish itself slowly begins to be metamorphosed, that religion, in self-defense, props itself up on its dogmatism and rejects its relativity. Like a chrysalis that feels the forces of transformation welling up inside it and attempts to reject them, religion rejects metamorphosis, it rejects the end of its ephemeral form and becomes "a realm of morality" (*Int* 6).

I wrote a novel about a Catholic priest, for whom the agonizing question that remained with him even during his prayers was not that of knowing whether he should work in a factory, or whether he should get married, but of knowing whether, if he had lived in Jerusalem in the third decade of the Christian era and had been a priest of the religion of that time, he would have remained a member of the church to which he belonged or would have followed Christ and his new church. It will take many generations for men to cease feeling the need to see their own religion as immortal, and for the cultural printed circuits to admit that religions, like civilizations, join the royal procession of great and noble mortals. Many already entertain the idea, but it usually remains an idea: it is thought, not yet experienced. It is like a graft on a fruit tree that has not yet taken and cannot yet produce any fruit. It will take generations before the faithful go into their temples to pray with fervor and with faith, experiencing their religion in their innermost depths as an ephemeral and mortal translation. There is even the fear, unfortunately, that religious fanaticisms will first be exacerbated. And there is also the fear that Christian ecumenical movements will not encourage this metamorphosis of religious culture. Their search for unity, sometimes at all costs, leads Christian religions, especially Catholicism, to minimize that which makes them unique and original. Instead of being a recognition and frank affirmation of the plurality and relativity of religions, instead of being a proclamation of the mortality of religions, this ecumenicism often resounds as a reaffirmation of the intangibility of Christian revelation and its superiority over all other religious translations. The religions of the Far East, by their very nature and the message they deliver, teach that all forms, including their own, are successive and ephemeral. This is yet another reason for the attraction they hold for Western youth.

It is not enough to admit that religions are mortal, nor that all absolutes are relativized; we must also accept the consequences and recognize that gods are "the highest power of man's creation" (*L'Express*, 21 May 1955), they are "torches lit one by one by man to light the path that leads him away from the beast" (*Les Nouvelles littéraires* 3 April 1952). All the ideas about God that man has already accepted and all those he will accept are ideas *imagined* by man. Just as pictorial and sculptural forms of God are products of the imagination of the artist who created them, so the verbal forms of God that each religion proposes are products of the imaginary of their founder and his disciples. And the Christian mystery of the incarnation can be seen as the arrival upon earth of a transcendent God, but more especially it can be seen as a reminder that it is always the human that engenders the form in which man sees the divine. A truly religious mind should never forget that the divine in which he has faith can be neither represented nor described. He should never forget that all formulations of the divine are products of the human mind. Mystics who speak of the divine by saying what it is not are aware of this truth, and Thomas Aquinas teaches the same when he states that all he has written is but straw compared to what he has *seen*. After having *seen*, he never speaks again. Unfortunately, the Church to which he belonged attached more importance to his writings than to his silence. Even religions based on revelation should admit that all representations of God, including their own, are produced by the human imaginary, for if God revealed himself, He did so to men who translated that revelation into a human language.

Malraux, to explain the place he gives in his works to his returns to earth and to the resuscitations he experienced, says they "belong to the realm of epiphanies" (*L* 147), but he immediately adds a thought that demands profound meditation: "The Revelation," he says, "is that nothing can be revealed. The unknown realm of the unthinkable has neither shape nor name . . . What epiphanies correspond to the epiphany of the unthinkable? Those of life" (ibid.). Whoever wishes to become open to the epiphany of the unthinkable must first freely admit that all the forms and all the names man might give to the unthinkable are creations of the human mind. The Christian God, by temporarily assuming human form before being transfigured, affirms this majestically.

After having the revelation that nothing can be revealed, and that the unknown of the unthinkable has neither form nor name, Malraux quickly completed *The Timeless* and ended his meditation on the significance of art. He then wrote: "The language common to statues of Christ and Shiva . . . is the totality of art as an enigma of surviving presences—as an All-Encompassing of all works of art" (*Int* 384). And he immediately added: "as is music." This final remark begs our attention. Malraux's sensibility to music has often been misunderstood and sometimes denied. Sophie de Vilmorin's statement, however, is crucial and unimpeachable. In the book by Patrice Howald, she adds: "André Malraux granted great importance to music. Often he listened to it lovingly, but he could not undertake everything. He had chosen to speak of painting and sculpture, but he loved music passionately." Alain Malraux's testimony is also unimpeachable. André Malraux had told him: "Music has revealed myself to me by certifying that I exist." To be able to evoke "that subterranean region in which music takes man's head between its hands and slowly lifts it towards human fellowship" (*DW* 48), one must possess an exceptional sensitivity to music. Malraux possessed that sensitivity. He only allowed it to be expressed in an allusive fashion and was somewhat cautious of it. In an attempt to understand why, we may shed supplementary light on Malraux's personality.

To fight against madness in his prison cell, Kassner sings Bach and Beethoven. His memory is full of those composers. Gradually, the music leads him to "a lasting communion," a "world victorious over pain," to a collected manifestation in which all is mingled, "even as life and death merge in the immobility of the starry sky" (*DW* 45–46). But Kassner is a hero who wants to act, and when his lucidity is assured he distances himself from music, for it makes him "sink, from serenity to serenity, to the abject domain of consolations." If Malraux had allowed music to take the place in his life it might have occupied, he would have undoubtedly also been tempted to sink serenely into that domain. But he rejected all consolation and sought to open up a victorious domain.

In the last lines of *Man's Hope,* Manuel becomes aware of his metamorphosis and of the infinite possibility of man's destiny immediately after listening to some music (*MH* 509–11). In the final pages of *Man's Fate,* Gisors, following the metamorphosis brought about in him by the death of his son, had been delivered from life and death, had entered "the worlds of contemplation where all is vain," and had discovered music which alone could speak to him of death (*MF* 356–58). I believe Malraux instinctively protected himself from the contemplation music can encourage when one feels it as strongly as he did. Moreover, after 1961 he may not have wanted to let music speak to him too much of the death of his two sons, who had been killed in an automobile accident. During his adolescence and his entire life as a novelist, Malraux waged a remarkable battle to deliver himself from death, but he didn't want to deliver himself from life—on the contrary. I suspect Malraux was more willing to allow himself to listen to music after his stay at the Salpêtrière hospital than before. After his hospital stay he could in fact write: "Weary of the rustling voices of death, on awakening I watch life renewing itself on my fingernail" (*L* 149). Music could then speak to him of something other than death, and he could listen to it as he listened to "the language common to statues of Christ and Shiva," as "the All-Encompassing of all works of art." He had climbed all the steps in his ascent toward the Unformed.

The deep roots of reemerging materialism in the nineteenth century, and those of the tragic or the absurd invading the second third of the twentieth century, can be found in the jolt the human mind received with the realization that every formulated absolute was a human creation, that only the relative existed, and that henceforth every religious spirit refusing the relativity of its faith could be seen as lying to itself. For most people, the impossibility of an absolute Absolute will engender the absurd or the tragic, either materialist or not. But not for Malraux. In 1959 he declared to Jacques Olivier: "In the end, it is as if religions were nothing other than successive libretti of an immense music, as if that mysterious music were only transmitted to us through the communion of works of art" (*Le Figaro littéraire*, 6 June 1959). For Malraux, the relativity of imagined absolutes and the mortal character of religions do not stifle that "immense music." On the contrary, they reveal its presence even more. Like a music lover who can use several interpretations of the *Quartet of Spheres* to probe ever deeper into the mystery of Beethoven, Malraux was able to use the relativity and mortality of religions to listen ever more attentively to the "mysterious music" he heard.

Anyone who has claimed that Malraux's ideas are similar to those of Pascal has been too hasty. Either such critics were unfamiliar with *The Timeless* or *Precarious Man*, or they had failed to see the blossoming of what was germinating under *The Voices of Silence*. Pascal, in reconciling the science of the mathematician and the consciousness of the mystic having experienced "the night of fire," made his Wager. All-too often, people have not noticed that Pascal's Wager was double-edged. He gambled not only on the existence of God but also on one of the imagined representations of that God. Malraux's attitude was radically different. He heard the sounds of the language man carries within and which transcends all civilizations, all religions, and all the gods that have already been imagined. He willingly admitted that man has not yet decoded the ciphered secret of that language. He didn't even assert that man will one day be able to decode that language entirely; yet he foresaw a growing, swelling spiritual event. Malraux's wager—for him it was a foresight—was that man will soon give new spiritual expression to the existence of a language common to all forms, those created by "the crafty bountifulness" of nature as well as those fashioned by the human imaginary, which includes the forms created by man as a representation of the divine.

"For about ten years the world has been sensing and muttering that something is going to happen in the spiritual realm," said Malraux in 1974 during his dialogue with Guy Suarès (*VO* 169). The world had, in fact, been sensing this for some time, and Kandinsky had already expressed it in 1912 in the final lines of his treatise *Concerning the Spiritual in Art*. But the exact date the world began to sense its advent matters little; what is important is that the world also began to mutter about it. Although he spoke often, almost continually, of this spiritual event, Malraux never sought to specify the modalities it might take. He knew that would have been useless. He knew and repeated that the nature of spiritual revolutions is to be "eruptions." One can foresee their coming but not their forms. "Great upheavals in the soul by their very nature challenge any ability to foresee" (*HP* 322). When they have occurred, "the entire past is metamorphosed, it belongs to them: the world changes its past" (*VO* 164).

"The crucial problem of the end of the century will be the religious problem" (*Preuves*, March 1955). Malraux said this in 1955—this date is important—and he constantly repeated it between 1970 and 1976. He also repeated in various ways that the twenty-first century will see the blossoming of a major spiritual phenomenon. But he pointed out, and this precision is essential, that that phenomenon will not "necessarily be the birth of a new religion." This spiritual event, he said, could be to religions what religions have been to what preceded them. Malraux sensed that "a religious renaissance would be based on givens that we do not possess" (*VO* 33), and that the religious problem will be presented "in a form as different from the one we are familiar with as Christianity was from ancient religions" (*Preuves* March 1955). The passage from a magical universe to a sacred universe was one of the great metamorphoses of the spirit. The passage from the sacred to the divine universe was another. The three or four centuries of the Imaginary of Fiction that the West has come to know may appear as the ultimate phase of a new fundamental metamorphosis of the spirit. Malraux sensed this was possible, but he possessed the wisdom, indeed the serenity, to admit that the chrysalis must not seek to imagine what the sensations of the butterfly will be. He serenely admitted that we may have to endure rather than govern the next metamorphosis (*HP* 323). At the ultimate stage of his earthly spiritual journey, Malraux admitted that man today

Religions Are Also Mortal

is a precarious being placed in uncertainty, but he invited us to see along with him that that man is not necessarily a tragic figure in an absurd or overwhelming cosmos. Shortly before his death, Malraux issued a challenge in the last sentence of his last work: "Will we resign ourselves to seeing man as an animal incapable of *not* wanting to conceive of a world which by its very nature escapes his mind? Or will we remember that crucial spiritual events have always confounded all predictions?"

18

Metamorphosis as Universal Law

❦

AT THE BEGINNING of *Anti-Memoirs,* Malraux evokes his observation of the upheaval of the world: as an adolescent he saw the sparrows swooping down on the horse-drawn buses in the gardens of the Palais-Royal; a few decades later he met Commander Glenn on his return from a space voyage. And he asked himself how his life would respond "to these dying gods and rising cities" (*A-M* 3). Four years after asking himself that question he made this surprising confession to Yves Florenne in May 1971: "I only want to die knowing what I've thought about life" (*Le Monde,* May 9–10, 1971).

We must take enough time to reflect upon the profound meaning of that confession in order to sense the fantastic and beneficent reversal it proposes. It expresses a radical change in the perspective imposed by most, if not all, religions up to that time. For millennia, humans have wanted to die only knowing what they thought about death and what happened afterwards. Malraux, on the contrary, wanted to know what he thought about life and to die only after he had found that out. For him, it wasn't what happens after death that gives meaning to life, it was life that gives significance to death. Eighteen months after confiding in Yves Florenne, Malraux was taken by ambulance to the Salpêtrière hospital. While he was there he felt he was on the threshold of death, that is, he had contact with death; then he experienced a third return to life. A year and a half later he then said to Jean-Marie Dunoyer: "I am attempting to make a life, the life of someone at a moment in history when one becomes aware of Metamorphosis as Universal Law" (*Le Monde,* March 15, 1974). He lived for two and a half years longer, and "making a life"

Metamorphosis as Universal Law

for Malraux meant completing *The Timeless* and writing *Precarious Man*. He wrote with a certain feverishness, like a man whose days are numbered, and with a certain serenity, like a man for whom things have found their rightful place. Since 1975 he had known and said that "the moment when the completely unthinkable begins" is the moment of death (*L'Herne*, p. 158). "In the end, insofar as life and death are concerned, it may be a much more optimistic thought than it first appeared, because if you begin by saying that to conceive of death is absolutely impossible, but if at the same time you put that in the perspective of metamorphosis, then the blend is livable."

All Malraux's works, in fact, should be read in the light of Metamorphosis as Universal Law, for metamorphosis is constantly present in them all. Malraux himself declared, "The essence of my thought is metamorphosis" (ibid.). His early writings are rich in comic, *farfelu* metamorphoses. In 1929, in the controversy over *The Conquerors*, Malraux specified that Garine sets up metamorphosis as a value against values of order, consideration, and foresight. During the 1930s, most of Malraux's speeches on culture or art referred to metamorphosis. The idea of metamorphosis is often expressed in *Man's Fate, Man's Hope,* and *The Walnut Trees of Altenburg* and represents the focal point of all his writings on art. In *Precarious Man,* Malraux wonders whether tomorrow man might not live in an Imaginary-of-Metamorphosis just as he once lived in an Imaginary-of-Truth and then in an Imaginary-of-Fiction. Metamorphosis is always present in the works and life of Malraux from his adolescence until his death.

The image of metamorphosis imposed itself on the adolescent Malraux, who used it to make the *farfelu* sparkle, that is, in a way it would have been radically different without. Heir to an Aristotelian, Christian, and Cartesian world, Malraux long resisted before totally accepting metamorphosis. While reading his works, one even has the impression that he was trying to reject it. He felt it at work in the world of art; he could not see extending it to life. Despite the ancient cultures of Egypt, Latin America, and Africa, despite the honored avatars of India, Western culture has rejected and even scorned metamorphosis. Shakespeare, for example, often uses the word "metamorphosis," but when Prospero commands Ariel to metamorphose himself into a nymph, or when Ariel celebrates the metamorphosis of the King of Naples, French translators prefer to use the verb *changer,* "to change." In the late nineteenth and early twentieth centuries, metamorphosis still provoked shock, as demonstrated by the prefaces written for translations of the ancient Egyptians' *Book of the Dead*. Egyptologists at that time underlined the absurdity and the schizophrenia of the beliefs expressed in the book they had just translated. And even today the idea of metamorphosis still shocks many people.

The Western mind considers metamorphosis to be a fable or a superstition, or, at best, a literary convention in tales and legends. People fail to see that there are three types of metamorphosis in Apuleius' *The Golden Ass:* the metamorphoses brought about by sorcerers or magicians such as Meroe; the uncontrollable metamorphoses brought about by the servant Fotis; and the metamorphoses performed by Isis, the goddess of goddesses, she who is honored in the final chorus of *The Magic Flute*. At most, Westerners agree to acknowledge metamorphoses brought about by sorcerers, but they relegate others to the realm of fables or to fairy tales, in which, after losing their childhood innocence, they can no longer believe. The Catholic Church has done everything in its power to banish metamorphosis from the cultural universe of Christendom. The ass is no longer the guest of the Nativity, nor the means for the Flight into Egypt, nor the vehicle for the climb to earthly or celestial Jerusalem, nor *The Golden Ass;* it has become a symbol of stupidity and laziness, and its cap is the cap of dunces. The Councils of Constantinople II, in 553, of Lyons in 1234, and of Florence in 1439 condemned belief in the preexistence of souls before their incarnation and affirmed as an intangible truth of faith that the soul, after death, is sent immediately to heaven, to purgatory, or to hell. These articles of faith served mainly to combat the belief in possible metempsychoses, but they also served to banish metamorphosis from the official culture. In Catholic education, the first chapter of *Genesis* triumphed over the second. In the first chapter, the Creator creates grass, trees, animals *after their kind*, and he orders them to be fruitful and multiply *after their kind;* then, seeing that it was all good, he creates man. In the second chapter, on the other hand, the breath of Yahweh on a speck of dust from the ground creates man *before* he creates plants and animals. Yahweh *then* has the animals march in front of man so that man can give them a name, can name them. Then and only then, man not having found a companion worthy of him among the animals, Yahweh plunges him into a deep sleep, takes one of his ribs, and turns it into a woman. The Catholic catechism took what suited it from each chapter and turned it into a watered-down mixture.

Anyone who can read these all too-familiar biblical images with an open mind will clearly see that there are very few images as metamorphosing as that of a speck of dust becoming a man or of a man's rib

Metamorphosis as Universal Law

becoming a woman. We should all be able to admit that to ask a practicing Christian to believe that the bread and wine of the Eucharist *really* become the body and blood of Christ is to ask him to believe in a transubstantiation, a transformation, a metamorphosis. The Real Presence is a metamorphosis. The faithful Egyptian who believed in the real presence of Osiris in the waters of the Nile did not believe in a mystery, for he could believe in metamorphosis. We should also all be able to admit that the Christian mystery of the Incarnation is a symbol of metamorphosis, perhaps the most expressive symbol of it. To truly believe that through an act of the Holy Spirit the Word was made flesh is to believe in the metamorphosing power of the Spirit! (No doubt some time will elapse before it is possible to study in depth and in complete peace of mind the reasons that led the Catholic religion to obscure metamorphosis when its most important dogmas are metamorphoses.)

The *Book of the Dead*, the Tibetans' *Bardo Thodol*, and even the *Popul-Vuh* of the Quiche Mayans show what spirituality, a culture, and a civilization can be when, far from considering metamorphosis as a superstition, they turn it into one of the laws of life. And it is not surprising that the West is rediscovering these books at the same time it is beginning to "become aware of Metamorphosis as Universal Law." Visits to the Far East and the popularity of Latin American literature testify to this. For "the Man of Corn" and for South American literature, metamorphosis is a cultural given, just as the Last Judgment is a cultural given in the West.

For a Westerner, metamorphosis is at best a literary myth. Ovid himself doesn't seem to believe in it. Out of caution he cites the words of Pythagoras: "Nothing keeps the same appearance forever, and nature, in its perpetual renovation, rediscovers in forms the material for new forms. The sky and all that is under the sky changes form, the earth as well, and all that is on the earth, including us" (Ovid, book 15). Ovid recorded tales and legends the way our modern ethnologists do, and, like them, he didn't really believe that those tales and legends expressed any truth. He sought and found material for formal poetry in them. He neither sought nor celebrated the poetry in the profound significance of those tales and legends. It was not within his scope to have realized that the stones—clay—that Deucalion and Pyrrha threw behind them were metamorphosed into men because Deucalion was the son of Prometheus and Pyrrha the granddaughter of the Earth. Zeus wanted to keep the power to metamorphose for himself and his Olympian court. He bound Prometheus, who had brought fire to men thus enabling them to feed the forge in which forms are created and to maintain athanors in which matter is sublimated. Fortunately, Aeschylus alerted us that Prometheus would one day be delivered and that Zeus would learn that no one rules with impunity.

Ovid is completely representative of Greco-Roman culture, which no longer believed in metamorphosis and saw it merely as material for wonderful, entertaining stories. Modern Catholics act in the same way when, pressed with questions, they recognize they no longer truly believe in the Real Presence of the body of Christ in the bread of the Eucharist and that they receive that bread as a symbol rather than as a reality.

Despite nearly twenty-five centuries during which the cultures and religions of the Greco-Roman world prevailed while considering metamorphosis to be a superstition, we may note with André Pieyre de Mandiargues that "in the folklores of the whole world there are metamorphoses, as if men had not hoped for anything else with such fervor" (*Cahier Renaud-Barrault,* no. 101). And if it is still too early to hope that Westerners will truly renew their ties with metamorphosis, it should no longer be too early to ask skeptics to sympathize with Renan, who wrote to Flaubert on September 8, 1874, that in the metamorphoses described by Ovid he found "a profound relationship with nature" and felt questioned by those "mobile and ravishing images."

We ordinarily relegate metamorphosis to the realm of the fantastic and see it as the source of brutal and aberrant transformations. Raymond Roussel, in *Locus Solus,* has shown the falseness of such a view. At the beginning of the book the eminent scholar Martial Canterel leads his visitors into the park on his property. He gradually has them witness scenes—minutely described by Roussel—which at first appear fantastic, almost mad, irrational, and in any event brought on by an unbridled imagination. Roussel then retells the story of each scene from another perspective, and this time it becomes clear, logical, obvious. Gradually the reader must abandon his logical certainty, which rests only on the appearance of phenomena. He is then ready to meet the fortune-teller Noël (the name is significant) and his rooster Mopsus. He is able to witness the metamorphosis of fine metal cylinders into a supple and silky fabric. This metamorphosis, too, becomes a perfectly normal phenomenon explained by the nature of things and elements; in addition, this phenomenon provides some relief and a little happiness to a stricken old man. Metamorphosis is logical; it is beneficent; only the insufficiency of our knowledge prevents us from admitting this.

Metamorphosis as Universal Law

Zoology and botany, far from considering metamorphosis to be in the realm of fables, have long considered it a reality. Other sciences are beginning to accept or to question it, among them the most unexpected of all—mathematics. Since the publication in 1790 of Goethe's *Attempt to Explain the Metamorphosis of Plants,* botanists have known that metamorphosis is the law of the plant world; they know today that stems, leaves, flowers, and fruits are all derived from a metamorphosis, the transformation of meristems. They also know that the unfolding of a metamorphosis is slow, gradual, and not brutal or sudden. Since the voices of Elie Faure, Focillon, and Malraux have been heard, it is finally being admitted that metamorphosis is the law of the world of art works, in which it acts on the scale of centuries. Since 1977 when the mathematician René Thom published *Structural Stability and Morphogenesis,* it has become obvious that mathematics, especially topology, is currently seeking fundamental equations of metamorphosis. Granted, mathematicians will probably call them equations of René Thom's "catastrophe theory," but we must avoid misinterpreting the meaning of "catastrophe," which etymologically is not a disaster but an unfolding. Racine had no disaster in mind when in his prefaces he spoke of the catastrophe of his plays.

Without knowing the most recent developments and investigations in contemporary scientific thinking, Malraux arrived at a thought whose full depth and consequences have not yet been measured, one that enabled him to write shortly before his death that we withdrew from the nineteenth century and its way of thinking the moment we became aware of our past by way of metamorphosis rather than by way of history (*HP* 283). We have now begun to see "metamorphosis as our past." Malraux asked himself one of the essential questions of our time when he wondered, in 1976, whether a new attempt to understand man would not begin "when the awareness of metamorphosis comes to dominate evolution and to create its own history" (*AC* 223). (One senses that Malraux weighed each word of that statement: awareness, dominate, evolution, its own history).

For a time it was believed—and some people still hope—that biology will provide man with the explanation of himself that he had once hoped to find in history since the time he stopped looking for it in religions. Malraux was one of the first to sense that a biological totalitarianism, if it should ever see the light of day, would be more totalitarian and more sinister than historical totalitarianisms had ever been. He knew that shaky individualism, after seeking the secret of man in history, was now seeking it in the succession of species, and he feared the "subtle determinism" that was affecting the unconscious more than the attempts at historical determinism had affected it (*Revue des Deux Mondes*, February 1975). For Malraux, the theory of natural selection, regardless of the names it is given or the covering used to hide its insufficiencies, was a theory that was "too logical for the world and for the recent discoveries in biology" (ibid.).

Today, all the theories of evolution based on natural selection seem shaken by the advances made in biology, genetics, paleontology, and mathematics. In 1947 at the Princeton congress on evolution, neo-Darwinism still seemed triumphant and the journal *Evolution* was created. Thirty years later at the 1980 Chicago congress, natural selection appeared more modest and assumed a defensive position. Theories of probability, notably those of Heitler, have shown that it is improbable that chance is at the origin of mutations, which doesn't mean that necessity must be reintroduced. We know today that genetic heterogeneity and chromosomal heterozygosity occur within the same species; consequently genetics, though it can describe the changing of genes in a species, cannot explain the appearance of new species. For a geneticist today, the gene no longer appears as a transmitter of form, but as a key that opens or closes the possibilities of realizing a form or a morphogenetic project. The gene is no longer at the origin of genesis. And a biologist like Rupert Sheldrake is led to propose the "theory of morphogenetic fields" to explain the morphogenesis that genetics no longer explains.

For scientists who study the formation of embryos, the difference in organisms between species poses far fewer problems than does the similarity in organs which can be observed in young embryos of very different species. In paleontology, with the work of Elchedge and Gould, it seems that species, far from evolving imperceptibly and progressively, remain stable for a rather long time before being replaced by other species. The famous "missing links" that had vexed Darwin, and that Teilhard de Chardin conveniently called "the original whites," seem not to have existed and to have been mere intellectual artifices created to defend theories of natural selection. Darwin, himself, influenced by negative criticism and comments on the first formulation of the *Origin of the Species,* subsequently recognized in 1859 that there were other evolutionary processes. In *The Descent of Man* he admitted that he had probably attributed too great a role to natural selection or the survival of the fittest. Along with Stephen Jay Gould, we must ask ourselves whether a new general theory of evolution may not be emerging (cf. Gould's 1980 article "Paleobiology"). It is even becoming difficult to suggest the contrary. Will awareness of metamorphosis guide the science of evolution? It is not impossible, and Malraux was right when he wondered whether a new attempt to understand man would not be undertaken at the very moment "when the awareness of metamorphosis comes to dominate evolution and to create its own history" (*AC* 223).

The nineteenth century now appears fanatic in its devotion to continuity. It sought the continuity of species just as it sought that of history. For a time, twentieth-century biology, genetics, and paleontology were caught up in the flow of a continuity to be achieved at all costs. In the second half of the century they have been disengaging themselves from it. Today, the central problem of particle physics is that of discontinuity, quanta. Today, the central problem of all life sciences as well as that of the historical sciences, including the history of art, is the discontinuity of evolution. The discontinuity of the way in which men have looked at the portal of Autun, and the metamorphoses of that portal are more important and more significant than the hypothetical relationship between that portal and its predecessors. It is finally being admitted that Athens is not the childhood of Rome and that the historical past is made up of irreconcilable parts. Perhaps it will soon be admitted that we shouldn't seek to forge "missing links" out of nothing just to find an intellectual continuity between the ichthyostegid of the Devonian Era and the salamander of the Quaternary.

Quantum physics has abandoned the notion of linear time upon which science had been constructed from the time of Descartes. Physicists today no longer know what time is. They must even accept the idea that reversible time can be hypothesized in an attempt to explain facts observed in the laboratory. Indeed physicists can no longer be zealots for continuity. Their science has emerged from its infancy and has had to abandon a vision of time that was convenient but terribly reductive. Unfortunately, astrophysics, which is still in its early stages, seems to want to fall back into the rut of continuity. The models and cosmologies being conceived by some astrophysicists attempt to construct a continuous history of the universe, from the "big bang" to the present, from "the primordial soup" to cervical complexity. Where necessary, these astrophysicists also imagine missing links so they can forge a Darwinist vision of the evolution of the universe. When their science too has also emerged from infancy, they too, no doubt, will be able to accept a discontinuous history of the expansion and contraction of the universe. The enigma confronting astrophysics today rests on the absence of a quantum theory of gravity, which, if it existed, would enable scientists to use generalized relativity and quantum physics simultaneously. To construct that theory, astrophysics will probably have to disengage itself truly and completely from a linear notion of time and from the continuity which is its daughter.

Genetics has been interested primarily in the study of the permanence of forms and in their transmission through heredity. Morphology deals with the creation of forms. And it may be forced to admit, as the history of art reluctantly had to do, that creation proceeds more through ruptures than through continuity. When we remember that the founder of morphology was Goethe, we realize that Malraux worked and meditated on art the way Goethe worked and meditated first on plants then on animals. Malraux hunted for the source of the appearance and metamorphoses of forms in art; he laid the foundations for a morphology of art, which is why he was so harshly attacked by pure art historians, who only sought the continuity in or the relationships between artistic forms. For similar motives, Goethe and Malraux were compelled to enlarge the field of their investigations. After studying the morphology of plants and discovering that they obeyed the laws of metamorphosis, Goethe undertook the study of animal morphology and brought to light the metamorphosis of the jawbone and of the cranial vertebrae. At that time he envisioned writing a treatise of generalized morphology. After more than forty years of reflection and meditation on the metamorphosis of works of art, Malraux was led to question "the crafty bountifulness" of the creative power of nature and to accept the placement of all forms—those of Rembrandt as well as those of driftwood, of Ellora as well as of calcedonian agates—into the immense melting pot of Metamorphosis as Universal Law.

The work of René Thom shows the extent to which the science of forms—morphology—becomes the science of sciences when all forms are encompassed within it: the apparently static forms of minerals, the dynamic forms of the plant and animal kingdoms, but also forms of the semantic and psychic worlds. René Thom has probably laid the foundations of metaepistemology, which has haunted scientists from the time of Piaget and for which the equilateral triangle of the "ancestral monoid" of the mathematician Pierre Miallet provides an architecture that is at the same time highly scientific and highly symbolic. With the equations of René Thom, the dynamics of certain forms and of many other future forms, their structural stability or, on the contrary, their structural transformation, can be described by the use of an abstract model of mathematical symbols. Today it has become possible to see a form as a dynamic system maintaining its form through the interplay and action of totally abstract attractors. Let these attractors be captured or bifurcate from their usual field of action, and there then appears a true morphogenesis, a new creation of form. A morphogenesis is a conflict of informal attractors. Biology, like mathematics, is beginning to be persuaded of this. It is no longer seeking to explain the structure by the molecule but, rather, the molecule by the structure. The theoretical hypothesis of morphogenetic fields proposed in 1920 by Waddington, and that of "morphic resonance" proposed in 1984 by Rupert Sheldrake, already enable us to imagine a group of experimental verifications which will someday invalidate or confirm this vision of morphogenesis. Already today the mathematical and abstract models of D'Arcy Thompson and René Thom strongly suggest that the creation of new forms and the maintenance of old forms depend on fields of action and chreodes (from *chre,* necessary, and *odos,* path), whose subtle combinations bring about not only the crafty bountifulness of nature but also that of our brains. Like magnetic or gravitational fields, the fields that create forms are immaterial, abstract. And anyone who reflects and works on them belongs to the nobility of "researchers in search of immaterial realms," whom Kandinsky, as early as in 1912, had designated as the conquerors of tomorrow.

Bergson has underlined the striking convergence between the forms of organs in a living being and those of tools created by man; for example, between the heart and the pump, the lung and the bellows, the fist and the hammer. Rupert Sheldrake would explain that convergence by a phenomenon of morphic tuning. René Thom wondered whether a form of forms might exist, an archetypal chreode which extended into families of forms, and whether, on the tree of these families, those tools and organs might occupy homologous positions. Malraux, too, at the most advanced stage of his meditation on forms created by artists, had to ask himself whether there might exist "a language of forms which transcends civilizations" (*Int* 311), and whether there might exist forms that he preferred to call primordial rather than archetypal. In 1912, Kandinsky demanded the right for abstraction to reach the *inner necessity* of forms. As early as July 9, 1786, Goethe wrote to Mme von Stein: "I am beginning to perceive the form with which nature seems to play and, as it plays, to produce all the diversity of life." René Thom's *archetypal chreode,* Malraux's *primordial forms,* Kandinsky's *inner necessity,* and

Metamorphosis as Universal Law

Goethe's *Ur-Forme* all seem to sing the same hymn—the one that will rise up in the Cathedral of the Abstract when all its stones and keystone have been laid.

René Thom's rigorous equations give a phenomenal foundation to the intuitions of Goethe and Malraux. He too, but through calculations, ended up with the sense that there are primordial, abstract structures, independent of any substratum—algebraic beings, he said, which aspire to existence, to become phenomena, and which are at the source of the creation of forms. If this were truly the case, and if René Thom's equations could be extended to an increasing number of forms, then Metamorphosis as Universal Law would be the majestic and infinitely varied unfolding of archetypal chreodes, the unfolding of astract beings which humanity sought to reintroduce by calling them gods but which the high priests of Egyptian antiquity had already named "divine mathematical combinations." Metamorphosis as Universal Law would be the unfolding of "the informal form" that Malraux discovered in *The Timeless* (*Int* 226). And Kandinsky would have been right to boldly assert that abstraction is "the realism of the visionary."

For some, the idea of an abstract form aspiring to existence, waiting for an opportunity to become incarnate, is a spiritualist idea and comes out of a metaphysical presupposition. For others it is quite simply an aberrant idea. And yet if we reflect profoundly on this idea, it almost becomes obvious and acquires the greatest of qualities—simplicity. To approach it, we need only think of Rembrandt's *Slaughtered Ox* or Flaubert's *Madame Bovary,* for example. If Rembrandt created the forms of the *Slaughtered Ox* by an artistic morphogenesis, wasn't it because he carried within him a *still abstract form* that aspired to become a painting, to be given an existence? If Flaubert trans-formed the news item of "the Delamare woman" into Madame Bovary, wasn't it also because he carried within him an *informal form* that aspired to become a novel? To respond here that *The Slaughtered Ox* is a painting simply because Rembrandt was a painter and that *Madame Bovary* is a novel because Flaubert was a writer would be to completely fail to recognize the true mechanisms of creation. We should say, rather, that Rembrandt was a painter because his power to incarnate an abstract form was a pictorial power, whereas Flaubert was a writer because his power of incarnation was a literary one. We must go even further and recognize that the power to incarnate an abstract form is not exclusive to artists; this power is more evident in them, more eloquent, that's all, even if "all" covers the fact that to become more evident the power has to be cultivated at the price of sometimes harsh, terrifying battles. The artist is someone who fights to the bitter end for the incarnation and who accepts no subterfuge to escape it, even if he sometimes wishes that the cup of bitterness would leave him.

For centuries many philosophers, and today biologists, have sought to resolve the problem of which came first, the chicken or the egg? Today it is possible to see that the answer to that enigma is *basically* only of *secondary* importance. Both the chicken and the egg are only different temporal moments in the metamorphosis of an informal form; they are merely successive moments in the realization, the actualization, of a chreode that aspires to take form. And the problem raised is only a temporal problem. It simply raises the problem of the cerebral choice of a position on a linear axis of a time/convention of the mind.

The most powerful and most convincing example of Metamorphosis as Universal Law is the fundamental equation of the twentieth century: $E = mc^2$. There is nothing shocking about believing in the metamorphosis of energy. Between the muscular energy that pulls the string of a bow, the kinetic energy of the flying arrow, and the caloric energy spent by the arrow striking the target, there is no continuity of energy, no evolution of energy; there is metamorphosis. Energy takes forms which are variable and irreductible. Even if it is possible, by using a quantum theory, to explain the persistence of this energy, it is impossible to deny that its successive forms have not evolved but have been metamorphosed. But if E truly equals mc^2, if matter truly contains potential energy just as carbon, wood, and atoms contain it, if energy truly conceals potentialities of matter as is shown by particle accelerators, why is the same metamorphosis one accepts for energy denied to matter? If $E = mc^2$, the metamorphoses of E reveal the metamorphoses of mc^2. For a quantum physicist this question no longer poses a problem since he can no longer define matter.

The metamorphosis of everything that current usage continues to call matter continues to amaze us. The metamorphosis of Daphne into a laurel tree, of Egeria into a fountain, of Romulus's javelin into a tree planted on Mount Palatine, still appear to be pleasant fables. Zeus metamorphosing himself into a swan to seduce Leda is also amazing, but less so, for it is acceptable that the god of gods should possess a power unknown to man. For millennia, artistic power has essentially been "the power to incarnate the gods" (*AC* 225). That power was then erased before its victorious rival, "the power to incarnate the imaginary" (again, in Malraux's vocabulary the imaginary is a realm of forms).

These two powers have no longer appeared as rivals, or even to have different natures, since the forms of gods as well as those of the unreal have been seen as forms created by the human imaginary. The power, artistic or not, to incarnate the gods is an attribute of the power to incarnate the imaginary, which itself is one of the manifestations of *the power of incarnation of the informal form:* "Humankind has longed for the incarnation of creative genius" (*AC* 225). The formation of the informal form was not accomplished in a day or in six days; it is being accomplished and will be accomplished every day. It is in constant action, in the artist, who breaks with earlier forms to propose his own, in nature, which never repeats the same forms, and in the cosmos, where its true unfolding is just beginning to be perceived. The finite and temporal genesis of a world that was to be made fruitful is erased in the presence of a cosmogenesis in action, of a cosmic morphogenesis.

All morphogenesis, whatever it might be, any creation of new forms, is above all a disorder in comparison to an established order. Out of concern and a need for clarity, the human mind gladly conceived of the universe as an Order and sought for its immutable laws (etymologically, *cosmos* means order). The human mind must also conceive of the universe as a process, that is, as an incessant appearance of disorders. Scientists are already admitting this, as evidenced by the colloquia they organize on "order and disorder." They know that in an organism order maintains the structure while disorders maintain life. Without disorders, life wilts. Without them there can be no creation of forms. Without what we are still calling disorder there would never have been the manifestation of a creative power. All prophets, those who foresee a new form of thought and reveal it, have first been perceived as disturbances. Christ, too, first appeared as a disturbance. The appearance of a new species, which fascinates us today, was once a disorder in the stability of the species. Rembrandt's *Night Watch* upset an established order, which rejected his painting.

Order puts everything in its place. Order is command, injunction. It is also almost immutable classification. It is an injunction to structure to repeat itself in an identical fashion. Disorders are possibilities, licenses, permissions without which life, worn down by erosion and entropy, would not be regenerated—without which creative power would not be incarnated. The stability of forms and their transformation appear as the salutary and invigorating interplay of Injunction and Permission, of Repetition and License. When nature invents a new species, it grants itself permission to do so, it has license to give a morphogenetic chreode free rein, to let a creative power be incarnated. It also does so when it sculpts a piece of driftwood, when it fashions the abstractions of a chalcedonic agate, or when it creates the expansion or contraction of galaxies. The anxious, thirsty quest for laws of order have enabled man to improve his knowledge of matter. That knowledge in turn has led to the current questioning by quantum physics, which is attempting to discover the dynamic equations of processes and the aleatory laws of permissions and possibilities. To propose that laws of order are a necessary limit to the appearances of momentary disorders caused by the incarnation of a creative power is acceptable on condition that the modalities of disorder are also accepted and cherished as the necessary brake to the repetitive, invasive, and totalitarian power of order. The full and complete acceptance of disorder *and* order can alone enable man to reconcile an anxious quest for cosmic order with a confident adherence to life.

"Order was one of the royal myths of Europe" (*Int* 236) Malraux contended, before noting that the architecture of Chinese geomancers and the purity of Buddhic works of art "suggest a more penetrating order than that of the Greek geometrists, the Thomist constructors, and the classics." The meaning of the notion of order is changing. Its immutability must be erased in the presence of dynamism. The idea of order used to favor stability; it is beginning to accept dynamism and process (*Int* 367). The West inherited the statue in the center of the square from Rome. Modern urbanists and architects looking for values around which they can organize their plans don't yet know to whom they should entrust that statue. Their research, like much other current research, is helping to "deliver us from our obsession with the center, with the idea that every center is order and every polyphony is disorder" (ibid.). Westerners have set out on the path which will enable them to cease being obsessed only with the center of gravity, the point where mechanical forces operate, and to also hear the polyphony of all centers of attraction and all fields of action, those that maintain structure and those that liberate possibilities of morphogenesis.

After stating that imaginaries—the realms of forms which inhabit man—"succeed each other by metamorphosis rather than by filiation" (*HP* 211), Malraux proposes that we accept that the true aim of metamorphosis is "to tame the universe." Man's attitude toward the universe fluctuates between the Western will to subdue the universe, which amounts to a subjugation, and the Oriental ideal of melting into it, which often leads to submission. But it is slowly being discovered, thanks notably to Egyptian, African, and South American cultures, that there are relations with the universe other than those of subjugation or submission. If one agrees that the forms in which a creative power is incarnated obey the laws of metamorphosis, that Metamorphosis is Universal Law, a law of all worlds, the inorganic earthly or cosmic world as well as the organic world, the physical world as well as the psychic world, if one agrees that metamorphosis is a law of the rock and of the plant, a law of the species and of works of art, then metamorphosis does indeed change man's relationship with the universe, and its aim is "to tame the universe." Didn't the fox ask the Little Prince to tame it? Wasn't it he who taught him how to do so? Wasn't it thanks to him that the Little Prince, before leaving, was able to teach his friend how the millions and millions of stars could laugh like a joyous glockenspiel?

In *The Timeless,* Malraux forcefully describes how the accelerated projection of a film on the blooming of a flower gives one the feeling that the flower has a "will" (*Int* 371). But we still hesitate. "We sometimes believe in that invisible but real will, but we sometimes attribute it to the technical artifices of film or television" (ibid.). It is possible to continue further, and boldly, on the path indicated by Malraux. We need only imagine having a timeless movie camera and filming Cape Finisterre, the Gorges du Tarn or the canyons of Colorado for millions of years, then fast-forwarding the film in order to reduce the images to the dimensions of human time; to project it while transforming some geologic millennia into a few human minutes, just as the acceleration of a video tape suffices to transform a few days of a flower into a few minutes for man. The accelerated projection of that imaginary film would show the movement of Cape Finisterre and would give us the feeling of a struggle between "the will" of the rock and "the will" of the water. Would we still attribute these "wills" to technical artifices? Or might we say that the accelerated projection of the floral unfolding and the geological erosion sufficiently intensifies our perception and thus enables us to see the will-to-act of a creative field of forms, a morphogenetic field and its chreodes? These wills-to-act perform in a time which is not that of man. Accelerated projection is not just a technical trick; it is an instrument, a telescope that enables man to perceive those wills-to-act which, without accelerated projection and a condensation of time, remain outside man's faculties of perception. Accelerated projection, because it condenses time, also opens "the doors of perception" (cf. Huxley).

In order to have all the wills-to-act of the universe appear overtly and simply, it suffices to modify the scale of our perception of a span of time just as we modify the scale of a map according to what we want to see or indicate. We need only experience the days of flowers and the millennia of rocks the way one experiences human minutes. In one of the three surreal tales of the *Nabot de Purperac,* I wrote about a young woman who, every summer night, had a rather mysterious and somewhat ambiguous date with an owl, which landed on the trunk of an old olive tree at the precise moment when the moon reached the top of a tall chestnut tree. To outwit her impatience while waiting for her hooting dialogue with the owl to commence, the young woman trained herself to modify her perception of time in order to see the moon rise more quickly in the sky. Readers who have revealed their reaction to this scene have given me comforting proof that voluntarily modifying one's perception of time is a human faculty, real, normal, and that only the fact that it isn't cultivated by our cultures makes it seem paranormal.

For the action of metamorphosis to become evident, we must be able to free ourselves from the convention used to measure time; we must be able to experience all time, and should not measure the duration of one time by that of another. We must sink into time, according to all mystics who have known illumination and ecstasy. All quantum physicists who question the reduction of wave packets or Schrödinger's equations have been led to question our notion of time once again and give marvelous hope to man: tomorrow, sinking into time and experiencing illumination will no longer be reserved only for mystics who have overcome all the terrifying trials of the *Dark Nights* or the *Temptations of Saint Anthony;* tomorrow, awakening will no longer be the privilege of those who have been able to use the grasses or cactuses that nature offers in abundance without destroying themselves; tomorrow, when quantum physics has discovered them, it will be possible to learn the equations of the reduction of wave packets, it will be possible to learn scientifically how to sink into time, to *make one's own time.*

"We deal with animals only in order to domesticate them, and with things in order to subjugate them—in spite of St. Francis, a glowing exception" (*Int* 230). Malraux was right when he spoke during his conversations with Jean-Marie Drot about "the near metamorphosis at Assisi." (One day someone should find out why it was a "near metamorphosis," why it was necessary to pretend in convents that the chronicles of Celano and Perouse—whose destruction St. Bonaventure had ordered—didn't exist. If man becomes capable of perceiving different times just as he has become capable of perceiving paintings created according to different perspectives and even without any perspective at all, he will then regain contact with the will of the flower, with that of water, with all the wills in the universe, and man will also be able to speak of "my brother, the wind," and "my sister, the rain." He will understand why Bachelard dared to attempt the psychoanalysis of all those wills and thus fulfill the magnificent wish Camus expresses in *The Myth of Sysyphus:* "If man recognized that the universe, too, can love and suffer, he would be reconciled with it."

During his last trip to Japan, Malraux said to Professor Terukazu-Akiyama as they were walking up to the Joruriji temple, "These monuments are bound to nature and correspond to it closely. In India we can't find nature like this. Only the cosmos exists there" (Catalogue Malraux et le Japon éternel). A few days later, at the Eukaku-ji monastery, Malraux expressed better what he was perceiving: "It is curious," he said, "that there is high spirituality here, but no impression of the sacred." And when asked whether that came from Zen Buddhism, he replied: "Not necessarily. What is important is the relationship with nature. Here, nature enters the very interior of the temple, whereas in India it is the cosmos that dominates the monument." In the garden of a Trappist monastery as in the park of Versailles, man seeks to dominate nature and to rope it in. In Ellora as in the streets of Bombay, the cosmos dominates man, who in turn accepts that domination as a supreme finality. In Japanese temples and gardens, Malraux perceived a man and universe who had tamed each other, who had been reconciled. And we can better understand what Malraux perceived if we agree that the most expressive symbol of man having tamed the universe and of the universe having tamed man is the bonsai tree, whose strength and power would be capable, in time, of destroying all human creation if they had not been tamed by the delicate care that flows back to him who has dispensed it.

Contemplating a bonsai cedar in a bowl emerging out of a few centimeters of earth does not make one think of a miniature tree. On the contrary. It slowly leads one to sense an almost completely interiorized, almost entirely potentialized strength, "the inner truth" of the tree. It opens up roads of access to the inner truth which is usually overshadowed by the majestic unfolding of the forms of a woodland cedar. When one has truly contemplated a bonsai cedar, one sees a woodland cedar in a different way. A clairvoyance of the cedar has been acquired. Beyond the appearance of the woodland cedar, one becomes capable of seeing the inner reality of the cedar tree. Contemplating the appearance of the bonsai cedar and that of the woodland cedar makes one sense a "something" that is definitely not concrete, something that makes both trees cedars. As Malraux said, and he must have experienced it intimately or he would not have been able to express it in this way, "beyond everything concrete" is not only a concept, it can be a state of consciousness; "to the feeling (not the idea) of appearance responds the feeling of what makes, and what made, appearance" (ibid.).

Another example will perhaps be more revealing for Western minds, that of the clarinet quintet that Mozart composed shortly before his death. The score of this quintet is not the music Mozart created, it is a transcription. Musicians who play the score give an acoustic "appearance" to the music. Other musicians give it another appearance. Today's music libraries, by providing the various appearances that have been given to that quintet, facilitate our approach to and perception of it, provided we can be interested in more than just appearances, just interpretations, which, unfortunately, is the case with too many music lovers.

In November 1957, in a letter cited by Joseph Hoffmann, Malraux wrote: "Consciousness posits nonappearance, whatever name we give it, at the same time as it posits appearance." Logical reason might object to Malraux's claiming that if consciousness begins by positing appearance, it is in effect forced to then posit nonappearance, and that one must be able to avoid becoming a slave to an idea of appearance in order to avoid becoming a slave to an idea of nonappearance. Unfortunately, this objection has allies in all composers in search of concrete music and in all musicologists who try to see Beethoven's Sixth Symphony as an acoustic painting showing brooks and meadows. Music is beyond the realm of appearance, and if today, more than ever before, the zealots of appearance seek to confine music to that realm, might it not be in the unconscious hope and with the tenacious illusion of being able to recover a realm which has always been the most solid contradiction to all those who sought only a concrete reality without anything beyond the concrete? The fact that consciousness and, today, the science of quantum physics are forced to posit appearance and, hence, nonappearance is irrefutably demonstrated by human love. In the presence of two beings united by true love, we can observe the gestures, the looks, the words, the silences of love, but we can never observe the love itself. Love is beyond the gestures it inspires. It is possible to see the manifestations of love, but not love itself. And if we consider this carefully enough, we can see that this language, once reserved for poets, has also become the language of quantum physicists. In an attempt to explain what they observe, some scientists appeal to "hidden variables," either localized or generalized in all of space; others appeal to a reality, a "veiled real," of which matter and spirit are but two manifestations; others accept the fact that their science does not bear on reality itself but on the knowledge one can have of it; still others propose theoretical explanations, which question the common notions of space and time. Implicitly or not, all have had to admit that something exists beyond appearances.

Contrary to what common usage might lead us to believe, an appearance is not an illusion, it is a relativity. Today everyone knows that matter is energy organized in a space/time. The way in which this matter appears to us depends upon the space/time we use to look at it. Consider a block of marble and look at it in the space and time imposed by the human senses; it will appear as a solid and immobile block. Consider it now in the enlarged space and the accelerated time to which we have access through electronic microscopes and particle accelerators, and it appears as a rapid circle of elements separated from one another. And if we can look at it through several different space/times at once, we experience the appearance in us of the immaterial of the material. What the nineteenth century called the real, what mystics have always called appearance, is merely a vision dependent on chosen or imposed relativity in order to become aware of an organization, a relationship.

"What escapes from historical time questions appearance" and thus obliges us to confront that which is beyond appearance (*Int* 134). Shortly after writing this in *The Timeless*, Malraux made a statement which, if we pay close attention to it, can help transform our vision and perception. "Rembrandt," he wrote, "kept repeating his portrait in order to deliver himself from appearance; Cézanne tirelessly repeated Sainte-Victoire in order to deliver himself from time" (*Int* 137). After reading this statement it seems impossible to me that one could listen to Bach fugues without thinking that Bach tirelessly repeated them in order to free himself from the passing of time, and even impossible not to wonder whether the seed does not tirelessly repeat the plant, or the galaxy does not indefinitely repeat the star, also in order to free themselves from space and time. Olivier Messiaen was right in calling his magnificent quartet *Quartet for the End of Time*.

If scientific thought in the nineteenth century believed it possible to grant preferment to appearance and consider it the single, unique reality, twentieth-century scientific thought has been able to return appearance to the rank it should rightfully have. Anyone today, even not ordinarily looking into an electronic microscope or at the screen of a particle accelerator, can be aware of having at least two different perceptions of matter, all matter, all concrete reality. Through an initial perception it is possible to see a block of marble as a compact, resistant whole, which hurts if one is violently hit with it. Through a second perception it is *also* possible to see that block of marble as an arrangement of elementary particles identical to other particles which, when combined in other ways, create a snowflake or a piece of fabric. Marble, snow, fabric—all bodies, including the human brain—are composed of the same elementary particles, and what makes up the particular reality of each of these bodies is not the particles that compose them but the relations, the correlations, between those particles. In a block of marble, in which we have become used to seeing the continuity of a homogeneous and immobile material, we must *also* see the discontinuity of particles separated by huge empty spaces where fields of force are at work. Where we have become used to seeing marmoreal continuity and immobility, we must *also* see corpuscular discontinuity and undulatory vibration.

Through the initial perception of daily and habitual experience provided by the senses when left to themselves, reality can be seen as palpably concrete. Through a second perception, acquired through experiences in which the sensual field of investigation is powerfully amplified by instruments, concrete reality can *also* be seen as the interplay of correlations, as something beyond the concrete, something that doesn't appear on cathodic screens but whose trace one can observe. We readily admit that it is impossible to expose what is beyond the concrete, that which makes *The Slaughtered Ox* something other than varicolored matter spread onto a canvas, or makes Mozart's quintet something other than a succession of notes. We will also have to admit that it is impossible to expose what is beyond the concrete of what we continue to call reality. The interplay of correlations using the same particles, which sometimes engenders marble, sometimes snow, and sometimes the rock picked up by Armstrong on the moon, is an interplay that cannot be given appearance. The mathematical symbols used to express this interplay, that which is beyond the concrete, neither represent it nor give it appearance; they only symbolize it.

Twentieth-century science teaches us to go even farther. With Planck's hypothesis, with the discovery of the discontinuous quanta of energy, with Young's experiments as well as those of Aspect, we must accept that appearances—reality—are only realized probabilities. Reality is a probable that has been realized. It is essential here not to misinterpret the nature of probability and its significance. The probability that a certain side will come up on a die one has thrown is not the uncertainty of its outcome; it is the expression of the distribution of all the outcomes if the game lasts long enough. If by a total effort of imagination we condense into an extreme point the entire duration of the game, then the probability of the appearance of the side of the die would become the *certain* figure of its appearances. Mathematical formulas of probability accomplish this total effort of imagination. Probability appears as uncertainty or chance because we consider it at a given moment or for an insufficient amount of time. If, on the contrary, we lengthen the time of observation or, which amounts to the same thing, we condense our perception of time, then probability becomes the form toward which a series of temporal events are directed. Probability is not chance; it appears to be governed by chance when the length of observation is insufficient or the perception of time is too diluted.

If we now leave aside the amusing probabilities of dice tossed, cards drawn, or numbers chosen, which merely involve the probability of one event among a limited number of events, and if we broach the infinitely more complex probabilities of the appearance of new events among an infinite number of possible events, we discover that mathematics, in order to calculate these complex probabilities, uses uncertain variables. So mathematicians construct probability trees, which are surprisingly like biological trees of genetics, analogic trees of the most abstract algebras, and also like mythological trees, those of the Garden of the Hesperides or of biblical Paradise, those which in all mythologies and all regions are called the "tree of life" and the "tree of knowledge."

All these trees of mythology and biology, of probability and algebra, are ultimately only a way of looking at the ancestral monoid revealed by the mathematician Pierre Miallet, with which it becomes possible to realize the biological, logical, and psychological force of uncertainty. By sufficiently contemplating these trees and that ancestral monoid, it becomes possible to see three almost untenable truths: over each of these trees a whole tree rises majestically; each part of these trees is the culmination of a whole, which seems to converge toward it; each element of these trees and the whole that converges toward it seems to have a desire for other elements in order to continue with them in indefinitely forming *the uncertain tree of Life*. (Today a biologist such as Henri Atlan already calmly accepts the need to introduce uncertain variables into the models he conceives in an attempt to account for the self-organized and secreting living systems in order to organize their information and significance).

Reality is a probable that appears. It is subject neither to necessity, which doesn't exist when time is concentrated, nor to chance, which is only perspective from which probability is envisioned when it is perceived in a diluted time. The roulette wheel stopping at the number 3 is, in human time, a chance of the probability of appearance possessed by the number 3. Reality is the appearance of the uncertain that is celebrated throughout Malraux's last two books.

Before the roulette wheel stops, hitting 3 was uncertain. Afterwards, the outcome has become an actuality. It is a possible that has become real, a potential that has become actual. In the same way, the correlations that cause particles to form marble or snow or gray matter are uncertain probabilities that have become actualities, potentials that have become actual. Using our senses alone, we can only perceive actualities and reflect upon them. Amplified by microscopes, telescopes, and particle accelerators, the sensations received through our senses enable us to achieve the awareness of the potentials that have engendered the actualities. Our senses enable us to observe either the light, the heat, or the action we can bring about by plugging a lamp, a heater, or a motor into an electrical outlet. They will never enable us to observe the difference in potential between the two poles of the outlet, a difference that can be converted into light, heat, or action. Through reflection we have realized the difference in potential that exists in an electrical current even though our senses will never enable us to perceive it.

Through our senses we perceive reality, appearance, the actual. Through consciousness alone we can conceive of potential. Today, "science without consciousness" can be translated as knowledge of actuality without an awareness of potentiality. By going from the optic microscope of Louis Pasteur to the electronic laboratory of Niels Bohr, from the gravity of Newton to the relativity of Einstein, from the historical materialism of Marx to Planck's discontinuity of matter, science has gone from a sovereign reality to an uncertain actuality. Today, the "new scientific mind," thanks to the piercing eye of particle accelerators, perceives actualities and conceives of potentialities similar to those that the inner eye of mystics had revealed to them.

This comforting convergence of science and consciousness comes about at the very moment when, unfortunately, the eye of countless enthusiasts of audiovisuals is satisfied only with actualities. The great role Malraux foresaw for audiovisuals, which fills the final chapters of *The Timeless,* can only be fulfilled when the news of potentialities on television screens is as accepted—if not more so—as is the news of actualities. That day may be less distant than we might believe. The difference in potential of an electrical current, familiar today since it has been learned in school, seemed strange to the average man at the end of the nineteenth century. Similarly, a difference in potential from which actualities spring forth, those of mineralogy as well as biology, those of psychology as well as astronomy, still seems strange to the waning twentieth century, but such a difference will very likely be taught in a few decades in the classrooms of renovated schools. Metamorphosis, far from being considered a fable or an exclusively Olympian power, or yet the power of a sorcerer or a fairy, will then be seen as the appearance of an actuality, sudden in its manifestation but lengthily prepared by an augmentation or a diminution of potential. If Daphne is metamorphosed into a laurel tree in an instant, if her actuality changes form, that metamorphosis is the culmination of a long process that began many years earlier.

A careful reading enables us to see the very different nature of the metamorphoses found, for example, in Ovid, Apuleius, the ancient Egyptians, and Lautréamont. In Ovid, the metamorphosis of Io into a heifer and that of the heifer into Io is carried out by Jupiter; it is ordained, imposed from outside, now as punishment, now as protection, now as reward. In Apuleius, when Lucius is metamorphosed into an ass, he is under the influence of a magical unguent, and when the donkey that has become the Golden Ass after a series of trials is metamorphosed into Lucius, it happens through the will and the power of Isis. In the ancient Egyptians' *Book of the Dead,* in order for man to go through the cycle of metamorphoses, to be able to climb into the barge of Re, he has to have learned, with the help of the gods, how to exercise the power of metamorphosis he carries within. In Lautréamont, metamorphoses owe nothing to an external power; they are a coagulation, a condensation, of a will-to-live that has not had the chance to be exerted.

In all these cases, metamorphosis appears as the actualization of a power, a force. In Ovid, the actuality that results from metamorphosis was produced by an external force, that of the gods. For the ancient Egyptians, as in Lautréamont, metamorphosis is the action of an inner power which, to a degree, has not been actualized. In Ovid, metamorphosis is a determinism imposed on man. For the ancient Egyptians it is a supplementary freedom, a liberation man conquers when he has learned to actualize all the potential he carries within.

A comparable difference separates Darwin's *Origin of the Species* from Goethe's *Metamorphosis of Plants.* For Darwin and his successors, the form and structure of an organism depend on the interplay of external forces to which that organism has adapted with the help of its inner

Metamorphosis as Universal Law

possibilities. For Goethe, form and structure are the result of potential forces that the organism possesses within, which he renders actual according to external conditions. Darwinism and Goetheanism are fundamentally not as contradictory as a hasty approach might lead one to believe. Theories of natural selection can be seen as attempts to explain the appearance of an inner potential through external factors. They explain *how* a possible form became actual, and *how* an actual form disappears from actuality; they do not seek to explain *why* a form was possible, *why* it was in a potential state. Goethe, on the other hand, stresses the potential forces contained in a seed or a jawbone, and seeks to account for the unfolding of these forces rather than the external conditions that have favored or hindered that unfolding. And if one dares translate the prologue to the Book of John, "And the Word was made Flesh," by "And the potentiality took on actuality," one might say that Darwin was concerned above all with the flesh, whereas Goethe was concerned above all with the word.

An example too simple for scientists but familiar to others enables us to realize the incessant interplay between the actual and the potential, which constantly engender each other. When a hand is holding a balloon filled with helium, the muscular force is an actuality, which contains the balloon's potential to rise. When this potential to rise, which asks only to be realized, forces the tired hand to let go, the tired actuality of the muscular force ceases, whereas the balloon's potentiality to rise is liberated. The balloon's ascent in turn becomes an actuality which, in turn, comes into conflict with other potentialities: the resistance of the air, the dilation of the gas, etc. The unused muscular force becomes a potential available to engender other actualities: to pick up a stone, hold another balloon, etc. It is possible to continue indefinitely imagining the subtle and uncertain interplay of potentials and actuals that can be engendered both by the balloon and by the hand. Even if the balloon bursts, even if the hand is wounded, even if they lose their form to the point of returning to particles, there is no end to the engendering of potentialities by actualities and of actualities by potentialities.

When we see the royal interplay of actuality simultaneously preventing and preparing for the blossoming of a potential, and that of a potentiality freeing itself from an actuality, then we can also see that the metamorphosis constantly present in all mythologies, all literatures and all legends is the imaged expression of correct intuitions, of immediate perceptions, and of convictions that had to be hidden because they were no longer accepted. The ancient Egyptians' belief in metamorphosis now appears not as the schizophrenia that nineteenth-century scholars made fun of, but as the experienced and *sensed* consciousness of another kind of schizophrenia, that of potential and the actual endlessly engendering each other. This belief in no way devalues reality but, rather, assigns it its status: reality is appearance, the appearance assumed by an actualized potential. Reality is an actuality.

In his 1970 book *Malraux par lui même*, Gaëtan Picon writes: "Malraux seems always to have been in search of a plenitude of being, which he tries to find only in action but which action cannot provide him" (p. 119). Malraux added in the margin: "Indeed. But when completed it may provide (and not only to me) the currency for that feeling." Malraux's response is superb. Let's look at it from a different angle to see all its facets: action, when completed, provides the currency for the plenitude of being, the means of exchange and communication with the plenitude of being. Despite Malraux's response (but he may not have known it when he was writing his book), Gaëtan Picon continues: "At once a man of the senses (of acts, of the moment, of history) and a man of inner plenitude (of the absolute), Malraux can only pursue that inaccessible harmony in vain, a harmony he seeks all the more avidly as he is separated from it." On this point Gaëtan Picon is mistaken. Malraux did not vainly pursue harmony between the act and the absolute. That harmony is not inaccessible. The moment, history, action, the act—all belong to the realm of actualities. Inner plenitude belongs to the realm of potentiality. And when in 1974 Malraux declared that he was trying to create a human life at the very moment when man was becoming aware of Metamorphosis as Universal Law, when Malraux encountered the uncertain while completing *The Timeless* and writing *Precarious Man*, he found the harmony he had so ardently sought between inner plenitude, the height of potentiality, and action, the act, the actual.

An ancient Chinese tale tells of the adventure of an old nobleman dining alone in an inn. His fingers are covered with precious rings; from his belt hang two sabers with magnificent sheaths and handles encrusted with rare stones. Four robbers come into the inn and sit down not far from the rich old man. They decide to insult him beyond what his honor can allow him to endure; forced to avenge himself, the rich old man will have to challenge them, the robbers will defend themselves, and soon the lone old man will meet his end. The rings and sabers will be theirs. The robbers' insults are flung without any reaction from the old man. The robbers shout even more inflammatory insults. Then the rich old man, using the two chopsticks he has been employing to eat his rice, catches a fly in the air, kills it, and delicately places it on the edge of the table. Seeing the mastery of that gesture, the robbers prefer not to confront the old man, and they leave the inn.

The rich old man has acquired such skill that the strength within him can remain potential. Through its potential alone his strength acts and obtains the essential result—the departure of the robbers—and avoids useless acts—a fight. All legends and mythologies of all countries tell the stories of heroes who, through trials, have cultivated mastery over themselves and have become capable of apparently superhuman feats. In *The Odyssey*, Homer often says that the mere sight of Ulysses froze his adversaries with terror, which enabled him to exterminate them one by one, often alone against them all. A man who can transform trials he has endured into ever greater potentialities is capable, upon liberating them, of obtaining actualities that appear beyond the power of other men.

Nietzsche's exasperation with Christ, god/man, who was slapped and ridiculed, is the exasperation one experiences in face of a power that refuses to act, a potential that refuses to transform itself into action. Conversely, in the presence of Christ, man/god, who refuses to petrify his tormenters by merely looking at them, who refuses to remove the crown of thorns with a simple wave of his hand, and who, above all, accepts that the cup not be taken from him, one can also see an incarnation, an actuality that aspires to rejoin the world of pure potentiality, the world in which, all actualities having been consummated, no other actuality is desirable. And it often seems to me that Nietzsche, showing deep emotion, must have seen the Passion in that way during the last eleven years of his life, which passed slowly, with no action either in words or in writing. The word no longer sought to become flesh. And the will to power, having become entirely the desire for potential, no longer sought to manifest its power. It also seems to me that Nijinski, in the protective and purifying silence he maintained for many years after his triumph in *Afternoon of a Faun,* showing the same emotion, must have had a similar vision of the Passion and cosmic Dance.

Along with the legends and mythologies that seduce us with tales of the slow, difficult ascents of man's potential, there are also the tales that make us shiver at the sight of men who go from fall of potential to fall of potential and who become capable only of constantly diminishing and fading actualities. In the realm of literature, Kafka shows us the almost unbearable spectacle of that slow degradation of potential in *The Metamorphosis,* and the degradation of the life that results from it: Gregor is a modest salesman; everything weighs heavily upon him, and he cannot feel well because of his irresistible need to sleep; he is slowly metamorphosed into a hideous creature who takes hours to move a few centimeters or to eat his meager ration.

The way one feels and thus the acts one feels capable of performing depend upon the potential one possesses. Ever since sciences ceased being concerned only with apparent reality and began to concern themselves with potentiality too, they have widened their horizons and often reverse the direction of their inquiries. We now seldom hear that the appearance of the human brain is the consequence of the animal's standing erect; on the contrary, we wonder whether the animal's standing erect might not be the consequence of a brain that was in a potential state and aspired to find a form worthy of its potential. We are beginning to rediscover our sense of direction and to realize that a doctor does not become a doctor because he has had medical training but, rather, that he has training because he wants to become a doctor. The training is chosen to reach an objective. And our age cruelly reveals the tragedies and unemployment which come from people being trained without having a truly chosen objective. To become a doctor one must undergo adaptation and selection, but neither one nor the other can become realities, actualities, if there is not first the will to take on "the form" of a doctor. Some might object to this example and claim that in man there is reasoning, consciousness, and thus the possibility for will. Yet it should not be forgotten that the accelerated projection of a blossoming flower, or of granite erosion, suggests to us, against our will, the idea of the "will" of the flower or the "will" of the rock. Conversely, an extremely sloweddown projection of the film showing the years of training of a future doctor would suppress any impression of will in that student. Will being the force that causes us to make efforts today to attain an end tomorrow, we need only stretch the space between today and tomorrow for will no longer to appear, no longer to be apparent, which doesn't mean that it doesn't exist. Conversely, we need only shrink that space sufficiently in order for the sight of that will to become almost unbearable. Try to imagine the emotion and, probably, the terror we would experience if an accelerated projection enabled us to see in fifteen minutes the work of a few trees in the tropical forest encompassing and submerging the

Banteai-Sre temple. Tolkien, in *The Lord of the Rings,* that great twentieth-century epic of the Knights of the Round Table, could imagine it, feel it, and invite us to feel it with him.

If we really want fully to understand the acquired knowledge and the interrogations of contemporary science, we must face two questions: (1) Is the will of a doctor's son who wants to become a doctor truly of a different nature than the "will" of a cedar seed wanting to become a cedar? (2) Is the will of a mutant individuality that will result in a new species, as paleontologists say, truly of a different nature than the will of a preacher's son who wants to become the painter Van Gogh, or of a preacher's daughter who goes through the leaden, dark years that make her an active member of Baader's Circle? Even if it is too early to provide scientific data to answer these two questions, it is already impossible not to ask them. Chance cannot be at the origin of mutations—as Heitler has shown—and we are forced to grant some credence to the idea of mutations "in the direction of . . . ," that is, to the idea of the actualization of a potential.

Gaston Bachelard, in his study of Lautréamont, boldly asserted that a living being possesses an "appetite for form" as great as the being's appetite for matter. Bachelard, a philosopher and poet of the "New Scientific Spirit," knew that the appetite for something is the first impetus which directs one toward that thing, "the movement that leads one to look for that which can satisfy an organic need" (*Le Robert* dictionary). A living being possesses an "appetite for form," and that appetite will put it in motion until it has found the form that satisfies its need (p. 57). That organic need, or instinct, Bachelard continues, will be maintained long enough for the energies in play to be materialized into organs. Matter, with the stimulus of "the appetite for form," is "inhabited by the formal cause." Rupert Sheldrake called it the *formative cause.* François Jacob described "the cell that dreams of being divided." The *dream* of François Jacob's cell seems quite close to Bachelard's *appetite for form* and to René Thom's *calculated chreode.*

Since the time of Aristotle, science has favored the study of the cause that produces now an effect that will be observed later (even if only a second later), in other words, the efficient cause, and it has more or less been left to religions to speak of the cause that explains how something happens now to attain a given goal, in other words, the final cause. Yet thousands of phenomena or events can be observed daily that occur *not because of* something that has just happened, *but for* something that is going to happen. The moisture in the earth is drawn toward roots, is then transformed into sap and directed toward the flower *in order to* nourish the pistils and the stamen; the pistils and the stamen are not nourished *because* the moisture in the earth has gone toward the roots. To say that a cat stalks a mouse *in order to* catch it is as true as saying the mouse was caught *because* the cat had stalked it. The truth of the stalking cat appeared before the truth of the caught mouse. To say: "I am taking the plane *in order to* go to Heliopolis" is true before "I am in Heliopolis *because* I took the plane." The final cause is manifest *before* the efficient cause, paradoxical as that may seem to unprepared minds.

Earlier scientists hesitated to posit the goal to attain as an explanation of observed phenomena or of actualities in the process of being made manifest, for, from future goal to future goal, they ended up with an Absolute Final Cause, which determined everything and suppressed both liberties and permissions. Things are quite different for the scientific minds of today, which calculate probabilities and live with uncertainty. A final cause does not determine; it makes something probable, it gives the uncertain its freedom. Wanting to go to Heliopolis does not force one to take an airplane, and leaves open the possibility of taking a boat. In the cosmic symphony of potentialities that engender actualities and of actualities that nourish potentialities, the working of the uncertain neither conditions nor determines any actuality; it respects the probabilities of all.

Since regaining contact with the timeless we carry within ourselves and no longer push outside, we have been able to see that the questioning of the nature of causality is really a questioning of time. Efficient causality flows down the river; it seeks to explain tomorrow by today; it hopes to predict the future. Final causality goes back upstream; it seeks to understand yesterday by today. Choosing one or the other of these causalities therefore amounts to choosing, without even being conscious of the choice, the perspective from which we observe a phenomenon that we position in linear time. To explain that one is in Heliopolis because one took a plane is a perspective favoring the anteriority of having taken the plane. To explain that one takes a plane to go to Heliopolis is a perspective favoring the posteriority of being in Heliopolis.

By favoring the efficient cause and rejecting the final cause, Western science from the sixteenth to the twentieth century condemned itself to gradually becoming a science that seeks to know only in order to predict, that scrutinizes and explains the past in order to appropriate the future. That is why it became a science engendering action and technology.

Metamorphosis as Universal Law

But it also became a science without consciousness. Conversely, a science favoring the final cause and neglecting the efficient cause becomes a science of consciousness and engenders contemplation above all else.

If we escape from a linear conception of time, there is no longer a one-way relationship between facts, between the engendered and the engenderer. In nonlinear time, the son can be the father of his father, and the mother can be the daughter of her son. When we scrutinize the depths of our inner selves, we perceive actions, failed or successful, words spoken or stifled, which have been experienced in chronological time but are stockpiled in nonchronological time. And if we are capable of enduring these apparitions, we become aware of actions that are both the effect and the goal of earlier actions. They constantly engender each other, not in an eternal return to the same thing, but in a timeless repetition of the identical being incarnated into changing forms. Paradoxical as that may appear at first glance, studying efficient causes is to turn towards ω, whereas studying final causes is to turn towards α. One must be able to do both, but while remembering that men of little faith are more concerned with the end than with the beginning, and while remembering that what is *one* is not causal.

Metamorphosis as Universal Law is a law that magnificently contains both the "because" and the "why"; it contains both voices—that of the child receptively asking "why?" and that of the parent responding with assurance "because." The law of metamorphosis contains both the final cause and the efficient cause. Every time a word is made flesh, that flesh aspires to be made a word; every time flesh is made a word, that word aspires to be incarnated into flesh. Every potential aspires to create an actuality, and every actuality participates in the augmentation or diminution of the potential it contains. And in the eternal "potential-actual-potential" cycle, which must be preferred over the "actual-potential-actual" cycle since the possible *is* before the realized *exists*, each phase, however minimal its importance might be, secretes a difference in potential, which can be a plus or a minus, an ascent or a fall. An Oriental would say that the Karma of an act can be either positive or negative and survives beyond the act. A Westerner would say that an act participates in the redemption of the sin and brings one closer to heaven, or that it perpetuates the sin and brings one nearer to hell.

When dominant, churches, schools, and aesthetics accept metamorphosis with difficulty, for they prefer to maintain acquired forms and fear the questioning new forms entail, forms that have just become actualities. Established churches, schools, and aesthetics have a basic fear of rising potential and acknowledge metamorphosis only if it is regressive. They can deal better with Kafka, whom they honor, than with Apuleius, of whom they are ignorant. In the past two centuries, however, a few great voices for metamorphosis have once again made themselves heard: Goethe, Nerval, Lewis Carroll, Flaubert in *The Temptation of Saint Anthony,* Lautréamont, Kafka, Rilke in *Sonnets to Orpheus,* Richard Strauss, Jung, Valéry in *My Faust,* and Malraux—"I am attempting to create a life at the moment when we are becoming aware of Metamorphosis as Universal Law." With all these voices, to which scientists of today are providing harmonic accompaniment, it becomes possible to share the wish expressed so well by Bachelard: May "the living being, interdependent on diverse forms, live a transformation, accept metamorphoses, lay out a truly acting, strongly dynamic formal causality . . . The mind must rediscover the youth of form, the vigor, the joy of formal causality. It must reach a quivering formal causality which develops projects in all directions" (*Lautréamont*).

Among the great voices that in the past two centuries have once again begun to sing the praises of metamorphosis, there is one that must be highlighted. It fills our imaginary even when we hear it without understanding its profound meaning. It is the voice of the mathematician Lewis Carroll and his *Alice in Wonderland.* Alice first comes up against the inexplicable because she keeps trying to explain it by using identities that are repeatedly belied by continual metamorphoses. Only after her conversation with the caterpillar can Alice discover in herself and through herself the mechanism of the metamorphoses she has just experienced. In this way she can enter into the most diverse logics and no longer find them illogical. She has entered into the universe where the smile of the Cheshire cat appears without the appearance of the cat's body. After traveling through all of Wonderland, Alice can accede to the Land on the other side of the looking glass. She must go through all the squares of the chessboard, one by one, to arrive at the Eighth Square, where, as the Red Queen has told her, they will both be queens. After each square Alice must cross a stream. In mid-journey, in the Fourth Square, after going through the woods where everything loses its name, after leaving Tweedledum and Tweedledee, Alice learns from the White Queen what a final cause is—she learns that one can be hurt now because one will prick one's finger later, which is, in essence, only the other side of the looking glass, that is, to be hurt later because one has pricked one's finger now. Alice is, nevertheless, somewhat disconcerted by this disturbing logic, and when she says so to the White Queen, the latter feels sorry for her for having a memory that functions only in one direction. Alice then begins to understand how things really happen, and she can continue her journey toward the Eighth Square, where she too will be queen.

"Metamorphosis is the total activity of any being," claims Bachelard (ibid., p. 150). Everyday language, simple, direct, often immediate, sometimes offers profound truths that go unheard from inattentiveness or force of habit. In everyday life we sometimes answer a habitual "How are you?" with a no less habitual "I'm in good shape." To be in good shape, in form, to be in possession of one's possibilities, to feel capable of the acts one wishes to perform, what more can we wish for? And this is why we must hope that a great philosopher will soon undertake *The Critique of the Being in Form* which would undoubtedly show that *Being and Nothingness* is an impossible pair.

The Ancient Egyptians knew that "metamorphosis is the total activity of any being." Their *Book of the Dead* taught the faithful how to acquire "the mastery of Forms and Metamorphoses" (*Book of the Dead*, chap. 17), how to become "the living integral of all the potentialities of the past" (chap. 16), and how to contain within "all the potentialities of the future." The faithful one who had learned to "travel at will through the cycle of Metamorphoses" (chap. 78) finally arrived at "the Lake of Fire," and the power of his words enabled him to contemplate successive forms. He had acceded to "the Region of Generalized Potentiality" (chap. 80). He could say: "I speak and my magic word immediately becomes an accomplished deed." At the end of his life, Paul Valéry rediscovered this great inspiration. His Faust finds Mephistopheles rather outdated. Mephisto doesn't evolve, doesn't follow the movement of human thought, and keeps using the same tricks. Valéry's Faust has arrived at the stage where he can assert: "And now I am what I am, and I don't believe otherwise." He can open up "the inner wings that mark the true passing of time. They carry the being I am from what it was to what it will be." He can "see" beyond appearances, beyond a pine tree in the sun, beyond a roof of gleaming tiles. He has gone beyond the stage when one attaches importance only to "precise forms which the slightest move can transform." Mephisto, rather out of date, cannot propose much of interest to a Faust who has reached this stage. But Faust still has to learn what is essential. He might learn it from the *Solitary,* from him who has arrived at "absolutely incommunicable reality" and who can utter the supreme invocation:

> A moi Splendeurs du pur, à moi peuple superbe
> Puissances de l'instant, Sainte diversité!
> Forces sans formes, puissances sans prodiges
> Exterminez mystères, énigmes et miracles.[1]

But Faust remains Faust and falls back onto his error. Despite the fairy who reminds him,

> La Parole a pouvoir sur la Métamorphose
> Tu devrais le savoir, toi qui sais toutes choses[2]

Faust continues to deny. "No" was his first word; it will also be his last.

Immediately after telling Jean-Marie Dunoyer that he was attempting to "create a life at a moment in history when we are becoming aware of Metamorphosis as Universal Law" (*Le Monde*, March 15, 1974), Malraux cited Nietzsche: "Those moonstruck by the hidden world don't want to understand that there is nothing more profound than appearances"; then Malraux added, "I think he meant: appearances have their own laws because they are successive moments of metamorphosis." This comment illuminates Malraux's quest from the beginning to the end of his meditation in *The Metamorphosis of the Gods*. In the introduction to the first volume, following a passage of intense poetic beauty, he wonders: "What is there, then, in common between the atmosphere of pious communion with which the medieval dusk flooded the naves and that massive intimation of transcendence which is conveyed by the Egyptian architectural complexes?" What is there common to "all forms embodying an aspect of the inapprehensible? It is their revelation of the presence of an Other World, not necessarily infernal or celestial, nor merely a world beyond the grave; rather a supra-real world existing here and now. For all alike, in differing degrees, the "real" is mere appearance, and something else exists that is not appearance—and does not always bear the name of God" (*MG* 7–9). During the twenty years it took to write the three volumes of *The Metamorphosis of the Gods*, these questions were always present, and often vexing, in Malraux's mind until the time when, at the end of the third volume, he found it possible to hazard a response. He thought he had then found what is common to "all forms embodying

---

1. ["Spendors of purity, proud ones, come all of you here, / Instantaneous powers, Holy in your diversity! / Formless forces, powers that assert no miracle / Put mystery to death with its riddles and marvels." Paul Valéry, *Plays*, translated by David Paul and Robert Fitzgerald (New York: Pantheon, 1960).]
2. ["You ought to know, you who know everything,/ That Words have the will's power to metamorphose." Ibid.]

an aspect of the inapprehensible." He had isolated that "Other World," that "supra-real world existing here and now," that something else "that is not appearance—and does not always bear the name of God." After resisting for a long time, he had to admit the existence of "primordial Forms" (*Int* 311), and, as if he himself were shocked or disturbed by the response that had arisen in him, he formulated it as an interrogative.

Throughout his meditation on the forms created by all arts of all time, Malraux was split between reality, appearance, and that something else that "exists, that is not appearance—and does not always bear the name of God." He never gave up hope that it would be possible either to give value to one of these two realms, by subjugating the other to it, or to fuse them both into one. It was in Japan, in 1974, that he was content to let them coexist, and to link them without any antagonism, for it was during that trip that he experienced "Inner Reality" in his innermost self, whereas until that time he had worked with it only as a concept. In front of the Nachi waterfall he moved from the idea to the awareness, from the thought to the lived, from the cogitated to the experienced. Behind the appearance of forms, and without any devaluation, he entered into communion with the Inner Reality of forms, with "the language of forms which transcends civilizations" (*Int* 311), with, one might say, the *Word of forms*. He heard "the language of the Inner Reality that exists before art but which art reveals" (*Int* 224).

Having experienced Inner Reality, Malraux then rediscovered, but on a much higher spiritual level, what had been the theme of the central chapter of *Man's Hope:* "To be and to act." He reaffirms that "it is indeed *being* and *acting* that are separated by the fundamental division" (*Int* 130), but then testifies: "There exists an All-Encompassing which the word "acting" is inadequate to grasp; ... an All-Encompassing traversed by causality, reason, time, design ... The All-Encompassing of gods and of death, nonchronological time, the eternity of religions. It is more vast than the sacred. Perhaps we can approach it by assembling within it all those things we have no hold upon, the inapprehensible that religions inhabit but do not fill" (ibid.). Anyone who reads, rereads, and meditates on these beautiful words of Malraux will surely be struck by the possibility of their becoming one of the basic hymns to be sung during all the Easter services of a new spirituality, which will also have accepted the fact that its culture and means of expression have entered the cycle of metamorphosis.

The Generalized Potentiality of the ancient Egyptians, Goethe's primordial plant, Valéry's "Formless Forces which put mystery to death with its riddles and marvels," Malraux's primordial Forms and his All-Encompassing—all might appear as the intuitions of artists, but since the mathematician Pierre Maillet revealed the ancestral monoid, we have been permitted to wonder whether those intuitions are not now being proved. If this is so, it is forbidden *not* to wonder about the surprising and comforting synergy that causes the convergence of "the correlations of appearance" (*Int* 130) revealed by particle accelerators, the mathematics of René Thom and Pierre Maillet, Bergson's *Two Sources of Morality and Religion,* the meditations of Goethe, Flaubert, Valéry, and Malraux, the music of Richard Strauss, and the spirituality of the ancient Egyptians.

In *The Temptation of the West,* Malraux writes: "In his ecstasy, the thinker does not identify himself with the absolute . . . ; he merely defines as absolute the furthest point of his sensibility" (*TW* 92). Malraux did not "think" Metamorphosis, he sensed it with his sensibility, he perceived it through his senses, he lived it, he experienced it. Metamorphosis as Universal Law represents the furthest point of his sensibility, which is why, while discussing Japanese art, he could write that "appearance leads to the absolute" (*Int* 235). The study of plants leads to the *Ur-Pflanz*. The contemplaton of works of art, sepia agates, and driftwood leads to the "common language of forms which transcends civilizations" and culminates with Primordial Forms. The cycle of metamorphoses leads to the Lake of Fire, where formless Forces put mysteries, riddles, and marvels to death. The knowledge of actuals leads to the potential. "Inner Realities converge; those of all that we see or sense are united in the essence of the universe" (ibid.).

This stirring proclamation in *The Timeless* deserves to be written as a poem:

> The inner realities
> of all that we see
> or sense
> are united
> in the essence of the universe.

The perception of inner realities and of their convergence leads to man's reconciliation with the universe; to that reconciliation which Camus hoped for and Malraux experienced. A man and a universe who had been divorced and who have reconciled are a man and a universe who

Metamorphosis as Universal Law

can proclaim loud and clear the new alliance they have formed with each other.[3]

3. While correcting the proofs of this book I discovered the remarkable thesis on Malraux defended in 1981 by Gilles de la Houssaye, entitled "Awaiting an Impending Metamorphosis." I cite from it here: "What is metamorphosis? What finer answer can one give than that given in India: 'Every wave reflects the moon according to its wave form, as every man reflects Being.' Every form hides Being by reducing it to a specific form. On the other hand, the change in forms unveils Being. All works proclaim a hidden secret at the heart of humanity, and that secret, like life, assumes all forms."

19

The Absolute Agnostic

❧

MALRAUX LIKED TO CITE a statement Braque made when he was eighty years old: "The most important thing in a painting is always what one cannot say." It is also what is most important in a musical score, as is seen in the dialogues of true musicians who seek to express the inner reality of a score; for the most part, they are dialogues through onomatopoeia. "What one cannot say" is also what is most important in a novel or a poem. At the conclusion of his long meditation on these "inexpressibles," Malraux had to admit that "what one cannot say" follows a work throughout all its metamorphoses. But he was faced with what was certainly the question of his final years, a question that could have called everything into question: "Does the informulable of a work transcend metamorphosis?" (cf. *AC* 245).

With this question, Malraux moved a little higher on the spiral of his spiritual ascent. He now looked at the metamorphosis of works of art from a new perspective, which integrated his earlier perspectives yet went beyond them. A work of art doesn't change its form, and if it has entered into the river of metamorphosis, it is because of the different ways people look at it. In itself it contains enough richness, possibilities, and potential to nourish all the changing views of those who have stopped to look at it. What is trans-formed, metamorphosed in that work, is the way in which it appears *to us,* the appearance *we* give it. "What one cannot say about it," its "unformulable," transcends metamorphosis. The river of metamorphoses that bathes creation springs from "a source deeper than all our means of capturing it" (*Int* 329). And when Malraux was concluding *The Timeless* and *Precarious Man,* he admitted he was no longer trying to discover whether Metamorphosis is Universal Law but was seeking, was avidly setting out on the quest for, the unformulable that transcends metamorphosis, the quest for "the inapprehensible that religions inhabit but don't fill" (*Int* 130), the quest for that "All-Encompassing traversed by causality, reason, time, design" (ibid.), the thirsting quest for that "source deeper than all our means of capturing it."

Malraux is said to have been haunted by the myth of Prometheus. That may be so, but we should recall that in the genealogy of the gods Prometheus is almost in the same line as Zeus; both descend directly from Uranus and Gaea. Especially must we recall that Prometheus did not seek to offer men immortality or eternal youth; he tried to deliver them from their obsession with death by giving them a share of one of the powers reserved by the gods for themselves. That is why Zeus, jealous and authoritarian, sentenced Prometheus so harshly. But Prometheus was able to endure his punishment with the virtue of hope: he knew that the eagle would never peck out his liver; he knew that it was not even within Zeus's power to cause Prometheus's death; he knew that Zeus tried to hide the limitation of his power from men and from the other gods by making them believe in an eternal punishment; and, finally, Prometheus knew that the day he would be delivered—for he would indeed be delivered—Zeus would learn the distance between "reigning" and "serving" (*Aeschylus* 248).

Today, those who tame atomic fire are no Prometheuses; they are rather Hephaestus-Vulcans and, like them, create weapons and thunder. The Prometheus of today would provide men with a portion of the metamorphosing power that all the gods of all the Olympuses have always attempted to keep for themselves in order to seduce or to terrify men. The Prometheus of today would provide a portion of that informulable which transcends metamorphosis and is its source. That is why every Zeus and every Hephaestus seeks to lock them up or exploit them. If Prometheus had listened to Oceanus's words of caution and submission, he would have been exploited and have rediscovered the fasti and the gold of Olympus. For a time, between 1958 and 1969, Malraux frequented the gilded ministerial palaces, but during that time he published only *Anti-Memoirs* and made scarcely any progress with *The Metamorphosis of the Gods*. During the same years, however, he underwent some terrible spiritual crises, which are not generally known about. These crises, often comparable to those Mozart went through, will only be made known when a really serious biographer can communicate them with the tact and justice they deserve (as Hocquard did with the spiritual crises that Mozart managed to overcome). After 1969, having gone to Verrières-le-Buisson and having found an admirable real presence in Sophie de Vilmorin, Malraux was able to resume his (Promethean?) quest for metamorphosing power.

About a year after saying that Garine upheld a "value of metamorphosis" in contrast to the bourgeois values of consideration, order, and precaution, and after specifying that for his part he absolutely refused to substitute a proletarian ideology for a bourgeois ideology, since he was concerned only with contrasting certain values of metamorphosis to those of permanence, Malraux wrote to Walter Langlois in September 1930: "Perken incarnates a man who in his quest 'for a universe of forms' is in touch with his destiny." That statement could be applied to Malraux himself. Unlike Perken, who did not find his universe of forms, Malraux did find his own. Perken had already rejected values of permanence, but he had not yet acceded to values of metamorphosis. Malraux achieved his ascent to those values.

To make values of metamorphosis one's own when one is heir to values of permanence assumes a spiritual adventure riddled with traps and risks. To live through it and survive, Malraux had to overcome numerous crises, "dark nights." One of the worst, no doubt, was the one that almost crushed him in 1965, which he overcame by embarking on *Anti-Memoirs*. A modest, restrained echo of that crisis appears in *Anti-Critique*: "By widespread questioning we hope ... to perceive the ferment which saves the work of art from oblivion ... We are fascinated to watch the precarious fireflies of survival haphazardly flitting in the darkness. Immortality was less surprising" (*AC* 249). Values of permanence were reassuring. Metamorphosis as Universal Law and the values of metamorphosis that emerge from it are still unsettling. More than anyone else, Malraux had the right to speak of "the fear of losing one's depth, provoked by the idea of an endless metamorphosis" (ibid. 247). Gisors experiences this at the end of *Man's Fate* when he realizes that "the power of thought is not great against metamorphosis" (*MF* 332).

A mind used to permanence, eternity, or immobility can't help being unsettled, even dumbfounded, by metamorphosis, which requires total acceptance of the ephemeral and the uncertain. With great lucidity and honesty, Malraux doesn't hide the fact that even if the world of the Orient as well as that of the West, the world that has been nourished on eternity as well as the world that has been nourished on immobility, begins to become aware of Metamorphosis as Universal Law and to realize that values of metamorphosis can exist, the world has not yet found an ordering value in metamorphosis. That will be the task of our successors, "who will most probably read our writings in the light of metamorphosis" (*AC* 230), but if they "find in them the values which give them a sequential meaning, let them be sure that it is a thing which escaped us."

As was taught by the ancient Egyptians, as well as by Paul Valéry, if we don't want to become prisoners of an *idée fixe,* if we want to be fully realized, we must agree to travel through the cycle of metamorphoses, we must not seek constantly to repeat the same thing. The values of metamorphosis will be values of discontinuity. Wanting at all costs to find psychic continuity is no less dangerous than wanting to find historical continuity or biological or paleontological continuity. When values of discontinuity have been formulated, we will probably stop trying to believe at all costs that the adult is necessarily the continuity of the child, and will stop educating human beings to remain the same throughout their lives. To reject discontinuity in oneself, to fear the metamorphoses of oneself, is the desire to keep the same actuality, the rejection of the action of potential. Cinderella's sisters rejected metamorphosis and accumulated no potential in themselves. Their shoes remained leather. They were never to wear the glass slipper. No pumpkin would ever be metamorphosed into a carriage to carry them to the ball of life.

The values of metamorphosis will also be values of plurality. "The Imaginary Museum is no longer looking for the polestar but for a constellation" (*Int* 302). That statement from *The Timeless* echoes Malraux's even more explicit statement at the beginning of *Anti-Memoirs:* "I have found again and again a fundamental riddle, subject to the whims of memory which—whether or not by chance—does not recreate a life in its original sequence. Lit by an invisible sun, nebulae appear which seem to presage an unknown constellation" (*A-M* 6). (While reading that statement one must see the full weight and dimension of every word.) Plurality is such a recent concept for the Western mind that it is still difficult for Westerners to accept it fully and to rid themselves of the need to find an orienting polestar. The West believes it has contrasted plurality to unity; in fact it has contrasted it to uniformity—to the unique, single form. Hence, it will take generations for the false opposition between monism and pluralism to disappear. Alain Daniélou has shown how the plurality of Hindu gods is a powerful expression of the unity of the cosmos. So is the plurality of Egyptian gods and that of the three persons of the Trinity. Accepting values of metamorphosis enables one to accept the apparent contradiction between the unity of the Principle and the plurality of Forms, between the unity of the Generalized Potential and the plurality of manifested actualities.

Because he had truly accepted Metamorphosis as Universal Law, Malraux could see museums and libraries as "cathedrals of Metamorphosis." In this, too, he was ahead of his age, which still sees the Louvre only as a museum or the Mazarine as a library. When the Romans saw the catacombs animated by an astonishing life, when they began to see tiny chapels surmounted by the cross of Jerusalem rise out of the earth, they could not yet conceive of the ordering value that Christendom was to become. Like the Romans, those unable today to see museums and libraries as "cathedrals of Metamorphosis" or to see that cultural centers are gradually becoming chapels of metamorphosis cannot imagine that Metamorphosis will become an ordering value. They cannot imagine that the values of Metamorphosis sought by Garine may one day cover the terrestrial and sidereal space of abbeys and of Our Lady of Metamorphosis, filled with the chant of Rilke's *Sonnets to Orpheus:*

> Choose to be changed. With the Flame, with the flame be enraptured,
> Where from within you a thing changefully-splendid escapes.[1]

"To experience the sensation that our modes of thought might not be those we know provides a freedom whose importance could become unique" (*Les Nouvelles littéraires,* July 31, 1936). Here again we must see the full significance of the word "sensation" as Malraux uses it. He doesn't evoke the concept of a thought that could be quite different; he *experiences*—in 1936—the sensation that it could be thus. During forty years of reflection and meditation on metamorphosis, Malraux forged modes of thought that were not those people are normally familiar with, which is why so many of his readers are unable to enter fully into *The Timeless* or *Precarious Man.* But to those who make the effort to get into his mode of thought—and we should here give "mode" the meaning it is given by musicians—Malraux "provides a freedom that could become uniquely important." At the end of his life, Malraux might well have said what Goethe confided to Eckermann on July 15, 1831, on the subject of metamorphosis: "Its mysteries are of an unfathomable depth, but man is increasingly able to penetrate those mysteries." It was the enigmatic value of art, which Malraux had come upon, that led him truly to accept

---

1. [Rainer Maria Rilke, *Selected Works,* vol. 2, *Poetry,* translated by J. B. Leishman (London: Hogarth Press, 1960).]

The Absolute Agnostic

Metamorphosis as Universal Law. We are reminded of "the sacred Enigma" that Goethe celebrated in an elegy composed in an attempt to convey, through poetry, to reticent philosophers and scientists what the metamorphosis of plants truly was:

> But if, there, you decipher the sacred signs of the goddess,
> You will then see them everywhere, though different.

It appears perfectly normal a posteriori that Malraux, having fully accepted the discontinuity of forms and their plurality, came upon the precarious. In *Anti-Memoirs* he justifies the title of that work by stating that he had, without knowing it, resuscitated the word *farfelu*. In his last book he also resuscitates the word "precarious." It was only after the seventeenth century that the adjective "precarious" took on the meaning of uncertain, unstable, ephemeral. Before the seventeenth century "precarious" denoted a right that was exercised at the will of a revocable authorization, and the *precarium* was the parcel of exploitable land allotted to a peasant who had presented his *precaria,* his "prayer." One must read and reread *Precarious Man and Literature,* Malraux's last book, in which he meditates on the word, no longer on the form, remembering always that the Man in question in the book is a man who exploits a parcel; that the parcel allotted to him depends upon the precaria he has presented; and that that parcel could be taken away from him. Man had believed he was the proprietor of the earth, and he was beginning to believe he was the proprietor of space. In fact he is merely exploiting a precarium, and if he does so without having presented his precaria, his exploitation is invalid.

The expression "precarious man," which Malraux chose as the title of his book, appears only on the last page of the book. It crowns a long meditation on the uncertain, a meditation begun at the end of *The Timeless.* If we wish to understand Malraux's thought and to follow his quest, we must see the full significance of the word "uncertain." Malraux invites us to do so when he writes that "we are dupes of our vocabulary, which concedes to us the choice between meaning and the absurd" (*HP* 329). If one throws the die only once, getting the number 3 is uncertain; it remains uncertain if one throws the die an insufficient number of times. But if one can throw it a sufficient number of times, the outcome becomes *certain.* Uncertainty is only uncertain in time. It is only uncertain for those whose perception of time is limited. It is only uncertain within the human condition. But for those who enter "into that time," for those who can condense time in themselves, uncertainty is no longer uncertain, nor is it the unexpected subject to chance; it is one of the multiple forms the probable can assume. Uncertainty gives form to the plurality of the probable.

Mathematics can conceive of spaces in 3, 4, 5 ... n dimensions, and it can condense time absolutely. The equation of a parabola contains within it and in it alone all the positions a point can take in all past, present, and future instances. The formula of a parabola condenses time absolutely, as do formulas for the law of large numbers and equations of probability. They are a crucible that sublimates seconds and centuries, a crucible in which uncertainties appear, in full light and in complete certainty. A mathematician using his formulas, symbols, and equations lives and works in completely condensed time, though not always aware of it. The mystic too lives in absolutely condensed time. It is easy to understand how Pascal's adding machine led him to the mystical experience of his "night of fire." We would need all the knowledge of a mathematician and all the consciousness of a mystic to perceive the full value of Malraux's statement, "One cannot understand the uncertain if one confuses it with a skepticism, because this all-encompassing uncertainty reigns at the paradoxical summit of limited certainties" (*HP* 316).

As if confronted by a compelling landscape, we must pause here and reflect. The uncertain is an "all-encompassing uncertainty." Uncertainty because we are in time and are unable to condense our perception of time. But an "all-encompassing" uncertainty, for if we succeed in transmuting our perceptions and in making the absolutely condensed time that Bergson was seeking appear in the crucible of our sensations, then that uncertainty would encompass all our limited certainties, it would *rule over* them. An all-encompassing uncertainty, the uncertain is royal, and its royalty is sacred.

In *The Timeless*, Malraux searched so avidly for the All-Encompassing of all the forms of creation, the All-Encompassing of the secret and coded language of forms, the All-Encompassing of Primordial Forms, that we can hardly fail to see the full significance Malraux assigned to the expression "the uncertain, that all-encompassing uncertainty."

Einstein, despite his theory of relativity, remained enclosed within the interrogative exclamation he often repeated: "What is so extraordinary is that all that should have a *sens!*"[2] In that statement he favored exclamation at the expense of interrogation, which prevented him from

---

2. [I am maintaining the French word *sens* in preparation for the argument that follows.—Trans.]

The Absolute Agnostic

going deeper in his dialogue with Niels Bohr or with the scholars of the Copenhagen school. Few words are as ambiguous as *sens*. In French, the word *sens* serves to designate the organs that enable us to perceive as well as the direction toward which one is going and the significance one attributes to ideas or symbols. Unfortunately it has become common to forget the first meaning of *sens* when we use the last two. When we ask about the *sens* of history, or the *sens* of the human adventure, it is difficult to distinguish whether we are asking about the direction in which that adventure is going or about the meaning, or sense, of that adventure. We want to give meaning to the human adventure only on condition that it is given a direction. We want to give it meaning only on condition that it is given a point of departure and a point of arrival. The precarious man of uncertainty can free himself of this confusion. There is no direction to the uncertain, which doesn't mean it has no meaning. The uncertain doesn't start from one point and go toward another. The uncertain is not subject to a sense of progression, it is subject to condensation, to extreme "potentialization." All the chances in a lottery drawing can be condensed into a formula, a single formula that expresses, outside of time, the generalized potential of all drawings that at some moment in human time can become actualities—a single formula which doesn't subject the drawings to chance or necessity. In itself and by itself, this formula encompasses beyond time all drawings that can occur within time. It encompasses the certainty of potentiality and the uncertainty of actualities. It encompasses all potential drawings and all realized outcomes.

Malraux often cited Einstein's exclamation because he himself experienced the temptation to adopt it. But the last twenty pages of *Precarious Man*, the last pages Malraux ever wrote, resound as an ultimate and fantastic effort finally to free himself from the temptation to believe that "all that should have a *sens*." After looking for an answer all his life, Malraux ended up admitting in a luminous, enlightening way that "the true response," instead of providing a *sens,* could well be a response "immunizing man against the question" (*HP* 314). Until recently, religions, like philosophies and ideologies, have also proposed answers that would provide "a sense or a direction" and required adherence. But haven't these religious answers "covered up a silence that might contribute to form man as much as adherence to a religion does"? (ibid.).

"Reject the question of *sens*. There is nothing to suggest that a civilization cannot develop within such a rejection" (ibid.). (If Malraux had had the time to work on the manuscript of *Precarious Man* as he worked on his other writings, he might have expressed himself more as he usually did; he might have written: Accept that you should not ask the question of sense, or direction; there is nothing to suggest that a civilization cannot develop within such an acceptance.) The idea of "rejecting the question of *sens*" is so shocking for some that they refuse, even for a moment, to accept it as a hypothesis for thought. Formed by two-and-a-half millennia devoted to giving sense, or direction, to the world and to man, they can consider neither man nor the world as successive, discontinuous, uncertain actualities. Malraux too had trouble freeing himself of his cultural heritage; he too sought for a long time to give *un sens* to "all that," but he could accept the sacred royalty of "the all-encompassing uncertainty" of the uncertain, and he suggested we follow along with him when he finally admitted that "in the presence of the uncertain, neither the world nor man have *un sens* since its very definition is the impossibility of *sens*—through thought as through faith" (*HP* 329).

In 1974, that is, midway between the Salpêtrière and *Precarious Man*, Malraux confided in Guy Suarès, "What has been written about the Absurd postulates that man needs his consciousness to legitimate the universe. But that is by no means a given" (*VO* 34). (The verb "to legitimate" must have been chosen with particular care.) Until now, religions and philosophies have begun by postulating implicitly or explicitly, that man has to have the universe legitimated. And if we wonder why philosophies and religions have posed that postulate, we find only one truly satisfying response: they posed it because they granted more importance to the questions raised by death than to those raised by life.

It is not at all certain that the universe needs to be legitimated. The only people who seek to legitimate love are those who have never really experienced it. Those who truly know love do not seek to legitimate it, they seek to live it, ever more profoundly. They do not wonder about the sense, or direction, of their love, they manifest it in actions. Having accepted love as a fact that has been manifested to them, they live it and acquire an intimate knowledge of it. Those, on the other hand, who seek to know where their love came from and where it is going kill it with analysis. By an excessive desire to legitimate the universe, man has deprived himself of experiencing and living it. By forcing us to realize that the postulate of a universe having to be legitimated is by no means certain, Malraux has opened the way to a true rebirth of the world.

Our age has fallen heir to all cultures, all arts, and all religions of all time, not "despite the uncertain, but because of it" (*HP* 329). But the dawn of the uncertain is only just breaking, and Malraux rightly confided to Victor Franco, "I believe that thought, true thought, must succeed in giving form to the uncertain. Currently, our forms of thought have no hold over the uncertain" (*Journal du Dimanche,* November 28, 1976). For many centuries, physics and mechanics had no hold over uncertainty, nor did human thought. Today, scientific thought has become familiar with uncertainty and constantly improves its hold over it. Through a comparable movement, precarious man must enhance the forms of thought and sensibility that have a hold over the uncertain. If we remember that for Malraux the imaginary is a realm not of dreams but of forms, we will understand that, celebrating "the adventures of the imaginary" in *Precarious Man,* he already sensed that by following the imaginary-of-Truth of the Sacred Arts, and by following the imaginary-of-Fiction of the Arts of the Unreal, an imaginary-of-Metamorphosis could develop that would be that of the uncertain (*HP* 108). If we accept this imaginary-of-Metamorphosis, it becomes possible to understand Malraux's final testimony, which fills the last pages of *Precarious Man:* "Death is an invincible mystery; life, an uncanny mystery" (*HP* 326).

Listening to the profound voice of Malraux's works, we discover that Malraux's entire existence was marked by a gradual deepening of the "uncanny mystery" of life. In *Paper Moons,* Malraux showed how wanting to kill Death changed nothing for nothing. In the *last* page of *The Royal Way,* Perken challenges the sovereign character of Death and reduces it simply to the death of an individuality. In the *last* pages of *Man's Fate,* Gisors wants May to learn to love the living and not the dead. In the *last* pages of *Days of Wrath,* Kassner entered into a fellowship with the eternity of the living, withdrawing from the eternity of the dead. In the *last* page of *Man's Hope,* Manuel feels "the seething life around him charged with portents" (*MH* 510). In the *last* pages of *The Walnut Trees of Altenburg,* the awareness arises that the secret of life would not have been "less poignant if man had been immortal." In all studies on art, reflections and meditations are organized around the presence in the world of the life of works which should belong to the world of death. And, finally, in the *last* pages of *Lazarus* we find one of the most beautiful hymns to life that Malraux ever composed: "Weary of the rustling voices of death, on awakening I watch life renewing itself on my fingernail ... At the moment of keeling over (I had actually left the ground), I felt death recede; I was penetrated, possessed—overwhelmed—as by an unknown presence, like Boaz by the immense blessedness that descended from the Chaldean firmament—by an inexplicably consoling *irony,* which momentarily outstared the worn-out face of death" (*L* 149).

It is highly significant that all the *last* pages of all Malraux's novels but his first are a hymn to life, and that the essence of all his nonfiction is a deepening of the mystery of life. Usually, if the occasion warrants, men celebrate life during their youth, continuing to a degree during their adulthood, but as soon as old age approaches they begin either to dread death or to question it. Malraux provides a contrasting, and uplifting, example. As an adolescent, then as a young man, he seemed obsessed by death, but he already saw it as the queen of a *farfelu* kingdom. At forty he had the revelation of the uncanny mystery of life and of its secret, which was independent of mortality or immortality. At seventy and more, he marveled at the progress of life and looked ironically at the worn-out face of death. What an example! But also how different from Sartre, who, at about the same age, wrote in *Words,* "I see clearly, I have lost all illusion ... For about ten years I have been a man who is awakening, cured of a long, bitter, and sweet madness, who can't get over it, and who can't remember his former wanderings without laughing, and who no longer knows what to do with his life." The existentialist arriving at the conclusion of his existence no longer knows what to do with *his* life. At the same moment in time Malraux was not concerned with *his* life; he was watching the advance of *life.* He extended an invitation to the "epiphanies of life" (*L* 147), and above all he formulated the wish, or the vision, that one day, if "on every radio and television set, in the presence of men ready to listen at last, the ultimate prophet would yell at Death: 'There is no nothingness!'" (*L* 148). *In the presence of men ready to listen at last . . .*

Metamorphosis wears away the face of death and unveils that of life. In *The Songs of Maldoror,* beings are metamorphosed under the impulse of a vitality whose use has not yet been discovered, that is, under the impulse of a desire to live that has remained victimized and repressed (cf. Bachelard). But along with these Lautréamontist metamorphoses provoked by an exacerbated "will to live" there are metamorphoses that result from mastering the art of living, knowing *how* to live. The ancient Egyptians' *Book of the Dead,* Apuleius's *Golden Ass,* and the entire Imaginary Museum offer the loftiest illustrations of metamorphoses due to knowing how to live. Lucius, who wanted to be metamorphosed into a bird, was turned into an ass because he didn't know how to live, as his earlier voyages prove. Having turned into an ass while keeping the psyche of a man, he is subjected to the worst torments, which ultimately

The Absolute Agnostic

teach him to live; he becomes the artisan of his metamorphosis into a man and then into a priest of Isis.

When victimized, the will to live ultimately serves nothing but itself and ends up in violence. Violence in Sade and Masoch, in whom a will to live is diverted into a cerebral will to pleasure, that impoverishment of true vitality and of its means of reproduction. An even greater violence in Lautréamont through the uncontrolled emergence of an animal vitality and a primal will to live. Knowing how to live, on the other hand, has no need to resort to violence to make life burst forth and participate in its immortality. The time seems to have arrived to undertake a rereading of all myths and legends, including fairy tales, in which metamorphoses appear. Such rereading could be guided by Goethe's *Sacred Enigma,* Gerard de Nerval's visions, Flaubert's temptations of Saint Anthony, Rilke's Sonnets, Valéry's *Solitary,* Malraux's *Precarious Man,* but also by the philosophical and poetic reflections of Bachelard, the research and meditations of Henri Corbin and Mircea Eliade, the equations of René Thom, who sought the integral of the creative fields of forms, and by the ancestral monoid of Pierre Miallet. The time seems to have arrived to undertake the topology of metamorphosis, to draw the fresco of metamorphoses-ascents and of metamorphoses-falls, of metamorphoses engendered by a will to live, which often consumes vitality, and of those engendered by knowing how to live, which like a *Jacob's Ladder of vitality and creation* seems to show the royal path to the more-than-life.

Here and now, without waiting for that immense topology, it is possible to reread all the tales of metamorphosis and see that legends of rocks or clods of clay that metamorphosed into men, or of men that metamorphosed into plants or animals, are images of learning life in all its forms through experience, images of a slow and sometimes painful approach to learning what life truly *is*. They are images that teach us that centaurs and chimera, far from being a synthesis of several forms of life, are the product of a dangerous illusion: the illusion of believing that one can acquire a knowledge of life by living several forms of life simultaneously, the illusion of wanting to destroy stages in the Cycle of Metamorphoses. Such images teach that man may be situated at the summit of vital "complexification" but is not thereby exempted from seeking to acquire the same kind of relations with space, time, and life that minerals and plants have. Daphne, metamorphosed into a laurel tree, maintains as permanent acquired knowledge the perception of time and space that belongs to the woman Daphne, but she also acquires the perception of space and time belonging to the laurel tree. The woman Daphne takes root in the earth and offers herself up to the blowing wind. And she can wish nothing better for her lover than that he also should be able to know that caress. The fisherman Glaucos, metamorphosed into a fish, can be divinized; he has been liberated from one of the limits imposed on man: to live *on* a surface. He has acquired the privilege granted only to fish and birds: to live *in* a volume. He has acquired an additional liberty, as mathematicians say in this case. These are images that teach that metamorphosis into a Golden Falcon or a Royal Phoenix is necessary if we are calmly to say:

> Yesterday gave birth to me
> Here it is that Today
> I create Tomorrows.
>
> (*Book of the Dead*, chap 179)

In all civilizations and cultures, man has established a symbolic correspondence between an animal, or a species, and an instinct. The bestiaries of the Middle Ages as well as those of antiquity were constructed upon that correspondence. Those of today are, as well. The recent science of animal behavior, as Bergson said and, after him, Roger Caillois, tends to see the psychism of an animal as a monovalent psychism. Animals have a monomania, which is their instinct. Their behavior is alienated from their instinct. This concept offers immense possibilities of interpretation of all tales about people being metamorphosed into animals. Thanks to metamorphosis, man can know the instinct of that animal, and in knowing it he is able to dealienate himself from it. Placed at the summit of the hierarchy of animals, man contains all animal instincts. The myths and legends of the metamorphosis of man into an animal thus become an expressive image of man's need if he wishes to attain complete knowledge of how to live, to dealienate himself from animal instincts, and to learn how to master them. Conversely, Oriental myths of reincarnation into an animal are images that illustrate the fate which awaits man when he has not been able to truly dealienate himself from one of the instincts he contained.

Myths, tales, and legends telling of metamorphoses are bearers of another vision of vitality, another perception of vital dynamics, another perspective on creative evolution. When Alice succeeds all by herself, and with the simplicity of a child, in clearing up the deliberate ambiguity of the advice given her by the caterpillar, she is no longer the victim of thoughtless changes in form; she is able to master her stay in Wonderland and then to pass *to the other side of the looking-glass*. Lewis Carroll,

The Absolute Agnostic

who was a mathematician, published his book six years after Darwin's *Origin of the Species*. Today, understanding of the will-to-live and of knowing how to live found in plants, animals, and men seems greater in *Alice in Wonderland* than in *The Origin of the Species*. Particle accelerators and Young's experiments have begun to speak a language nearer to that of the Red Queen than to that of neo-Darwinism.

"Art begins when life ceases to be a model and becomes raw material" (*AC* 255). To live one's life is also an art; and in this realm, too, art begins when one approaches life the way one would approach a raw material to which one will give form, hoping to have it enter into the cycle of metamorphoses. In a conversation with Tadeo Takemoto, Malraux said that "humanity has had two great problems: one was salvation and the other serenity" (*Appel*, December 1973). Immediately afterwards he stressed that salvation is "something of serenity in death," whereas serenity is "something of salvation in life." Salvation and serenity seem to have been reconciled and unified in Malraux, who was able to write: "No question interrogates man in a more pressing way than the one that asks him the meaning of life, since it is death that asks it of him" (*HP* 312). It is not the contemplation of the wilted or the dead leaf which introduces us to the metamorphosis of plants; it is the acceptance of plant life. It is not the death of a Sunday painting that questions us about metamorphosis. We should confidently read and reread the surprising dialogue between Malraux and de Gaulle:

DE G. . . . Why need life have a meaning? . . . Since they began to think, what answers have the philosophers produced?
M. Doesn't the answer belong rather to religions? If life must have a meaning, it is surely because that alone can give a meaning to death . . .
DE G. Death: you know what death is?
M. . . . My relationship with death is far from clear . . . But the idea of death itself forces the real metaphysical problem, the problem of the meaning of life. (*FO* 38–40)

As long as man has questioned himself about death, that is, probably as long as man has been man, few profane and agnostic voices have proclaimed such a serene victory over death. Nietzsche, Rimbaud, and Gide had prepared the way; Nietzsche with the *The Gay Science;* Rimbaud by exclaiming "What an old maid I'm becoming, lacking the courage to love death" and in announcing that "to every being several other lives seemed due" (*Mauvais sang, Alchimie du verbe*); Gide with his gentle words, "Nathanael, I will speak to you of instants. Have you understood how forceful is their presence? An insufficiently constant reflection on death has not attributed enough value to the smallest instant of your life" (*Nourritures terrestres*, book II). Malraux went even further. Beginning with *The Temptation of the West*, he showed how the European mind, after destroying God and abolishing all that might stand in man's way, finally found itself in the face of death like Rancé before the dead body of his mistress; man then discovered he could no longer be enamored by death, "and never has there been as disquieting a discovery" (*TW* 121). In *Man's Hope*, Malraux attributes to old Alvear "a very profound feeling in the face of death, which has never been expressed since the Renaissance: curiosity." Each of Malraux's returns to earth enabled him to wear down the face of death with the flint of life. Two of these returns were secret and less spectacular than those he has written about, but they were crucial and painful; he experienced the first when he resisted the temptation to commit suicide following the death of Louise de Vilmorin, and the second when the death he seemed to be seeking in Bangladesh eluded him. He then had to accept living, which enabled him slowly to make his way toward an ultimate awareness: it is always life that wins, not death, as his doctor believed (*L* 114).

To live "the ephiphanies of life" to which Malraux summoned everyone, it is essential to have truly rid oneself of all individualism, to have rid oneself of all the images, sermons, and words that have led one to believe that an individuality was important enough to be worthy of entering into eternity. An individuality is an actuality. The flesh of an individuality is not the glorious flesh of the Resurrection, as demonstrated by the pilgrims of Emmaus, who did not recognize Christ after he was resurrected and for whom a sign was needed. Eternity cannot be an eternity of actualities. In the final two pages of *Precarious Man*, those in which Malraux, shortly before dying, evokes for the last time the possibility of a "spiritual metamorphosis" (*HP* 330), an essential spiritual event, Malraux confronts man with the crucial question that man refuses to look at directly, whether from the arrogance of the individual or from intense individualism. Here is the question in all its blinding simplicity: "Does the summons of death, irrefutable by the individual, preserve for a culture its depth of a bronze drum?" (*HP* 329). Wouldn't the individual, obsessed by the summons of death, behave like one of the millions of cerebral neurons that die each day in us, believing that its death is the death of the mind in which it existed? The "We civilizations, we know we are mortal" of Spengler and Valéry "is unaware of metamorphosis" (ibid.), and Malraux delivers man from an obsession by proposing to translate that statement by "We caterpillars, we know we are temporary." The "We individuals, we know we are mortal" that has obsessed the Westerner for centuries must now be translated by "We individuals, we know our actuality is temporary." Fully to accept that the summons of death is only irrefutable by the individual can totally reestablish man's attitude toward life and death. A civilization or a culture which might truly accept this would most likely consider past civilizations, including our own, as "immense metaphysical ages," as "an era of death" (*HP* 330). That civilization could open up an era of life and rediscover the true sense of Christ's message, "I am the Life." Then perhaps the god Malraux evoked in the future tense, rather than the conditional will descend: "The god who presides over the most profound metamorphosis of all, that which will have changed *the empire of death* into a modern museum" (*A-M* 53).

Villon once said: "He who dies, dies in pain." That was true. And Bernanos used that statement admirably to tie together his *Dialogue of the Carmelites*. "But by gradually emancipating itself from pain, death loses much of its Pascalian virus" (*HP* 325). This radical change, too, in man's relationship with death opens the way to yet undreamed-of continents and intervenes at the very moment when techniques of contraception are radically changing man's relations to the life he transmits. After remarking that no civilization has posed death as a ritual fact, Malraux said to Tadeo Takemoto, "How normal it would be to encounter an entire civilization in which there was no death" (*Appel,* December 1973). One needs great self-control, here, to accept the simplicity of the adjective "normal" that Malraux chose, which gives the statement its serene fullness.

I hesitated for a long time over the meaning of the title *Mirror of Limbo,* under which Malraux grouped *Anti-Memoirs* and *The Cord and the Mice,* the two books in which he talks about his life. For some Catholic theologians, limbo is the place where children who have died without being baptized remain, enduring, despite their innocence, the consequences of original sin; it is also the resting place of the souls of adults who were righteous but did not receive the supernatural grace needed to enter into eternal beatitude immediately. In common usage, limbo is used to describe an indeterminate region, an uncertain state. Of which limbo exactly does Malraux provide the mirror? The answer is found at the end of *Precarious Man:* "Before the twentieth century the West lived in unlimited metempsychosis. Proclaiming the Resurrection, the Last Judgment, it believed it had rejected reincarnations at the same time as the vague places—the Elysian Fields, Sheol, the immortality of the Enlightenment—to which the soul emigrated. It remained tied to that limbo, however, by a realm so vast and so obvious that it never grasped it: it conceived of death as a change" (*HP* 313). The mirror of limbo is the mirror of that "vast metaphysical era," of that "era of death" which our successors will perhaps view with shock. The image of man reflected in the mirror of limbo is that of a man "attuned to the questions which death raises about the meaning of the world" (*A-M* 6), the image of a man who believed he had rejected vague places but who remained tied to them. On the other side of the mirror of limbo our successors will perhaps find a man who is in agreement with the questions life raises about the meaning of the world. They will then come out of limbo to enter an era not of the metaphysical but of the physical, since today it is the study of the physical that reveals a forever invisible world, a sur-real as real as reality. They will then enter an era not of death but of life.

"My Brother the wind," "my brothers the birds," "my sister the rain"—and we must add "my brother the rock"—belong to life, not death. They belong to the physical, not the metaphysical. They are actual, and their actuality, when it can be contemplated, reveals the potential within them. We must pass through to the other side of the mirror of limbo in order to obliterate the image of vague places and finally to hear the song of Rimbaud, the young student:

> Car l'Homme a fini, l'Homme a joué tous les rôles.
> Au grand jour, fatigué de briser des idoles
> Il ressuscitera, libre de tous ses dieux,
> Et comme il est du ciel, il scrutera les cieux.
> L'idéal, la pensée invincible, éternelle,
> Tout le dieu qui vit sous son argile charnelle
> Montera, montera, brûlera sous son front.
> Et quand tu le verras sonder tout l'horizon
> Contempteur des vieux jougs, libre de toute crainte,
> Tu viendras lui donner la rédemption sainte.[3]
>
> (*Soleil et Chair*, III)

---

3. ["For Man is finished! Man has played all roles! / By day, weary of smashing idols / He will revive, free of all his gods, / And as he is from heaven, he will scan the skies! / The Ideal, the invincible, eternal, thought, / Everything; the god who lives under his clay of flesh, / Will rise, will rise, and burn under his brow! / And when you see him sounding the whole horizon, / A despiser of old yokes, free from all fear, / You will come and give him holy redemption." *Rimbaud: Complete Works, Selected Letters,* translated by Wallace Fowlie (Chicago: University of Chicago Press, 1966).]

The Absolute Agnostic

On the other side of the mirror of limbo, transformed by his passage, man will be able to hear the prophet who has come to proclaim the eternity of the living, and he will no longer encounter the group of Perkens who point at the starry majesty of the night and say that to exist "against all that" is the same thing as existing "against death." On the other side of the mirror of limbo, man will be able to live *with* all that and *with* death.

From *The Voices of Silence* to *The Timeless,* Malraux untiringly scrutinized all the stages of "the Copernican revolution," which brought to light "the fact of creation" as an autonomous and sovereign fact (*Int* 246). Since the opening of the Imaginary Museum, "the fact of creation" is the sun of art; it is no longer its satellite. But at the end of *The Timeless,* Malraux was forced, almost against his will, to admit a striking extension of the "fact of creation." He admitted that "the unconquerable power of creation, which man contrasts to mortal appearance," is no longer a privilege man alone possesses (*Int* 164). "The inexhaustible power of creation, which travels through centuries" (*Int* 161), "the insistent continuity of creation" (*Int* 144)—Malraux saw these powers in driftwood sculpted by the sea, in the designs of agates, as well as in chalcedonic signs; "they reach the final cape of our world of art." "The crafty bountifulness" of the cosmos, too, is a creator of forms; it, too, repeats already created forms, wears out old forms, and creates new ones; it, too, appears to manifest chreodes of primordial forms.

Malraux then acceded to the Jacob's ladder of all the facts of creation. He, who had brought to light the world of art in all its splendor as an autonomous world reflecting only itself, reintegrated the world of art into the whole world and placed it on the peninsula of the cosmic adventure. The creative power of the artist and the creative power of the cosmos are of the same nature. Granted, the sea sculpting a piece of driftwood or the terrestrial crucible creating an agate "provide us with fewer masterpieces than has genius" (*Int* 252), but the Sunday painters, too, have left us fewer masterpieces than have Michelangelo and Van Gogh.

In the final chapters of *The Timeless,* Malraux uses various approaches to seek almost impatiently—since he didn't have much time left—for the profound significance of all those facts of creation. "Art sometimes wonders what the agates and the abstracts together allude to" (*Int* 282). Contemplating the inexhaustible power of creation possessed by man and the cosmos, Malraux wondered: What is that power of creation? Where does it come from? What does it mean? To follow his successive approaches to that mystery, we should be aware of the thought Malraux expressed one day to Roger Stéphane. Malraux never repeated that thought in his books, but it illuminates his thinking: "It does not go without saying that God, the character called God, the entity called God, is the creator. And the very fact that we might separate God from Creation means we have already begun to carry out incredible transformations" (*Le Point*, no. 219). Separate God from Creation! Malraux was entirely consistent with himself, and he was willing to go as far as the light cast by the Imaginary Museum. He showed that an artist's power of creation is a power that reflects only itself, even if it seeks to "attain" as much as to express. He then linked together all the facts of creation existing in the cosmos. And he ended, of course, by admitting that the power of creation of the cosmos is also a power that reflects only itself, in other words, that God can be separated from Creation.

We are inevitably reminded, here, of the words of Valéry's Serpent:

> Sun! ... Oh Sun, you glaring error! ...
> By way of delights impenetrable
> You, my proudest accomplice,
> And loftiest of all my snares,
> You protect all hearts from knowing
> That the universe is merely a blot
> On the pure void of Non-being! ...
> As though bored with the pure theater
> Of Self, God broke the barrier
> Of his perfect eternity:
> He became He who fritters away
> His Primal Cause in consequences,
> And stars his Unity.[4]

Separate God from Creation! How can we not recall the last sermons of Meister Eckehart: "God operates, but the Deity does not; it has, moreover, no work to carry out ... When I arrive at the source of the Deity, it is there that God disappears ... If God is called 'God' it is by the will of creatures. It was only when the soul became a creature that it had a God." And how can we not recall Professor Raja Rao declaring and teaching from the University of Texas that the concept of God is an objectification, that where there is ego there is God, and where there is no longer ego there is the Absolute. In *The Timeless*, Malraux notes al-

---

4. [Paul Valéry, *Poems*, translated by David Paul (Princeton, NJ: Princeton University Press, 1971).]

The Absolute Agnostic

Goldmund. After traveling throughout the world, enjoying all pleasures and overcoming all dangers, Goldmund returns once again to the monastery where he grew up. There he finds Narcissus, the head of the monastery, a man of high spirituality who has led an exemplary life. A true friendship has united Narcissus and Goldmund for many years. Exhausted, Goldmund senses he is going to die and awaits death with curiosity, which astonishes Narcissus. Although talking has become difficult for him, in an ultimate effort Goldmund attempts to make Narcissus understand how strongly he feels he is on his way to meet his mother. Throughout his life he has pursued the dream of sculpting "the beautiful statue of the great maternal Eve." He now knows the form he will give her. But Eve doesn't want this. She doesn't want him to reveal her secret. Goldmund understands very well why, and he dies without regret, thanks to her. Just before dying, he has the strength to utter a final statement, which burns in the heart of his friend, the apparently holy and irreproachable man: "But how do you expect to die some day, Narcissus, since you don't have a mother? Without a mother one cannot love, without a mother one cannot die." Goldmund's final statement would surely burn in Narcissus's heart like a purifying flame, perhaps allowing Narcissus to accede to the wisdom of which Lao-tzu spoke: "He who has reached the mother (matter, the body) knows her son (the vital spirit contained within) through her. He who knows the son and preserves the mother will reach the end of his days without accident."

During the syncope that had prostrated him at the Salpêtrière hospital, Malraux felt "disembodied" (*L* 140). He had lost everything—the sense of his body, of his identity, of bearings to the right, the left, below, above—everything except "life." And from that experience Malraux derived a consciousness, that "consciousness of life is not consciousness of the person" (ibid.). To become conscious of life, conscious of what the vital flow at work in the cosmos truly is, one must go beyond the framework of the person, one must sense life independently of one's own. It then becomes possible to speak "to death on an equal footing," to look ironically at "the worn-out face of death."

Shortly after relating that consciousness, which was going to transform the way he would henceforth view life, Malraux wrote two essential statements, around which his meditation during the final years of his life was organized: "The tragedy of agnosticism does not lie in the fact that we regard death as unthinkable, but in the fact that we cannot bring ourselves to do so" (*L* 143). "Agnosticism can only speak to death on an equal footing if it, too, bases itself on faith" (*L* 146). It takes great strength of mind to agree that agnostic thought can be based on faith, to agree that an agnosticism can be a religion. Between *Lazarus* and *Precarious Man,* 1972–76, totally accepting that "our fundamental consciousness is only the consciousness of being alive" (*L* 142) and not the consciousness of having to die, Malraux became an absolute agnostic. He opened the doors to an absolute agnosticism for which "the absolute unknowable is not a realm of doubt, it is as imperious as the successive faiths of humanity" (*L* 145).

After becoming conscious of life, after seeing the worn-out face of death go away, Malraux no longer spoke of a riddle that haunted him as it had haunted Dostoyevski, which recurred in various forms in his earlier works: "If it is true that for a religious spirit the camps, like the torture of an innocent child by a brute, pose the supreme riddle, it is also true that for an agnostic spirit the same riddle springs up with the first act of compassion, heroism, or love" (*A-M* 407). When one has become conscious of Life, that riddle is no longer posed: love is part of life; the torture of a child by a brute no longer causes one to give up; the goddess Kālī with her protruding tongue dances on a corpse; and the heart of a mandala contains the seeds of all its lobes, lobes of love as well as of hate. The uncertain actualities engendered by potential do not affect generalized Potentiality; they affect only themselves. The Sphinx is reborn from its ashes, and its royal immobility is in no way affected by the riddles that one may or may not ask oneself in its presence.

The consciousness of Life also enabled Malraux to erase an assertion he had advanced in the 1950s. At that time he had admitted that an art of the "Great Navigators" was thinkable, but he had asserted on several occasions that a culture of "Great Navigators" was not, that a culture of interrogation *alone* could not exist (*VOS* 604 and *Liberté de l'Esprit,* June 1950). After 1972, having become conscious of Life, Malraux was no longer concerned with substituting one causality for another, one explanation for another, but with accepting "the questioning which causalities and conditionings must submit to" (*AC* 228). He even went so far as to write, "It doesn't much matter whether my impressions win approval, so long as my questions cannot be ignored" (*PM* 216). Neither metamorphosis nor uncertainty require an answer. Answers serve to give form to that which has none. Answers are actualities. And although like all actualities they are ephemeral and uncertain, they engender forms of dogmatism, which kill life. "Whosoever shall not receive the kingdom of God as a little child, he shall not enter therein"; hence, for children, no "because" can stifle the "whys."

Abbreviations

AC	*Anti-Critique (Néocritique)*
A-M	*Anti-Memoirs (Antimémoires)*
Con	*The Conquerors (Les Conquérants)*
CS	*The Cord and the Mice (La Corde et les souris)*
DW	*Days of Wrath (Le Temps du mépris)*
FO	*Felled Oaks (Les Chênes qu'on abat)*
HP	*Precarious Man (L'Homme précaire et la littérature)*
Int	*The Timeless (L'Intemporel)*
Ir	*The Unreal (L'Irréel)*
JE	*Of a European Youth (D'Une Jeunesse européenne)*
L	*Lazarus (Lazare)*
Laz	*Lazare*
LP	*Paper Moons (Les Lunes en papier)*
MF	*Man's Fate (La Condition humaine)*
MG	*The Metamorphosis of the Gods (La Métamorphose des dieux)*
MH	*Man's Hope (L'Espoir)*
MI	*The Imaginary Museum (Le Musée imaginaire de la sculpture mondiale)*
OF	*Eulogies (Oraisons funèbres)*
PM	*Picasso's Mask (La Tête d'obsidienne)*
RF	*Farfelu Kingdom (La Royaume Farfelu)*
RW	*The Royal Way (La Voie royale)*
TN	*The Black Triangle (Le Triangle Noir)*
TW	*The Temptation of the West (La Tentation de l'occident)*

Abbreviations

VOS   *The Voices of Silence* (*Les Voix du silence*)
VS   *Les Voix du silence*
VO   *The Voice of the West* (*La Voix de l'occident*)
WTA   *The Walnut Trees of Altenberg* (*Les Noyers de l'Altenberg*)

Works by André Malraux

Note: The English-language translations listed after certain works are the editions used in the present translation.

1921　*Lunes en papier.* Paris: Editions de la Galerie Simon.

Les Hérissons apprivoisés, Journal d'un papier de jeu de massacre. Signaux de France et de Belgique, 1, no. 1 August 1921): 171–77.

Ecrit pour une idole à trompe (unpublished)

1926　*La Tentation de l'occident.* Paris: Grasset. Translated by Robert Hollander as *The Temptation of the West.* New York: Vintage, 1961. (Reissued, with a new Foreword by Jonathan D. Spence; Chicago: University of Chicago Press, 1991.)

1927　*Ecrit pour un ours en peluche*, no. 4 (Summer, 1927): 114–24.

D'une Jeunesse européenne. Paris: Grasset.

1928　*Les Conquérants.* Paris: Grasset (definitive French version with Postface by Malraux published in 1949 by Grasset). Translated by Winifred Stephens Whale as *The Conquerors.* Boston: Beacon Press, 1956. (Also translated by Stephen Becker, 1976. Reissued, with a new Foreword by Herbert R. Lottman; Chicago: University of Chicago Press, 1991.)

Royaume farfelu. Paris: Gallimard.

315

Works by André Malraux

1930 *La Voie royale.* Paris: Grasset. Translated by Stuart Gilbert as *The Royal Way.* New York: Vintage Books, 1935.

1932 *Oeuvres Gothico-Bouddhiques du pamir.* Paris: Galerie de la NRF.

1933 *La Condition humaine.* Paris: Gallimard. Translated by Haakon M. Chevalier as *Man's Fate.* New York: The Modern Library, 1936.

1935 *Le Temps du mépris.* Paris: Gallimard. Translated by Haakon M. Chevalier as *Days of Wrath.* New York: Random House, 1936.

1937 *L'Espoir.* Paris: Gallimard. Translated by Stuart Gilbert and Alastair Macdonald as *Man's Hope.* New York: The Modern Library, 1941.

1939 "Laclos." In *Tableau de la Littérature française, XVII et XVIII siècles*, 417–28. Paris: Gallimard.

1943 *Les Noyers d'Altenberg.* Lausanne: Editions du Haut-Pays (republished by Gallimard in 1948). Translated by A. W. Fielding as *The Walnut Trees of Altenberg.* London: John Lehmann, 1952. (Reissued, with a new Foreword by Conor Cruise O'Brien; Chicago: University of Chicago Press, 1991.)

1946 *Esquisse d'une psychologie du cinéma.* Paris: Gallimard.

1947 *Le Musée imaginaire.* Vol. 1 of *La Psychologie de l'art.* Geneva: Skira.

Dessins de Goya au Musée du Prado. Geneva: Skira.

1948 *La Création artistique.* Vol. 2 of *La Psychologie de l'art.* Geneva: Skira.

1949 *La Monnaie de l'absolu.* Vol. 3 of *La Psychologie de l'art.* Geneva: Skira.

1950 *Saturne.* Paris: Gallimard. Translated by C. W. Chilton as *Saturn: An Essay on Goya.* London: Phaidon Press, 1957.

1951 *Les Voix du silence.* Paris: Gallimard. Translated by Stuart Gilbert as *The Voices of Silence.* New York: Doubleday, 1956.

1952 *Le Musée imaginaire de la sculpture mondiale: La Statuaire.* Paris: Gallimard.

Works by André Malraux

1954   *Le Musée imaginaire de la sculpture mondiale: Des bas-reliefs aux grottes sacrées,* Paris: Gallimard.

Le Musée imaginaire de la sculpture mondiale: Le Monde chrétien. Paris: Gallimard.

1955   *Le Musée.* Paris: Editions Estienne.

1957   *La Métamorphose des dieux.* Paris: Gallimard. (This work was later titled *Le Surnaturel. La Métamorphose des Dieux* then became the general title of three essays: *Le Surnaturel, l'Irréel,* and *L'Intemporel.*) Translated by Stuart Gilbert as *The Metamorphosis of the Gods.* New York: Doubleday, 1960.

1967   *Antimémoires.* Paris: Gallimard. (This work became volume one of *Miroir des Limbes.* Its definitive version was published in 1972 in Gallimard's Folio series.) Translated by Terence Kilmartin as *Anti-Memoirs.* New York: Holt, Rinehart and Winston, 1968.

1970   *Le Triangle noir.* Paris: Gallimard.

1971   *Les Chênes qu'on abat.* Paris: Gallimard. Translated by Irene Clephane and Linda Asher as *Felled Oaks: Conversations with de Gaulle.* New York: Holt, Rinehart and Winston, 1971.

Oraisons funèbres. Paris: Gallimard.

1973   *Roi, je t'attends à Babylone.* Geneva: Skira.

1974   *La Tête d'obsidienne.* Paris: Gallimard. Translated by June Guicharnaud and Jacques Guicharnaud as *Picasso's Mask.* New York: Holt, Rinehart and Winston, 1976.

Lazare. Paris: Gallimard. Translated by Terence Kilmartin as *Lazarus.* New York: Holt, Rinehart and Winston, 1977.

L'Irréel. Vol. 2 of *La Métamorphose des Dieux.* Paris: Gallimard.

1975   *Hôtes de passage.* Paris: Gallimard.

1976   *L'Intemporel.* Vol. 3 of *La Métamorphose des Dieux.* Paris: Gallimard.

La Corde et les souris. Vol. 2 of *Miroir des Limbes.* Paris: Folio Gallimard.

L'Homme précaire et la littérature. Paris: Gallimard, 1977.

"Néocritique." (English title: "Anti-Critique.") Postface to *Malraux: Life and Work*, edited by Martine de Courcel. London: George Weidenfeld and Nicolson Ltd.

Index

Absolute agnostic, 288–312
Abstract expressionism: uncertainty and, 311–12
Absurd: difference and, 43, 192; rejection of, 41–47
"A-chronism," 148
Action: as alternative to absurd, 44–46; as instrument of conscious thought, 46; as metaphysical requirement, 47. *See also* Revolution; Revolutionary action
Actual: potential and, interplay of, 275–76
Adventure: as individual intoxication, 48–50
Advertising: organization of debasement in, 110, 111
Agnostic: absolute, 288–312
Agnosticism: faith and, 309–12
Airplane: as catalyst for cosmic reconciliation, 208–10
Alice in Wonderland: metamorphosis in, 282–83
All-Encompassing: art and, 219; cycle of metamorphosis and, 285
Antidestiny: art as, 218, 222
Anti-Memoirs: art as world of metamorphosis in, 25; political change in, 65;

power in, 180; propaganda in, 83–84; relations between culture and civilization in, 133–35
Appearance: assumed by actualized potential, reality as, 276; nonappearance and, 269–70; as relativity, 270
Art: as antidestiny, 218, 222; autonomous existence of power of creation and, 223; as conquest, 224; enigma of, 236–37; as expression of truth above and beyond appearance, 226–27; fellowship of, 231; fellowship of differences and, 232–33; as fellowship with destiny, 240; freedom of, 221; metalanguage emitted by, 239; precariousness of, 235–36; primordial forms of, 240, 242; struggle of, against destiny, 216, 218; time and, 148–49; work of, temporalities of, 218; worlds of, unity of, 220
Artist: demiurgic power of, 229–30; independence of artistic creation from, 229–30
Artistic creations: Malraux's novels as, 5–7
Astrophysics: time and, 159–60
Audiovisuals: consciousness formed by, 156

319

Index

Bachelard: on metamorphosis, 282, 283
Biographical approach: to Malraux, 7–8
Bonsai tree: man and universe taming each other in, 268
Bourgeoisie: Malraux and, 118; values and, 16–17
Breton, André: literary surrealism of, 165

Camus, Albert: on absurd, 43–44; on reason and irrationality, 162–63
Carroll, Lewis: metamorphosis and, 282–83
Catholicism: metamorphosis and, 254–55, 256
Cause: efficient, 279–81; final, 279–81
Childhood: mask of, 210–11
Christianity: rejection of, 99–100; solitude and, 167–68
Chronological time: history and, 144–46
Civilization: and culture, relations between, 132–33; culture compared to, 122; and nature, relations between, 204
Coin of the Absolute, The: religion and, 245
Colloquy: metamorphosis and, 192–93
Communism: as adversary, 217–18
Communist party, French: attack of, on Malraux, 117–18
Community: fellowship and, 194; individual and, interaction of, 185–88; theme of, evolution of, 190–91
Conquerors, The: illness in, 91; intent of, 6–7; outcome of revolution in, 90–91; propaganda in, 83; resistance against depersonalization and dehumanization by parties in, 81–82; revolution in, 62, 63, 66; terrorism in, 50–52; wisdom in, 57–58
Consciousness: audiovisuals in, formation of, 156–57; fraternal, 154–76; metamorphosis of, 46–47; potential conceived by, 273; science and, convergence of, 273–74; will to, value of, 158. *See also* Consciousness of life
Consciousness of life, 310; wonder and, 311

Contractual obligations: human relationships as, 23, 29–30
Cosmos: life and, reconciliation of, 208–10
Creation: artistic, independence of, from creator, 229–30; facts of, significance of, 305–6; separation of God from, 306. *See also* Creative power
Creative power: autonomous existence of, art and, 223; disorder and, 264–65; gods and, 306–7; intemporal nature of, 149; in Malraux's battle with destiny, 216; as metaphysical power of man, 230; mystery of, 305–7
Creative process: history and, 129
Cultural revolution: end of dehumanization and, 72–73
Cultural society: preparation for, 190
Culture(s): as agreement of sensibilities, 124–27; all, Malraux as heir to, 207–8; and civilization, relationship between, 132–33; civilization compared to, 122; communication and, 122–23; meaning of, changes in, 121–22, 124; nature and, reconciliation of, 202–3; organizing power of, 131, 132; past, Malraux's knowledge of, 10; roles of, 125–26; work of, 122–23. *See also* Metamorphosis of culture

Days of Wrath: airplane in, 209–10; fellowship in, 193; fulfillment in revolution in, 89–90; temptation of resignation in, 102–4
Debasement, organization of, 109–13; protecting humanity from, 216
Debray, Régis: on Malraux, 118–19
de Gaulle, Charles: Malraux as government minister to, 96
Dehumanization: end of, cultural revolution and, 72–73
De Kooning's abstract expressionism: uncertainty and, 311–12
Democracies: organization of debasement in, 110, 111
Demons: psychology and, 31

Index

Destiny: art's struggle against, 216, 218; fellowship with, art as, 240
Dictatorships: organization of debasement in, 110
Differences: absurd and, 43; evolution of, theme of, 191–92. *See also* Differences, fellowship of
Differences, fellowship of, 177–96; achievement of, in art world, 232–33; metamorphosis of culture and, 194–96
Discontinuity: values of, values of metamorphosis as, 291
Discontinuous history: concept of, 139; new perspective on, 141–42
Disorder: creative power and, 264–65
Dream factories: repudiation of, 166
Dream merchants: organization of debasement and, 111–12

Earth, Malraux's returns to: acceptance of life and, 302; reconciliation with life and cosmos and, 210–11
Efficient cause, 279–81
Election campaigns: organization of debasement in, 110, 111
Energy: metamorphosis of, 263
Evolution: discontinuity of, 259; theories of, 258–59
Expressionism, abstract: uncertainty and, 311–12

Facts: and ideas, reciprocity between, 130
Faith: agnosticism and, 309–12
Farfelu: in Malraux's battle with destiny, 216
Farfelu Kingdom: meaning of, 2–3
Fatality: history as, 74–76
Fellowship: of art, 231; community and, 194; with destiny, art as, 240; theme of, evolution of, 190–91. *See also* Fellowship of differences
Fellowship of differences, 177–96; achievement of, in art world, 232–33; metamorphosis of culture and, 194–96
Final cause, 279, 280–81
Forms: in art, new, creation of, 228

Fraternal consciousness, 154–76
Fraternity: Christianity and, 167–68; communal, 170–71; exercise of power and, 179, 181, 183–84; in *Lazarus*, 169–70, 176; in *Man's Fate*, 171–72, 175; in *Man's Hope*, 168–69; scorning of, 69–73; in *The Walnut Trees of Altenburg*, 169
French Communist party: attack of, on Malraux, 117–18

Garaudy: on Malraux, 117–18
General interest: individual interests subjugated to, 188
God(s): mortality of, 14–15; separation of, from creation, 306
Group: individual and, relationship between, 185–88

Heritage: as metamorphosis, 207
History: creative process and, 129; discontinuous, 128–53; as fatality, 74–76; as incarnation of human will, 143–44; Malraux's feelings about, 135–39; Malraux's knowledge of, 10; time and, 144–46. *See also* Discontinuous history
Hostility: against property owners, revolution and, 61
Hugo, Victor: on facts and ideas, 130
Humiliation as goal, 110. *See also* Will: to humiliate

Ideas: and facts, reciprocity between, 130
Illness: in *The Conquerors*, 91
Illusion: lyrical, 89–105
Imaginary: meaning of, 123
Imaginary Museum: audiovisuals and, 156; autonomous existence of painting and, 223; communion offered by, 150; creative power and, 149; forms from appearance in, 225; illusionary nature of continuity of individual in, 140; possibles of past and future in, 222; relativity of religions in, 244, 245
Individual: community and, interaction of, 185–88; tyranny of, 21–37

Index

Individual intoxications: rejection of, 48–59. *See also* Intoxications, individual

Individualism: breakdown of, Malraux on, 35–36; psychological, 31–33, 35

Individualistic thought: rise of, 21–22

Inner reality: experience of, 285; revelation of, 241–42; search for, 241

Inner self, 33–34

Innocence: face of, 210–11

Institutions: Malraux on, 120

Intemporal: creative power as, 149; living in, 152–53; questioning of time and, 146–47

Intoxications, individual: adventure as, 48–50; lies as, 54–56; rejection of, 48–59; terrorism as, 50–54; wisdom as, 56–59

Irrational, 160–61; realm of, 163–64; rise of, in novel, 161–62

Knowledge: Western concept of, 155

Language: of appearance and language of truth, distinguishing between, 226–27

Lazarus: fraternity in, 169–70, 176

Liberation: political choice after, 217

Lies: as individual intoxication, 54–56

Life: birth to, 97–99; cosmos and, reconciliation of, 208–10. *See also* Life, consciousness of

Life, consciousness of, 310; wonder and, 311

Literature: understanding, 9

Love: belief in existence of, 171–72

Lucidity: lies and, 55–56

Lyrical illusion, 89–105; revolution as, 90

Maisons de la culture: Malraux's goal for, 232

Man: metamorphosis of, 96–97, 109–20; metaphysical power of, creative power as, 230; nature and, relations between, 201–3; reconciled, 197–211; tragic existence of, 13–20. *See also* Shaping of man

Man's Fate: demand of party for obedience in, 79; fraternity in, 171–72, 175; lies in, 54–56; love in, 171–75; male-female relationships in, 24–28; nationalism versus individual in, 78; possessive individualism in, 23; relationship between individual and group in, 186, 187–88; revolution in, 62–64, 66; solitude in, 167; terrorism in, 51–54; theme of, 15; wisdom in, 59

Man's Hope: airplane in, 208–9; aspiration "to create men" in, 78; conflict between revolutionary action and ideals in, 85–88; disillusionment in, 91–92; divorce between man and party in, 79; fraternity in, 71–72, 73, 168–69; man at loss in, 18; metamorphosis of man in, 96–97; opposition between fraternity and hierarchy in, 82; power as fraternal superiority in, 179, 181; "quality of man" and, 158; revolution in, 63–66; theme of, 15; title of, significance of, 116–17

Mao: on culture and civilization, 133–35

Marx, Karl: culture and, 130–31

Masses: man consumed by, 77–88; revolutionary fighters and, separation between, 113–14

Mauriac, François: on Malraux, 205

Metalanguage: emitted by art forms, 239

Metamorphosis: as actualization of power, 274–75, 276; in *Alice in Wonderland*, 282–83; as appearance of actuality, 274; Catholicism and, 254–56; Colloquy and, 192–93; as constant theme, 253; of energy, 263; as furthest point of sensibility, 286; goal of, 265–66; heritage as, 207; knowing how to live and, 298–301; law of, efficient and final cause in, 281; as literary myth, 255–56; of man, 96–97, 109–20; rejection of, by religions, 245–46; science and, 257; time and, 267; unformulatable that transcends, quest for, 289; as

Index

universal law, 252–87; of values, 245; values of, as values of discontinuity, 291; Western view of, 253–56. *See also* Metamorphosis of culture

Metamorphosis of culture: fellowship of differences and, 194–96; need for, 105–13; organization of debasement and, 113; science and, 126–27

Metamorphosis of the Gods, The: Sphinx experience and, 226–27

Metaphysical power of man: creative power as, 230

Metaphysical problems: revolution as solution to, 92–96

Mirror of Limbo: meaning of, 303–5

Morphogenesis: metamorphosis and, 260–62, 264

Morphology, 260–62

Mother-goddesses: theme of, 307–8

Mothers: theme of, 307–9

Music: Malraux's sensitivity to, 247–49

Mysticism: Oriental, rejection of, 100–102

Nationalism: individual and, 77

Natural selection, 258–59

Nature: man and, relations between, 201–3

Nazi camps: organization of debasement in, 110

Nehru: on political change, 65; power and, 180

Obligations: contractual, human relationships as, 23, 29–30

Order: disorder and, 264–65

Organization of debasement, 109–13

Organizing power: of culture, 131, 132

Oriental mysticism, rejection of, 100–102

Ownership: power and, 177, 178

Pascal: on man, 17

Permanent factor: Malraux's search for, 19–20

Physics: quantum, time and, 259

Picasso: Malraux on, 228–29

Picon, Gaëtan: on Malraux, 276

Plurality: values of, values of metamorphosis as, 291–92

Politics: abandonment of, 95

Possessiveness: fellowship and, 194

Potential: actual and, interplay of, 275–76; actualized, appearance assumed by, reality as, 276

Power: actualization of, metamorphosis as, 274–75; of artist, demiurgic, 229–30; authorities opposed to, 183; as exercise of "fraternal superiority," 179, 181; "foul fatality" and, 178–79; metamorphosis of, 180; metaphysical, of man, creative power as, 230; ownership and, 177, 178; participation versus subordination and, 182–83. *See also* Creative power

Precarious Man: Picasso and form in, 228–29

Primordial forms of art, 240, 242

Probability: realized, reality as, 271–73

Propaganda: man's stupefication by, 82–84

Proximity: temporal, 149–50

Psychological individualism, 31–33, 35

Psychological techniques: man's stupefication by, 82–84; of organization of debasement, 110, 111

Psychology: demons and, 34

Quantum physics: time and, 259

Reality: as appearance assumed by actualized potential, 276; as realized probability, 271–73

Reason: attack on, 17

Reconciled man, 197–211

Reification: of individual, 24

Relationships: human, as contractual obligations, 23, 29–30; male-female, in *Man's Fate*, 24–28

Religions: metamorphosis of, rejection of, 245–46; mortality of, 243–51; mu-

Religions (*continued*)
  sic and, 249; renaissance in, prediction of, 250
Renaissance: religious, prediction of, 250; upheaval caused by, 13–14
Resignation: temptation of resignation in, 102–4
Resistance: involvement in, 104
Revolution, 60–66; action and ideals of, conflict between, 85–88; cultural, end of dehumanization and, 72–73; fulfillment in, 89–90; as solution to metaphysical problems, 92–94
Revolutionary action, 60–66; separation of everyday life from, 113–14
Revolutionary struggle: in Malraux's battle with destiny, 216
Royal Way, The: absurdity in, 41–42; adventure in, 48–49; relationship of man and nature in, 197–98
Ruins: fascination with, 198–99

Sage: individual intoxication and, 56–59
Sartre, Jean-Paul: on human tragedy, Malraux compared to, 19; on militants, 78
Science: consciousness and, convergence of, 273–74; metamorphosis and, 257; metamorphosis of culture and, 126–27
Self: inner, 33–34
Senses: perceptions of, consciousness and, 273
Sensibility: metamorphosis as furthest point of, 286; reason versus, 164–65
Shaping of man: absence of, 126–27; as goal of society, 190
Society: cultural, preparation for, 190
Solitude: attack of art on, 231; Christianity and, 167–68; love as deliverance from, 172–75; in *Man's Fate*, 167
Sphinx experience: reflections on art and, 226–27
Surrealism: Malraux and, 165–66

Tame Hedgehogs, The: man at loss in, 17–18

Technology: fascism and, 70
Temporalities: of work of art, 218
Temporal proximity, 149–50
Temptation of the West, The: rejection of Christianity in, 99; rejection of Oriental mysticism in, 100–102; wisdom in, 56–57
Terrorism: as individual intoxication, 50–54
Thom, René: on forms, 260–62
Time: astrophysics and, 259–60; history and, 144–46; metamorphosis and, 267; notions of, 147–49; quantum physics and, 259; transcendence of, 151–53; work of art and, 218
Timeless, The: enigma of art in, 236–37
Totalitarianism: struggle against, 75–76
Totalization: totalitarianism versus, 76
Tragic existence: of man, 13–20
Tyranny: of individual, 21–37

Uncertain: all-encompassing uncertainty of, 294–96
Unformulatable: that transcends metamorphosis, quest for, 289
Unity: desire for, doubt of legitimacy of, 44
Unreal, The: art as sovereign world in, 224–25
USSR: organization of debasement in, 110

Valéry, Paul: on metamorphosis, 283–84
Value(s): of discontinuity, values of metamorphosis as, 291; metamorphosis of, 245; of plurality, values of metamorphosis as, 291–92; work as, 204–5. *See also* Values of metamorphosis
Values of metamorphosis: Malraux's acceptance of, 290–91; as values of discontinuity, 291; as values of plurality, 291–92
Voices of Silence, The: art as antidestiny in, 218, 222; creation of forms in art in, 228; history in, 136, 137; metamor-

phosis of values in, 245; revolution in, 61–62

Walnut Trees of Altenburg, The: birth to life in, 97–99; emergence toward life in, 95; fraternity in, 169; revelation of life in, 199–201; wisdom in, 58

Will: as force for actualization of potential, 278–79; human, history as incarnation of, 143–44; to humiliate, 110
Wisdom: as individual intoxication, 56–59
Women characters: evolution of, 24
Work: as value, 204–5